INTERNET BUSINESS GUIDE

Second Edition

D1403364

Internet Business Guide

Second Edition

Rosalind Resnick
Dave Taylor

sams
net

201 West 103rd Street
Indianapolis, IN 46290

For the friends of Rosalind—wherever they may be!
—Rosalind Resnick

For the jewels of my life: Linda, Karma, and Jasmine
—Dave Taylor

Copyright © 1995 by Sams.net Publishing

International Standard Book Number: 1-57521-004-5

Library of Congress Catalog Card Number: 95-70179

98 97 96   4 3 2

Interpretation of the printing code: the rightmost double-digit number is the year of the book's printing; the rightmost single-digit, the number of the book's printing. For example, a printing code of 95-1 shows that the first printing of the book occurred in 1995.

Composed in Palatino and MCPdigital by Macmillan Computer Publishing

Printed in the United States of America

Trademarks

President, Sams Publishing	Richard K. Swadley
Publisher, Sams.net Publishing	George Bond
Acquisitions Manager	Greg Weigand
Development Manager	Dean Miller
Managing Editor	Cindy Morrow
Marketing Manager	John Pierce

Acquisitions Editor
Mark Taber

Development Editor
Fran Hatton

Production Editor
Katherine Stuart Ewing

Editorial Coordinator
Bill Whitmer

Technical Edit Coordinator
Lynette Quinn

Formatter
Frank Sinclair

Editorial Assistant
Carol Ackerman

Technical Reviewer
Ryan Scott

Cover Designer
Jay Corpus

Book Designer
Alyssa Yesh

Production Team Supervisor
Brad Chinn

Production
Michael Brumit
Mary Ann Cosby
Terrie Deemer
Louisa Klucznik
Kevin Laseau
Paula Lowell
Brian-KentProffitt
SA Springer
Tina Trettin
Mark Walchle
Dennis Wesner

Indexer
Greg Eldred

OVERVIEW

CONTENTS

ACKNOWLEDGMENTS

I'd like to offer my special thanks to all the people who generously contributed their time and expertise to help me write this book, most notably my lead researcher, Heidi Anderson, who surveyed over 100 business owners about their experiences on the Internet; my other researcher, Dave Asprey, who took all our screen shots; my programmer and partner Ryan Scott, who patiently answered my technical questions about the Web and suggested numerous cool sites to include; Yanek Martinson of SatelNet Communications, Tom Benham of CyberGate, and Michael Tague of Computer Witchcraft, who generously provided access to their servers; Debra Young of CompuServe; Margaret Ryan of America Online; Brian Ek of Prodigy; and Teresa Gann of eWorld.

—*Rosalind Resnick*

I'd like to again thank my partner, Linda, for helping with this writing project. If we're not careful, we'll start to enjoy the process! I'd also like to acknowledge the help I received from my ever-reliable mates Kevin Savetz, James Armstrong, Marvin Raab, and Tai Jin. Dave Asprey and Heidi Anderson were also a great help as we went through extensive revisions on this second edition of our book.

In a true testimony to the Internet and how it's changing how we do business, I've never seen a single page of this book on paper: All discussion, development, composition, and editing has been done through e-mail and file transfer, with the pipeline between CompuServe, Netcom, and Indiana access provider Metropolitan Data Networks getting quite a bit of traffic.

Thanks also to Joel, Mike (the new guy), Tom, Crow, and the rest of the Mystery Science Theater crew for helping me keep some semblance of sanity, and Sting and Thomas Dolby for ensuring that it was never too quiet around the office.

—*Dave Taylor*

ABOUT THE AUTHORS

Rosalind Resnick

Rosalind Resnick (rosalind@harrison.win.net) is a former *Miami Herald* business reporter and now a freelance writer, author, and consultant specializing in business and technology. Her articles have appeared in *The New York Times, Forbes, Nation's Business, Internet World, Computer Life, Home Office Computing, PC Today,* and other major newspapers and magazines. She is the author of *Exploring the World of Online Services* (Sybex, 1993), a beginner's guide for small businesses; editor and publisher of *Interactive Publishing Alert*, a twice-monthly newsletter about electronic newspaper and magazine publishing, and a consultant to businesses and publications seeking to set up a presence on the World Wide Web. The online business column she writes for the *Miami Herald* is distributed nationwide through the Knight-Ridder wire service. She lives in Hollywood, Florida, and has two daughters, Julia, 5, and Caroline, 2.

Dave Taylor

Dave Taylor (taylor@netcom.com) has been involved with the Internet since early in 1980 when he first connected and learned how to use e-mail. Since then he's been a Research Scientist at Hewlett-Packard Labs, reviews editor for *SunWorld* magazine, and is now president of Intuitive Systems. He has published more than 500 articles, is a columnist for *Internet World* and *Marketing Computing*, and has three other books: *Creating Cool Web Pages with HTML, Teach Yourself UNIX in a Week,* and *Global Software.* With his Masters in Educational Computing, he's also busy teaching Internet courses, keeping the Internet Mall up-to-date, trying to train his dogs to talk, cooking gourmet vegetarian foods, and watching innumerable old movies.

INTRODUCTION

Last year, when we wrote the original *Internet Business Guide,* the field was relatively uncrowded.

Now, there are dozens of Internet business books on the market—and more on the way.

The reason isn't difficult to see: There are now over 5,000,000 host computers, 50,000 computer networks, and between 40,000,000 and 50,000,000 computer users on the Internet today, according to the Internet Society's most recent statistics. That's more than double last year's tally—and the Internet keeps growing at a rate of more than 10% a month with no signs of slowing.

So if you've got our book in your hands and you're looking for a good reason to plunk down your money and buy it, we'll give you six!

- As does our original edition, this new *Internet Business Guide* is designed to help business people like yourself use the network to make money, cut costs, and run your company more productively. If you're looking for a book to teach you HTML, this isn't it. However, if you're looking for book to teach you how to build a Web site that rings up sales and generates traffic, you've come to the right place.

- Our new edition features shorter chapters and lots more of them, making it easier for you to surf around and find what you're looking for.

- Again, as did our first edition, this new Guide tells you not only why to use the Internet for business but how. We go beyond management theory and case studies to give you the lowdown on getting the best deals on Internet access, Web site creation, Internet advertising, and more.

- To help answer the persistent question, "Is anybody making money on the Internet?," we've surveyed more than 100 businesses about their experiences on the Internet. You can read about our findings in Chapter 14, "Is Anybody Making Money on the Net?" and find dozens of individual company profiles scattered throughout the book.

- We offer a realistic assessment of the Internet market today, not advice on how to get rich quick. We also tell you how your company can use the Internet to improve communications, customer service, and market research.

- We don't just write about doing business on the Internet; we actually do business on the Net ourselves. Rosalind uses the Internet to publish an electronic newsletter, Interactive Publishing Alert, and, together with her partner, Ryan Scott, has launched a company called NetCreations to put businesses on the Web. Dave is proprietor of The Internet Mall—with more than 2,000 stores listed. As president of Intuitive Systems, he works with firms to develop exciting and innovative Web and Internet sites.

Intrigued? Read on!

The Internet Business Guide: Your Personal Passport to Doing Business Online

Now that you've gotten a taste of what the Internet can offer, let's look at what this book can offer you. In a nutshell, our purpose in writing this book is to offer you a guide through the maze of commercial, cultural, and technical issues surrounding the use of the Internet.

We'll take you on a tour of the tremendous number of valuable resources now available on the Net, including many that you won't find anywhere else at any price. As in our first edition, we won't shy away from nuts-and-bolts technical information; you'll learn everything you need to know about working with Internet mailing lists, Usenet newsgroups, and the World Wide Web. You can even watch over our shoulders as we use the FTP (file-transfer program) to download press releases from companies on the Net and then sign up for and participate in a mailing list that discusses the Internet's commercialization.

Who Should Read This Book?

This book is for anyone who wants to make his or her business more efficient and profitable. Whether you're a home-based startup or a Fortune 500 company, a computer-savvy network administrator or a marketing VP who has never gone online before, there's something in this book that can either make you money or help you save it.

You don't need to be a computer expert, you don't even need to have logged in to the Internet or connected to a commercial online service specific information service—though we're willing to bet that you've encountered the Net at some point and just didn't realize it. Our goal here is to present a vision of the Internet and how businesses can work within its community and technologies in a way that benefits everyone.

Even if you're already an Internet expert, we believe that there's plenty in our book that you'll find valuable and thought-provoking, too. From novel ways to build your client base with e-mail to how Usenet can help you identify what your competitors are up to, this book has something for practically everyone.

How Is This Book Organized?

We've organized this book to help you master the art of doing business on the learn about the business face of the Internet with minimal time and trouble fuss. Our hope is that you will read it straight through, but if there are particular sections you find exciting, feel free to flip directly to them!

Part I, "Getting Started," gives you an overview of the commercial Internet, its phenomenal growth, and the first steps you'll need to take to get your business on the Net. Chapter 1, "How Internet Business Came to Be," tells how the Internet evolved from a sleepy academic backwater to the bustling thoroughfare it is today. Chapter 2, "Hooking Up to the Net," offers practical information on picking an Internet access provider and a pricing plan, and evaluates the pros and cons of the three major access alternatives (shell, SLIP/PPP, and leased line). Chapter 3, "Finding the Interface That's Right for You," looks at text-based, graphical, and hypermedia front-ends for the Internet and helps you pick the best one for your company's needs.

Part II, "Internet Tools," shows you the wide range of different software programs and services available on the Internet. So many, in fact, that it's split into: Chapter 4, "What Tools Are Available," which gives you a heads up on the range of tools; Chapter 5, "Communications Tools," which tells you about electronic mail, Usenet, and other ways you can communicate with others on the Internet; Chapter 6, "Marketing Tools," which helps you understand the strengths and differences between Gopher, the World Wide Web, and similar tools; and Chapter 7, "Research Tools," which shows you how to find information using the existing services, including Archie, Veronica, and Web search systems.

Part III, "Communicating Your Message," focuses on the how and why of interacting with others through the computer system. Chapter 8, "The Power of E-Mail," explains the power of using electronic mail as a vehicle for keeping up with your clients, customer support, and more. Chapter 9, "The Electronic Schmooze," tells how your business can raise its visibility through individual participation in mailing lists and Usenet groups, and Chapter 10, "Business Netiquette," explores some of the things that businesses need to keep in mind when working online.

Part IV, "Marketing on the Net," shows you tips and tricks for getting your company's message out without getting scorched by Internet flame-throwers. Chapter 11, "Marketing *Do's* and *Don'ts*," helps you use the soft sell to win friends and customers on the Internet. Chapter 12, "Setting Up a Web Site," tells you everything you need to know about creating an interactive billboard or storefront on the World Wide Web. Chapter 13, "Getting Your Business Noticed," tells you how to drive Internet users to your Web site through print and online advertising.

Part V, "Net Sales," shows you how to ring up sales on the Internet and how to sidestep the pitfalls that online entrepreneurs typically encounter. Chapter 14, "Is Anybody Making Money on the Net?," shows you what sells and what doesn't on the Internet and helps you identify profitable niches for your company's products and services. Chapter 15, "Storefronts and Cybermalls," gives you an overview of the Internet retailing options now available and shows you how companies are successfully using the Internet to attract new customers, ring up sales and, in some cases, even deliver electronic merchandise directly to the customer's computer. Chapter 16, "Getting Paid (Safely)," tells you all about credit card encryption, digital cash, and other secure ways of transacting business online.

Part VI, "Bringing the Internet In-House," explores the business advantages to be gained by working with the network. Chapter 17, "Mining for Business Information," shows you how to gather free, up-to-the-minute market intelligence on the Internet. Chapter 18, "Providing Customer Support," tells about one of the most exciting aspects of the network: working with customers through e-mail. Chapter 19, "Network Security," highlights the importance of vigilant security and talks about common ways to ensure your private data and network stay that way.

Part VII, "The Commercial Nets," shows you ways in which you can integrate your use of commercial services such as CompuServe, Prodigy, America Online, and The Microsoft Network with the Internet to enhance your company's ability to do business. Chapter 20, "Business Opportunities on the Commercial Nets," tells you about sales and marketing options on these for-profit networks. Chapter 21, "How the Other Half Lives," features profiles and demographic information about The Big Three plus Apple's new eWorld online service.

Part VIII, "The Future of Internet Business," has the authors peering into the cyber-crystal ball to predict the future. Chapter 22, "Hurdles to Be Overcome," is a realistic look at the strengths and weaknesses of the Internet and the companies hooking up today. It's a must-read chapter. Chapter 23, "Trends and Predictions," wraps up with what we believe are the most interesting and exciting trends on the way in the bustling cyberspace Internet community.

We've also included two appendixes: Internet On-Ramps, a comprehensive list of Internet access providers worldwide, and Tools and Resources, a detailed list of software programs and information sources designed to help you with everything from using an e-mail autoresponder to building your own Web site.

What Conventions Are Used?

To ensure that you can quickly find information within each chapter and throughout the book, we use a variety of typographical conventions and small margin illustrations. Throughout the book when you see lines of output in monospace

```
this is a typical line of computer output
```

it means that it's the output of a specific Internet program or application. If you see it in monospace boldface

```
Here's what you would type
```

it's exactly what you would type.

The graphics conventions are

 Note: These boxes will highlight interesting information to make your work with the Internet more productive and business communities more enjoyable.

 Tip: Tip boxes suggest ways to streamline your interaction with the Internet or find valuable information.

 Profile: An abstract business book without real-life case studies of companies doing business on the Net would be of little value, so we've included extensive profiles of businesses large and small, real businesses that are really using the Internet today, all tucked into these profile boxes.

In our new edition, we also include "data cards," which give you quick snapshots of companies doing business on the Net. A data card looks like this (any relationship to any company doing business on the Net is purely unintentional):

Company Name: NetShirts Unlimited

Type of business: T-shirts

Location: Cambridge, Massachusetts

Owners: Jim and Jenny Jones

URL (or e-mail address): http://www.shirts.com/

Internet tools: E-mail, newsgroups, World Wide Web

Length of time doing business on the Internet: Since November, 1994

Reason for going on the Net: The potential to target new markets and expand our existing sales channels

Internet business strategy: To market Internet-related T-shirts online, to boost company awareness by posting to newsgroups, and then drive Internet shoppers to our cool site on the Web.

Time and money invested: $1,000 to pay a design firm to set up our Web site, $100 a month to host our pages on a local server.

Net results: $2,000 a month average sales.

Future plans: To sell additional products such as baseball caps and mouse pads on our Web site

Lessons learned/Net philosophy: If you don't know where you're going, it's impossible to get lost.

Contact address: shirtseller@netcomaol.com

It's an Art, Not a Science

As you read this book, keep in mind that doing business on the Internet means developing the right mix of marketing, research, sales, and staff. It's really more of an art than a science.

Right now, most of the companies tapping into the Internet are still experimenting, and there are no hard and fast rules to Internet business success. Some firms will succeed; others will fail. We can't tell you who the winners will be, but we can help you learn how to properly evaluate the various business opportunities there.

The most important difference between success and failure on the Internet, after all, is the same as it is for any other business venture—meeting the demands of the customer in an innovative and cost-effective manner. Of course, it also helps to have a little bit of luck.

Our advice is to approach the Internet with an open mind, just as you would an overseas business trip. Wander around a little. Take in the sights. Join a discussion group and post a few notes there. Tap into a database that looks intriguing. Start an e-mail exchange with a colleague in Japan or Hungary. Put up a Web site. Most of all, don't be afraid to step off the beaten track, because, on the Internet, the old adage is especially true, "If you don't know where you're going, it's impossible to get lost." As we've learned time and again, when you travel on the Internet, you're guaranteed to be surprised at where you end up. For a growing number of businesses, that destination is proving to be an extremely profitable place to be.

GETTING STARTED

HOW INTERNET BUSINESS CAME TO BE

These days, it's difficult to pick up a newspaper or magazine without reading about the Internet, the World Wide Web, and the enormous potential for businesses to market products and services worldwide at a fraction of the cost of traditional advertising channels.

Businesses are no longer asking *whether* they should set up a presence on the Internet but *how*. E-mail addresses are becoming as commonplace as phone numbers on business cards. Net surfers now number in the millions. And just about every company, it seems, has a home page on the Web—or is planning to get one.

How a year has changed things!

When Dave Taylor and I wrote the first edition of the *Internet Business Guide* last spring, relatively few businesses had any idea what the Internet was all about and only a handful were using it for sales and marketing. Back then, the big flap was over Canter & Siegel, an Arizona immigration law firm that had riled the sensibilities of Net veterans by "spamming" thousands of Usenet newsgroups with electronic junk mail promoting their "green card" services.

Now, hundreds of "cybermalls" are springing up all over the Internet, and thousands of entrepreneurs, peddling everything from bouquets to beachfront real estate, are rushing onto the Internet hoping to make money. The reason: Savvy marketers are now discovering what teenage computer nerds have known for years: Hop aboard the Internet and kiss your printing and postage costs goodbye. On the Internet, an interconnected "network of networks" that links over 20 million users worldwide, your company pays one flat monthly fee to blast out as many copies of your marketing message as you like to wherever you want them to go without spending a dime at the post office or copy shop. With the Web, the Internet's hypermedia system, companies large and small showcase page after page of full-color photos, drawings, charts, animation, and audio and video clips at a fraction of the price of an advertisement in a printed newspaper or a magazine.

Although the Net is still brimming with offbeat stuff put up by college students and computer geeks, the once-pristine communications link is looking more and more like the Home Shopping Network all the time.

How many companies are doing business on the Internet? It's impossible to really know, but, as of April 30, 1995, there were 49,636 commercial domains registered with InterNIC, the Internet's central registry, according to Internet Info, a Falls Church, Virginia, market research and consulting firm. These include DDB Needham Worldwide, Bellcore, Georgia-Pacific, International Paper, McCaw Wireless Data, Burger King, Estee Lauder, Miller Brewing Company, Nike, Ocean Spray Cranberries, The GAP, Warner Brothers Records, First Union National Bank, National Westminster Bank and the law firms of Bell, Boyde, & Lloyd; Choate, Hall & Stuart; Cooley, Godward, Castro, Huddleson, & Tatum; and Paul, Hatings, Janofsky, & Walker. Even the National Basketball Association and the National Hockey League Enterprises are on the Net.

The purpose of this book is to show you how your company can get on the Internet *today* and how you can use the network's many tools, features and resources to make money and cut costs. Although doing business on the Internet is still far from a perfect science, the huge opportunities and the relatively low cost of establishing a presence there make it riskier to wait and see than to take a chance and dive in now.

A Brief History of Net Commerce

Unlike commercial online services such as CompuServe and Prodigy, the Internet is not a for-profit company. It's a computer cooperative that isn't owned by anyone. The Internet was born in 1969 when a group of Department of Defense researchers linked four computers at UCLA, Stanford Research Institute, the

University of Utah, and the University of California at Santa Barbara to create a network to communicate with one another about government projects. Because the researchers were part of the Department of Defense's Advanced Research Projects Agency, the network was dubbed ARPAnet. Three years later, more than 50 universities and military agencies were linked together on the network, and other computer networks began to appear around the country and the world.

As ARPAnet evolved, as the military and the educational networks diverged, and as agencies such as NASA began to experiment with computer networks, the networks began to interconnect. (That's how the Internet got its name, by the way.) At the same time, the Internet's infrastructure began growing, too. In the mid-1980s, the National Science Foundation built high-speed, long-distance lines that connected supercomputing centers across the United States, eventually replacing the original ARPAnet network. In time, NSFnet was joined by other networks at dozens of universities, research laboratories, and high-tech companies.

For years, commercial traffic was forbidden on the Internet. That is, companies were barred by "acceptable use policies" from using the government-funded network to sell or advertise their products and services. In 1991, the federal government made it known that it no longer intended to restrict the network's backbone to use in research. This policy shift created an incentive for three major Internet access providers—Performance Systems International Inc. (PSI), Uunet Technologies Inc., and General Atomics Cerfnet—to create their own commercial backbones to skirt the government-controlled NSFnet that banned business traffic. These providers, along with nine others including Sprintlink and Nearnet, formed the Commercial Internet Exchange (CIX).

Today, millions of ordinary consumers have access to the Internet, and the once-pristine network is fast becoming dotted with storefronts, shopping centers, and sprawling cybermalls springing up on practically every virtual street corner. These days, merchants hawking books, bouquets, games, jewelry, CDs, concert tickets, pizza, and even lobsters are setting up shop in hopes of wooing the global network's more than 30,000,000 potential shoppers.

Risks and Rewards of Doing Business on the Net

For all the Internet's commercial opportunities, there are also some very real risks to doing business on the Internet—security being the biggest one. Late in 1993, for instance, electronic "crackers" broke into the Internet and began stealing account passwords for a variety of different machines. By the time anybody noticed, the bandits had already learned thousands of passwords, the keys to public and private computer accounts throughout the world. In February of this year, hacker Kevin Mitnick was arrested and charged with computer fraud and access-device

fraud, including stealing an estimated 20,000 credit card numbers and thousands of data files from the Internet.

On a commercial online service like Prodigy, where only paying subscribers are allowed to access the service, your customers can be assured that their credit-card numbers are safe from cyber-thieves when they place an online order. Not so on the freewheeling Internet, an open network that makes it relatively easy for hackers to break in and take whatever strikes their fancy. Though few instances of Internet credit card robbery have been reported so far, it doesn't take too many Kevin Mitnicks to scare online shoppers away. Given the choice between shopping in a dangerous neighborhood and a place with police protection and brightly lit parking lots, most people will go the safer route.

Business Opportunities on the Net

The Internet offers businesses an impressive number of competitive advantages, including these six key benefits: electronic mail, access to research, tracking competitors, inexpensive remote collaboration, enhanced customer service, and low-cost marketing and advertising.

Let's look at them one-by-one.

Electronic Mail

Much of the traffic on the Internet today is electronic mail. Indeed, it's been estimated that well over 4,000 messages are sent each second on the Internet. That's 28,800 messages in the typical eight-hour business day.

Being able to send messages in seconds to a user anywhere in the world is probably the single most important reason so many companies find the Internet so appealing.

The Internet is also cheaper and more cost-efficient than comparable commercial online networks such as CompuServe, GEnie, or MCI Mail. Once you're connected to the information highway, there are no additional per-minute or per-message charges. In the world of commercial online services, by contrast, flat-fee plans by which users send unlimited messages are quickly giving way to pay-as-you-go schemes as the services learn to compete in this new market.

There's another important aspect to this, too: In addition to enabling your employees to communicate in an effective and inexpensive manner, the Internet links your company with the Internet's more than 30,000,000 users. Even if only 1% are vaguely interested in what you have to sell, we're talking about a lot of people!

Research

Imagine that every book in your local library were actually a gateway to another library and that each of those libraries had another two to fifty times as many volumes as the first one. That's what makes the Internet such a treasure trove of information for your business.

For starters, the Internet provides

- Access to the Library of Congress and just about every major university library in the United States
- Business-oriented databases such as Commerce Business Daily, the Federal Register, and the U.S. Chamber of Commerce's Economic Bulletin Board
- U.S. and Canadian Census data
- Supreme Court decisions
- World health statistics
- Security and Exchange Commission corporate financial reports
- International weather forecasts (including up-to-the-hour satellite pictures)
- United Nations information
- Transcripts of daily White House press briefings

The Internet contains more than statistical data, however. The network's lifeblood is its widely varying and often freewheeling discussion forums, split between bulletin boards (called *Usenet newsgroups)* and mailing lists (often known as *listservs* after one of the popular software programs that runs them). Both offer forums packed with experts discussing the latest developments in their fields. There are Internet discussion groups about almost anything you can think of— entrepreneurship, computer programming, franchise opportunities, Eastern European trade and politics, semiconductor manufacturing, continuing employee education, and over 10,000 other topics.

Competitive Tracking

One of the most important ingredients of business success is being aware of what your competitors are doing. Frequently asked questions include

Are my competitors working on a new product?

What areas of research are they contributing expertise to on the network?

What do customers say about their products, both good and bad?

All this information and more is available for free on the Internet, awaiting your careful analysis.

Collaboration

The Internet can also help your company work with colleagues throughout the world to develop new products and services. By using the Internet to exchange and search for information, many businesses are facilitating collaboration and lowering the costs of research and development.

When IBM does development work with other companies, for example, its engineers use the Internet to communicate with counterparts rather than set up an expensive private data connection.

The Internet also offers a cost-effective way to match buyers and sellers worldwide. One such service is the Globalnet Trade Opportunity Database, an online directory of companies doing business internationally. Currently, Globalnet has 3,500 Florida manufacturers online and now intends to go national. It also features a database containing the names of 35,000 registered buyers representing foreign governments or companies stored in a database to help manufacturers find buyers worldwide. Each manufacturer pays $30 to $100 for Globalnet to set up a *home page* linked to the Globalnet directory. For more information about putting up a home page, see Chapter 12, "Setting Up a Web Site."

An even more ambitious project is being launched by the United Nations (UN) Conference on Trade and Development to connect trading sites in 50 countries. The UN Trade Point Programme will set up connections via the Internet and other telecommunications links to help companies crack new markets and locate new sources of raw materials. One of the program's goals is to use EDI to reduce by more than 25% the estimated $300,000,000,000 cost of international trade paperwork by the year 2000.

Marketing and Advertising

With more than 30,000,000 users worldwide, many of whom are affluent and highly educated professionals, the Internet is a fertile field for companies advertising everything from silicon chips to luxury cars.

Businesses that explicitly target the Internet's technocratic culture can gain a competitive edge and boost sales. Some companies also have found that supplying a free sample of what they're offering can whet the appetites of Internet users for a product or service they're willing to buy. It's the same idea as giving away a taste of an ice cream flavor at a soda fountain; bait the hook right and the customers will reel themselves in.

These days, the hottest marketing opportunity for businesses on the Internet is the World Wide Web. Thanks to this network-wide hypermedia system, it's easier than ever for businesses to display information and attract customers on the Net. Once a backwater, the Web has exploded to nearly 14% of all Internet traffic over the NSFnet backbone. If Web growth continues at its current 30%-a-month clip, Web traffic will surpass that of all other Internet applications this year.

By creating a home page on the Web, companies can flash their message to the world like a giant billboard on the information superhighway. Potential customers who stop and look can access a rich marketing message through which they can sift through layer upon layer of information to find out more about the company's products and services. What's more, a growing number of companies are raking in big bucks selling advertisements on their sites; Netscape Communications Corp., developer of the hugely popular Web browser, is selling spots on its site for $40,000 for three months to the likes of General Motors, EDS, MasterCard, AT&T, Adobe, and Netcom On-Line Communications Services.

Advertising on the Internet can be perilous, however, especially for those who don't know or don't respect the Internet culture. Witness the Canter & Siegel law firm that blitzed the Internet with thousands of unwelcome newsgroup postings and became Internet pariahs. Advertising on the Web, by contrast, is considered politically correct because potential customers come to you, not the other way around.

Remember that business success on the Internet comes from treading lightly and learning the culture before launching any commercial ventures. There are many opportunities for profit, but there is just as much potential for failure, too—failure that can ultimately prove quite damaging to your company.

Customer Service

Increasingly, companies are turning to the Internet to set up customer support bulletin boards offering technical advice, monitoring customer satisfaction, providing new product information, and making software upgrades available electronically.

For many companies, it's a cost-effective way to do business. By supporting customers electronically, these companies avoid the expense of 800 numbers and corporate newsletters announcing upgrades. Customers, meanwhile, save on long-distance phone calls. What's more, simple upgrades can be quickly distributed to your customer base at no expense—a technique used extensively by Apple with its Macintosh software suite.

Business Risks on the Net

Although there are unquestionably many advantages of doing business on the Internet, there are also many risks and problems. In addition to the business-averse Internet culture, there are also security breaches, traffic jams, and reliability problems that crop up from time to time.

Right now, security is probably the most pressing concern that businesses have about connecting to the Internet. Unlike commercial online services, which have computers and databases open only to registered users, the Internet's thousands of computers can be accessed by anyone with an account anywhere on the network. Though this makes information easy to distribute and share, it also makes the Internet vulnerable to hackers and vandals who periodically break into the network's computers and steal files and other valuable data.

Although Internet break-ins may be impossible to stop, the good news is that two strong, new, security protocols—Secure HTTP and Secure Sockets Layer—are making a reality of safe credit card transactions on the Internet. Heading off a standards war that could have stalled the growth of Internet commerce, Netscape Communications Corp., America Online, CompuServe, Prodigy, and IBM recently announced their investment in Terisa Systems, a Menlo Park, California, company that licenses and markets technologies that enable secure transactions on the Internet. Terisa will develop a unified approach designed to integrate both the Secure HTTP protocol of Enterprise Integration Technologies and Secure Sockets Layer from Netscape.

Then there are the traffic jams. On the Internet, as on any real-world roadway, traffic tie-ups occur when thousands of people try to tap into a particular computer at once. One example is the Illinois National Center for Supercomputer Applications computer, which offers free copies of the popular Internet browsing software, Mosaic. So many users try to download the software from the machine that it often slows to a veritable crawl trying to meet the demand. Other times, due to its traffic load, it simply refuses entry to users trying to connect. Internet computers and data providers are working to add capacity, although it seems a safe bet that however fast networks are expanded, there will always be places where user demand will exceed computer capacity. Call it "rush hour on the information highway!"

Another occasional problem is network reliability. Unlike centralized for-profit services like CompuServe and Prodigy, there's no guarantee that your message or data will get to where you send it in a timely manner, and there are precious few reliable ways of checking or confirming receipt. Our experience shows that the system is nonetheless quite reliable, with hundreds of messages transmitted without incident to Eastern Europe, India, and the People's Republic of China for every message that vanishes or bounces back.

The Future of Internet Commerce

As you've just seen, the Internet today is a highly effective tool for communications, information-gathering, and multiple-site collaboration, but it still has a way to go before it gains acceptance as a secure and reliable place to do business. Cultural obstacles also remain, though they're gradually lessening as the Internet community begins to realize that commerce is here to stay.

The biggest barrier to doing business on the Internet today, we believe, is differentiating your message from the tsunami of information that washes over each user every time they come near the network and standing out from the crowd in a way that allows your company to be viewed as a contributor to the growth of the network and online community, not a detractor from its original vision and goals.

Within the next few years, the Internet, or whatever the name the information superhighway takes, will be a busy thoroughfare for all kinds of voice, data, and video traffic. But because the Internet is not yet a mass market and the technological infrastructure is not fully developed or easy to use, those companies likeliest to profit in the short term are businesses with heavy communications needs and those that sell information products and services, such as publishers, software designers, and online information scouts. At the same time, practically any business can benefit from at least some of the services and information sources available on the Internet today.

HOOKING UP TO THE NET

How much would you pay for the key to the world's largest library? What would it be worth to be able to send, without paying postage, all the mail you wanted anywhere in the world? What price would you put on the opportunity to announce a new product or tell your company's story to an audience of several thousand of the top movers and shakers in your field? $1,000? $10,000? $1,000,000?

Try $20 a month—or less.

That's the going rate for basic individual Internet access these days. For about $20 a month (and sometimes as low as $10), most Internet access providers let you send and receive as much e-mail as you want, download as much free software and information as you like, and stay online as long as you want. You'll never pay a penny more as long as it's a local phone call away. Although some businesses may choose to pay more for high-speed dedicated connections, the cost of even the most expensive Internet link rarely exceeds $1,000 a month—unless you're planning on becoming an Internet access provider!

Sound like a great deal? You bet it is! In fact, it's such a great deal that hundreds of thousands of people are signing up each month for Internet access, causing lots of anxiety at CompuServe, Prodigy, and America Online, services that make their money by billing customers for connect time. (Not to be left out, the commercial services are rolling out Internet access, too, but we'll talk more about that in Chapters 20, "Business Opportunities on the Commercial Nets," and 21, "How the Other Half Lives.")

Of course, logging onto the Internet isn't as easy as signing up for a commercial online service such as Prodigy. Because the Internet is a computer cooperative, not a for-profit company, there's no "800" number to call to get a free start-up kit; plus, you can buy several different types of Internet connections plus a wide range of services and pricing plans.

The good news is that accessing the Internet is far easier than it used to be. Whereas once Internet access was restricted to a small group of university researchers, today the Internet is open to anyone who can afford a $20-a-month connection. These days, rocketing into cyberspace is as simple as deciding which services you want and choosing the best way to get them.

Getting Connected: Your Ticket to Ride

In this chapter, we take a look at the three basic types of Internet connections and identify which offers the most for your business. The three basic options are

> Dialup accounts (through Internet access providers and commercial online services)
>
> Dialup network extensions—particularly Serial Line Interface Protocol (SLIP) and Point to Point Protocol (PPP)
>
> High-speed leased lines connecting your network to the Internet directly

Each has its pluses and minuses, and your choice will be colored by the tools and services you want to access, the amount of money you're willing to spend, the kind of interface you want, the degree of user-friendliness you prefer, and the amount of time you want to spend online. Generally speaking, the higher the speed of your connection and the more data traffic it can carry, the more you'll have to pay. The slower the link and the less traffic it carries, the less you'll have to spend.

In this chapter, we explore what each type of connection has to offer and how much you're likely to pay for the service, and we offer a list of vendors that can help you connect to the Internet. An extensive listing of commercial Internet access providers offering a variety of connectivity options is provided in Appendix A, "Internet On-Ramps."

Internet Economics 101

Because the Internet is a network of networks, it's not surprising that many organizations are already accessing the information highway, sometimes without even realizing it.

For these people—oscilloscope designers at Hewlett-Packard, assembly line workers at Xerox, undergraduates at Harvard, Ph.D. candidates at Stanford and MIT, and federal government employees—the connection to the Internet is free; they don't have to pay a monthly fee or any connect-time charges to access the wealth of resources and information on the network.

"Free" is really a misnomer, though; the Internet certainly doesn't operate without cost. Just like the interstate highway system and any other aspect of the national infrastructure, somebody—in this case, the government, universities, telecommunications companies, and large businesses—had to ante up the money to build the Internet's network of roadways. Now, somebody—namely, every network user—has to pay for its upkeep.

Who pays for the Internet? The answer is threefold:

The government. The federal government started it all when the Defense Department Advanced Research Projects Agency (ARPA) created the original ARPAnet. The National Science Foundation backbone (NSFnet) followed in the early 1970s, linking the ARPAnet with academic researchers. Soon however, the National Science Foundation (NSF) is scheduled to begin an overhaul of NSFnet and of the Internet itself. On April 30, 1995, NSF's contract with Advanced Network and Services Inc., its network manager, expired. Because the agency wants to change the way it supports the network, smaller regional networks connected to the NSFnet backbone have been told to find other connections. To ease the transition, the government is funding mid-level service providers such as New England's NEARnet and the Southeast's SURAnet. The bottom line: Private-sector communications companies will take over maintenance of the information superhighway.

Commercial providers. The various commercial Internet access providers are the second important source of funding for Internet maintenance and development. Because the government originally banned commercial traffic on NSFnet, a group of companies seeking to use the growing network for commercial purposes formed a loose cooperative venture called the *Commercial Internet Exchange* (CIX). The goal of the CIX is to build and maintain its own parallel backbone network wherein commercial traffic could appear without violation of the NSF network usage policies. Today, in return for paying CIX a flat fee of $10,000 a year,

Internet connectivity "resellers" can buy unlimited Internet access, which they can then resell by the hour or on a flat-fee basis to individuals and businesses.

Individuals. In the early days, the list would have stopped here, but today the Internet encompasses more than 25,000 different networks, connecting more than 30,000,000 users, and individual-user connectivity fees are becoming an important source of Internet revenue. Most individuals, businesses, and other users pay monthly fees or per-hour charges for Internet service. Prices vary depending on the speed and capacity of the Internet link: People who access the Internet through a simple dialup connection pay as little as $20 a month—or less. Internet service providers and larger corporations might pay $1,000 a month or more for a complete network-to-network bridge, a personal on-ramp as it were.

Most of the well-known commercial networks—CompuServe, America Online, and AppleLink—charge users a base monthly fee plus connect-time charges and often, additional charges for those users that access specialized databases, discussion forums, and other features.

If you're used to that environment, you'll be delighted to know that the standard policy for Internet service providers is a monthly access fee with no hidden or supplemental charges. No additional payment is required if you happen to receive more than, say, 20 e-mail messages in a month. Instead, Internet pricing is based on the speed, power, and capability of your connection. Generally speaking, the higher the speed of the connection, the more you have to pay.

Note: Although $20-a-month Internet access may give technologically savvy individuals and small businesses everything they need, it's a less than ideal solution for larger companies and less-computer-adept users. These simple dialup accounts are the "worst" for businesses wanting to ship large amounts of data over the Internet, perform multiple tasks in parallel (that is, have more than one program running at the same time), or allow more than one employee at a time to log onto the network and access the Internet's many features through the standard DOS, Windows, or Mac interface. If that sounds like your business, you'll probably find that it's worth investing in a more powerful and expensive Internet connection.

Analyzing Your Internet Needs

Sexy car advertisements aside, it's always a good strategy to analyze your needs before you decide what kind of Internet connection to get. If you're buying a new automobile, basic questions include budget, fuel efficiency, size, utility, reliability, and so on.

The best strategy is to spend some time identifying your information needs and budget before making your decision.

You need to consider whether

> You want to hook up one person, a small group, or a larger department or company.
>
> You want your business to broadcast information, such as advertising, to other Internet users.
>
> You want simple connectivity for your company.
>
> You want to access the World Wide Web with its cool graphics and hyperlinks.
>
> E-mail and Usenet groups are sufficient for what you want to do.

Here's a checklist to get you started in assessing your Internet connectivity requirements. Your answers to these questions will determine the type of Internet connection your company needs.

> How big is your company? How big might it become in the foreseeable future?
>
> Is your business located all in one office, with your computers connected on a single local area network, or do you have multiple sites scattered throughout the state, country, or even the world?
>
> How many people at your company are going to need Internet access? everybody? the corporate library staff? the owner?
>
> What Internet features are you planning to use most often? electronic mail? discussion groups? information-gathering? marketing? remote-site collaboration? file-transfer? real-time conferencing?
>
> Will your employees need to perform multiple tasks on the Internet simultaneously? Will more than one employee need to log on at the same time?
>
> How much money can you afford to spend on Internet access every month? How much are you spending on phone, fax, overnight delivery, and other communications tools now?

Keep in mind that whether you're the owner of a small business operating out of a spare bedroom or a high-powered executive heading a multinational corporation with offices around the globe, you're almost certain to cut your overhead by connecting to the Internet.

No matter what your business, the more you learn about the Internet's capabilities, the better you can restructure your company's communications system to take advantage of the international infrastructure that's already up and running.

Choosing an Internet Access Provider

As you do when you buy a car or hire a real estate broker, you must consider a number of factors when you choose an Internet access provider. The key, of course, is whether the provider offers the type of connection that you seek, but that's not the only element to consider.

Before we discuss the different types of Internet access, let's talk a little about the things that you should look for when selecting an Internet access provider.

The six key factors we recommend you consider are

- Network reliability
- Network performance
- Network security
- Network restrictions
- Local phone access
- User services and support

Each of these is covered in the following sections.

Network Reliability

If you run a business, you know what it's like when your computer system crashes or a lightning storm causes your power or phone line to go down: The business grinds to a halt. The same thing can happen to your Internet connection if the network that's providing your access goes on the blink. If you rely on Internet e-mail for your communications needs, a network failure can leave you out of touch with your employees, your colleagues, and most importantly, your clients and customers.

There are a variety of reasons that portions of the Internet can break down or otherwise go offline. In the last few years, portions of the network have failed due to power outages, downed telephone connections, and poor weather conditions.

> **Tip:** Reliability is an important question to consider when you're evaluating Internet access providers because different companies have different online records. Talk with the provider and several of his or her customers to find out how reliable the system is. Persistent problems indicate that the system is growing so fast that there aren't enough phone lines to handle all the calls or that the system is too small.

Network Performance

Network performance is the speed at which your Internet access provider can carry the e-mail and other data you want to send. There are two aspects involved—the speed with which you can connect to the provider and the speed of the connection the provider has to the Internet. For obvious reasons, it's important that your service provider has a very high speed connection to the Internet, lest your data sit idly on the system waiting to be dispatched to your customers or colleagues.

The speed of a network connection is measured in *bits per second* (bps). Because a single character of data is composed of eight bits of information, a slow 9,600 bps connection, for example, would transmit 9,600 / 8 or 1,200 characters per second (in reality, it's often less than that due to system overhead). This chapter is about 28,314 characters, for example, so with a noise-free 9,600 bps connection, it would take about 23.6 seconds to transmit it to your machine. Contrast this with a 28,800 bps connection, which would require a transmission time of only 7.9 seconds. Internet service providers should have considerably faster connections to the Internet; a T1 connection between your service provider and its Internet connection is the minimum you should accept (at that speed this chapter could be transmitted in under a second).

Network Security

Despite what you may have read about crackers and pirates swooping down on unsuspecting Internet users and pilfering passwords or reading private e-mail, chances are quite slim that your company's computer system will be broken into.

Nevertheless, it's vital to find an Internet access provider who will work with you to set up "firewalls," passwords, and other network security measures if you decide to connect your computer system directly to the Internet. Security is also a reason that a provider who has been on the Internet a while may prove a safer choice than a brand-new access provider. If you're planning to sell your goods or services online, you'll also want to consider strategies for transmitting credit card information in a secure manner.

> **Note:** For more information about Internet security, both for users and businesses, read Chapter 19, "Network Security."

Network Restrictions

Earlier, we talked about acceptable use provisions of various networks, particularly how they apply to the government-funded NSFnet Internet backbone. The Acceptable Use Policy (known informally as AUP) is a critical issue for any Internet access provider; before you begin to work with an access provider, make sure that the provider has access to a network that permits commercial traffic.

Major access providers have their own AUP policies, and we strongly recommend that you carefully read these policies before signing up for a particular service, regardless of how you anticipate using the Internet.

Local Phone Access

One advantage of using the Internet for information gathering and dissemination is its low cost and flat monthly fee.

Your cost savings can vanish instantly, however, if you choose an access provider that's a long-distance phone call away. Although the various telecommunications companies might appreciate your use, it's a sure bet that your first phone bill will be enough to make you rethink your Internet connection strategy!

This isn't a problem if you sign up with an Internet access provider in your city, but it's something to think about when considering whether to hook up with a national or international Internet network.

The good news is that many of the biggest Internet providers are beginning to offer local dialup access and toll-free numbers in a variety of locations throughout the United States. For example, Netcom Communications Service, with computers in the San Francisco area, has local dialup numbers in Los Angeles, San

Diego, Seattle, Portland, New York City, Las Vegas, Chicago, and Austin, Texas. Netcom and other providers, including AlterNet, CERFNet, Performance Systems International, and WinNET Communications offer Internet access via toll-free 800 lines. This can be a double boon if you travel and want to remain connected without paying for long-distance phone calls.

User Services and Support

Although Internet access is fast becoming a commodity, Internet providers vary widely in terms of the services they offer. For example, some networks offer the full range of Internet tools and features, including Archie, FTP, Gopher, telnet, Usenet, and the World Wide Web; others offer only Internet e-mail and a small selection of newsgroups. Some access providers offer subscriber newsletters and information updates as well as Internet training courses and technical support by telephone and online.

Before you choose a network access provider, it's important to check references. You wouldn't purchase a car based only on the information you learned from the salesperson, so don't sign up for an access provider without doing your homework.

One good way to learn about the service is to request the names of a few customers from the Internet access provider and ask them how well the access provider has met their needs. It can also be useful to check the network's reputation by posting messages to online bulletin boards or by attending meetings of local computer user groups. Finally, ask the Internet access provider for a service guarantee and find out—in advance—what kind of procedures the firm has for resolving problems quickly.

Doing your homework up front can save you considerable frustration—and money—down the road.

The Three Types of Internet Connections

Now, it's time to get down to the nitty-gritty—choosing the type of Internet connection that's right for you and your business. There are three basic kinds of Internet connections.

- An online, or dialup, account with an Internet access provider
- A SLIP or PPP connection, enabling your company's computer or local-area network to connect to the Internet directly for full Internet connectivity.

■ Leased-line (T1) service, offering Internet network access at speeds as fast as 1.544 megabits per second. At this speed, by the way, it would take less than a second to transmit this chapter from one computer to another over the Internet.

Online Accounts

Online accounts, sometimes known as "shell" accounts, are probably the best value for individuals and small business owners who don't plan to log onto the Internet for more than a few hours each day.

With an online account, you use your computer and modem to dial your Internet access provider's computer system, which is linked directly to the Internet. Your computer never actually connects to the Internet directly.

Hundreds of companies nationwide sell access to the Internet for as little as $10 to $15 a month, and, depending on the company and the pricing plan, you can buy either a set number of connect-time hours per month or unlimited Internet access. If you work for the government or a university, you may even be able to get a shell account for free.

Check out Appendix A, "Internet On-Ramps," for the Internet access provider nearest you.

The main advantages of this type of dialup connection are low cost, unlimited access to e-mail and other Internet services, and protection from network-wide system crashes and security problems. If your provider's computer crashes, your PC won't go down with it; you don't have to worry about hackers or viruses, either.

With a shell account, you can access most of the tools and data the Internet offers—even though your computer isn't directly connected. You can send and receive e-mail, download files from remote computers (known as file-transfer protocol), log into another computer remotely (telnet), search thousands of databases in cyberspace called gophers, and surf the Web in text-based format.

The big drawback to this kind of connection is that you can't access the hypermedia splendors of the World Wide Web—at least, not without obtaining and installing special software. Another problem is that it's slower than a more powerful Internet connection and lacks the capability of running multiple Internet sessions simultaneously. If you need a dozen Internet accounts for your employees, however, an online account for each user may end up actually costing you more than a SLIP or PPP connection, as you'll see later.

> **Note:** Now it's possible to get graphical access to the Web without paying higher prices for a SLIP or PPP connection. Two of the leading "pseudo-slip" programs are Remsock and The Internet Adapter (TIA), both of which can run on an Internet access provider's host computer. You can download Remsock ($15) from `ftp://oslonett.no/Shareware/Windows/Comm/remsock.zip`
>
> For information about TIA's availability, send e-mail to `tia-info@marketplace.com`.
>
> There's also SlipKnot, a Web browser with TCP/IP and most of the WinSock translation handled internally. SlipKnot resides on your terminal. SlipKnot is available from `http://www.interport.net/slip-knot/slipknot.html` or `ftp://ftp.netcom.com/pub/pbrooks/slipknot/slnot110.zip`. Be aware, however, that these programs do not work with all Internet access providers.

Online accounts are available from three different sources—an Internet access provider, a commercial online service, and a university, government, or nonprofit organization. Here are the pros and cons of each:

Internet Access Providers

Pros:	You get full Internet access, not just the e-mail that the commercial online services provide. You usually pay a flat monthly fee as opposed to per-minute charges based on usage. You're likely to find an AUP that's consistent with your requirements.
Cons:	Many Internet access providers still don't offer easy-to-use Windows, DOS, or Macintosh front-ends for online accounts or navigational programs, forcing you to struggle with an ungainly text-based system or download a shareware program. It also means that you might have to compose and reply to your mail online, a nuisance when you're accustomed to commercial services like CompuServe and their handy offline text editors and filing cabinets. Because many local Internet access providers are small companies with few modems and phone connections, you may get busy signals if you try to dial in during peak hours.

Commercial Online Services

Pros: You don't have to pay an additional monthly fee to set up a dedicated Internet account somewhere else. You also get a nice-looking, easy-to-use DOS, Mac, or Windows interface. Prodigy and CompuServe now offer access to the Web and most other Internet tools; America Online just rolled out a preview version of its Web browser to its members.

Cons: If you're not careful, you may end up with a bad case of "sticker shock" at the end of the month. Though CompuServe recently rolled out a $24.95-for-20-hours plan, the service charges an additional 10 cents for every Internet message you receive, whether you want that piece of mail delivered or not. Join a few mailing lists and start getting e-mail from customers. Soon you'll find yourself paying $50 a month or more just for e-mail. Prodigy and America Online charge monthly fees plus hourly charges for a package of services that includes Internet access.

University, Government, Non-Profit Groups, or Freenets

Pros: It's free.

Cons: It's hard to get an account on a government or university system unless you work or study there or know someone who does. There are also limits on the amount of time you're allowed to spend on the system at any one "sitting," and you may have a hard time getting past the busy signals during peak usage times. Most importantly, the acceptable use policies of these organizations usually prohibit any business or commercial use.

To have your own dialup account, you'll require an account on an Internet access provider, a high-speed modem (14.4 kbps minimum), and some terminal emulation software (typically around $100, though less expensive and even free packages are available. We recommend VersaTerm for Macintosh and Procomm Plus for PC and Windows). In the latter category is a bewildering variety of options from dozens of firms. Your best bet is to ask your future service provider for a recommendation, and, indeed, many of the biggest Internet service providers can sell modems at a special discount rate. Dave has VersaTerm Pro on his Macintosh and connects with a Telebit Worldblazer at home and Telebit QBlazer on the road. Rosalind uses WinNET Mail front-end software, Crosstalk for Windows, and the 14.4 kbps modem that came bundled with her Dell Dimension XPS P90 computer.

SLIP/PPP Connections

However powerful the computer on your desk may be, it's really no more than a "dumb terminal" when all the files, processing, and applications are running on a remote computer connected to the Internet.

If you have a high-speed dialup connection to the Internet, however, you can use the power and capabilities of your desktop machine to run Internet programs. Instead of sending individual characters through the modem, dialup IP actually extends the Transmission Control Protocol/Internet Protocol (TCP/IP, the nervous system and underlying foundation of the Internet itself) to work with dialup connections.

What does this mean? It means that instead of being limited to text on your screen, you can transmit graphics, audio, and various other forms of digital information. Further, TCP/IP enables you to use multiple Internet tools at once, so you can compose an e-mail message while checking out the latest news on Usenet and in, a third window, searching for a file with Archie, for example.

There are two types of dialup Internet Protocol (IP) connections: SLIP and PPP. Both provide a full Internet connection capable of sending and receiving data from the tens of thousands of other computers on the network. Using this more powerful form of dialup connection, your computer can "talk" directly with other computers on the network in the Internet's universal "language"—the TCP/IP protocol. What's more, other computers connected to the Internet can dial your computer directly.

SLIP and PPP connections offer many advantages. One is that you can perform many network-related tasks at once. For example, you can download a program file from one computer on the network while accessing data from a Gopher site housed on another. You can also set up your system so that e-mail is delivered directly to your company's computer, enhancing security. You can also choose your own domain name—for example, Dave chose `intuitive.com` for his firm—which may be useful for marketing. Rosalind and her partner, Ryan Scott, chose `netcreations.com` for their new company that helps businesses set up interactive advertising sites on the Web.

Another advantage is the ability to use sophisticated graphics software interfaces, such as Mosaic or Netscape, to access a wide spectrum of information with a click of your mouse. These days, a number of commercial software programs can serve as front ends for Macs and PCs. With Netmanage's Chameleon, for example, you can access the Internet through an easy-to-use Windows interface; Spry's Internet in A Box is also a popular choice.

SLIP/PPP connections are available from the same Internet access providers who offer shell accounts—and they've dropped dramatically in price over the last year. You can now get a SLIP/PPP account for $20 a month, though there may be a limit to the number of hours you can spend online without paying extra. Full-time connections, however, may run into a couple hundred dollars depending on how often you go online and how many users are connected.

Besides the higher price, another drawback to SLIP/PPP accounts is the need to install the TCP/IP software on your computer before you can connect—a daunting prospect for novice Internet users. Fortunately, there are a number of new software programs coming onto the market that make TCP/IP installation as easy as slipping a floppy in your A: drive. For example, Internet in A Box enables even novice users to set up and configure their entire software package in about five minutes simply by loading in diskettes and following on-screen instructions.

SLIP and PPP software for DOS, Windows, Macintosh, and UNIX computers—known as *client* software—can range in cost from nothing to hundreds of dollars depending on the features, ease of use, and complexity of the program. TCP/IP software is included in almost every version of UNIX, though not all UNIX packages include the specific SLIP or PPP client software. In all cases, your best bet is to work with your Internet access provider to obtain the latest version of the connectivity software you need for your particular platform.

Leased-Line Connections

Although connections through a regular phone line are inexpensive, they aren't particularly fast. Dialup connections, either a simple online account or a high-powered SLIP or PPP connection, are adequate for many purposes but insufficient for companies planning to offer lots of electronic information on the network or connecting a large number of employees to the Internet.

Fortunately, there's an alternative—leased lines. Leased lines are the connection of choice for Internet power users—large companies with lots of users spread out over multiple sites or sites with a lot of data to transmit.

With a leased line, your company can hook up their local-area network to the Internet, enabling any or all of your employees to access the Internet whenever and for whatever task they need. As with a dialup IP connection, a leased line exposes your computer system to all the Internet's risks and problems, which means that you'll need to take security precautions.

The main advantage of a leased line is speed, enabling you to move large amounts of data in a short period of time.

A T1 line can transmit data at speeds as high as 10 megabits per second. A T3 line can go even faster, zapping data from one end of the wire to the other at speeds as high as 357.5 megabits per second.

To put this in perspective, this chapter which takes 23.6 seconds to transmit on a 9,600 bps dialup connection would move so fast over a T1 or T3 line that its journey would be over before you could start your stopwatch.

There's a price for this performance, however, and much of the cost comes from the local telephone company. The going rate for a full T1 connection is $2,000 to $3,200 a month, and you'll pay an additional $400 or so a month for the wire itself. If you want the speed of a T1 but don't mind sharing the bandwidth with other users, we suggest looking into getting a fractional T1 line. Fractional T1s are available for as low as $400 a month.

A less expensive alternative is a 56 kbps line, which offers many times the speed of a dedicated dialup link. A 56K line, as they're often known, typically costs between $300 to $1,000 a month; the local phone company tacks on another $100 a month for a digital line.

To set up a leased-line connection, you need a computer running TCP/IP software on a local area network. The networked computer—the "server" in this case—is hooked up to a router that also connects to the telephone link, a phone line with a digital conversion device on each end. The telephone link is hooked into a router or gateway at the network provider's end of the circuit. Installing a leased line is a complex, time-consuming job, and we strongly recommend you work with a skilled network administrator. Many Internet service providers can offer recommendations of local groups and individuals that can help.

The Future of Internet Pricing and Connections

With its flat-fee pricing, multiple connectivity options, and unlimited access to e-mail, files, databases, and computers throughout the world, the Internet is clearly the biggest communications bargain available today.

But that may not always be true. As more and more individuals and businesses log onto the Internet, bogging down the information highway with an ever increasing quantity of data traffic, many people are beginning to question whether the "free lunch" that exists today can continue—or if, ultimately, users will have to buy their Internet access by the minute or by the byte just as subscribers to commercial online services do today.

We believe that connect-time-based access providers will become more prevalent than they are today but that there will still be flat-rate Internet access providers willing to offer competitive rates for those companies ready to hook their businesses onto the information highway.

FINDING THE INTERFACE THAT'S RIGHT FOR YOU

Until recently, the Internet's text-based UNIX interface made the network difficult for all but the most technologically astute computer users to navigate.

Not any more.

Over the last year, a cornucopia of point-and-click interfaces has burst onto the scene, offering users everything from offline e-mail creation to hypermedia links to audio and video clips. Forget about typing arcane commands at the system prompt; now, surfing the Net is almost as easy as navigating Prodigy or CompuServe.

For Internet novices, there's never been a better time to cruise the information superhighway. Not only are there dozens of Windows, Macintosh, DOS, and UNIX front-end programs that make the Internet easier to navigate, there are also hypermedia browsers such as Mosaic, Netscape, Air Mosaic, and WebSurfer that you can use to point-and-click your way through the full spectrum of graphics, sound, and video clips on the World Wide Web.

From GUI to MUI

Last year, the hot news from cyberspace was point-and-click graphical interfaces that made online services easier to navigate.

These days, it's snazzy, new multimedia interfaces with which you can experience the full spectrum of graphics, sound, and even video clips.

In less than a year's time, we've gone from GUI to MUI.

If you've been navigating the Internet in silence, you're in for a treat—or a shock, as the case may be. Thanks to a host of new front-end programs from Internet access providers such as Netcom, Pipeline, and WinNET Communications, software companies such as Spry (Internet in A Box), Netscape (Netscape Navigator), and Spyglass (Enhanced Mosaic), and commercial online services such as Prodigy, CompuServe, and America Online, surfing the Net is more graphical and exciting than ever before. Forget about the blank screen and the system prompt— unless, of course, you're a UNIX guru like Dave. (Rosalind prefers to do Windows.) These days, accessing photos, sounds, and video clips is as easy as clicking a hyperlink with your mouse.

The Internet's hottest interface is the Mosaic-style browser, a point-and-click front-end for the network's World Wide Web hypermedia system. Mosaic and spin-offs such as the Netscape Navigator take the clunky, text-based Internet and transform it into a thing of beauty, so that you can point and click effortlessly through thousands of online shopping malls, art museums, bookstores, and the electronic equivalent of four-color magazine ads—experiencing sights and sounds along the way. Thanks to graphical Web browsers, even small businesses can set up online shops for a fraction of the cost of leasing real-world retail space. There are also plenty of graphical interfaces for Internet e-mail, databases, and search tools that make the network easier to navigate.

Types of Interfaces

Although there are dozens of Internet interfaces available both commercially and as shareware, all of these front-end programs break down into three main categories. They are

> Text
> Graphical (point-and-click)
> Hypermedia

Though text-based UNIX interfaces are boring to look at and tricky to use, they're very handy once you master them. The big advantage to text-based interfaces is their interchangeability. In other words, you can use the same basic commands with any Internet provider that offers access through a UNIX shell. What's more, you can use a text interface to access every feature of the Internet, from e-mail to newsgroups to Internet Relay Chat (IRC) to the World Wide Web.

Consider: Your Internet access provider may not offer a graphical interface, requiring you to use a text-based file-transfer protocol (FTP) program to download one. Even if you have a graphical program, an advanced Internet tool such as telnet (remote login) may only be available in terminal emulation mode, requiring you to type text-based commands. Or perhaps you're away from home and need to log in through a friend's UNIX shell account that lacks a graphical front-end.

One of the most popular text-based e-mail programs is Pine, a full-featured, easy-to-use editor for composing e-mail and sorting it into folders. It even comes with an address book. (There's also Elm, an e-mail program originally authored by Dave Taylor.) One of the better newsreader programs (for accessing newsgroups) is nn. Though it can be tricky for novices to learn, once you've memorized the commands, it serves its purpose well. With Lynx, you can surf the Web without the time and expense of installing a SLIP connection (though you'll have to download the graphics and view them later).

Despite the Internet's wealth of information, its UNIX-based interface has long made it difficult to navigate for all but the most technologically astute computer users. Now that the Internet is opening its doors to online novices and business users, an impressive collection of easy-to-use Windows interfaces is coming onstream. Some of these are stand-alone products—such as Qualcomm's Eudora and Netmanage's Internet Chameleon, a scaled-down version of the $499 Chameleon 4.0 package—that work with any Internet access provider; others are software-server combination packages, offered by Internet providers such as Netcom, Pipeline, and Performance Systems International.

The third type of interface is hypermedia, which, for most Internet users, means National Center for Supercomputing Applications (NCSA) Mosaic and its commercial spinoffs. With a graphical Web browser, you simply point and click a highlighted phrase and you're immediately transported to another document, image, or digitized audio or video clip on the computer you're accessing or on a computer halfway around the world. For example, you might click a familiar smiling Macintosh icon and be connected to the Apple Computer central Web server in Cupertino, California. Clicking `Olivetti` might move you to a computer system in Italy, and the phrase, `click here to see the latest products from Toshiba`, could zap you across the Pacific to Japan. You also can use Mosaic to access other Internet tools such as Gopher, World Wide Web, FTP, Usenet newsgroups, Archie, Wide Area Information Services (WAIS), and Veronica. It doesn't really surprise us that a nation of channel-surfers and remote-control junkies would cozy up to the Web.

Easy On-Ramps to the Infobahn

Here are seven Internet access programs that provide easy on-ramps to the infobahn.

Text

With all the hoopla about the new graphical user interfaces, it's easy to ignore that old standby, the text-based interface. True, you've got to wrestle with UNIX commands at the system prompt, but text-based programs are fast, and they get you where you want to go.

Where text-based interfaces really shine is interchangeability. In other words, you can use the same basic commands with any Internet provider that offers access through a UNIX shell. (This is slowly changing, however, as providers increasingly write their own text interfaces.)

Another advantage is that a text interface enables you to access every feature of the Internet, from e-mail to newsgroups to Internet Relay Chat (IRC) to the World Wide Web. One of the most popular text-based e-mail programs is Pine, a full-featured, easy-to-use editor for composing e-mail and sorting it into folders. It even comes with an address book. One of the better newsreader programs (for accessing newsgroups) is nn. Though it can be tricky for novices to learn, once you've memorized the commands, it serves its purpose well.

The drawback to text-based interfaces is two-fold: 1) They're difficult for novices to master; and 2) They can't display graphics. For example, text-based FTP is difficult to use without memorizing long strings of archaic commands.

Lynx (see Figure 3.1), a text-based program for surfing the Web, doesn't let you view the Web's many multimedia marvels.

Pipeline

The folks at Pipeline are freethinkers, and it shows in their innovative Internet interface. The brainchild of *New York Times* science writer James Gleick, Pipeline's Internaut software doesn't look like any of the other Internet interfaces on the market. (Pipeline, formerly an Internet access service as well, was acquired by Performance Systems International earlier this year; the Pipeline software can be used with other Internet access services as well.)

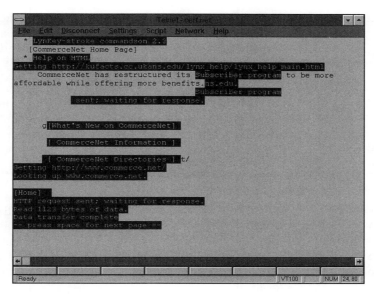

Figure 3.1. Surfing the Web with Lynx.

Like other Internet programs, Pipeline gives you graphical interfaces for e-mail, newsgroups, Gopher sites, FTP, the World Wide Web, and IRC, plus search tools like Archie. There's even the capability to engage in real-time "talk" sessions, which aren't supported by most Internet software.

One of Pipeline's unique features is its small footprint. Rather than hogging a full screen, the program opens a small window containing the opening screen and then pops open a new window every time you visit a new location in cyberspace. Each window remains open and fully functional until you close it, so you can revisit any area without having to go back and reaccess it. Also, there's no need to put an electronic "bookmark" in an area you plan to revisit because you can simply minimize the window and return to it at your leisure.

Pipeline's e-mail utility is superb as well. It supports multiple mail folders and comes with a handy address book. It also automatically saves a copy of every e-mail message you send, creating an electronic archive for future reference. Whenever you compose a message offline, the message automatically goes into the program's outgoing mailbox and gets sent the next time you dial in.

Pipeline's newsreader and FTP interfaces are also strong. The newsreader closely resembles Windows File Manager, with each newsgroup displayed as a directory and each message as a file. With Pipeline, you can download the subject header of each newsgroup posting and then log off, so that you can select the messages you're interested in while offline. When you reconnect to the Internet, Pipeline goes in and downloads the messages to your computer for offline reading, a savings for Pipeline users who dial in from outside New York.

Pipeline's FTP utility is one of the best around. Instead of limiting you to viewing one directory at a time, Pipeline enables you to view an unlimited number of directories of an FTP site, each in its own window. With Pipeline's "talk" feature, you can contact anyone who's logged on anywhere on the Internet and conduct a "live" chat session by typing back and forth.

Internaut Version 2.07 adds a long-awaited Web browser to complete its Internet package.

Internaut works over the national CompuServe network and can be activated from most local dial-up accounts. Internaut's Web browser isn't particularly powerful; it uses menus instead of buttons, for example, and doesn't automatically save data to your hard drive for faster recall the next time you access the site (a process known as *caching*). On the other hand, it has a great bookmark organizer to keep track of your favorite sites.

One of Internaut's big advantages is that you don't need to establish a SLIP/PPP connection or install a program like Trumpet in order to start surfing the Web. Internaut uses a protocol called Pink Slip, which enables you to access the Web over a standard dialup phone connection. Although the Pipeline browser (see Figure 3.2) can't compete with the feature-rich Netscape, Internaut is an excellent overall choice if you're looking for an easy on-ramp to the Internet's tools and features.

NCSA Mosaic

The first Web browser on the scene, NCSA Mosaic is still the best known, though newer, faster browsers—notably Netscape—have begun to pass it by. Nevertheless, Mosaic isn't resting on its laurels; its developers at NCSA are working hard to keep it current.

The latest version, a beta release called Mosaic V. 2.0, is far more stable than the original, a RAM hog that frequently crashed when asked to display a graphics-rich page. NCSA has also added a powerful *hotlist* manager (a hotlist is a list of favorite sites that you can access with a click of your mouse) (Figure 3.3) that lets you organize your favorite Web pages into folders. If you can use Windows File Manager, you'll find Mosaic's hotlist a breeze. Best of all, it's free—unlike many of its commercial cousins.

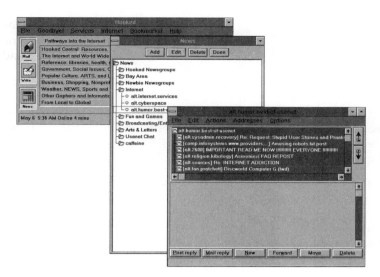

Figure 3.2. Reading newsgroups with Pipeline.

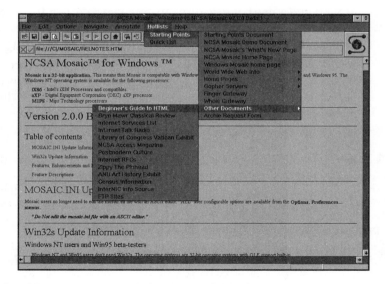

Figure 3.3. NCSA Mosaic now includes a powerful hotlist manager.

But although NCSA Mosaic is much improved, it's far from perfect. It still takes more memory than any other browser, and it lacks Netscape's slick look and feel. Finally, Mosaic requires that you connect to the Internet through a program like Trumpet Winsock before you can run it; installing Trumpet requires more Net-savvy than most Internet novices can muster.

Netscape Navigator

Netscape Navigator is the coolest browser on the block—hardly surprising considering that it was created by the same talented team that pioneered the original Mosaic program at the NCSA. Their long experience shines through in every feature of Netscape, from its new, easy-to-use navigational buttons to the way it loads pages onto the screen while you watch. Netscape is quick and easy to install thanks to a well-written setup program and takes up less than 2 MB of storage space on your hard disk. It's free to download, or $39 for registration and technical support from the company.

Netscape's most striking feature is the way it loads Web pages onto your screen. Other Web browsers make you wait until a page is completed before you can start viewing it, but with Netscape, you can view pages while the download is still in progress. Unlike other Web browsers, Netscape doesn't limit you to the Web alone. It also enables you to access e-mail, newsgroups, Gopher, FTP, and other Internet tools.

Another valuable feature of the program is that it automatically transports you to its home page whenever you log on (unless you go in and change the default setting). The Netscape home page features an excellent tutorial for new Netscape users as well as a host of other Internet informational resources and pointers to cool, new Web sites. Especially helpful is a menu option with which you can search the Internet using five different search engines.

Netscape's latest version, version 1.1N, contains a number of new features designed to please businesses and consumers alike. For Web page designers, Netscape offers the capability to dress up pages with colored text, background fills, tables, and animation and to employ dynamic document updating so that users can view continuously changing data such as stock quotes and weather maps. The new Netscape also features encryption technology, which safeguards your credit card number when you order a product online provided that the merchant's pages are housed on a secure server such as Netscape's NetSite software.

Netscape is not without its limitations, however. As with Mosaic, you'll still need to find and install a TCP/IP software stack (such as Trumpet Winsock) in order to connect to the Internet and get Netscape to run. But once you get Netscape up and running, you'll view the Web the way it was meant to be seen! (See Figure 3.4.)

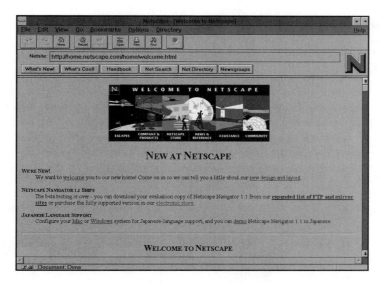

Figure 3.4. The Netscape home page features links to cool sites, search engines, and useful information about the Web.

Internet in A Box

Spry's feature-rich Internet in A Box is the Cadillac of Internet connection packages. Not only does it come shrink-wrapped, but it also includes two software manuals and a special edition of *The Whole Internet User's Guide,* the highly acclaimed book by Ed Krol. As for software, Internet in A Box includes AIR Mosaic, Spry's version of the Mosaic browser, and five other top-notch interfaces for accessing Internet tools. On top of all that, Internet in A Box also features a first-rate image viewer and an excellent UUencoding/decoding utility for transmitting binary files.

The e-mail utility included with Internet in A Box is excellent. Designed for online or offline mail creation, it's a godsend for business travelers and students who need to keep in touch with their colleagues or classmates while they're on the road. Spry's e-mail program features a folders setup matching the one in Windows File Manager, making sorting mail a snap.

To make newsgroup browsing more manageable, AIR News enables you to sort the groups into folders called "personal groups." Unfortunately, the current version of AIR News doesn't allow newsgroup postings to be downloaded and read offline.

Spry's Gopher, FTP, and telnet interfaces are excellent, too. AIR Gopher, for example, features buttons labeled with both a word and a picture describing their function. Network File Manager, the FTP interface, is one of the best and easiest on the market (see Figure 3.5). Just click the icon and Network File Manager splits the screen with Windows File Manager. To download a file from the Internet, you simply copy it from one directory to another.

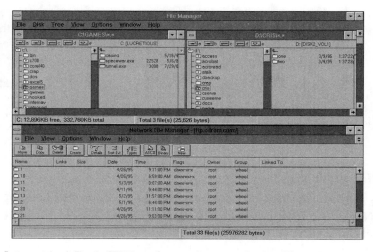

Figure 3.5. Internet in A Box's FTP interface makes transferring files a snap.

The only drawback we could find to Internet in A Box is its cost. At $149, it's far more expensive than any other Internet application suite on the market. On the other hand, we believe it's worth the lofty price tag; you get what you pay for, after all.

NetCruiser

NetCruiser—the graphical interface for Netcom, which is one of the largest Internet access providers in the country—is a big budget production from start to finish. Unfortunately, NetCruiser won't work with anything but Netcom accounts. Though Netcom is a national provider with local nodes around the country, you have to pay an extra $4.90 an hour to dial Netcom's toll-free number if there's no local node in your area.

With NetCruiser you can send and receive Internet e-mail, browse Gopher sites, read and post to newsgroups, and access FTP, telnet, and the World Wide Web. There's also a nifty utility called Site Chooser with which you can locate resources on the Internet by pointing to their geographical locations on a map. Internet features are accessible by clicking a row of command buttons at the top of the screen, and you can use multiple features at the same time. For example, we were able to compose an e-mail message while loading a Web page to our screen.

NetCruiser's e-mail utility is pretty standard except for one stand-out feature: You can set the length of each line in your message. Although this may seem trivial, it's actually fairly important because many Internet users have trouble reading mail with lines longer than 80 characters. Reading newsgroups with NetCruiser is truly a pleasure; the layout makes it intuitive and easy to use even for Internet novices.

NetCruiser's Gopher, FTP, and telnet interfaces all feature the handy Site Chooser utility (see Figure 3.6), which makes it easy to find what you're looking for. The IRC utility features a convenient row of buttons for joining discussions or initiating private talks but would benefit greatly by incorporating a Site Chooser utility to help novice users locate the IRC groups they would like to join.

NetCruiser's Web browser is a close cousin to NCSA Mosaic. The navigational buttons look a little different but perform the same basic functions. Unlike Netscape, the NetCruiser browser loads a page while you wait and displays the first part and then disables scrolling until the entire page is loaded to your screen, making you wait to view the entire page. NetCruiser's browser also has a few other limitations that make it less than ideal for business use. For example, it has trouble handling forms—a serious drawback for any company interested in selling products and services through online order forms.

Figure 3.6. With NetCruiser's Site Chooser, you can locate resources on the Internet by pointing to their geographic locations on a map.

Prodigy

Prodigy, long a laggard in the Internet access game, has come from behind by becoming the first of the Big Three online services to roll out Web access. Prodigy's home-grown Web browser is actually quite respectable; like Netscape, it loads text before pictures so that you can read while waiting for pictures to download, and displays pictures image by image as they arrive. What's more, surfing the Web on Prodigy is pretty fast—not because of Prodigy's access speeds (though Prodigy recently announced ISDN connectivity) but because Prodigy's computers house copies of the most frequently accessed Web sites to its own computers in a process known as *caching*. Because some Web sites are updated frequently, the Prodigy software also offers you the option of loading a page directly from its home on the Net. The end result is that you can have fast access when you want it and accurate viewing when you need it.

The biggest advantage of the Prodigy browser, though, is convenience. Unlike Netscape and NCSA Mosaic, there's no need to download the program from the Net and figure out how to install it. Simply log onto Prodigy as you always do, type WEB at the jumpword prompt, and choose Browse the Web from the menu choices on the right side of the screen. If you don't have a copy of the Prodigy browser on your hard drive, Prodigy will automatically ship you one while you wait.

Prodigy's browser isn't fancy, but it's a godsend for Internet novices (see Figure 3.7) who would rather spend their time surfing the Web than trying to figure out how to make their own surfboard.

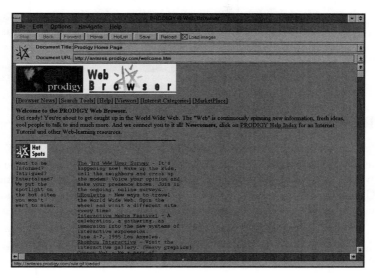

Figure 3.7. Prodigy's browser is ideal for Web novices.

 Note: In April, 1995, CompuServe rolled out a version of its new NetLauncher Web browser (actually, a version of Spry's Air Mosaic that works with the CompuServe Information Manager navigational software) and two aggressive Internet pricing plans—aggressive, that is, by CompuServe standards. One plan offers three hours of PPP Internet access for $9.95 a month plus $2.50 for each additional hour of usage; the other plan offers 20 hours of Internet access to Internet services for $24.95 with additional usage billed at $1.95 an hour. Meanwhile, America Online, which pioneered easy-to-use graphical interfaces for newsgroups, Gopher sites, and other Internet features, recently released a "preview" version of its Web browser. Unlike Prodigy's and CompuServe's browsers, America Online's browser is built right into the service's existing multimedia interface, making it simple for novices to master. The AOL browser also contains a nifty Favorite Places feature that you can use to create bookmarks for future browsing in both AOL and Internet features. You'll trade some functionality, however, for ease of use. For example, AOL's browser doesn't include an "open location" button that enables you to type the Internet address (URL) of an Internet location you would like to visit (though the AOL home page features lots of links and search tools); if you're new to browsers, it probably wouldn't occur to you to delete the address at the top of the screen and type your own.

Looking Ahead

What's the future of Internet interfaces? Clearly, the old days of UNIX shells and test-based command lines are rapidly drawing to a close. It's also clear that Mosaic and other hypermedia browsers will play a major role in the Internet's future. Ultimately, all Internet tools—not just the Web—may be accessed through graphical Web browsers, eliminating the need for separate interfaces for each.

Although a standard Internet interface may never emerge, the growing number of access programs on the market increases the likelihood that you'll find the Internet interface that's right for you.

Contact Information

Shopping for an Internet interface?

Here's where to get the seven Internet access programs mentioned in this chapter.

Internet in A Box

Spry, Inc.
316 Occidental Avenue South, Suite 200
Seattle, WA 98104
Phone:　1-800-SPRYNET
URL:　`http://www.spry.com`
e-mail:　`info@spry.com`
Price:　$149 (includes two manuals, a 500-page Internet book, and 90 days free tech support)

NCSA Mosaic

NCSA Mosaic
National Center for Supercomputing Applications at the
University of Illinois
Phone: No contact phone number
URL: `http://www.ncsa.uiuc.edu/SDG/Software`
           `/Mosaic/NCSAMosaicHome.html`
Price: Free

NetCruiser

Netcom
3031 Tisch Way, Second level
San Jose, CA 95128
Phone: 1-800-353-6600
e-mail: `support@ix.netcom.com`
Price: Software is free, Netcom access costs $25 setup fee plus $19.95
           per month

Netscape Navigator

Netscape Communications Corp.
Mountain View, CA
Phone: 1-800-NETSITE
e-mail: `order@mcom.com`
FTP: `ftp.mcom.com`
URL: `http://home.netscape.com`
Price: Free for personal, academic, and research use, $39 for support
           license.

Pipeline

Pipeline
150 Broadway—Suite 610
New York, NY 10038
Phone: 1-212-267-3636
e-mail: `info@pipeline.com`
Price: Free if downloaded, $5 for diskette

Prodigy

Prodigy Browser
Prodigy Services Company
Phone: 1-800-PRODIGY
URL: `http://www.astranet.com/`
Price: Free to Prodigy subscribers

Text-Based (UNIX) Interface

Freely available software is resident on most Internet access providers' machines, and you don't need to buy or install it.

INTERNET
TOOLS

WHAT TOOLS
ARE AVAILABLE

Although the global connectivity of the Internet is a key element in its growth and interest from the commercial sector, it's the tools—the applications that utilize that connectivity—that really transform the Internet from a mass of wires into the business network of the future.

A bewildering hodgepodge of words such as Gopher, Archie, WAIS, and Usenet, Internet tools can seem quite intimidating. But once you understand what these tools have to offer and how they fit together, you'll readily see how they can help you do business online.

Layers and Levels

To understand today's Internet tools, it's valuable to take a step back in time and consider how Internet computers communicated with one another when the network first began. Back then, high-speed data connections were essentially non-existent, and a small number of UNIX-based minicomputers shared information using the primitive networking technology and slow data lines that comprised ARPAnet. In those days, most of the Internet's terminals weren't PCs or Macs but dumb, text-only terminals and line-by-line typewriter/printer combinations known as teletype machines. Fortunately, the need to share graphical information was minimal because there was no way to view or work with it, anyway.

The early Internet tools, therefore, addressed the most basic needs of multicomputer connectivity—a way to transfer files back and forth and to connect to remote computers through the network and use their resources directly. The first tools created for the ARPAnet (the forerunner of the Internet) were FTP, a simple file-transfer program that worked with text-based commands to list files and transfer information, and telnet, which offered Internet users the ability to use any other computer on the network as if it were their own.

With the advent of today's Internet tools, it's easy to forget how innovative these two applications were at the time. Indeed, the ability to work remotely with computers was a watershed; for the first time, users could be anywhere on a network and utilize all its resources.

Meanwhile, a group of college students was using UNIX minicomputers and growing frustrated with the limitations of FTP. They hooked up modems to their computers and started experimenting with a new network that came to be known as UUCP, or UNIX-to-UNIX Copy Protocol. UUCP also offered a file-transfer mechanism, one that enabled users to copy files using intermediate host computers along the route. (Eliminating the need to dial the remote system directly saved these early Internet users lots of money on long-distance phone calls!)

Built on top of this phone-based file-transfer system was Usenet, a tool for enabling group discussions.

Now fast-forward a decade or so. Today, practically every Internet user has a high-speed connection and even home computer users can enjoy 28,800 bits-per-second access to the network. The Internet tools themselves, however, haven't changed much. Of the dozen or so tools now used by online marketers, only a small fraction have emerged in recent years. The newest, of course, is the World Wide Web.

As the network speeds have become faster, the older UUCP protocol has been superseded by the "language" of the higher speed ARPAnet wires—the TCP/IP protocol. TCP/IP is really two systems that run in layers on top of one another.

The lower level is IP, or Internet Protocol. It specifies the timing and size of the blocks of information sent along the wire and handles collisions, and so on. The upper protocol is TCP, or Transmission Control Protocol. TCP handles the breakup and reassembly of data transmitted, ensuring pieces don't get lost along the way and are put back together in the correct order.

The following text explains how the different tools fit into this picture.

Communication Tools

The most popular use of the Internet is communication. E-mail messages (see Figure 4.1), mailing lists, and Usenet newsgroups help tie the Internet community together—and make online marketing possible.

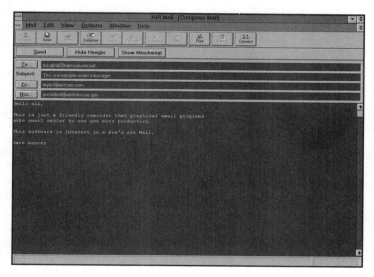

Figure 4.1. Electronic mail is the easiest and most popular way to communicate.

If you have an Internet account, you have an electronic mailbox—a file containing all the messages sent to you from anyone else on the network. New messages are deposited in your mailbox automatically, day or night, whether or not you're logged on.

Swapping e-mail is the single biggest use of the Internet, and it's also the most versatile. You can make contacts, generate sales leads, negotiate contracts, find suppliers, and even find solutions to technical problems. A single message can

be sent to a number of different recipients simply by naming them all on your distribution list. (It's as though you have a very efficient secretary who automatically makes as many copies of a document as you need.)

To distribute your message more widely, you can use what's known as a mailing list. There are thousands of mailing lists accessible publicly on the Internet plus thousands more that are used privately within companies, organizations, and groups of colleagues.

However, a mailing list with hundreds of users can quickly become unwieldy. That's where Usenet newsgroups (see Figure 4.2) come in.

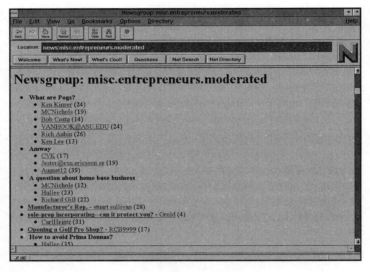

Figure 4.2. All the news, compliments of Usenet.

There are two parts to Usenet, just as there are two parts to the TCP/IP protocol. The lower level is called Netnews; that's the software that transmits individual Usenet "articles" (the equivalent of messages or memos). Operating above that is the content itself, the articles. This is Usenet itself, and, just as a library with no books wouldn't be very interesting, Netnews without the Usenet discussions on top would be a pretty dull place.

But Usenet is far from dull. Currently, there are more than 14,000 Usenet newsgroups distributed throughout the network. As with other Internet tools, Usenet started out as a primitive text-based interface that was difficult to master. Today, reading and posting to newsgroups has become much easier thanks to a wide variety of easy-to-use graphical interfaces that make Usenet as simple as pointing and clicking with your mouse.

Internet communication is more than simply exchanging messages, however. The original two Internet tools—FTP and telnet—also play a key role in transferring data.

Unfortunately, text-based FTP remains difficult to work with, confusing users with a host of dir, get, put, and ls commands (see Figure 4.3).

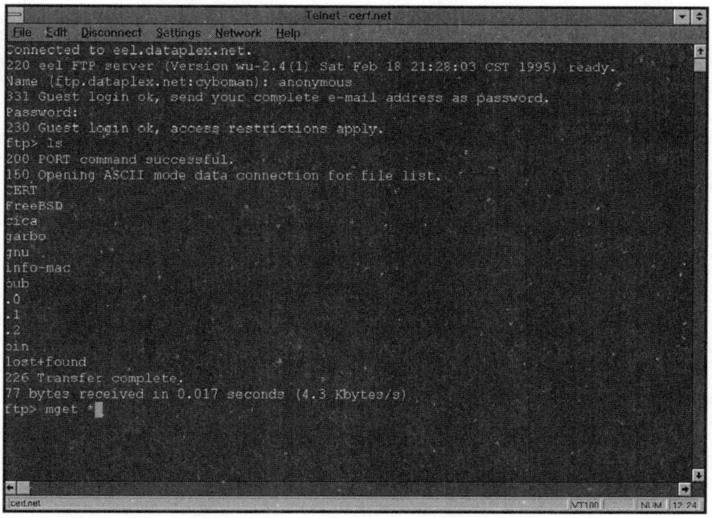

Figure 4.3. Transferring files the old-fashioned way.

The good news is that Windows-based FTP interfaces (see Figure 4.4), such as the one included with Spry's Internet in A Box, now make transferring files a snap. Just click an icon and Spry's Network File Manager splits your screen with Windows File Manager. To download a file from the Internet, you simply copy it from one directory to another.

Now let's move on to telnet. There are many ways to access the far-flung databases in cyberspace, but the most popular and easiest is a tool called *telnet*, for telephone network. The program works by connecting you to a remote computer and then sending to that computer everything you type on your screen; once you're logged on, everything from the remote machine appears on your local display (see Figure 4.5). With telnet, you can dial into thousands of computers connected to the Internet—even those overseas—without ever worrying about remembering phone numbers or racking up long-distance phone bills. Electronic mail addresses require you to know names of users and the full names and domains of their computers; with telnet, you only need to know the computer's name.

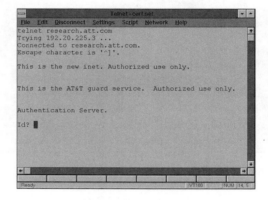

Figure 4.4. Today's graphical interfaces make FTP much easier.

Figure 4.5. Connecting to a remote system with telnet.

Sitting in California, for example, you can use telnet to connect directly to the United States Library of Congress Information System (LOCIS) and search its card catalog. You can also try connecting to the Wharton School of Business at the University of Pennsylvania to search for business information or the holdings catalog at the University of Melbourne in Australia. Once you have an Internet account, you can also telnet directly to a variety of commercial networks such as CompuServe and Dialog. You'll still need to open an account on these services before you can access the information stored there, however.

Marketing Tools

The communications tools we've just discussed offer a valuable way of sharing ideas with others, but businesses also need a means of advertising and marketing their products through the online equivalent of storefronts and mail order catalogs. That's where Gopher and the World Wide Web come in.

Gopher, primarily a text-based tool (though there are some graphical interfaces for it now), can serve as a one-stop shopping source for all kinds of information. A menu-driven document-delivery system, Gopher enables you to browse the Internet's resources, read text files, and access or distribute data of all kinds (see Figure 4.6). With Gopher, you "burrow" through a series of nested menus to find the information you need on any computer system connected to the network running Gopher software. The most powerful aspect of the Gopher service is that any system can include a variety of links to other Gopher servers. The result is a network-wide information source called *Gopherspace*. Gophers also provide gateways to other Internet information systems such as WAIS, Archie, Whois, and the Web and to network services such as telnet and FTP.

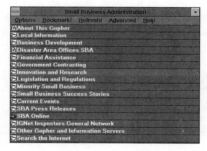

Figure 4.6. Visiting the Small Business Administration with Gopher.

Gopher offers an easy and useful way to distribute company press releases, product catalogs, and software updates. Gopher technology can also be used to create online storefronts to sell books, games, and other items.

For all its advantages, however, Gopher has a very serious flaw—it can't display graphics, only text. Imagine reading a magazine containing page after page of text with no fonts or graphics and pretty soon you'll begin to see why millions of Internet users are rushing headlong toward the Web.

The newest of the Internet tools, the World Wide Web, or the Web, as it's commonly known, is the first universal multimedia platform for publishing information on the network. The Web is built of thousands of *pages* of information distributed throughout the network, with each page containing audio and video clips, graphics, and/or text-based information. On the Web, words can be presented in bold, italics, and a variety of fonts, and any word or phrase can serve as a hypertext button to move the user from place to place with the click of a mouse.

The Web also solves one of Gopher's other problems—identifying files. The way Gopher works, the entry for each item of information is confined to a single line of text. If a paragraph of explanation is required to fully understand a particular file or software package, Gopher is not much help. The Web, by contrast, features an addressing system that identifies documents through Uniform Resource Locators, or URLs. For businesses, a URL can work like an 800 number, pointing potential customers to a company site containing files, pictures, audio and video clips, and other information as well as Gopher and FTP sites and Internet resources available in other formats.

The Web also offers another advantage for businesses—the ability to display multimedia documents (see Figure 4.7). Want to include pictures, video, and a sound clip in your online advertisement? You can do it on the Web. Want to offer links from your company's home page to other sites on the Net? You can do that, too.

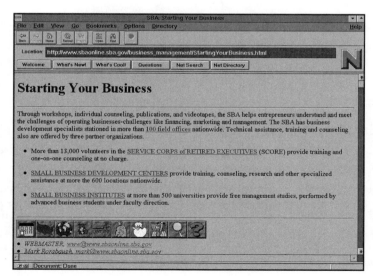

Figure 4.7. Companies use the Web to display multimedia documents.

Research Tools

Besides communications and marketing tools, the Internet also offers a variety of tools to track down information and gather competitive intelligence.

For businesses, the ability to quickly cull through thousands of Internet archives to find a specific document can be an invaluable time-saver.

There are Internet search tools for FTP, mailing lists, Usenet newsgroups, Gopher sites, and the Web.

The simplest of these tools is Archie, a centralized database that indexes the more than two million documents, programs, and other information available via FTP. If you read about a free program, shareware utility, or other useful file in a newspaper or magazine, Archie is a good place to start your search. The only drawback is that you may have to guess the name of the file containing the information you're looking for because Archie indexes FTP documents by filename, not a program name or description.

Usenet offers two search methods. Stanford University provides a free search system that automatically flags articles matching your criteria—and informs you via electronic mail once you set up your user profile. Recently, a company called InfoSeek launched a Web-based service that enables you to search Usenet articles by keyword to find information about topics you're looking for (see Figure 4.8). Check it out at www.infoseek.com.

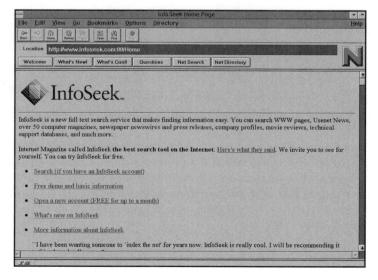

Figure 4.8. InfoSeek enables you to search Usenet articles by keyword.

Gopher, perhaps the best indexed of the Internet tools, can be searched with a tool called Veronica. The basic concept is simple: Certain sites accessible through Gopher have a huge database containing an entry for each menu item on each of thousands of Gopher servers throughout the Internet. Type a keyword or two, and you get a list of all the Gopher menu entries that match. The downside is that Veronica often pulls up many more items than you need or want.

The top of the Internet research "food chain" is the Web, and there are two popular types of Web search tools. The first, exemplified by the popular Yahoo site (see Figure 4.9), is a topical catalog of Web site abstracts submitted by the Web page designers and operators. Although the Yahoo index contains fewer than 40,000 sites as we go to press, the quality of the information and clarity of the results make it a pleasure to use.

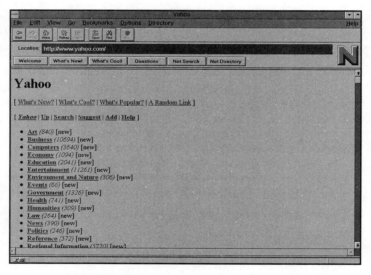

Figure 4.9. A visit to the Yahoo Web Index.

By contrast, Lycos, WebCrawler, and other search engines seek to index the World Wide Web through active, rather than passive, means. The WebCrawler project involves seven computers that search out Web sites 24 hours a day, add them to the master index, and then surf on to new sites (see Figure 4.10). The result is a staggering index of over 4,000,000 Web documents, Gopher sites, and FTP archives that can be searched for free.

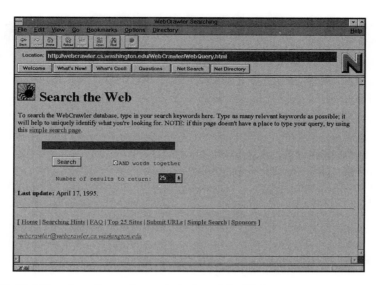

Figure 4.10. WebCrawler offers a dynamic index of the Web.

Summary

Because the Internet has grown based on the needs and interests of its user community, it's quite different from commercial online services such as CompuServe or America Online. That's why there are so many different tools available to the Internet entrepreneur, ranging from the primitive (FTP) to the marvelously sophisticated (the World Wide Web). Each has its place in your Internet toolkit, however, and savvy entrepreneurs and marketers recognize the necessity of using a combination of these tools to yield the best results.

The next three chapters will explore these tools in greater depth and give you an overview of the strengths and weaknesses of the Internet. Chapter 5, "Communications Tools," covers electronic mail, Usenet, FTP, and telnet. Chapter 6, "Marketing Tools," examines Gopher and the World Wide Web, and Chapter 7, Research Tools," explores Archie, Veronica, Yahoo, and many other Internet research tools.

COMMUNICATIONS TOOLS

There are a thousand different ways to use the Internet for business purposes and just as many companies trying each one. Unlike a real highway, composed of relatively few lanes, the information highway is littered with more tools, services, and parts than a jet engine.

For some companies, doing business on the Internet means using the network's international electronic mail system to send memos and documents from corporate headquarters to satellite offices. Different tools offer dramatically differing capabilities. How each company opts to use the network depends as much on the needs, interests, and technological savvy of the particular business as it does on the capabilities of the tools and sales outposts throughout the world. For other companies, doing business means searching Internet-accessible databases for market data, competitive intelligence, and university research reports—all without paying a dime. For still others, doing business on the Internet means exchanging ideas with colleagues around the world in specialized public and private discussion groups and "networking" online to get new clients. And for some aggressive entrepreneurs, it means sending low-cost targeted mailings or promoting their products and services to small groups of potential buyers who hang out on specialized Internet newsgroups.

And that's not counting all the entrepreneurs who are selling Internet-related products and services to newcomers in need of help. These days, thousands of companies large and small are offering everything from Internet access, training, and consulting to books, magazines, computers, software, and flowers that can be ordered online.

The logistics of setting up a storefront in the local strip mall or office building are fairly straightforward, but doing business on the information highway is nowhere near so simple. Unlike the real world of bricks and mortar, there's no compass or roadmap to point you or your potential customers in the right direction. Despite the Internet's enormous potential as a worldwide marketplace, the Internet is still, to a large extent, an uncharted frontier. Imagine New York City without street signs, the Kalahari Desert without a map, and hieroglyphics without the Rosetta stone, and you're starting to get an idea of what navigating the Internet can be like if you don't know what you're doing.

If you're driving down Interstate 95 to attend a meeting in downtown Fort Lauderdale, for example, all you need to do is find the sign that indicates the desired exit ramp. Even if you get hopelessly lost, you can always pull off the highway, pull in at a gas station and ask for directions. Cruise the Internet, by contrast, and you can spend hours poking about without finding what you want and with no virtual gas station or road map to guide you. And unlike commercial online services such as CompuServe and Prodigy, there's no toll-free technical support department you can call for help when you get lost on the Internet.

(To understand why navigating the Internet can be so confusing, imagine how hard it would be to find your way around if your local roads were rebuilt and re-routed every few days!)

Complicating the picture are the wide variety of Internet information services that you can offer existing and potential customers—everything from a simple product specification sheet stashed in an ftp archive to a set of elaborate multimedia documents interwoven into the World Wide Web. Before your customers can find your information, they'll need to know precisely which Internet services you offer and in what format to retrieve them. You can't send e-mail to an ftp archive, for example, and you can't use Gopher to read a World Wide Web document.

But don't despair! The good news is that there are a growing number of Internet tools and navigational software programs becoming available that make it much easier to find the information you're seeking and to get where you're going. If you pack the right tools and learn how to use them, you'll be cruising the information highway in no time. Decisions on how to make your own corporate data available are more complicated, however. We'll address them in Chapter 9, "The Electronic Schmooze," and in Chapter 11, "Marketing *Do's* and *Don'ts*."

In the rest of this chapter, we'll zero in on the many communications tools and services available through the Internet. When possible, we'll show you the nuts and bolts of what we're doing, but don't worry if you don't catch everything the first time around. The key is to try to understand the basic concepts and how you can use these communications tools to boost sales and cut costs.

In writing this chapter, we wrestled with the problem of choosing which interface to use to demonstrate how you can put these tools to use in your business. After much debate, we settled on the text-based command-line interface used when dialing up a UNIX shell account because it's still the most universal. However, we've also included examples of point-and-click graphical interfaces for the PC and Macintosh and Windows to show you how to do things the easy way.

Around the World with E-Mail

As recently as 20 years ago, English teachers were decrying the death of letter writing and that coldly impersonal technology—the telephone. The good news is that the death knell was premature and now written communications is enjoying a renaissance thanks to the Internet's electronic mail system. Based on statistics recently released by the National Science Foundation, more than 4,000 e-mail messages are sent *each second* on the Internet. These days, it seems that just about everyone is hooked up to the network in one way or another. More than 160 countries now have e-mail access to the Internet, and we're sure that, once the extraterrestrials move in, they'll get wired, too.

Being able to reach lots of people is certainly one benefit of Internet e-mail, but for many companies, a bigger advantage is cost. Not only do you save on postage and printing, but by paying a monthly fee to an Internet access provider, you can send and receive all the e-mail you want without paying extra for the messages or the time you spend online composing them. That's a refreshing change from commercial online services where you pay by the hour or the byte. (CompuServe, for example, charges its subscribers 10 cents for every Internet e-mail message they receive.)

The third advantage is ubiquity. Through the Internet, you can send e-mail to people with accounts on CompuServe, America Online, MCI Mail, AppleLink, eWorld, Prodigy, GEnie, AT&T EasyLink, Europe Online, and other commercial networks even if you don't have accounts there. You can also swap mail with colleagues and friends connected to government, military, and university e-mail systems and even people who dial in through computer bulletin boards. This means that you don't have to pay to subscribe to a dozen online services just to reach their subscribers or to log on and off each one each time you want to send a message to one of its users. Thanks to the Internet, sending e-mail is quickly becoming the next best thing to being there.

For example, Dave makes his living as a freelance writer and editor, and every morning he starts his day by logging onto his Netcom account to check for e-mail. On a typical day, he gets messages from Prentice Hall, sent from CompuServe; messages from colleagues at universities and online services; clients who use MCI Mail and commercial Internet systems; a message or two from friends overseas; press releases from eWorld; client queries from Prodigy; and notes from family members accessible through the Internet gateway to the United States Military Network (MILNET). There's no extra charge for receiving these messages—even when they're huge—and just about all of them are delivered in his mailbox within seconds of being sent. Better yet, a variety of messages from colleagues who subscribe to Internet mailing lists come into his mailbox, too, offering information comparable to high-priced newsletters but free of charge. Without the Internet to link everyone together, Dave's virtual world would be much smaller.

Using the Internet Post Office

Although there are many programs you can use to send electronic mail, they all have some features in common. Each mail system works by requesting one or more e-mail addresses for the recipients, offers you the ability to specify a brief (five- to ten-word) subject, and then enables you to compose or upload a message from your personal computer. In Internet parlance, these messages are composed of a message *header* and a message *body*; think of them as the envelope and the letter inside. Later in the book, we tell you more about e-mail's features and capabilities, but for now, let's spend some time considering the components of an electronic mail address and take a quick peek at a couple of the most common electronic mail programs.

To send mail to someone, you must have that person's Internet e-mail address. All addresses are composed of three parts: the person's name or account name, the name of the computer they use, and their domain, which describes how their computer is hooked to the Internet. For example, `taylor@netcom5.netcom.com` is a typical Internet e-mail address. Here `taylor` is the account name, `netcom5` is the name of the computer Dave uses to receive electronic mail, and `netcom.com` is the domain name. The at-sign, or ampersand (`@`), serves as a separator; the basic format is `user@host.domain`.

The domain is read from right to left (for example, `com` and then `netcom` in the previous example) with the most important, highest-level information at the far right. Thus, in the example, `com` would be the top-level domain. There are seven common domains used in the United States: `com` is for commercial sites and service providers, `edu` is for educational sites, including all K–12 schools and colleges, `mil` stands for military sites or other computers on MILNET, `gov` denotes government systems, `net` indicates that it's a different, autonomous network. (Remember that the Internet is a network of thousands of networks, not a single network such as Prodigy or America Online.) Finally `org` is for non-profit and other private organizations. Most international electronic mail follows a similar domain-naming strategy, but the top-level domain is the two-letter International Standards Organization (ISO) country abbreviation. For example, `mx` is Mexico, `au` is Australia, `uk` is the United Kingdom, `no` is Norway, `fr` is France, and so on.

Here are some examples of Internet addresses:

```
mtaranto@noc.sura.net
plieb@umd5.umd.edu
jstraw@navy.mil
tai@nsa.hp.com
cat@kodak.com
jackson@dftnic.gsfc.nasa.gov
```

These examples refer to a user on the SURA network, the University of Maryland at Delaware educational facility, the United States Navy, the Network Software group of Hewlett-Packard, Kodak, and the GSFC division of the National Aeronautics and Space Administration. Notice in the Navy and Kodak e-mail examples that the actual computer name has been omitted: Many sites are set up so that you can send mail to a user at the domain, and the site will route to the appropriate machine automatically. Indeed, the example we showed you earlier, `taylor@netcom5.netcom.com`, would be better written as `taylor@netcom.com` because the Netcom computer automatically routes e-mail to individual machines within the company.

That's what an Internet address looks like. How does a mail message look? Look over our shoulder as Dave sends a brief message to Rosalind. Dave will be using the Elm Mail System on a UNIX computer through his dialup account. Text shown in boldface is what's typed on the UNIX system.

```
% elm rosalind@harrison.win.net

Subject of message: Quick question about Chapter 5
Cc:

Please enter your message, using '.' to end it.

Rosalind, I'm revising some of our earlier text in Chapter 5 and wanted to kn
ow how strongly you felt about the holographic illustration you've included i
n the current draft? I also wanted to remind you that our next deadline is in
four days...

Dave
.

message sent.

%
```

Another important capability of electronic mail is automated mail servers that are available on the Internet—both for retrieving documents and information and for companies wanting to distribute information through those means. Most of these services simply require customers to know a specific e-mail address for the service and nothing else. For example, the Internet Shopping Network offers an electronic software shop on the Internet through e-mail: a message without any content sent to the address `info@internet.net` results in

```
Message 1/6  From info@news.internet.net        May 27 '94 at 5:44 am -
480
                     re: Internet Shopping Network


HERE IS THE INFO YOU REQUESTED FROM:

THE INTERNET SHOPPING NETWORK

GENERAL INFORMATION

The Internet Shopping Network is an electronic shopping system available on t
he worldwide Internet.  It is set up like a virtual mall with a variety of st
ores selling various products.

Today, the network offers twenty thousand computer software and hardware prod
ucts available from nearly one thousand different companies.  More than 95% o
f these products, representing more than $500 million dollars worth of invent
ory, are in stock and can be shipped to you the next business day.

Anyone can browse the stores and catalogs of the shopping network from anywhe
re on the internet.  All you need is an internet connection and a copy of a W
eb browser like Mosaic -  and you can connect.  The connection address is htt
p://shop.
internet.net

 65 lines more (35%). Press <space> for more, 'i' to return.
```

From there, it's easy to see how to request specific documents and information from the server. A message with the subject `send prices`, for example, might result in a price list being sent back automatically within seconds of the request and without any human intervention. Later in the book, we'll look at how to set up these automated mail servers, what we like to think of as e-mail robots.

Tip: One e-mail robot that's worth meeting right now is Embot, a simple UNIX-based server written by Dave Taylor. Send it a message at `embot@northcoast.com` to learn more about it.

Joining the Crowd with Mailing Lists

Once you understand how to use the Internet to send messages to friends and colleagues, it isn't much of a leap to imagine sending the same message to dozens, hundreds, or even thousands of users. Imagine that you're sending a letter through the U.S. Postal Service and the postal workers have a really fast copying machine at their branch and a big list of addresses. If you were to send a letter to, for example, all the homeowners in your neighborhood, you would need to send only one copy of the letter. Then the post office would duplicate it and send copies to every registered homeowner—for free. That's exactly how mailing lists work on the Internet. A central computer somewhere on the network maintains a list and anyone on the list can then send e-mail easily to everyone on that discussion list by addressing it to the so-called list-server machine.

You would be surprised to find out how much work is required to maintain current names and addresses for a magazine such as *TV Guide*. Electronic mailing lists on the Internet are also quite involved, but the good news is that there are computers to help the process considerably. The most common software program used to maintain lists on central computers is called LISTSERV (without the trailing *e*). To sign up for a list that uses the LISTSERV software, you would send an e-mail message directly to the LISTSERV program itself, requesting that you be added (or removed) from the specified list.

As you can imagine on a network with more than 30,000,000 users, there are mailing lists on just about everything under the sun. At last count, there were close to 9,500 mailing lists, ranging from medieval literature and consulting to Microsoft Word for the Macintosh and commercialization of the Internet.

You can obtain your own list of Internet mailing lists by sending a request to the LISTSERV program that resides on the BITNET network information center computer. Send the message to LISTSERV@BITNIC.BITNET with the message body (not the subject—an important distinction) containing the words list global. It should look like this:

```
% elm listserv@bitnic.bitnet
    Subject: none
    Cc:
    Please enter your message, press '.' to end
    list global
    .
    %
```

It will take 15 minutes to an hour to process your request and the resulting list of lists will be enormous. Here's a sampling of the first page or two:

```
Network-wide ID     Full address        List title
---------------     ------------        ----------
'I-AMIGA-UIUC...    I-AMIGA@UIUCVMD     Archive of I-AMIGA list elsewhere on net (Do+
'NEW-SUPERCOM...    S-COMPUT@UGA        (Peered) SuperComputers List (UGA)
'UPDATE-ELECT...    UPNEWS@MARIST       Update Electronic Music Newsletter renamed t+
A-GROUP             A-GROUP@UMSLVMA     The A-Group (Kind of like the A-Team)
AAAE                AAAE@PURCCVM        American Assoc. for Agricultural Education (+
AAAE-C              AAAE-C@PURCCVM      American Assoc. for Agricultural Education (+
AAAE-E              AAAE-E@PURCCVM      American Assoc. for Agricultural Education (+
AAAE-S              AAAE-S@PURCCVM      American Assoc. for Agricultural Education (+
AAAE-W              AAAE-W@PURCCVM      American Assoc. for Agricultural Education (+
AAASHRAN            AAASHRAN@GWUVM      AAAS Human Rights Action Network
AAASMSP             AAASMSP@GWUVM       AAAS Minority Perspectives on Ethics in Scie+
AACRL               AACRL@UABDPO        Alabama Association of College and Research +
AACUNY-L            AACUNY-L@CUNYVM     AACUNY-L: Asian Americans Culture mailing li+
AAHESGIT            AAHESGIT@GWUVM      AAHE Info. Tech. Activities & Projects Steve+
AARPUB-L            AARPUB-L@JPNIMRTU   AAR Electronic Publication list
AASCU-L             AASCU-L@UBVM        American Association of State Colleges and U+
AASIG-L             AASIG-L@GSUVM1      GSU Academic Administrators
AATG                AATG@INDYCMS        American Association of Teachers of German
AAUA-L              AAUA-L@UBVM         American Association of University Administr+
AAVLD-L             AAVLD-L@UCDCVDLS    American Assoc of Vet Lab Diagnosticians
ABE-L               ABE-L@BRLNCC        Forum da Associacao Brasileira de Estatistica
ABEP-L              ABEP-L@BRUFSC       Associacao de Brasileiros Estudantes e Pesqu+
ABILITY             ABILITY@ASUACAD     Journal for the study and advancement of the+
ABLE-JOB            ABLE-JOB@SJUVM      St. John's University Job Opportunity List
ABLE-L              ABLE-L@ASUACAD      ABILITY Journal - Discussion & submission
ABOG-L              ABOG-L@UCSBVM       UCSB Academic Business Officers Group (ABOG)
                    ABOG-L@UCSFVM       UCSF Academic Business Officers Group
ABSAME-L            ABSAME-L@MSU        ABSAME-L
ABSJRN-L            ABSJRN-L@CMUVM      ABS Journal Committee
ABSLST-L            ABSLST-L@CMUVM      Association of Black Sociologists
ABUSE-L             ABUSE-L@UBVM        Professional Forum for Child Abuse Issues
ACADDR-L            ACADDR-L@MCGILL1    Academic Computing Centre Directors Forum
ACADEMIA            ACADEMIA@TECHNION   Academia   -   Forum on Higher Education in Is+
ACADEMIC            ACADEMIC@BRUFMG     Forum de Ciencia Computacional
ACADLIST            ACADLIST@CESPIVM2   Lista Secretarios Academicos UNLP
ACADNEWS            ACADNEWS@TECHNION   Acadnews   -   Bulletin on Higher Education in+
ACADV               ACADV@NDSUVM1       ACADV Academic Advising Forum
ACC-L               ACC-L@GITVM1        ACC-L: "Advanced Computer Controls Discussio+
ACCES-L             ACCES-L@UNBVM1      Associated Competitions for Can. Eng. Studen+
ACCESS-L            ACCESS-L@BRUFPB     List for MS ACCESS
                    ACCESS-L@INDYCMS    Microsoft Access Database Discussion List
ACCI-CHI            ACCI-CHI@URIACC     Consumer Economics and Chinese Scholars
ACDGIS-L            ACDGIS-L@AWIIMC12   Geographische   Informationssysteme
ACE-COM             ACE-COM@WSUVM1      ACE Communication Management SIG
ACES-L              ACES-L@UNBVM1       Atlantic Congress of Engineering Students (F+
ACEWEST             ACEWEST@WSUVM1      Ag Communicators in Education
ACH-EC-L            ACH-EC-L@BROWNVM    ACH Executive Council Discussion List
ACHNEWS             ACHNEWS@UCSBVM      Newsletter of the Association for Computers +
ACLA-L              ACLA-L@WSUVM1       Association of Collegiate Licensing Administ+
ACM-L               ACM-L@KENTVM        ACM-L List for discussing ACM; gatewayed to +
                    ACM-L@PACEVM        Association for Computing Machinery
ACMET-L             ACMET-L@TEMPLEVM    Academic Metal Crafts discussion
ACMMEX-L            ACMMEX-L@ITESMVF1   ACM MEXICO
ACMR-L              ACMR-L@UHCCVM       Association for Chinese Music Research Netwo+
ACMSTCHP            ACMSTCHP@SUVM       ACM Student Chapters
ACORN-L             ACORN-L@TREARN      ACORN computers Discussion List
```

> **Tip:** If your system can't send mail to the BITNET network, you can try an alternative address for the same request: `LISTSERV%BITNIC.BITNET@uunet.uu.net`. If you don't get a reply, it's possible that your system just won't let you get messages that large; ask your administrator about obtaining the information through other means. Finally, you can search the World Wide Web for accessible versions of this information too. Start with the URL `http://www.neosoft.com/internet/paml/`.

There are three main types of mailing lists: unmoderated, moderated, and digest format. With an unmoderated mailing list, any message posted to the list is distributed automatically to everyone subscribed to the list. As a result, you can expect an off-subject discussion once in a while.

Moderated lists, by contrast, have a moderator who screens all messages to ensure that they're appropriate for the list. If a message is appropriate, it's distributed to the list; if it's not, it's returned to the sender with an explanation. The disadvantage to this kind of list is that messages are not always distributed to everyone right away, but might sit for hours or days before being checked and forwarded by the moderator.

The third type of list is a variation on the second. Rather than each message being posted to the list individually, a large number of messages are bundled together into one large message that is distributed periodically. Dave prefers to receive digested lists; Rosalind likes to sift through her messages one at a time to make sure she doesn't miss anything newsy.

There are two main business benefits to Internet mailing lists—access to industry experts and access to potential customers. Mailing lists typically attract a wide variety of users, from top experts in a field to neophytes hoping to learn from them. Compare it to the trouble and expense of attending an industry conference or workshop and you'll find that subscribing to an active mailing list can save you considerable time and money. It's also nice to be able to bounce ideas off the experts for free —though it's important to recognize that a competitor may also be interested in your fledgling ideas.

The other big advantage to mailing lists is that you can use them to disseminate product- and service-related information to your target community without any of the usual expenses. Beware of breaches of netiquette, however. (See Chapter 11, "Marketing *Do's* and *Don'ts*," for an in-depth exploration of this topic). Remember that you also can create your own mailing lists—one of which could be a vehicle for disseminating your company's new product announcements. You could add customers to the list when they purchase a product from your firm.

Here's an example of how this can work: In the latter part of 1994, Rosalind launched a consulting business to help newspapers and magazines expand into online services and interactive media. In addition to the word-of-mouth networking she did among her contacts in the publishing world, she also joined four Internet mailing lists—two discussing Internet trends and developments (with an eye toward commercialization of the network), one about computer-assisted journalism, and another about online newspapers and magazine publishing.

Practically every day since then, she has devoted 30 minutes or more to reading the messages distributed on the lists, adding comments of her own, and, where appropriate, including information about her consulting services or her newsletter, Interactive Publishing Alert. It has proven a very efficient way for her to find out about online publishing and business trends; it also has given her a chance to network with colleagues and potential clients throughout the world at minimal cost and without leaving her home in Hollywood, Florida.

Internet discussion and mailing lists can be a direct-marketer's dream—if used judiciously. Unlike the bulletin boards on CompuServe and other commercial services, you don't have to wait until your prospective customers drop by and happen to glance at your company's information—they get your message automatically as subscribers to the list. Of course, this can be a double-edged sword. If you misjudge your market or word your press release in too promotional a way, you run the risk of alienating your entire target market in one fell swoop and apologies often aren't accepted.

Getting on the List

Joining an Internet mailing list is as easy as sending a single piece of electronic mail. There are no cards to fill out, no authorizations or qualifications, and best of all, no checks to include. Instead, you need only identify the name of the mailing list and the name of the computer that hosts the list. Most mailing lists are run through the LISTSERV list processing software (another popular list processor is called Majordomo), so you'll need to send your subscription request to the list processor—typically LISTSERV or Majordomo— rather than to the list itself.

For example, when Dave requested the comprehensive list of mailing lists from BITNIC (a message sent to `LISTSERV@BITNIC.BITNET` with the message body containing the words `list global`), he noticed that buried deep in the file was a mailing list called AAVLD-L that described itself as the "American Assoc of Vet Lab Diagnosticians." It sounded interesting, so Dave checked the list of mailing lists and saw that it was listed as `AAVLD-L@UCDCVDLS`, which meant that he could join it by sending a subscription request to the Listserv list processor program at that computer:

```
% elm listserv@ucdcvdls.bitnet
Subject: none
Cc:
Please enter your message, press '.' to end.
```

```
SUBSCRIBE AAVLD-L Dave Taylor
.
%
```

The message you'll send to sign up for a mailing list is almost identical to this one; the only changes you'll need to make are the e-mail address, the name of the list and your own name—and the name of the list processor, if it's different. If Dave wanted to sign up for the Net-happenings list, a clearinghouse for new products, services and activities of interest to the Internet community, he would send the following message instead. Note that this list is processed by the Majordomo program instead of LISTSERV.

```
% elm majordomo@dsmail.internic.net
Subject: none
Cc:
Please enter your message, press '.' to end.
SUBSCRIBE NET-HAPPENINGS
.
%
```

Subscription requests are processed within seconds of receipt most of the time. Don't be surprised if, less than a minute after you send your subscription request, you receive an acknowledgment similar to this one:

```
You have been added to list net-happenings@dsmail.internic.net.
The system has recorded your address as taylor@netcom.com
and in order for your messages to get posted, you will
have to send them from this address.
```

If after a few days or weeks, you decide that you don't like the list, the conversation isn't of value, or there are just too many messages to read each day, you can easily unsubscribe by sending another message to the list processor program, substituting UNSUBSCRIBE for SUBSCRIBE in the message body. To remove himself from the list, Dave could send the message

```
% elm majordomo@dsmail.internic.net
Subject: none
Cc:
Please enter your message, press '.' to end.
UNSUBSCRIBE NET-HAPPENINGS
.
%
```

Note: Because you can now send electronic mail to and from the Internet even if you subscribe to a commercial online service like

CompuServe, you can subscribe to an Internet mailing list through a commercial service, too. Be careful, however, because an active list can result in a large amount of e-mail being dumped in your box each day and some commercial services charge per-message fees for receiving e-mail.

Spreading the News with Newsgroups

If mailing lists are similar to an efficient post office that can make copies of your message and distribute it automatically to hundreds or thousands of recipients, Usenet is the public library where each book is actually a window opening onto a discussion of a specific topic. Currently, there are more than 10,000 Usenet newsgroups hosting far-ranging discussions on a bewildering number of topics—everything from HyperCard programming on the Macintosh to magazine writing, the best restaurants in San Francisco area, and the debate over abortion.

Similar to mailing lists, newsgroups are divided into two categories—moderated and unmoderated. Most groups are unmoderated, and anything anyone submits (or *posts* in Internet lingo) to the group is rapidly distributed to all sites on the network and read by everyone who participates in the particular discussion group. On moderated groups, all submissions are sent automatically to an individual or committee that screens the articles for appropriateness, and then, if the articles are acceptable, posts them to the group. Delays of many days are common with moderated newsgroups, but with Usenet groups having 5,000 participants or more, you might find yourself quickly seeking shelter from the barrage of information.

On an unmoderated Usenet group, you post an article on your local machine, which keeps a copy and sends another copy to its electronic neighbors. On receipt of the copy, each machine makes another copy of your article, adding it to the disk directory set aside for that particular discussion group and sending another copy to the other machines. In a matter of hours, an article you wrote on one machine can be duplicated thousands of times on thousands of computers on the network.

Like Internet mailing lists, newsgroups require subscriptions, but the good news is that your Internet access provider can subscribe for you. But here's the catch: There are a wide variety of text-based interfaces available for reading Usenet news and they differ dramatically from one other. With the proliferation of Mac and PC computers on the Internet, new graphical readers are also becoming available, further complicating the matter. Even worse, not all Internet access providers offer the same set of Usenet readers. For example, Dave prefers tin for reading Usenet news, but it isn't available on the computer he uses at Purdue University, only on his Netcom account. Therefore, he uses rn for Purdue-related newsgroups. Rosalind, by contrast, prefers graphical interfaces and uses WinNET Mail Plus to read newsgroups.

Our advice is to use a graphical newsreader if one is readily available. If not, we recommend tin, a friendly screen-based Usenet reader that works quickly and easily over inexpensive dialup lines. If you want to customize your newsreader—and you have some programming experience or a good consultant available—the rn or trn programs can be a good choice also.

As a result of the plethora of Usenet interfaces, we debated (through e-mail, of course!) which would be the best newsreader to use to demonstrate how newsgroups work. We concluded that tin offers the best balance between universal accessibility and ease of use. Don't be surprised, however, if not everything is obvious right away: Like all Usenet software, tin takes a while to master. Also, it's difficult to figure out which Usenet groups are available at your Internet access site. Your best bet is to ask your Internet access provider for a listing of the groups available, preferably including their descriptions (ask for a file called /usr/lib/news/newsgroups). The information you receive will probably look similar to

```
comp.ai.genetic         Genetic algorithms in computing.
comp.ai.neural-nets     All aspects of neural networks.
comp.ai.nlang-know-rep  Natural Language and Knowledge Representation. (Moder
ated)
comp.ai.philosophy      Philosophical aspects of Artificial Intelligence.
comp.ai.shells          Artificial intelligence applied to shells.
comp.ai.vision          Artificial Intelligence Vision Research. (Moderated)
comp.answers            Repository for periodic USENET articles. (Moderated)
comp.apps.spreadsheets  Spreadsheets on various platforms.
comp.arch               Computer architecture.
comp.arch.bus.vmebus    Hardware and software for VMEbus Systems.
comp.arch.storage       Storage system issues, both hardware and software.
comp.archives           Descriptions of public access archives. (Moderated)
comp.archives.admin     Issues relating to computer archive administration.
comp.archives.msdos.announce    Announcements about MSDOS archives. (Moderate
d)
comp.archives.msdos.d   Discussion of materials available in MSDOS archives.
comp.bbs.misc           All aspects of computer bulletin board systems.
comp.bbs.waffle         The Waffle BBS and USENET system on all platforms.
comp.benchmarks         Discussion of benchmarking techniques and results.
comp.binaries.acorn     Binary-only postings for Acorn machines. (Moderated)
comp.binaries.amiga     Encoded public domain programs in binary. (Moderated)
comp.binaries.apple2    Binary-only postings for the Apple II computer.
comp.binaries.atari.st  Binary-only postings for the Atari ST. (Moderated)
comp.binaries.ibm.pc    Binary-only postings for IBM PC/MS-DOS. (Moderated)
comp.binaries.ibm.pc.d  Discussions about IBM/PC binary postings.
comp.binaries.ibm.pc.wanted     Requests for IBM PC and compatible programs.
comp.binaries.mac       Encoded Macintosh programs in binary. (Moderated)
comp.binaries.ms-windows        Binary programs for Microsoft Windows.(Modera
ted)
comp.binaries.os2       Binaries for use under the OS/2 ABI. (Moderated)
```

(You can also use a program called choosenews that makes things a lot easier.)

Let's step through a brief example session with tin, starting at the first screen, which indicates which groups Dave subscribes to and how many articles have been posted to each group since the last time he read Usenet:

```
Group Selection (15)                              h=help

      1            netcom.announce              Announcements from Netcom Staf
      2     2      netcom.general               General discussions about Netc
      3     1      netcom.internet              Internet access at Netcom: FTP
      4            ed.vr
      5     606    misc.entrepreneurs           Discussion on operating a busi
      6            netcom.programmers           Discussions about software dev
      7            ucb.extension.class.telewriting
      8     1      biz.comp.services            Generic commercial service pos
      9            school.subjects.languages    English, Deutsch, Francais etc
     10     3      clari.feature.miss_manners   Judith Martin's Humourous Etiq
     11     22     clari.biz.briefs
     12     19     clari.biz.industry.print_media
     13     16     clari.biz.industry.services
     14     22     clari.news.education.higher
     15     11     clari.news.education

    <n>=set current to n, TAB=next unread, /=search pattern, c)atchup,
  g)oto, j=line down, k=line up, h)elp, m)ove, q)uit, r=toggle all/unread,
    s)ubscribe, S)ub pattern, u)nsubscribe, U)nsub pattern, y)ank in/out

                    *** End of Groups ***
```

If you look carefully, you'll see that Dave subscribes to 15 newsgroups and that the group misc.entrepreneurs, for example, contains 606 articles that have arrived since the last time he checked the group. To see what's in that group, Dave presses Return (because the group is already highlighted with the inverse video bar), which results in the following screen:

```
              misc.entrepreneurs (321T 606A 0K 0H R)          h=help

   1   +     Can you teach entrepeneur              Ben M. Schorr
   2   +     On commercial use of the 'net          Randal L. Schwartz
   3   +     COMPLETE BUSINESS ON DISK              Christopher D. Col
   4   +     Free Report! How to m                  Scott Tengen
   5   + 9   A straw-man: Use "Distribution: ad"    Thomas F Lee
   6   + 3   Vending Business Opp                   epsinc@delphi.com
   7   + 2   Earn Free Travel & Cash                epsinc@delphi.com
   8   + 2   CASH Generator                         epsinc@delphi.com
   9   +     FREE Closing Costs & Appraisals        epsinc@delphi.com
  10   + 5   ALMOST FREE MLM Newspaper Sample       epsinc@delphi.com
  11   + 2   PROTECTING YOUR DESIGN                 Michael Sellers
  12   + 4   Has anyone heard of Incomnet?          acanton@delphi.com
  13   +     Data Detectives Wanted                 Daniel Hunsinger
  14   + 3   The IDEA Association, Free Newsletter. Donald Miller
  15   +     Help: Bottle Mfr. and Bottling Company Charleen Bunjiovia
  16   +     where can I get a list of govt auctions, date Michael Grommet
  17   +     Apologies for reposting due to technical prob Brookfield Economi

    <n>=set current to n, TAB=next unread, /=search pattern, ^K)ill/select,
  a)uthor search, c)atchup, j=line down, k=line up, K=mark read, l)ist thread,
    ¦=pipe, m)ail, o=print, q)uit, r=toggle all/unread, s)ave, t)ag, w=post
```

Here Dave is right in the thick of `misc.entrepreneurs` and is looking at a table of contents of the group's new articles. Tin's most commonly used commands are listed at the bottom. To read a particular article, either enter the number to the left of the article you wish to read or press Return to read the article indicated now. Here's what you'll see:

```
Thu, 26 May 1995 11:37:00        misc.entrepreneurs          Thread  1 of  321
Lines 24                    Can you teach entrepeneur          No responses
ben.schorr@bcsbbs.com  Ben Schorr at The BCS BBS - Los Angeles, CA - 213-962-
29

CJ> Can it be taught in business schools or is it something an individual
CJ> is born with?

Now THAT'S an interesting question. I think it can be taught, but there
is a certain attitude that can be very difficult for people that don't
have it inherent as part of their personality.

I think that there needs to be a little bit of swashbuckler in an
entrepreneur that the meek may never be able to get ahold of.

Just a thought.

-Ben-
Ben M. Schorr                                21000 Osborne, #6
Director of Operations                       Canoga Park, CA. 91304

   <n>=set current to n, TAB=next unread, /=search pattern, ^K)ill/select,
       a)uthor search, B)ody search, c)atchup, f)ollowup, K=mark read,
       ¦=pipe, m)ail, o=print, q)uit, r)eply mail, s)ave, t)ag, w=post

                                              --More--(79%)[933/1175
]
```

Usenet is divided into nine primary hierarchies, or categories, focusing on computers (`comp`), science (`sci`), recreation (`rec`), miscellaneous topics (`misc`), alternative topics (`alt`), Usenet software and organizational discussion (`news`), social topics (`soc`), hotly debated topics (`talk`), and business (`biz`). The alternative newsgroups space (`alt`) is worth special mention because the groups there have even fewer constraints than the rest of the Usenet. Some of the alternative groups are just plain gross, like `alt.sex.bestiality`, but others can be valuable and interesting to business users, such as `alt.education.distance` and `alt.internet.services`.

For businesses, some of the most valuable newsgroups are the ones that deal with computer-related topics. For example, there are newsgroups for users of Sun, NeXT, DEC, and Macintosh computers; newsgroups for Windows, spreadsheet, and database users; and newsgroups for people who want to share information and exchange ideas about everything from virtual reality to artificial intelligence. The great thing about newsgroups is that there's no charge to access them—unlike CompuServe's technical support bulletin boards, for example, where you pay by the minute. A small number of companies are creating their own newsgroups as a way of offering low-cost customer support, but we favor other alternatives, as we'll discuss throughout the book.

Newsgroups can also be a valuable marketing tool to announce new products and boost your company's visibility online—but, as with mailing lists, overly promotional or off-topic messages will almost certainly result in hostile reactions from your potential Internet customers.

As commercial online services incorporate more Internet features and information in order to compete for subscribers' time and money, Usenet newsgroups are now becoming available to millions more online users. Currently, CompuServe, America Online, and Prodigy all provide access to Usenet newsgroups. However, these services generally make it difficult to subscribe to sex-related newsgroups and newsgroups on other controversial topics unless you already know the group's name.

Dialing the World with Telnet

Electronic mail and Usenet both focus on stimulating discussions, but there's a world of far-flung databases available through the Internet, too. One of the most popular, and easiest, ways is through an Internet tool known as telnet. The program works by connecting you to a remote computer, sending everything you type on your screen to that remote machine, and then displaying everything on that computer's screen on your local display. It's like being able to dial in to any of the computers on the Internet—even those overseas—without ever worrying about phone numbers or a long-distance phone bill. Although electronic mail addresses require you to know the name of the user and the full name and domain of their computer, with telnet you only need to know the computer's name.

Sitting in California, for example, you can use telnet to connect directly to the United States Library of Congress Information System (LOCIS) and search its card catalog. Didn't find what you wanted? Try connecting to the Wharton School of Business at the University of Pennsylvania to search for business information or the holdings catalog at the University of Melbourne in Australia. Some commercial services, such as CompuServe, now also allow users to use telnet to connect to their accounts directly without dialing the central computers. Don't be fooled, however; you'll still need to pay CompuServe before you're allowed in the door.

Telnet offers a wide variety of services of interest to business users. For example, your CEO mentions that she saw a book on managing interpersonal conflict and thought you might find it of value. You could ask her for a full citation (and risk appearing stupid), or you can use the Internet to find it. Let's see what you could find with a quick check of the Duke University Library. To connect, type `telnet ducatalog.lib.duke.edu` and wade through the first few screens of startup information until you reach the main screen.

```
                        MAIN SEARCH MENU    (1 of 2)
DUKE_CATALOG


AUTHOR      a=faulkner william       (enter last name first)
            a=american chemical soc  (you may truncate search statements)


TITLE       t=scarlet letter         (omit initial articles a, an, the)


SUBJECT     s=substance abuse
            s=king, martin luther    (searching for works about a person)

KEYWORD     To start the keyword search program, type K at the >> prompt.

DATABASES   To search other databases, including the catalogs of NCSU and UNC-
CH
            type d at the >> prompt.

QUIT        To leave the Library Catalog, type quit at the >> prompt.

Enter your search below. Press (RETURN) to continue or type ?? to see Help Me
nu.
>>
```

To do a keyword search, enter K and you'll see the following display on the screen:

```
WELCOME
         ENTER            TO SEARCH          EXAMPLE

         fi               KEYWORD            fi games

         fi ti            TITLE              fi ti america

         fi au            AUTHOR             fi au asimov

         fi su            SUBJECT            fi su united states


         **************************************************
         * Enter   DISPLAY  to display a record           *
         *         START    to start over                 *
         *         STOP     to finish                      *
         *         HELP     for more information           *
         **************************************************



1>>
```

Based on these examples, you should be able to find the book by searching for the keywords `managing` and `interpersonal`. At the prompt, type `fi managing interpersonal` and see what happens. Astoundingly, only one match turns up; the `display` command shows what information is available.

```
1>> fi managing interpersonal
       1> MANAGING INTERPERSONAL occurs 1 time in 1 record.

2>> display
Record #1
        Title: Managing interpersonal conflict / William A. Donohue
                 ; with Robert Kolt.
       Author: Donohue, William A., 1947-
    Published: Newbury Park : Sage Publications, c1992.
      Subject: Interpersonal conflict.
               Negotiation.
               Conflict management.
               Interpersonal relationships

LOCATION: Fuqua   -- CALL NUMBER: BF637.I48 D66 1992
      c.1                                                   NotCheckedOut

2>>


he - for help    fi - to find a term  di - to display results  sto - to stop
```

Now type `stop` to quit the library catalog and return to your regular session. Don't be too intimidated if it seems difficult to work with these library catalogs. As you'll see, there are easier ways to work with this type of database.

These days, many electronic merchants are using telnet as a way to let potential customers throughout the world work with their computer systems and software directly, inviting customers to their online storefronts for the price of a local phone call. (Many others, of course, are displaying information on the Web.) Thanks to telnet, shoppers can browse and order books, CDs, software, or flowers.

Suppose that you find a book you want through the New York Public Library and decide to go ahead and buy it. There's no need to leave the telnet program; just connect to `books.com`, the computer run by Book Stacks Unlimited of Cleveland, Ohio. Once connected, you'll be asked to type in your name, address, phone number, and other information to uniquely identify yourself for future transactions. The next display is the main menu, the central spot for user interaction.

```
*****************************************
*       Book Stacks Unlimited, Inc.     *
*               MAIN MENU               *
*****************************************

          <B>ook Store

          <M>essages

          <N>ews/Notes

          <F>iles/Magazines

          <U>tilities

          <H>elp

          <G>oodBye

Command:
```

We choose B to search for a book and learn that there are quite a variety of ways to accomplish this.

```
********************************************************
*                 The Book Store                      *
*                 200,000+  Titles                    *
********************************************************

  <A>uthor Search           <R>eview Your Selections

  <T>itle Search            <O>rder (when done)

  <K>eyWord Title Search    <C>heck Order Status

  <I>SBN Search

  <S>ubject Search \ Just Published


-------------------------------------------------------
        <P>revious Menu    <H>elp    <G>oodbye

Command:
```

We specify T to search by title, enter interpersonal conflict, and learn that the desired book is available through Book Stacks Unlimited.

```
YOU HAVE SELECTED THE FOLLOWING TITLE:

Author  : Donohue, William A./Kolt, Robert

Title   : Managing Interpersonal Conflict (Interpersonal Commtexts, Vol 4)


ISBN     : 0803933126
Volume   :
Subject  :
Dewey #  : 303.69
Publisher: Sage Pubns
Date Pub : 07/92
Binding  : Paperback
Edition  :
Bookmarks:    0
Price    : $ 16.50
Reviews  : 0

How many copies would you like? <R>eviews <ENTER> To Exit :
```

If you choose the book, you enter your credit-card number and log off. Three days later, the book arrives at your door via United Parcel Service. (You, meanwhile, are contentedly munching a slice of pepperoni pizza at your computer.)

Moving Files with FTP

Telnet enables you to connect to other computers—or enables other users to connect to your computer—but it doesn't help disseminate your company's files, documents, press releases, or software. The tool of choice for transferring files through the Internet is named after the protocol of the same name—file-transfer protocol, or FTP. As with telnet, FTP requires you to know the name of the computer containing the file or files you need. There are two basic ways to work with FTP: For confidential information distribution, files can be deposited in a specific account locked with a secret password, or if the information is intended for public distribution, it can be made available through a service known as anonymous FTP, which doesn't require an account or password. With anonymous FTP, you can search through the files in the archive and download any file, document, or program available on that remote computer. Many computer companies, including Digital, Apple, Sun Microsystems, and Silicon Graphics, use FTP to enable their customers to download software fixes, press releases, and other informational files.

For reasons that are beyond our understanding, the FTP program available through most dialup Internet access providers is very primitive, perhaps one of the most difficult tools to fully understand on the Internet. Thankfully, a number of attractive graphical interfaces have recently become available for DOS, Windows, and Macintosh systems, many of which are available for free or as shareware. In this section, we show you how to work with the UNIX FTP program because it's likely that's what your dialup account will require you to use. However, we also show you how the same collection of files would appear within the Mac fetch and Windows XferIt programs.

To transfer a file using UNIX FTP, you need to connect to the remote computer, type the word anonymous or ftp as an account (and by tradition, your e-mail address as the password), change to the directory where the file you want is stored, and then use the get command to download it to your local account. By default, all files are transmitted as text, which usually works fine. However, if you know that the file you seek is a program or other file that must not be altered by the transmission, you can switch into *binary mode* by using the binary command. By contrast, if you're sure what you seek is text—a document, for example—you might use the ascii command (ASCII is the set of characters used by most Internet computers, and it stands for American Standard for Computer Information Interchange).

Here's an example of how FTP works: While reading a recent article in a technology-oriented business magazine, you notice a note at the end, the text of the intellectual property portion of the North American Free Trade Agreement is available via FTP from wiretap.spies.com as file 'NAFTA/17.intellect'. Based on the content, it's pretty safe to bet that it's a text file, so here's what a UNIX session would look like (in FTP, cd changes directory and dir lists the files in a specific directory):

```
% ftp wiretap.spies.com
Connected to wiretap.spies.com.
220 wiretap.spies.com FTP server (Version wu-2.3(2) Wed May 4 14:08:55 PDT 19
95) ready.
Name (wiretap.spies.com:taylor): anonymous
331 Guest login ok, send your complete e-mail address as password.
Password:
230-
230-wiretap.spies.com
230-
230-Welcome to the Internet Wiretap FTP server.
230-Tar and compressed tar archive output is enabled.
230-
230-Gopher access to this material is available on port 70.
230-
230-Logging has also been enabled on file transfers.
230-Anyone uploading pictures to this machine will have
230-their kneecaps broken.
230-
230-Look at ".files" in each directory for a better
230-description of contents. Please note that ".cap" files
230-are intended for use by Gopher, and are generally
230-meaningless to FTP users.
230-
230-Read the files in About/ if you desire more detailed
230-information regarding the Internet Wiretap.
230-
230-Comments to: archive@wiretap.spies.com
230-
230 Guest login ok, access restrictions apply.
ftp> cd NAFTA
250 CWD command successful.
ftp> dir 17.intellect
```

```
200 PORT command successful.
150 Opening ASCII mode data connection for /bin/ls.
-r--r--r--  1 9013      42           63957 Mar  5 1993 17.intellect
226 Transfer complete.
remote: 17.intellect
68 bytes received in 0.01 seconds (6.6 Kbytes/s)
ftp> ascii
200 Type set to A.
ftp> get 17.intellect
200 PORT command successful.
150 Opening ASCII mode data connection for 17.intellect (63957 bytes).
226 Transfer complete.
local: 17.intellect remote: 17.intellect
65434 bytes received in 2.3 seconds (28 Kbytes/s)
ftp> quit
221 Goodbye.
```

The FTP program is helpful but complicated to use, as you can see. How might a graphical interface help with the problem? Figure 5.1 shows how a directory of files looks when viewed with a graphical FTP program on a PC running Windows and directly connected to the network. If you're like us, you'll agree that it's considerably easier to use and understand.

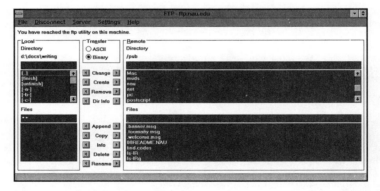

Figure 5.1. Working with FTP is much easier with a graphical interface, as shown.

Summary

Communication lies at the heart of the Internet and, indeed, at the heart of any successful business venture—online or in the physical world. We hope this chapter has given you a glimpse of some of the key communications tools available, and we strongly encourage you to become familiar with electronic mail before you begin your journey on the network.

In the next chapter, we take a look at some of the Internet's powerful marketing tools and show you how the World Wide Web and Gopher can help you advertise your business and ring up sales.

MARKETING TOOLS

In the previous chapter, you learned about the wide variety of communications tools available on the Internet. You can use these tools to interact with your clients and track market trends. But just as there's more to marketing than running a classified ad in the newspaper, there's more to marketing and advertising your business on the Net than using one-to-one communications tools.

Today, the most popular and exciting area of the Internet is the World Wide Web, a network-wide multimedia system that businesses can use to create interactive brochures, catalogs, storefronts, and even malls. Another popular Internet information source and marketing tool is Gopher, a text-based information distribution system. Underlying the Web and Gopher is an important network design paradigm that borrows from what's known as client/server architecture and the idea of transparent movement between computers on the Internet. *Client/server* is actually a pretty simple concept to understand. It splits the job of distributing and displaying information on the Internet into two operations, one occurring on the central "server" machine, the other on the "client" computer on your desk.

For Internet users, an example of client/server architecture is an e-mail program that uses a graphical interface. You use the client interface to compose the mail on your PC; the server software running on your Internet provider's machine then routes the mail to its destination. Client/server systems enable you to exploit the power of your desktop machine—particularly its interface and graphical capabilities—while simultaneously tapping the strength of the many computers elsewhere on the Internet.

But that's only part of what's going on with Gopher and the Web. The other half is something that's missing from e-mail, FTP, Usenet, telnet, and other programs—your ability to move from one server to another without a break in use or concentration. Think of it as reading a book with an endless number of pages. Every time you need more information, you click a hyperlink and it appears—whether the information is on your company's computer or on a computer halfway around the world.

One way to think of it is to imagine searching for the phone number of a friend of yours who works at a different company in a different country. If you relied on the phone, you would have to make several costly phone calls and hope that the company operators had their information sufficiently up-to-date to find your colleague's offsite phone number. On a system such as Gopher or the World Wide Web, however, finding your friend would be as easy as browsing through a list of companies and selecting the one you want. Click the company name with your mouse and suddenly you're looking at a list of their sites and plants. Touch the site you want and you'll view a list of company employees. Click the index and go right to the page that lists your friend's number. It's quick and painless with the "client" program on your PC connecting smoothly, silently, and instantly with other computers around the world.

It's the seamless connectivity to what we call information publishers (fancy names for servers) that really makes the Web and Gopher exciting new Internet tools.

But that's where the similarities between the Web and Gopher end. The differences between the two tools are immediately apparent once you see the two running side-by-side on your screen. Gopher offers a convenient way to deliver the same ASCII text-based information available through FTP archives and e-mail servers. The Web, by contrast, offers color, fonts, graphics, audio, video, page layout capabilities, and a wide variety of other design elements that make surfing the Web an addicting experience.

Gopher

Telnet is a terrific tool, as you learned in the last chapter, but it requires a considerable amount of knowledge about the Internet. In particular, you need to know a lot of computer names to be able to exploit the many services available, making it difficult to find the information you're looking for. The computer services group at the University of Minnesota encountered the same problem when they began making online documentation available to their students a few years ago, so they invented Gopher, a menu-based front end to documents, information, and services available on the Internet.

Think of Gopher as a one-stop shopping source for Internet information. A menu-driven document-delivery service, Gopher enables you to browse the Internet's resources, read text files, and access information of all kinds. By stepping through a series of Gopher menus, you can "burrow" through layers of information to find what you need on any computer system connected to the network and running Gopher software.

Similar to FTP, Gopher offers access to data through Mac, PC, and UNIX systems. First, we'll walk you through the menu-based dialup service, and then we'll repeat the procedure using TurboGopher (the Mac Gopher client) and WinGopher (the Windows client). The most powerful aspect of the Gopher service is that any system can include a variety of links to other Gopher servers. The result is a network wide information source that's known as Gopherspace. Gophers also provide gateways to other Internet information systems such as World Wide Web, WAIS, Archie, and WHOIS, and to network services such as telnet and FTP. One of the best things about Gopher is that when you access a Gopher site, the files listed on the menu could be housed anywhere—on your local server or on a computer system thousands of miles away. By simply choosing an item from the menu on your screen, you can access that information within minutes.

Here's the main menu of the Gopher site put up by the U.S. Census Bureau. We connect by typing gopher gopher.census.gov at the command line, and the screen shows

```
                Internet Gopher Information Client v1.12S

                   Root gopher server: gopher.census.gov

  —>  1.  About This Gopher Server ( Help and Information )/
      2.  About The U.S. Census Bureau/
      3.  Directory of Services and Information/
      4.  Our Organizations and Divisions/
      5.  Other Servers on the Web That Offer Census Data/
      6.  U.S. Government Gopher Servers/
      7.  University Gopher Servers/
      8.  Other Gopher Servers on the Web/
      9.  Internet Documents/
     10. Online Internet/Unix User Reference/

Press ? for Help, q to Quit, u to go up a menu                Page: 1/1
```

Tip: Web browsers can also access Gopher sites with a similar interface when you open the Web address gopher://hostname. In this case, you would use gopher://gopher.census.gov/.

Pressing 3 followed by Return chooses the Directory of Services and Information menu item, which immediately "zooms in" to that level, changing the center information on the screen to

```
         1.  What you will find in this menu.
  ->     2.  News Releases Hot Off the Press/
         3.  News and analysis from the Center for Economic Studies
         4.  International programs that collect global information/
         5.  Census Bulletin Board System <TEL>
         6.  Statistical Briefs like never before!!! (Postscript)/
         7.  Who's Who at the Census Bureau/
         8.  "We The People" Series!!! (Postscript)/
         9.  Financial data from state and local governments and schools
        10.  The Census Bureau Anonymous Ftp/
        11.  Census Bureau BBS Bulletins/
        12.  Sipp On Call/
```

Choosing 2 at this point enables you to see a list of news releases organized in 13 categories: Construction, Population, 2000 Census, Economic Census and Surveys, Education, Foreign Trade Monthly, Governments, Health and Health Care, Income, Wealth and Poverty, International, Housing, Agriculture, and Publications. Perhaps your business has an important foreign trade component; when you choose number 6, you see what's in Foreign Trade Monthly.

```
  ->     1.  About the January Press Releases (Jan '92 to '94).
         2.  U.S. International Trade in Goods and Services.
         3.  U.S. International Trade in Goods and Services 3 month avgs.
         4.  U.S. Services by Major Category — Exports.
         5.  U.S. Services by Major Category — Imports.
         6.  U.S. Trade in Goods.
         7.  Exports and Imports of Goods by Principal End-Use Category.
         8.  Exports of Goods by End-Use Category and Commodity.
         9.  Imports of Goods by End-Use Category and Commodity.
        10.  Exp/Imp/Bal of Goods, Petroleum, & Non-Petroleum End-Use Cat. Tot..
        11.  Exports/Imports of Goods by Principal End-Use Cat.(Const. $ Basis).
        12.  U.S. Trade in Goods.
        13.  Exports and Imports of Goods by Principal End-Use Category.
        14.  Exp./Imp./Bal. of Goods by Selected Countries & Geo. Areas '94.
        15.  Exp./Imp./Bal. of Goods by Selected Countries & Geo. Areas '93.
        16.  Exp/Imp of Goods by Principal SITC Commodity Groupings- '94 & '93.
        17.  Exports, Imports & Balance of Advanced Technology Products.
        18.  Imp. of Energy-Related Petroleum Products, Inc. Crude Petroleum.
```

You could easily choose any of these items to receive foreign trade data directly from the U.S. Census Bureau without ever leaving your computer. Despite its comical-sounding name, Gopher is one of the most popular and valuable tools on the Internet—and one of the most useful to businesses seeking to market their products and services online. Many Internet cybermalls are combination Gopher and Web sites; prominent examples include Branch Mall, The Internet Mall, and The Electronic Newsstand.

If you've got products to sell or information to distribute, you can set up your own Gopher site or rent space on someone else's. (For more information, see Chapter 15, "Storefronts and Cybermalls.") *The News & Observer,* a daily newspaper in Raleigh, North Carolina, last year created a Gopher site to allow its print subscribers (and anyone else who desires) to access an online edition of the newspaper. (It's available on the Web now, too.) To get there, type `gopher gopher.nando.net` at the system prompt. Here's a recent sampling:

```
            Internet Gopher Information Client v1.12S

              Root gopher server: gopher.nando.net

 —>  1.  READ ME!.
      2.  About this Gopher service.
      3.  About The News & Observer Publishing Co./
      4.  Today's edition of The News & Observer (a sampler)/
      5.  The Insider: North Carolina Government/
      6.  Other sources of news, sports and weather/
      7.  Education resources/
      8.  Exploring the Internet/
      9.  Government information/
     10.  Just for fun/
     11.  Kidslink/
     12.  Libraries/
     13.  MetroMUD: You're not in Raleigh anymore ... <TEL>
     14.  Misc. Triangle-area resources/
     15.  News and Observer Searchable Classified Advertisements/
     16.  Test Section/
     17.  The Armchair Traveler/
     18.  The Bookshelf/

Press ? for Help, q to Quit, u to go up a menu         Page: 1/2
```

Figure 6.1 shows how this screen would appear if we were using TurboGopher, a Gopher interface for the Macintosh. With this version, you can select items of interest with a click of your mouse, making information-hunting faster and easier.

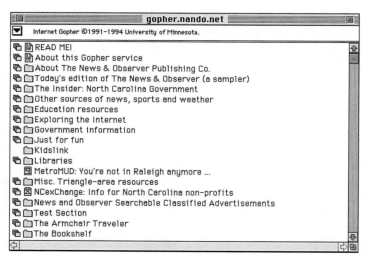

Figure 6.1. TurboGopher.

Winging Your Way with World Wide Web

Gopher is a valuable service for people using the Internet to find information and to make information available to others. The biggest problem with Gopher, however, is that the entry for each item is confined to a single line of text. That's a problem if a paragraph of explanation is required. That's where the Web comes in. The newest of the Internet information tools, the Web is the first truly universal multimedia environment for publishing information on the network. It offers a fascinating glimpse of the future information superhighway.

In a nutshell, the Web is built out of thousands of "pages" of information distributed throughout the network, each page capable of displaying audio and video clips, graphics, and text mixed as desired by the designer or publisher. Words can be displayed in bold, italic, and even different size type, and any word or phrase can be represented as a hyperlinked button capable of transporting the user to another document or image with the click of a mouse. This is best explained by illustration. Figure 6.2 shows the Web home page for the Macmillan Information SuperLibrary on the Internet (where you can buy another copy of this book without leaving your desktop!). Note the inclusion of eye-catching graphics. Clicking any of the words in the opening graphic moves you automatically to another document.

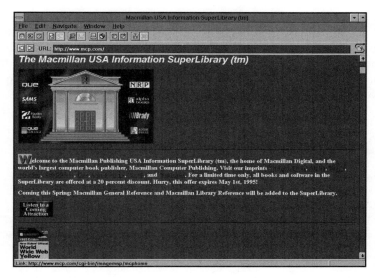

Figure 6.2. The Macmillan Information SuperLibrary on the Web offers a variety of books, including *The Internet Business Guide*.

Tip: You can visit the Macmillan Information SuperLibrary by visiting URL `http://www.mcp.com/`.

Once you're connected to a Web server, you can click a hyperlinked word, phrase, picture, or multimedia icon to access related documents elsewhere on that computer or on thousands of other computer systems throughout the world. On the Web, information can be shared internationally and disseminated to a large number of users at different sites. Because the Web is so easy to use, it has quickly become the method of choice for accessing a wide range of other Internet tools and services, including Gopher and FTP archives.

Originally designed for the high-energy physics community, the World Wide Web has rapidly spread to other fields and attracted a great deal of interest among newspapers, magazines, advertisers, and electronic merchants seeking ways to publish their information on the Internet in an eye-pleasing, accessible format. Internet-watchers predict that, by the end of the decade, even McDonald's customers may be clicking their Web servers to order a hamburger and fries. You never know: Pizza Hut has already set up a Web site at `http://www.pizzahut.com/`.

Although the Web is fun to surf, it contains some limitations that business owners should be aware of. For one, it can't be accessed through electronic mail, and many UNIX dialup accounts offer access to the Web only through a primitive character-based interface called Lynx that displays no graphics, audio, video, or fonts. The Macmillan page shown in Figure 6.2 looks quite different when only the words can be displayed:

```
                    Macmillan USA Information SuperLibrary (tm) (p1 of 4)

The Macmillan USA Information SuperLibrary (tm)

   See the new April SuperLibrary Newsletter

   [IMAGE]
   _____

   W elcome to the Macmillan Publishing USA Information SuperLibrary
   (tm), the home of Macmillan Digital, and the world's largest computer
   book publisher, Macmillan Computer Publishing. Visit our imprints -
   Adobe Press, Alpha, Brady, Hayden, New Riders, Que, Que College,
   Sams, and Sams.net. For a limited time only, all books and software
   in the SuperLibrary are offered at a 20 percent discount. Hurry, this
   offer expires May 1st, 1995!
— press space for next page —
  Arrow keys: Up and Down to move. Right to follow a link; Left to go back.
 H)elp O)ptions P)rint G)o M)ain screen Q)uit /=search [delete]=history list
 H)elp O)ptions P)rint G)o M)ain screen Q)uit /=search [delete]=history list
```

As you can see, even a Web site featuring cool graphics can lose its appeal quickly when viewed through a text-based browser. The good news is that, because of the excitement and enthusiasm surrounding the Web, thousands of people each day are upgrading their connections to SLIP, PPP, and leased lines so that they can view the Web in all its multimedia splendor.

The two most popular strategies for accomplishing this are through a SLIP (Serial Line/IP) or PPP (Point-to-Point Protocol) package running over a fast dialup modem line. Today, fast 28,800 bits-per-second modems are available for less than $200, and you can get a direct SLIP or PPP connection to the Net for $25 a month or less through a local Internet access provider or a commercial online service.

A year ago there was one program for accessing the Web in graphical format—Mosaic. Today, however, dozens of terrific programs are available for Windows, Mac, and UNIX workstations, including Netscape Navigator from Netscape Communications, WinWeb/MacWeb from EINet, Air Mosaic from SPRY (a division of CompuServe), TCP/Connect II from Intercon, Chameleon from Netmanage, Internet in A Box, The Internet Starter Kit, and many more. (For a detailed discussion of Web browsers, see Chapter 3, "Finding the Interface That's Right for You.")

Summary

Both the Web and Gopher offer businesses many exciting opportunities for marketing and advertising—opportunities far greater than those offered by Usenet postings and e-mail autoresponders. We don't recommend ignoring newsgroups or e-mail, of course, but we do believe that a balanced marketing strategy that incorporates a wide variety of Internet tools gives you the best chance of success.

In the next chapter, you'll learn about the many tools available to search for information on the Internet. We'll examine everything from Archie servers for FTP archives and Veronica servers for Gopher sites to Lycos, Yahoo, WebCrawler, the Internet Mall, and other tools and services for searching the Web.

RESEARCH TOOLS

For thousands of businesses, the Internet offers exciting, new opportunities to crack new markets and boost sales in existing ones. But it offers more: Research, competitive intelligence, government regulations, even "virtual" partners can be found on the Internet now. Online research can be quite a challenge, however, because there's no central index, database, or card catalog. In this chapter, we'll give you a running start by explaining some of the best and most useful Internet research tools.

Accessing Archives with Archie

FTP is the simplest of the information tools on the Internet, but it suffers from the same problem as the Internet's other information tools: How do you know which files are available and where? Indeed, this is part of a much more basic problem on the Internet, the problem of missing road maps and reconfigured highways that we've been talking about through this book.

A group of students at the McGill University School of Computer Science realized the problem with FTP archives, and with some ingenuity and programming
they solved the problem by creating a distributed ftp database system called
Archie. The Archie system automatically gathers and indexes the thousands of
ftp archives available and then distributes the comprehensive index to a variety
of Archie sites throughout the Internet.

Although Archie certainly helps find files available through ftp, there isn't much
information contained within the database. Filenames do not usually describe the
contents of the file, and unfortunately, that's all you have to work with. Some
systems are more thoughtfully organized, enabling you to infer some information about a file by its location.

Archie is but one of the many Internet information identification tools a savvy
business Internet user will want to learn. A quick example of what we mean when
we talk about directory naming and how it can assist: A directory such as `pub/`
`archives/mac/business/stocks` is a likely place to find stock market-related files and
applications. You can use this to help your searches: in this case if we search for
`mac` and `stocks`, we could match the files in this directory.

Archie's Internet archives database contains an entry including the name, location, host system, size, and file type of more than 2,000,000 files at more than 1,000
anonymous FTP archive sites. To give you some sense of how popular Archie has
become, public Archie servers currently receive more than 60,000 queries each
day. With more than 2,000,000 files in the Archie database, you won't be surprised
to find that it's massive, far too mammoth to be found on lots of different sites on
the Internet. Fortunately, that's not a problem because many Internet computer
systems offer public access to Archie for anyone who can use telnet to connect to
their machines. Here are some of the public access Archie sites:

Host Name	Site Location
archie.au	Australia
archie.edvz.uni-linz.ac.at	Austria
archie.univie.ac.at	Austria
archie.uqam.ca	Canada
archie.funet.fi	Finland
archie.univ-rennes1.fr	France
archie.th-darmstadt.de	Germany
archie.ac.il	Israel
archie.unipi.it	Italy
archie.wide.ad.jp	Japan
archie.hana.nm.kr	Korea
archie.sogang.ac.kr	Korea
archie.uninett.no	Norway
archie.rediris.es	Spain
archie.luth.se	Sweden

`archie.switch.ch`	Switzerland
`archie.nctuccca.edu.tw`	Taiwan
`archie.ncu.edu.tw`	Taiwan
`archie.doc.ic.ac.uk`	United Kingdom
`archie.hensa.ac.uk`	United Kingdom
`archie.unl.edu`	USA (NE)
`archie.internic.net`	USA (NJ)
`archie.rutgers.edu`	USA (NJ)
`archie.ans.net`	USA (NY)
`archie.sura.net`	USA (MD)

We're going to connect to the closest Archie site to see whether there are any files that help Macintosh users track their stocks and other securities. To connect to the Archie database, we use the telnet program, connecting to the host name specified in the preceding list. Using the Archie program directly through telnet can be quite confusing (as is FTP).

```
% telnet archie.internic.net
Trying...
Connected to ds.internic.net.
Escape character is '^]'.
            InterNIC Directory and Database Services

Welcome to InterNIC Directory and Database Services provided by AT&T.
These services are partially supported through a cooperative agreement
with the National Science Foundation.

First time users may login as guest with no password to receive help.

Your comments and suggestions for improvement are welcome, and can be
mailed to admin@ds.internic.net.

AT&T MAKES NO WARRANTY OR GUARANTEE, OR PROMISE, EXPRESS OR IMPLIED,
CONCERNING THE  CONTENT OR  ACCURACY OF THE  DIRECTORY  ENTRIES AND
DATABASE  FILES  STORED  AND  MAINTAINED  BY  AT&T.  AT&T EXPRESSLY
DISCLAIMS AND EXCLUDES ALL EXPRESS WARANTIES AND IMPLIED WARRANTIES
OF MERCHANTABILITY AND FITNESS FOR A PARTICULAR PURPOSE.

SunOS UNIX (ds2)

login:
```

As with all Archie servers, logging in here as `archie` will drop us into the Archie client program:

```
*****************************************************************************
            Welcome to the InterNIC Directory and Database Server.
*****************************************************************************
```

```
# Bunyip Information Systems, 1993

# Terminal type set to 'vt100 24 80'.
# 'erase' character is '^?'.
# 'search' (type string) has the value 'sub'.
archie> find stocks
# Search type: sub.
# Your queue position: 1
# Estimated time for completion: 00:50
working... /


Host sunsite.unc.edu    (152.2.22.81)
Last updated 11:07 22 Dec 1993


    Location: /pub/packages/TeX/fonts/postscript/adobe/Updates
      FILE    -r—r—r—    1315 bytes   22:42 14 Jul 1993
930709.StockSplit.press
```

Actually, dozens of matches are shown, all in the same format. This particular match is available at the ftp archive site sunsite.unc.edu in the specified directory. The match is 1,315 bytes in size. Looking through all the matches reveals the following:

```
Host wuarchive.wustl.edu    (128.252.135.4)
Last updated 11:27 22 Dec 1993

    Location: /systems/mac/umich.edu/misc/demo
       FILE    -r--r--r--  266426 bytes  15:15  5 Sep 1993
stockstack2.1g.cpt.hqx
```

Sounds promising. We could use FTP to connect to wuarchive.wustl.edu, change to the directory systems/mac/umich.edu/misc/demo, and then get the file stockstack2.1g.cpt.hqx to see whether it's what we're seeking. For now, just remember that there's a database of files available through the ftp archives, but it's not necessarily that easy to use.

Things aren't quite as bleak as they seem, however, because some terrific Archie front-end programs are available. The best is a utility called Anarchie, for the Macintosh. Figure 7.1 shows the results of the same search in Anarchie. Double-clicking any of the matched lines causes the program to connect automatically to the ftp archive, change into the correct directory, and obtain the file indicated. But Anarchie doesn't stop there; it automatically decodes and unpacks files, too!

Tip: You can get your own copy of Anarchie—pronounced an archy—by connecting via anonymous FTP to boombox.micro.umn.edu or use the URL http://wwwhost.ots.utexas.edu/mac/internet-ftp.html.

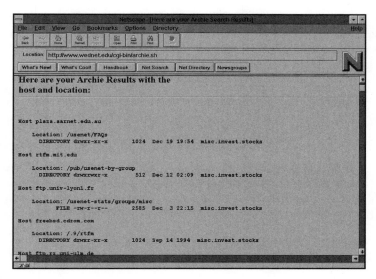

Figure 7.1. The best way to find and obtain files from ftp archives on a Macintosh: Anarchie.

Searching Gopherspace with Veronica

Unlike ftp and telnet data, and even mailing lists, the documents and information available in Gopher is uniquely suited for a comprehensive database and search capability. In Gopherspace, this is made possible through a search tool called Veronica. The basic concept is simple: A small number of sites accessible through Gopher house copies of a huge database containing an entry for each menu item on each of thousands of Gopher servers throughout the Internet. Type a keyword or two and Gopher returns a list of all the Gopher menu entries that match.

The problem is that, in an attempt to manage the overwhelming number of search requests, certain keywords are pre-searched or otherwise programmed to produce special results. If the keyword by itself would generate too many matches, Veronica won't go any further with your query except to respond too many matches or some similar phrase. This can be very frustrating when you're searching for Internet stock reports and use internet stock as your keywords. Most Veronica servers will see internet and immediately return a too-many-hits error. This problem can be minimized through a judicious choice of keywords, however.

Veronica is a simple search tool; all lists of keywords are implicitly considered as or choices, so that `internet stock` returns all entries that contain either `internet` or `stock` in their descriptions, hence the error. There is currently no way to conduct searches that build on one another.

Here's an example of what you might see on your screen if you used Veronica to search the NYSERNet system, one of several Veronica servers available to the public. Your first stop would be a menu item, probably at the first set of choices, called "Search Gopherspace using Veronica." Choose that and here's what you see:

```
        Search Gopherspace using Veronica

 —>  1.   Search gopherspace by veronica at NYSERNet <?>
     2.   Search gopherspace by veronica at SCS Nevada  <?>
     3.   Search Gopher+ ABSTRACTs (50 sites) via SCS Nevada  <?>
     4.   Search gopherspace by veronica at PSINet <?>
     5.   Search gopherspace by veronica at University of Pisa <?>
     6.   Search gopherspace by veronica at U. of Manitoba <?>
     7.   Search gopherspace by veronica at University of Koeln <?>
     8.   Search gopherspace by veronica at UNINETT/U. of Bergen <?>
     9.   Search gopherspace by veronica at U.Texas, Dallas <?>
     10.  Search Gopher Directory Titles using NYSERNet <?>
     11.  Search Gopher Directory Titles using SCS Nevada  <?>
     12.  Search Gopher Directory Titles using PSINet <?>
     13.  Search Gopher Directory Titles using University of Pisa <?>
     14.  Search Gopher Directory Titles using U. of Manitoba <?>
     15.  Search Gopher Directory Titles using University of Koeln <?>
     16.  Search Gopher Directory Titles using UNINETT/U. of Bergen <?>
     17.  Search Gopher Directory Titles using U.Texas, Dallas <?>
     18.                                    .

Press ? for Help, q to Quit, u to go up a menu          Page:1/2
```

We choose number 1 and then are prompted for keywords. Entering `finance stocks` produces quite a few matches. The first 18 are summarized on the screen of our dialup account as follows:

```
        Search gopherspace by veronica at NYSERNet: finance or stocks

 —>  1.   Top Technology Stocks by Volume and Change, 3-15.
     2.   Most active OTC stocks 7-20.
     3.   Finance Division (organizationalUnit)/
     4.   FIN  FINANCE/
     5.   Most active OTC stocks 3-17.
     6.   Finance Office (organizationalUnit)/
     7.   Search Finance <?>
     8.   Top Technology Stocks by Volume and Change, 7-2.
     9.   Stocks rise to record heights in London.
     10.  1993 Volume 17 Issue 1 Journal of Banking and Finance.
```

```
   11. Top Technology Stocks by Change at Midday, 7-22.
   12. 15 most active NYSE stocks 4-8.
   13. Read Bnking and Finance Assist. Center .. for EastWest Studies entr
y.
   14. 15 most active NYSE stocks 7-15.
   15. Stocks edge up in Japan.
   16. Stocks recover a little.
   17. Search ACCOUNTING AND FINANCE <?>
   18. Most active AMEX stocks 8-7.

Press ? for Help, q to Quit, u to go up a menu            Page: 1/12
```

Veronica is a valuable tool, particularly if you take the time to use various keywords (think synonyms) for your queries and try the same query at multiple Veronica sites. Not all sites are identical, however, and identical queries can produce widely varying results.

Searching the World Wide Web

Although quite a bit of information is available through Gopher, many businesses, government agencies, and other organizations are making their information available through the World Wide Web. The Web excels at displaying and linking text, graphics, photos, and even audio and video clips, but it's often difficult to locate the Web sites you want.

Various researchers and organizations have tried to solve this problem with impressive results. There are about six popular Web directories and search engines available today, each of which offers its own somewhat quirky interface and unique subset of the sites on the Web. In the following sections, we give you an overview of three of the best—Yahoo, Lycos, and WebCrawler—and then briefly explore a few other places to find information on the Web.

Yahoo

Yahoo is the brainchild of two Stanford University graduate students, David Filo and Jerry Yang, who wanted to solve the problem of managing their exploding lists of favorite Web sites—bookmarks or "hotlists." Yahoo, despite its irreverent name, has become one of the most popular starting points for exploring the World Wide Web—and one of the best, in our view.

Back in March 1994, Filo and Yang started comparing hotlists and they quickly realized that they had hundreds of entries. Keeping such a large number of entries organized within their hotlists was becoming impossible. In fact, it was becoming difficult to find things they had put on their own lists! Because they were Ph.D. candidates studying electrical engineering and possessed the necessary expertise, they decided to convert their hotlists into a database. They added custom scripts and programs to extract entries automatically in a format that was Web-compatible. They were on their way to bringing order out of chaos.

In the first few weeks after Yahoo went live, Internet users began stumbling onto it and suggesting new entries. That was just the beginning. About every month since then, the number of users accessing Yahoo has doubled. Early in April 1995, when Yahoo went commercial with an infusion of money from a venture capital firm, it had close to 40,000 entries in its database.

There are two ways to navigate in Yahoo—through its simple hierarchical menu system or by entering a query containing one or more keywords. The top-level menu is logical and well designed, as you can see here:

Art (829)
Business (10597)
Computers (3627)
Economy (1084)
Education (2032)
Entertainment (11201)
Environment and Nature (303)
Events (66)
Government (1321)
Health (737)
Humanities (309)
Law (264)
News (387)
Politics (242)
Reference (573)
Regional Information (5715)
Science (3817)
Social Science (145)
Society and Culture (1206)

The numbers in parentheses show how many links are in that particular category; they also offer an interesting glimpse of the landscape of the Web. Note that business, with 10,597 entries, is a most common entry. That's yet one more indicator that the Internet is becoming an important new venue for businesses seeking an edge.

The Yahoo site is pictured in Figure 7.2. You can check it out for yourself by connecting to URL `http://www.yahoo.com/`.

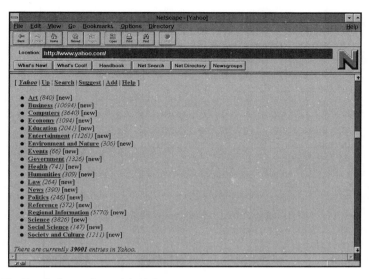

Figure 7.2. Finding information with Yahoo.

To get an idea of the information available within Yahoo, look at Figure 7.3, which shows the results of searching for stock bonds within the Yahoo database. Notice how neat and understandable the results are.

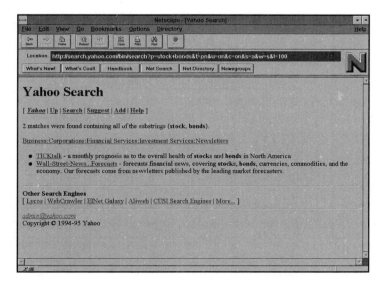

Figure 7.3. Easily understood search results—this time for stock bonds—within Yahoo.

WebCrawler

Yahoo is certainly valuable as a Web site directory, but imagine how much more valuable it would be if you added a server that automatically went onto the Web and searched for information.

In the world of science fiction, we would call this a self-aware directory, or using more recent jargon, an agent-based central listing service. Whatever you choose to call it, the vision is compelling; without any human intervention, the computer itself detects, acquires, and adds new information to the directory.

Some Internet directory services offer just such a capability, notably Veronica in Gopherspace and Archie for ftp archives. With the Web, however, the indexing process is more difficult because it's less obvious what information should be indexed and how it should be presented to the searcher. Imagine if each chapter of this book were a separate Web page and you searched for VERONICA. Would you want each match highlighted in the displayed table of contents? Would you prefer the first occurrence of the pattern within each chapter plus a few lines of context? Or would a long listing of all the matches better suit your purposes?

It's just these sort of questions that have prompted Brian Pinkerton at the University of Washington in Seattle to create WebCrawler (actually a suite of programs), which wanders the Web indexing everything it finds. The resulting database is accessible to everyone through the World Wide Web at `http://webcrawler.cs.washington.edu/WebCrawler/WebQuery.html`. WebCrawler is shown in Figure 7.4.

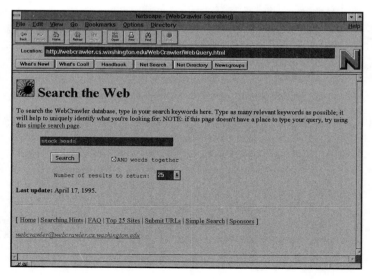

Figure 7.4. A massive database of Web information, accessible via WebCrawler.

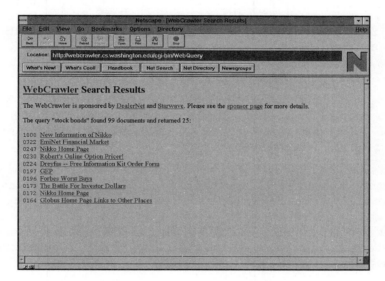
At the heart of WebCrawler is a WAIS Internet-capable database, which enables it to index hundreds of thousands of Web pages with relatively little disk space and processing required. Today the WebCrawler system runs on a Pentium PC running NeXTStep, with a single 500MB disk and 72MB of memory. Though the WebCrawler database is only 80MB in size, it contains information on more than 70,000 different documents residing on as many as 9,000 different servers. WebCrawler also keeps track of sites it hasn't seen yet, with its list of an additional 383,000 Web documents that haven't yet been indexed by the program.

To see how that changes the results of our earlier search, consider Figure 7.5, which shows the results of stock bonds within WebCrawler.

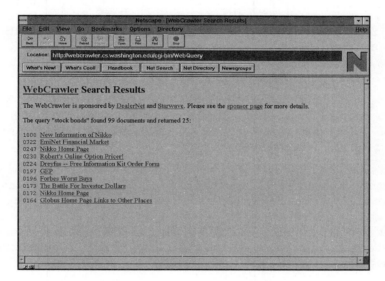

Figure 7.5. Searching for stocks and bonds with WebCrawler.

Lycos

Lycos is another crawler-like system that wanders the Web autonomously, keeping track of where it's been and where it wants to go. Accessing and indexing almost 10,000 documents each day, Lycos contains an online index of close to 3,500,000 documents. WebCrawler is similar at a philosophical level, but the scope of the two projects is dramatically different. Lycos runs across a cluster of 12 different computers, including several Sun SPARCstations and Pentium P90 workstations with two or three of these machines assigned to scout duties full-time. WebCrawler sits on a NeXT workstation and a PC.

The Lycos project, housed at Carnegie Mellon University in Pittsburgh, PA, started out as a program called LongLegs. Current funding for the project comes from the U.S. Government Advanced Research Projects Agency (ARPA), the Corporation for National Research Initiatives (CNRI), and Carnegie Mellon. Recently, the Lycos database has been licensed by Microsoft for inclusion in the Microsoft Network set to go live this summer.

Lycos gets its name from the Lycosidae spider, an unusual species that pursues its prey rather than passively spinning a web and waiting for lunch to drop in. We see this as an accurate—if perhaps a bit ominous—metaphor for the overall design of the search system.

What's most impressive about Lycos is the scope of what it has managed to find and index. As of June 1995, Lycos had catalogued close to 3,500,000 unique URLs. The program opens and explores any sites that are either Web, Gopher, or FTP files, giving it quite a range of data to draw from. It doesn't track e-mail addresses, telnet, or WAIS servers, however, so it's not quite the universal solution for finding information anywhere on the network. However, it's a tremendous resource for business users seeking research and information on the Internet.

Lycos suffers from one nagging problem, though. It's one that we suspect is inherent in the design of any crawler-type program: With close to 3,500,000 documents indexed and 10,000 new pages being added each day, information in the database begins to age. On the Internet, where information changes constantly, aging information translates to dead links, revamped pages, and other problems. Lycos offers a way for users to indicate that certain URLs have become inactive or disappeared and to add new (or updated) URLs to the search list, but it's something users have to do manually. As a result, don't be surprised if you visit Lycos only to find that some of the information it lists is no longer available any more. It's the flip side of the dramatic growth and expansion of the network; information can be hard to find even with these high-powered search tools.

Lycos also lacks sophisticated Boolean searches (for example, A and B but not C), but it does have a pattern language of its own. For example, if you enter a word you're looking for, Lycos automatically searches for that word plus many variants of it. The shorter the variant, the more occurrences of the word or the earlier the word appears in the snippet of information about the document, the more relevant Lycos believes the match. Enter two words and it will score documents containing more than one word more relevant than documents containing only a single word. You can search for one word but lower the relevance of another by putting a hyphen in front of the second word. For example, `cat -dog` would score most relevant documents with `cat`-like words but not `dog`-like words. End a word with a period to force an exact match, dropping the relevance of similar words. Append a dollar sign to a word, and you *increase* the relevance of prefix or suffix matching.

Figure 7.6 shows the main screen of Lycos, which you can find by visiting URL `http://lycos.cs.cmu.edu/`. Figure 7.7 shows a typical result for a search on `stock bonds` in its extensive database. Notice how the results compare with the Yahoo information we showed you in Figure 7.3.

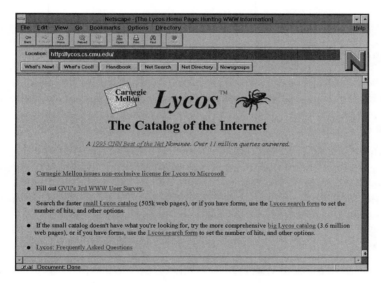

Figure 7.6. Searching for information on the Web with Lycos.

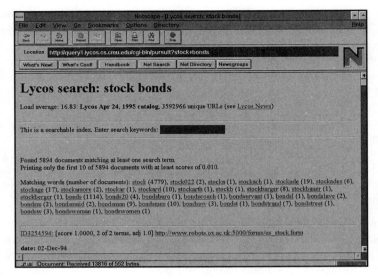

Figure 7.7. Lycos produces matches for a search on `stock bonds`.

Other Search Spots

A variety of other search spots are also available on the Internet, depending on what kind of information you seek. The Web seems to offer the widest variety of different search tools, with at least a dozen indexes in addition to the three already covered.

One that we find ourselves using a lot is the Internet Mall, run by co-author Dave Taylor. At the time of this writing, the Mall lists more than 2,500 stores and companies that are selling products or services on the Internet. Figure 7.8 shows a specific department within the Mall, this one a listing of small business services. The Internet Mall is found on the Web at `http://www.mecklerweb.com/imall`, or you can reach it by sending an e-mail message to `taylor@netcom.com` with the subject `send mall`.

Another great place to visit is EINet Galaxy. EINet also produces a very nice Web browser called MacWeb (for Macintosh users) and WinWeb (for Windows users). EINet Galaxy offers an interesting hybrid blend of information from the company and pointers to other spots on the Web and Internet. You can visit EINet Galaxy at URL `http://www.einet.net/` as shown in Figure 7.9.

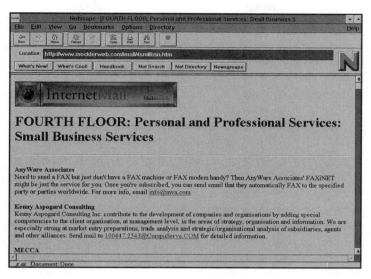

Figure 7.8. A spot for shops on the Internet: The Internet Mall.

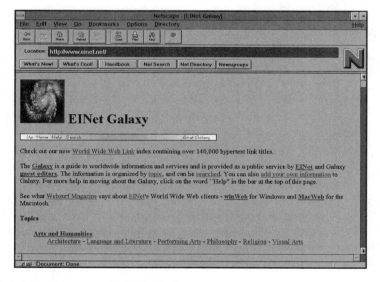

Figure 7.9. A different approach: EINet Galaxy.

If you're seeking information distributed by the United States Government or any of its many agencies, FedWorld is a valuable resource; check it out at `http://www.fedworld.gov/`. As you can see from Figure 7.10, FedWorld contains a staggering amount of information from more than 100 different government bureaus, departments, and agencies, though we have to warn you that the first screen is just a huge logo for the site.

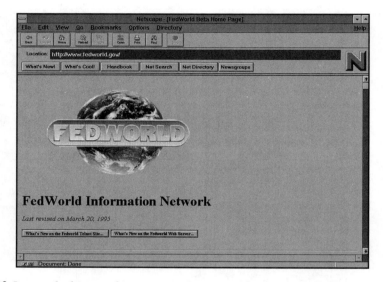

Figure 7.10. Ignore the big graphics image to tap a wealth of government information at FedWorld.

One of the best new sites that has appeared on the World Wide Web within the past few months is a Web-accessible database of postings from the popular Net-happenings mailing list. You can check it out at `http://www.mid.net/net/`. As companies set up sites on the Web, they often send announcements to the National Center for Supercomputing Applications' What's New Page or the Netscape What's New listing service. Both are worth a visit. Their URLs are `http://www.ncsa.uiuc.edu/SDG/Software/Mosaic/Docs/whats-new.html` and `http://home.mcom.com/home/whats-new.html`, respectively.

Two more sites of value are the Special Internet Connections Web Page, run by Scott Yanoff, at `http://www.uwm.edu/Mirror/inet.services.html` and Open Market's Commercial Sites index at `http://www.directory.net/`.

Summary

Ten years ago, only the largest companies had access to online news and information about their competitors and market conditions. Today, thanks to the Internet, even the smallest business owner and entrepreneur can access databases; gather technical information, programs and documents; monitor the news; and gather competitive intelligence. Using the search tools described in this chapter will give you a big head start in finding what you're looking for.

COMMUNICATING YOUR MESSAGE

THE POWER OF E-MAIL

As local markets evolve into a global marketplace, businesses large and small are searching for a quick, easy, and inexpensive way to communicate with employees, customers, and colleagues worldwide. These days, global networking often means patching together a hodgepodge of long-distance phone, fax, data-transmission, video conferencing, and overnight courier services and trying to integrate it all with the company's communications network back home—a complex and costly process. Even for giant multinationals, the cost of setting up a wide-area network to move voice, data, and video traffic around the world can often be prohibitive.

That's why the Internet is such an attractive alternative. With the Internet, your company pays a flat monthly fee to hook up to the network, enabling you to send all the e-mail, documents, graphics, audio, and video you want virtually anywhere in the world. Unlike commercial online networks, you're not charged by the byte or by the hour. With the Internet, you can forge ahead into new international markets confident that your profits won't sink in an ocean of long-distance phone bills.

How much money can Internet e-mail save your company? There are a number of different factors that come into play (such as the type of connection you choose), but telecommunications experts figure it this way: E-mailing a 200-word memo cross-country on the Internet takes less than 5 seconds and typically costs well under 10 cents, on average. Sending the same message by postal mail costs 32 cents, the same price as a 2-minute fax. An overnight package, by contrast, costs $17.

Of course, price isn't the only issue—especially for business. If it were, Federal Express would have gone out of business long ago!

Doing business on the Internet carries some risks; in terms of communications, these risks involve reliability, security, flexibility, and integration with local-area networks (LANs). Although Internet e-mail may be a low-cost way to reach out on a global scale, it's also a dicier way to go when your data absolutely, positively has to be there overnight (if not sooner).

The purpose of this chapter is to show you how to use the Internet to exchange messages, documents, graphics, video, and other files with employees, customers, vendors, and colleagues worldwide. We'll consider the *pros* and *cons* of Internet e-mail versus commercial network providers such as AT&T, MCI, Sprint, and CompuServe. We'll also discuss some of the challenges involved in integrating the Internet with your existing local-area network, showcasing solutions for small, medium, and large companies looking to set up Internet mail gateways.

Around the World with Internet E-Mail

For companies doing business internationally, Internet e-mail offers three key advantages: It's available all over the world, it's easy to use, and it's a lot cheaper than the commercial alternatives. According to Larry Landweber of the University of Wisconsin, who compiles a list of Internet-connected countries, 168 countries now have Internet connectivity, from France, Spain, Germany, and Italy to China, the Dominican Republic, and Zimbabwe. With more and more countries hooking up all the time, the Internet is fast becoming the Esperanto of electronic communications systems.

With Internet e-mail, you can use a wide variety of text- and graphics-based interfaces to send an electronic letter to one person or thousands of people. You can send text files and binary files. You can distribute memos, product announcements, brochures, job postings, and electronic magazines—all for a lot less than you would pay for postage or long-distance phone service. You can even send messages to people on online networks in which you don't have an account; for example, if you're a CompuServe subscriber, you can send a message to someone on America Online or vice versa.

Of course, Internet e-mail isn't just useful for international businesses. Even companies that do business locally can benefit. For example, Copytech Printing of Canton, Massachusetts, uses the Internet to swap messages with customers and vendors and to receive files for printing. Technical manager Jeff Weener says the Internet gives his company a competitive edge. "We're in the demand-print business where lead times are short," Weener says. "Internet helps with delivery and makes it easy to get files."

In Kansas City alone, Internet e-mail users include

> AlliedSignal Inc. is using the network to periodically update databases in five remote locations and send e-mail. The company fields questions about machine tools through a toll-free telephone number and then sends answers to its customers via the Internet.

> Sprint Corporation, the nation's third largest long-distance carrier, is hooking its internal computer networks to the Internet so that all its departments can communicate through the system. Sprint employees can now tap into Internet newsgroups to discuss professional development or telecommunications topics. Sprint also has used the Internet to set up an electronic information booth for employees. The booth features a variety of information about the company and its benefits.

> Ruf Corporation employees use the Internet to send e-mail to customers and talk with computer and statistics experts on Internet newsgroups.

In Pennsylvania, Internet e-mail users hail from industries as diverse as health care to petroleum. Students at Hahnemann University medical school in Philadelphia doing rotations at the hospital can use the Internet to tap into Hahnemann Automated Library and find out what's going on at their school. Buckeye Pipeline Co. in Emmaus, PA, uses the Internet to communicate with the American Petroleum Institute and other trade groups.

In Rosalind's home-based publishing business, she's used the Internet to communicate with business associates as far away as Australia and as close as those down the street. Last year, after posting a press release about her newsletter, Interactive Publishing Alert, an editor from South Africa's *Weekly Mail and Guardian* requested a subscription. Thanks to the Internet, she was able to swap notes with him without picking up the phone or worrying about time zones. What's more, she doesn't have to charge him extra for overseas postage because she distributes the newsletter by e-mail—which costs the same for subscribers down the block as for those across the globe.

With a busy travel schedule, Dave relies on Internet e-mail to keep in touch with his friends, colleagues, and clients throughout the world. It's common for Dave to hammer out contracts and the materials to be delivered to clients without a single piece of paper changing hands. Even invoices are distributed electronically. Clients in England or Japan can collaborate as easily as those in the same town.

Internet E-Mail versus the Rest of the Pack

Although there a number of commercial networks that offer worldwide connectivity— AT&T, MCI, Sprint, and CompuServe to name some of the major ones— the Internet is far less expensive and more widely available than they are. These days, even large corporations that rely on commercial networks are discovering the advantages of using the toll-free Internet instead, swelling Internet usage by about 15% a month. Companies as large as Lockheed—which pays $40,000 a year for a leased line that connects 5,000 of its 70,000 employees worldwide—to businesses as small as Alain Pinel Realtors—a California real estate brokerage that pays $180 a month to connect its 200 agents with local customers and vendors— are finding the Internet to be a cost-effective solution to their communications needs. Almost all of the major auto manufacturers are now utilizing the connectivity strengths of the Internet, too, including Toyota, Honda, Chevrolet, Ford, and Chrysler.

Cost isn't the Internet's only attraction for corporate users, though. Unlike many of the commercial e-mail products on the market today, the Internet was designed to handle large numbers of users and incorporates an addressing system to make that possible. The Internet's simple yet sophisticated addressing format divides each address into two parts—the name and the location. Locations always have an assigned domain portion—commercial, educational, military, and so on. SRI International, a government-funded research organization in Menlo Park, California, maintains the Internet directory and makes sure all names are unique.

By contrast, local-area network software packages such as cc:Mail and Microsoft Mail use a single, flat directory structure for addressing messages. There's no hierarchical organization; if there are two Joe Smiths, one has to use a different name. This type of addressing works fine for 100 or even 1,000 users, but what about 1,000,000? 20,000,000?

You might have heard of the X.400 messaging system, an internationally endorsed computer standard for addressing and building e-mail messages that is language- and transportation-system independent. It has some definite advantages over Internet e-mail, notably its support for foreign languages, but it's suffering from the chicken-and-egg problem, and too few sites use it for us to recommend that you choose it as a basis for your corporate e-mail. The Internet's addressing system also offers advantages over the widely used X.400 protocol. Unlike the not-for-profit Internet, X.400 is a commercial system, currently used by more than 200 public networks worldwide, including mail systems operated by MCI Communications Corporation and AT&T EasyLink Services. X.400 services are a more functional, more complex, and far more expensive route than the Internet and are at heart a commercial system, with many features designed specifically for the business of moving messages. Were it not for the Internet, X.400 would be the only real choice for worldwide e-mail.

If you have a registered domain for your business and decide to use a different carrier to access the Internet, you generally don't have to change your e-mail address. With X.400, you must include your carrier identification as part of your address. That's comparable to having to change your telephone number every time you switched long-distance carriers. The Internet also boasts another advantage: It's a single interconnected network. Once connected, you can send e-mail to anyone without restriction. By contrast, X.400 is made up of separate networks managed by different organizations. Each of these networks is called an ADministration Management Domain (ADMD). Usually a long-distance carrier or a government-owned telecommunications company owns an ADMD. ADMDs must bilaterally agree to be connected to one another, and not all ADMDs are interconnected, restricting your reach to those with X.400 connections.

Because of the Internet's low cost, widespread use, and addressing versatility, many experts are touting the Internet as a one-stop shopping mall for corporate telecommunications needs. Within a few years, the prediction of Tom Lunzner of SRI International might be true, "The Internet will replace the now-ubiquitous FAX machine."

How Internet E-Mail Works

To understand how Internet e-mail works, it's time to revisit the highway metaphor. As we noted in the introduction, the Internet isn't a centralized system such as CompuServe or America Online but a decentralized "network of networks," a collection of thousands of small regional networks connected by phone lines, cables, even satellites. The Internet's high-speed links carry a wide variety of data, including chunks of files (FTP), commands (telnet), discussion (Usenet), and even pictures and video (World Wide Web).

What makes all this Internet traffic possible is a set of common traffic laws called Transmission Control Protocol/Internet Protocol (TCP/IP), a language that almost all Internet-connected computers share. The best way to understand how the network works is to think of it as layers, with each protocol building atop the previous. At the bottom of the stack, serving as the foundation of the highway, is the Internet Protocol (IP), a specification that details how to send specific packets of information—called datagrams—across multiple networks. IP features a packet-addressing method that allows any computer on the network to forward a packet to another computer that is closer to the final destination. (At least, it's usually closer. On the Internet, routes can change at a moment's notice depending on computer loads, competing demands on the network, and other factors.) Another IP feature is the capability to break a datagram into small chunks, which is necessary because different networks may have different packet sizes.

It's important to recognize that, unlike Federal Express and other commercial carriers, IP is a "best efforts" packet delivery protocol. There's no method within the IP "layer" for verifying that a given packet arrives intact at its destination— or at all. In addition, IP routes each packet separately. Different packets, even within the same message, may traverse the network along different paths and may arrive at their final destination out of order.

Both of these problems are resolved by a high-level protocol—in this case, the Transmission Control Protocol (TCP). TCP exists to ensure reliable transportation of messages across Internet-connected networks. It handles the error-checking of IP packets and if necessary, requests retransmission of damaged or missing packets. It also handles the re-sequencing of out-of-order packets and discards any duplicate packets that may occur when too many packets are retransmitted. If IP is the concrete foundation of the information highway, TCP is the set of rules that allow specific lanes to be delineated, on- and off-ramps to be designed, and signs to be built.

The information highway isn't very useful without traffic of some sort—let's call them cybercars—and one important and popular type of cybercar is e-mail traffic. Unlike real cars, however, these e-mail messages travel by zooming from gas station to gas station, parking for seconds, minutes, or even hours at each stop. In computer parlance, this is called *store-and-forward* technology, and it means that your e-mail message isn't sent immediately or even directly to the recipient but rather is driven down the highway en route. The rules that govern the driving of these e-mail cybercars is called the Simple Mail Transfer Protocol (SMTP). It details the explicit steps one computer must make to connect to another computer and transmit an electronic mail message. Usually SMTP is built atop TCP/IP (the layering stuff we talked about earlier) but can use alternative means as appropriate, such as SLIP. (SLIP, you recall, is Serial Line/IP. The Serial Line protocol emulates TCP but with some differences, making it more suitable for phone-based connections.) One important advantage of SMTP is that, as a universal e-mail protocol, it enables highly dissimilar machines to exchange electronic mail without fuss or translation.

How does e-mail compare to the U.S. Postal Service? In many ways, it's surprisingly similar: People who use Internet e-mail don't exchange messages directly any more than the postal service picks up a letter from the mail box outside your office and carries it directly to the office park across the street. Your Internet access provider takes your electronic letters, trucks them to the nearest Internet "post office," sorts them, and distributes them. It may distribute them to your neighboring office park (because both buildings are in the same neighborhood and use the same post office), but more often, your e-mail message will stop at five or six Internet "post offices" along the way—just as if you mailed a postal letter from Tallahassee, Florida, to Sioux City, Iowa. Like postal mail, the recipient has to check his Internet electronic mail box to retrieve your letter, a letter courteously, if silently, delivered by the electronic Internet postman.

All postal mail carries the postmark of the post office that first received the letter, and often, if it's been routed through multiple post offices, it will bear one or two postmarks. An Internet e-mail message not only carries the mark of the original computer post office receiving the message but also includes information about each of the systems en route that saw and forwarded the mail. On the Internet, these postmarks are easily seen in each message by examining all the headers. Here's an example of this in an Internet message Dave recently received from a chap at the Virginia Department of Education. Look for the `Received:` lines:

```
From jhammond@vdoe386.vak12ed.edu  Mon Jun 19 08:02:19 1995
Return-Path: <jhammond@vdoe386.vak12ed.edu>
Received: from virginia.edu by mail.netcom.com (8.6.8.1/Netcom)
        id IAA02029; Mon, 19 Jun 1995 08:02:17 -0700
Received: from vdoe386.vak12ed.edu by uvaarpa.virginia.edu id aa25289;
        19 Jun 95 11:01 EDT
Received: by vdoe386.vak12ed.edu (5.65/1.34)
        id AA05854; Mon, 19 Jun 95 14:56:46 GMT
From: "D. Jon Hammond" <jhammond@vdoe386.vak12ed.edu>
Message-Id: <9506191456.AA05854@vdoe386.vak12ed.edu>
Subject: Help
To: taylor@netcom.com
Date: Mon, 19 Jun 95 10:56:45 EDT
X-Mailer: PENELM [version 2.3.1 PL11]
```

Notice how the mail was received by the original host, vdoe386.vak12ed.edu, at 14:56 GMT, routed from that system to uvaarpa.virginia.edu, received at that node at 11:01 EDT (which is 15:01 GMT), received by mail.netcom.com at 08:02:17 PST (GMT plus seven hours, this is also 15:02:17 GMT). Total transit time is under five minutes from Virginia to California, considerably faster than U.S. Postal Service mail.

Internet E-Mail Software

Unlike e-mail systems on many commercial online services, there's no single way to send Internet e-mail. It all depends on the type of system and software you're using. There are dozens of DOS-, Windows-, Macintosh-, and UNIX-based programs available for sending Internet e-mail. They all have some things in common, however. All Internet e-mail programs prompt you to fill in the recipient's address (the `To:` prompt) and the message header (the `Subject:` prompt) and then you can enter the message itself, known as the "body," or text, of the message. Many also offer you the ability to add other documents, or even audio, as attachments.

Let's further complicate the picture a bit here. Internet e-mail is handled by two kinds of programs: clients and servers. Don't panic, however, because the post office works the same way. There are people who show up at your home and handle specific mail transactions (delivery and receipt of outgoing e-mail), and there are the faceless thousands who work at central routing and delivery facilities throughout the world. Clients are the programs that you see when you work with e-mail on your desktop PC, and servers are the lower-level systems that take care of routing and delivery through the network. Good client programs offer a complete facility for managing your electronic mail, including address books, message folders, and more. Server programs queue your messages in a pile and periodically send them on electronic "trucks" to other computers on the Internet.

There are a wide variety of client programs, particularly for UNIX systems. Among the best are *mail* (also known as Berkeley Mail), the Elm mail system—Elm—*Pine*, and *mush*. All text-based, these handle the basics of e-mail messaging and can often be invoked by typing their names when you log onto your Internet access provider. Dave is partial to Elm for his UNIX accounts. Graphical programs include *ZMail, XMH*, and *MailTool* for UNIX systems. Many Mac and Windows clients are popping up, too: *Eudora* runs on DOS and Macintosh systems, and *Pipeline*, *NetCruiser*, and *WinNET Mail* are software-server combinations that provide an easy-to-use Windows interface. Rosalind uses WinNET Mail on her PC.

Berkeley Mail is one of the most widely available Internet e-mail programs for dialup access but also one of the most basic. It can be started by typing `mail` at the UNIX command prompt when you're connected to your Internet access account, or, if you specify an e-mail address when you start the program, you can compose and send a message to the specified recipient, as shown in this simple example:

```
% mail jorge@tyler.win.net
Subject: Still on for lunch?
Jorge,
Just checking in with you to confirm our lunch at Monty's in Miami today.
Send me a note if you need to change our plans.
Thanks,
Rosalind
.
Cc:
%
```

Here the mailer prompts you for a subject for the message with `Subject:`. We encourage you to use a succinct and meaningful subject for all your messages. Once the subject is entered, you can enter as many lines as you like. The last line of the message is indicated with a . by itself on a line. Once that's entered, the program asks if there are any other recipients that should receive copies of the message. In this case, there are none, so you press Return at the `Cc:` prompt and send the message. Then this client hands the message off to an e-mail server for delivery, probably a program called *sendmail* in this case.

There are other, easier programs for working with e-mail if you're on a UNIX account. Both Elm and Pine give you more control over handling and filing your messages. With the Elm Mail System, the messages that arrive in your mailbox are summarized: When the message was sent, who sent it, how long it is, and the subject of the message. To perform an action on a message, you scroll the selection bar up or down to highlight the message and press the appropriate key. Pressing D, for example, deletes a highlighted message; pressing R enables you to reply to the current message.

Here's what Dave's incoming mailbox looks like when he uses Elm:

```
        Mailbox is '/usr/spool/mail/taylor' with 29 messages [ELM 2.4 PL23]


  --> 1    Jun 17 Rosalind Resnick   (74)    Internet Business Guide -- Book Cov
er Info
      2    Jun 17 Kim Patch          (37)    a request...
      3    Jun 17 Rosalind Resnick   (25)    Business Guide cover art?
      4    Jun 17 Martha E. Anderson (43)    updated information
      5    Jun 17 Optel@aol.com      (27)    questions
  D   6    Jun 17 Rosalind Resnick   (114)   FEDGOVT> National Trade Data Bank v
i
      7    Jun 17 Rustici@aol.com    (31)    Re: Information on the Internet Mal
l
      8    Jun 17 Robert Wachtel     (119)   Possible listing or assistance
      9    Jun 16 Scott L. McGregor  (25)    How about a proposal for GATT/NII?
     10    Jun 15 LukeDuff@aol.com   (28)    Your book is great!

         ¦=pipe, !=shell, ?=help, <n>=set current to n, /=search pattern
 a)lias, C)opy, c)hange folder, d)elete, e)dit, f)orward, g)roup reply, m)ail
'
   n)ext, o)ptions, p)rint, q)uit, r)eply, s)ave, t)ag, u)ndelete, or e(x)it

Command: Quit
```

Pine is similar to Elm. Indeed, Pine supposedly is an acronym for "Pine Is Not Elm." Pine is available in DOS, Windows, and UNIX versions. Pine is similar to Elm in that it provides an easy-to-use menu interface so that you can issue commands with the touch of a key. Press C, for example, to compose a message. You can also use Pine to create folders with which you can organize your messages and maintain an electronic address book to store e-mail addresses.

Here's what the Pine main screen looks like:

```
PINE 3.87   MAIN MENU                          Folder: INBOX  2 Messages

      ?     HELP            -  Get help using Pine

      C     COMPOSE MESSAGE -  Compose and send a message

      I     FOLDER INDEX    -  View messages in current folder

      L     FOLDER LIST     -  Select a folder to view

      A     ADDRESS BOOK    -  Update address book

      S     SETUP           -  Configure or update Pine

      Q     QUIT            -  Exit the Pine program
```

```
Copyright 1989-1993.  PINE is a trademark of the University of Washington.
                    [Folder "INBOX" opened with 2 messages]
? Help                        P PrevCmd                    R RelNotes
O OTHER CMDS L [ListFldrs] N NextCmd                       K KBLock
```

Although text-based programs such as mail, Elm, and Pine are widely available (and they're almost always free because they're already installed on your Internet access provider's computer), you may prefer a graphical interface, especially if you're a Mac or Windows user and don't like typing commands at the system prompt. The graphically based e-mail programs can be easier to use, and you can cut and paste between applications, meaning that you can create a letter or document in your word processing package and then paste your prose into your outgoing message.

An even newer category of software are full-service Internet access packages, most often distributed in conjunction with Internet access providers like Netcom, Pipeline, or PSI. The Pipeline, for example, puts a pretty face on a full range of Internet services—including e-mail, newsgroups, Gopher, the Web, and even an Internet guide—and also provides a dialup server. WinNET Mail offers an easy-to-use front end for Internet e-mail and newsgroups. With WinNET's mail editor, you can maintain an offline address book, create folders for managing your mail and newsgroup messages, and compose and file messages offline.

Internet Addressing

As discussed earlier, Internet addresses have three parts—the user ID, the name of computer system, and the domain, or type of network. As a shortcut, think of addresses having the format *user@host.domain* (pronounce this as *user at host dot domain*). Usually the user portion of an e-mail address is a login address such as `taylor` or `ldunlap` or something similar, but in fact, it can be anything that the receiving machine understands, such as `cedric.higgins` or `the-boss`. It can be composed of any combination of letters, numbers, and a few punctuation characters, particularly a dot, dash, or underscore.

The host portion is often omitted and if present, is the actual "name" of the computer on which the user receives e-mail. To find out the actual host name for the system you use, try typing `hostname` to see what it says. Domains are the most interesting part of the address and are built from right to left, with the rightmost item indicating the top-level Internet domain. Examples: `com` is a for-profit commercial enterprise such as Apple Computer, Macmillan, or CompuServe, `net` is a different network, `edu` is for educational sites, `gov` is for government sites, `mil` is for military facilities, and `org` is for nonprofit and other private organizations.

For example, if you were on CompuServe, you could reach Rosalind by sending mail to `71333,1473`. But suppose that, instead of a CompuServe account, you had an account on America Online. You would address your mail to

71333.1473@compuserve.com and it would go to Rosalind through the Internet. By adding a domain specifier, you tell the AOL mailer that the recipient is on another system. The .com high-level domain indicates that it's a commercial address and compuserve specifies which of the more than 50,000 registered commercial domains is your intended destination. Note that, when you send mail through the Internet, CompuServe's commas (,) must be changed to periods (.).

Here's how you would send Rosalind an e-mail message via the Internet if you wanted to contact her on one of the other online networks on which she has accounts:

> Prodigy: vbtj94a@prodigy.com
> America Online: rosalindr@aol.com
> Genie: rosalindr@genie.geis.com
> Delphi: rosalindr@delphi.com

She also has two accounts with Internet access providers—Computer Witchcraft in Louisville, Kentucky, the company that developed WinNET Mail, and CyberGate in Deerfield Beach, Florida, a local Internet access provider. Her WinNET Mail address is rosalind@harrison.win.net, and her CyberGate address is rosalind@gate.net. You can also reach her at rosalind@netcreations.com; netcreations.com is her Web design company domain name.

A good place to find out the Internet addressing formats for other online networks, such as Bitnet, BIX, Easylink, Fidonet, and MCI Mail, is Scott Yanoff's *Internetwork Mail Guide.* It's available via anonymous ftp at csd4.csd.uwm.edu. Connect with ftp csd4.csd.uwm.edu, or use the Web URL ftp://ftp.csd.uwm.edu/pub/internetwork-mail-guide to see it in its plain text form.

Internet Directory Assistance

Although sending e-mail through the Internet is quick and easy, tracking down people's Internet addresses can be a time-consuming and frustrating experience. Unfortunately, the Internet has no comprehensive membership list as do CompuServe, MCI Mail, and the other commercial networks, and there's no universally accessed Internet White Pages or Yellow Pages directory that you can open to search for somebody's e-mail address (although several enterprising Netrepreneurs are attempting to put this sort of thing together).

For now, probably the quickest way to find somebody's e-mail address is to call them by phone and ask—not very high-tech, we'll admit. Nevertheless, there are several Internet "directory assistance" tools that you can try before you spring for that long-distance call. One very helpful program, called *Whois,* lets you type a person's name and, with a bit of luck, it responds with a directory listing for that person. The Whois services lists approximately 70,000 Internet users, though, with more than 30,000,000 people now on the network, the odds are that the person you're looking for won't be listed there.

An alternative way to look for an e-mail address is to use a program called *netfind*. Netfind is a white pages services that automatically searches through a variety of e-mail databases for you, although it is a bit tricky to use. Try it by connecting to the University of Colorado at `telnet bruno.cs.colorado.edu`.

There are a few other alternatives, including *finger*, which is of assistance in confirming addresses (try `finger taylor@netcom.com` to confirm that's the e-mail address of one of the co-authors). In addition, most university computers maintain a *ph* (PHone number) database that contains information about people who have Internet accounts at that site.

The Pitfalls of Using Internet Mail

By now, you're probably thinking, "If Internet e-mail is so great, why doesn't everybody just ditch their accounts on commercial networks and climb aboard?" The fact is many businesses are. At the same time, the Internet has some major drawbacks that are likely to keep CompuServe, MCI, and AT&T in the e-mail business for quite some time. The three biggest stumbling blocks to Internet e-mail are reliability, versatility, and compatibility.

Let's take a look at them one by one.

Reliability

Although the Internet provides a good, low-cost, e-mail alternative for routine business communications such as memos, press releases, and product brochures, it's risky for mailings requiring high levels of security and immediate delivery. Most Internet messages are delivered within minutes, but others can take days to deliver if a computer along the route is down for maintenance or other problems. And, unlike CompuServe, the Internet has no easily accessible "return receipt" function to make sure that the person on the other end actually got what you sent. What's more, with the Internet in the midst of a population explosion, the huge volume of message traffic is beginning to result in delivery delays, the online equivalent of traffic jams. Because the Internet is a collection of separately managed networks instead of a centralized commercial service, there's no control over the routing of data traffic and no way to tell what happens to your data once it's transmitted.

For now, many management information systems professionals remain skeptical of the Internet as a corporate communications tool. But then again, this is a group traditionally conservative in its adoption of new technologies and perhaps a bit anxious about some of its authority being usurped by a shared information highway.

Versatility

The Internet excels at sending text files—ASCII documents that don't contain any formatting, graphics, or embedded audio or video. When it comes to transporting binary files, however, the Internet's e-mail system falls short. To send a program, graphics, or other kind of binary file over the Internet, you first have to encode it—translate the binary information into text—using a special tool called *uuencode*. The typical steps involved are uploading the file to the Internet host, feeding the file to uuencode, e-mailing the uuencoded file to your recipient, and hoping they can decode it with *uudecode*.

Various utilities can uuencode and uudecode files without leaving your Mac or Windows system, notably StuffIt Deluxe for the Mac, but that only eases a single step: you'd still have to encode the file, upload it, and then e-mail the uploaded file. Receiving mail in this format is a bit easier, but it's unquestionably still a weakness of Internet use. On the other hand, as Dave finished his chapters he would uuencode the Microsoft Word files directly on his Macintosh using UUTool (a shareware program) and then e-mail them directly to the managing editor at Sams. A bit awkward but considerably faster—and cheaper—than mailing floppy disks each week. Rosalind's WinNET Mail program makes uuencoding and decoding binary files as easy as clicking her mouse.

Sending messages that include graphics, audio, or video clips through the Internet also is a problem, though the gradual acceptance of the Multipurpose Internet Mail Extensions (MIME) protocol is helping. MIME specifies a multiple media format for electronic mail messages in a way that is compatible with the Simple Mail Transfer Protocol (SMTP), allowing it to coexist with current mail systems. Current Internet e-mail systems don't provide the framework required for sound and video technologies; the MIME protocol offers the support these technologies require and provides future extensibility. MIME supports seven specific content types: text, multipart, message, image, audio, video, and application, encoding details of the content in both the envelope and body of the message. It will take many years before MIME is widely accepted, and even then it will still leave the basic dilemma of the dialup Internet user: How to receive graphics, audio, and more, when you have a slow connection to an unknown computer? It's also worth noting that since 1988, X.400 has included advanced e-mail features such as binary message attachments and return receipts.

Integration

Another big drawback to Internet mail—and one of the most serious for business people—is the difficulty of integrating the Internet mail system into a local-area network. If your firm is like most companies, you aren't running a TCP/IP based network currently but rather one based on NetWare, Vines, AppleTalk, or some similar package. Hooking your entire net up to the Internet can be considerably more difficult than you would think. Worse, not only does the underlying network vary, but the mail system you're using can cause problems, too.

Part of the trouble is that each LAN e-mail package uses a different addressing scheme, as does the Internet. Currently, there is no universal translator or common e-mail directory scheme, though many vendors have proposed their own systems as international, transnetwork standards. Incompatible addressing is only one of many problems destined to confront corporate network administrators attempting to bring the Internet "in-house." They must also attempt to balance cost, performance, reliability, compatibility, consistency, security, and support, while the array of available solutions constantly changes. That's because LAN-based e-mail systems have ignored worldwide standards such as the Internet's SMTP protocol in order to include sophisticated functions such as workflow processing, integrated scheduling, and the compression of attached files. The price has been the inability to work with each other and the rest of the e-mail world.

Although there's no question that it can be difficult to get a private mail system on a local network to interact gracefully and reliably with the Internet, it's also true that savvy network administrators are finding creative solutions to get things up and running. Dialup Internet connections for the PC and Mac are certainly becoming popular, but leased lines are usually the best bet for heavy Internet users or businesses. Alternatively, if you have a UNIX mail server at your site, you can set up a connection—a bridge—directly to the Internet. Once you have a leased line to the Internet, you can use an SMTP gateway to get from your LAN e-mail system to the rest of the world. Every major LAN-based e-mail system has a vendor-supplied SMTP gateway; ask the vendor for more information and take any claims of "easy connectivity" with a grain of salt.

Another hassle-free way to connect your system with Internet e-mail is through a value-added network provider such as CompuServe, which requires a Novell Message Handling Service gateway, AT&T Mail, or MCI Mail. Be warned that although this method is more reliable and secure, it also can be quite costly. CompuServe, for example, charges 10 cents for each Internet message received in addition to connect-time charges for time spent retrieving messages. Figure that a dozen people in your firm join a busy set of lists, and you could be looking at thousands of messages each week plus hours of connect time.

On the other hand, if you're a small company and you want some sort of Internet connectivity without too much fuss, connecting through CompuServe or a similar service can be a viable solution. Connecting through an online service allows a simple Internet connection plus relatively inexpensive message costs. If your firm sends a large volume of e-mail internationally, you may find the expanded international X.400 connectivity of a dialup service provider such as AT&T or MCI a better fit.

Once your firm grows beyond a certain size, paying the per-message charge through a commercial service can add up quickly to much more than a dedicated Internet connection, and it's a sure bet that this expense will just grow as your staff learns about the many riches available on the network. As a result, we strongly recommend that companies of any significant size connect to a public network carrier.

For now, many smaller firms are taking a middle-of-the-road approach when it comes to Internet connectivity and are using the Internet to supplement rather than replace the commercial networks they're using. Peter Stephenson, who last year wrote an article called "E-mail on a Budget" for *LAN Magazine* describes the compromise he struck. His LAN program, Lotus Development Corporation's cc:Mail, incorporates an MCI Mail gateway.

> I travel the world so I need a service that covers the world and connects to my private system. One such service—the Internet—provides this capability, but in many cases, it's awkward to use directly. When I'm in China, I can access the Internet. More importantly, people I work with can access the Internet. But not everyone does. So, for me, the Internet is necessary but not sufficient as a public carrier. Within the United States, another large system serves most of my colleagues who do not use the Internet. That service, also available in many other countries, is MCI Mail.

The Future of Internet E-Mail

Despite the highlighted drawbacks and difficulties, the Internet and particularly Internet e-mail are receiving lots of attention from software developers and network architects around the world, each of whom is trying to integrate the Internet more fully into existing applications, systems, and platforms.

One promising trend is the growing number of graphical interfaces that make Internet e-mail quicker and easier to use. One popular program is Eudora, a widely used shareware program developed by Qualcomm, Inc. of San Diego. The shareware version of the program was being used by more than 100,000 Internet users when the company introduced a commercial version with many more features, capabilities, and a higher level of reliability. The commercial version of Eudora includes mail filters and mail-management functions that you can use to download and sort Internet e-mail automatically. Thus, you can set up folders for each of your mailing lists, and Eudora will filter your messages according to their headers. You can also read, create, and edit messages offline.

What's more, Eudora supports common Mac and UNIX file transfer protocols such as uunenvied and *binhex*. Eudora was also one of the first Windows and Mac mail programs to support MIME. Eudora users can also correspond electronically with users of Microsoft Mail, Lotus cc:Mail or any other mail system that connects to TCP/IP networks.

The second trend is interoperability—breaking down the walls that now exist between the Internet and other networks.

One group that's working on improving the Internet's capabilities of interacting with other PC and Mac systems is the Internet Engineering Task Force (IETF). The IETF is working on its first standard protocol for accessing and manipulating electronic mail, a draft specifying an Internet message access protocol (IMAP) that covers commands for retrieving messages and manipulating mailbox activity in TCP/IP networks. IMAP will provide standard methods for creating, deleting, renaming, and checking the status of individual mailboxes on TCP/IP-based e-mail servers. The draft also specifies mechanisms for manipulating Internet mail messages and messages composed in MIME format, providing a way for TCP/IP networks to handle e-mail from different kinds of networks.

Meanwhile, private access providers are also busy trying to solve many of these interoperability problems. Gordon Bridge, president of AT&T EasyLink Services, notes that

> The Internet is influencing all of us to build more TCP/IP capability. EasyLink's InterSpan interconnect service, popular among Fortune 500 businesses, provides the largest public e-mail interconnect service in the world. That includes a way of connecting to the Internet. The InterSpan offering, which is multimedia-based, focuses on establishing business-to-business connections, such as electronic message backbones and gateways to LANs.

PC-based Internet access is also becoming easier and better integrated with commercial e-mail programs. If your company uses the popular Lotus Notes program, for example, you can add access to Usenet newsgroups with News Link from Corporate Software in Canton, Massachusetts. If you're a Windows user, you can buy Usenet news reader software from several TCP/IP providers, including Spry of Seattle, Washington. One Internet access provider, NovX InterServ, also in Seattle, offers a service called MS Mail that uses a dialup router to connect Microsoft Mail users directly to Internet mail.

The third trend is toward easier multimedia transmissions. Last year, Unipalm Ltd. announced Mail-It, a tool for sending multimedia files over the Internet. The Windows-based program is compatible with any UNIX-based electronic mail package via SMTP and supports both MIME and Microsoft's Messaging Application Programming Interface (MAPI). Mail-It is designed to appeal to users frustrated by the limitations of local-area network e-mail and want to take advantage of the worldwide wide-area links provided by the Internet. The program eliminates the need for expensive and difficult-to-manage gateway technologies but does require that you know what kind of mail system the recipient is using.

The MAPI feature allows e-mail to be sent while users work in a Windows application. MIME allows nontext attachments to be sent across the Internet from a desktop computer. MIME also permits the user to send multiple attachments in a single message. When Microsoft ships Windows 95, which will include the TCP/IP software needed for full Internet connectivity, Microsoft Mail users will be able to use Mail-It to communicate directly between Microsoft Mail and the Internet. UUCP users can use Mail-It Remote, which comes with an extra program that enables sending and receiving e-mail over remote serial links to the UNIX mail host.

The fourth trend is mobility. The Simple Network Paging Protocol (SNPP) will enable users to connect their e-mail systems to paging networks through the Internet for time-critical message transmissions. Adoption of the protocol by vendors would allow software developers to create applications that route important messages to pagers through the Internet, which is already used by many organizations to connect e-mail systems with gateways based on the SMTP. SMTP doesn't support message acknowledgment or immediate notification, however. SNPP enables users connected to the Internet to page mobile recipients with an urgent message and receive an acknowledgment from the paging network, according to Allen Gwinn, who wrote the protocol specifications. However, SNPP requires separate gateways and clients, an obstacle to its wide acceptance by the mobile paging industry.

Meanwhile, the Internet Anywhere Consortium has established a joint venture to develop a software and hardware systems solution to allow wireless access over Morbitex to the Internet, CANet news, mail, and data transfer services. Companies that contribute technologies and perform research and development efforts include Mortice Kern Systems Inc. (MKS), the Information Technology Research Center (ITRC), and Research in Motion Limited (RIM).

Whether all of these projects and programs succeed or not, it's clear that the trend is for Internet e-mail to be more pervasive, more easily integrated into your existing local-area network mail system, and easier to access from throughout the world. The Internet already connects much of the world.

THE ELECTRONIC SCHMOOZE

One of the most effective ways to market a product or service on the Internet is to join a discussion group and interact directly with current and potential customers. What we call "the electronic schmooze" is really no different from passing out business cards at your favorite trade shows—except that, instead of talking, you're typing. Because Internet discussion groups are as close as your computer, you can schmooze anywhere, anytime—from home, from the office, even at two o'clock in the morning wearing just your pajamas—without taking the time to shower, dress, or drive somewhere. And because the Internet is closely monitored by journalists, reporters, and editors from major newspapers and magazines, maintaining a high profile online is also an effective and inexpensive way to get your name out in the media.

Electronic schmoozing can take many forms. You can tack up a virtual press release about your company or your products; just remember to include more information than hype. You can also showcase your expertise and contribute to your industry by taking part in online discussions; not only are contributions of this nature less likely to result in strong negative responses—flames—but they're also part of what makes the Internet such an interesting community to join. Another way to network online is by answering questions, offering advice to other discussion group members and joining in topical conversations.

Whichever way you choose, Internet schmoozing can be a great way to drum up business, network with professional colleagues, even find a job or start a business.

As with any marketing approach, of course, there are some drawbacks. There's no guarantee that your comments and insights will be well received by the other members of the group. Worse, in some groups, any unintentional mistake that you make in your contributions, be they typographical or lapses in logic, will be speedily transmitted throughout most of the world. A more subtle drawback is that if you join a busy discussion group or two, you might find dozens to hundreds of messages filling your mailbox every morning, with contents ranging from the invaluable to a waste of electrons. Even with powerful electronic mail reading software and Usenet browsers, there's a considerable time investment involved.

The purpose of this chapter is to demonstrate how to use Internet mailing lists and newsgroups to "network" with customers and colleagues worldwide. We'll show you how to pick which discussion groups to join, how to join, how to post and respond to notes. Because it's possible that, in the thousands of discussion groups available, there still might not be one that is appropriate for your needs, we even offer a succinct primer on creating your own mailing list. Of course, no discussion of online interaction would be complete without a discussion of network etiquette—Netiquette, as it's known—so we'll share with you our own set of guidelines based on our combined two decades of using the Internet and other online services. Along the way, you'll see how other companies are turning Internet discussion groups into powerful sales and marketing tools. At the end of the chapter, you'll also find an annotated list of some of the Internet mailing lists and Usenet newsgroups of interest to specific businesses and professions.

Choosing a Discussion Group to Join

By now, you're no doubt familiar with the oft-used metaphor of the information highway. If you can imagine a highway system connecting thousands of towns and cities but without any signs indicating which is which and without any overall roadmaps, you'll start to get an inkling of one of the biggest problems on the Net. There are no central servers you can ask, "Which discussion groups talk about medicine?," for example. Worse, with more than 9,000 mailing lists and more than 10,000 Usenet discussion groups to choose from, even learning about a small subset of the potential lists on the Internet can be a challenge.

The good news is that there are some fairly painless ways to find out about Internet discussion groups. Perhaps the best way is to ask colleagues about groups that they find valuable. Another way is to find one group that is appropriate and post a question asking for pointers to other groups. Before you do that, however, do take the time to check for a Frequently Asked Questions and answers document in the group or on an FAQ server: These kind of questions are often answered there. There are also dozens, if not hundreds of books, which offer help in navigating the Internet. Many of them offer annotated lists of mailing lists and Usenet groups; go to your local bookstore and pick out a few you like. We recommend *Navigating the Internet* by Gibbs, Smith, and McFedries, published by Sams. Another valuable reference is *Internet: Mailing Lists* (Prentice Hall, 1993), edited by Edward T.L. Hardie and Vivian Neou. This guide, compiled and maintained by the Network Information Systems Center at SRI International in Menlo Park, California, contains names, descriptions, and subscription instructions of more than 800 Internet mailing lists, from opera and chess to engineering and library science.

This being the Internet, it shouldn't surprise you that you can obtain lists of discussion groups through the network itself, though this can be a bit tricky. The best-known list of mailing lists is maintained by SRI International and is called the List of Lists. Indeed, the book mentioned in the previous paragraph is essentially a nicely formatted printout of the list, though the online version is always more up-to-date. To obtain a copy of the List of Lists, send an e-mail message to `mail-server@sri.com`. In the body of the message, include `send netinfo/interest-groups`. The list can also be found on the World Wide Web by connecting to URL `http://www.neosoft.com/internet/paml/`.

There's another set of mailing lists that are often more academic in nature, hosted on BITNET, a large academic network that comprises one portion of the Internet. These lists have minimal descriptions, unfortunately—ten words or less—but you can join and quit a list without any human intervention. To obtain the global list of BITNET lists, send an e-mail message to `liserv@bitnic.bit.net` with the message body containing the phrase `list global`.

Obtaining a list of Usenet newsgroups through e-mail is a bit more difficult, but there are two avenues of exploration open to the intrepid Internet explorer. The best approach is to ask your Internet access provider for the location of the "newsgroups" file on his server (or you can look for it yourself; it's usually called `/usr/lib/news/newsgroups`) or any other document listing the groups received by your local system. Users of all-in-one Internet programs such as NetCruiser should be able to browse the list of available newsgroups without any fuss at all. On commercial services such as America Online and CompuServe, you can browse a list of newsgroups or search for newsgroups by typing words that describe the topic of the group you're seeking. Alternatively, a huge list of newsgroups is frequently posted to several Usenet newsgroups, including `news.lists`, `news.groups`, `news.announce.newusers`, `news.announce.newgroups`, and `news.answers`. Check around the beginning or middle of the month to find these lists.

Tip: Once you have downloaded an electronic copy of a discussion group list, use your word processor to open it as a text file. That way, you can do a keyword search for the topics you're interested in instead of scrolling through the file manually or printing it. Remember to look for synonyms, too; one list might talk about `medicine` and the next `doctor`, `hospital`, or `clinic`.

Joining and Participating in a Discussion Group

Once you've selected the Internet discussion group or groups that interest you personally or professionally, it's time to take the plunge. There are two kinds of discussion groups, mailing lists and Usenet newsgroups, and how you join will depend on which you've chosen. Joining a newsgroup is easy: Follow the instructions included with your Usenet program to select or quit reading any newsgroups you desire.

The majority of mailing lists on the Internet, including all the thousands of BITNET lists, rely on a program called a list server, in e-mail parlance a `Listserv`. To join any mailing list that uses this software, send a note to the Listserv program on the host machine requesting a subscription. *Never* send a message to the *list* itself requesting a subscription; your request will be forwarded to hundreds or thousands of subscribers and possibly provoke some hostile reactions!

Joining is pretty simple, but let's take a closer look at a list that both Rosalind and Dave subscribe to: Net-happenings. The Net-happenings list is hosted by Internic, and mail to be posted to the list is sent to the e-mail address `net-happenings@dsmail.internic.net`. To join the list, replace the name of the list with `majordomo`. A mail message to `majordomo@dsmail.internic.net` will do the trick. The body of the message should contain your specific request. `list` shows which mailing lists are maintained by the list processor on that computer, `subscribe` adds you to the list, `unsubscribe` removes you from a list, and `help` shows you the many other options available. To join a specific list, send a message to the list processor address indicating which list you'd like to subscribe to followed by your first and last name. For example, Rosalind signed up for the Net-happenings list by sending the message `sub net-happenings` to `majordomo@dsmail.internic.net`.

> **Tip:** You can save wear-and-tear on your electronic mailbox by signing up for the Usenet group `comp.internet.net-happenings`, which contains exactly the same articles as the mailing list.

If you've just subscribed to a Usenet newsgroup, you'll probably see a small number of articles already available. That's because your newsreader program (NetCruiser, Pipeline, rn, tin, nn, or any of the other possibilities) displays these articles automatically. If you have joined a mailing list, it will probably take a few hours before the first message from the list shows up in your mailbox. Either way, here's rule number one for any discussion group:

> RULE #1: Always read a discussion group's postings for at least a week before joining in any conversation or submitting any new topics.

When you're ready, participating in an Internet discussion group involves two activities—reading messages and posting messages. The technicalities of doing this vary depending on the kind of news and mail reading software you use or your Internet access provider offers.

With a mailing list, you can treat the messages you receive just like any other mail—read them, respond to them, delete them, or store them in a folder for future reference. One important tip: Pay close attention to the return address on the messages. Some lists are set up so that your response goes to only the author of the original message, whereas others send your response to the entire list! That's why, if you want to post your reply to the group as a whole, it's important to make sure that your posting is addressed to the list's address, not just the individual who posted the original message. Conversely, if you want to keep your reply private, address your note to the e-mail box of the individual who posted the note, not the list as a whole. The same applies when posting a note of your own.

With a newsgroup, you typically don't get postings delivered to your mailbox (although some programs, such as WinNET Mail, have that capability). Instead, you log onto your Internet account and use a newsreader such as nn to access them. For example, to read the postings on the `misc.entrepreneurs` newsgroup, an nn user would type `nn misc.entrepreneur` at the prompt. This displays a list of subject headings to help you decide which postings you want to read and which ones you would prefer to ignore. As with a mailing list, you can also reply to and post messages on a newsgroup. The difference is that more people might see your postings on a newsgroup because there's no need to subscribe; on the other hand, there's no guarantee that the colleagues or customers you're trying to reach will see them because your postings aren't delivered to their e-mail boxes.

Tapping into Internet Discussion Groups for Fun and Profit

Now that you've learned the rules of communicating in Internet discussion groups, it's time to take a look at how your participation can benefit you and your company. As we discussed earlier in the chapter, online networking is a great way to "work the room" without actually being there. There are four ways in which a business can use an online discussion group to its advantage—sales and marketing, trend-watching and information-gathering, customer support, and employee recruitment.

Sales and Marketing

Blatant advertising is a no-no on Internet discussion groups; however, subtle advertising that contains a healthy dose of information of interest to the list can slide by with no problem. With that in mind, there are three ways to advertise your products on a discussion forum:

- Post a press release announcing the formation of your company or the availability of your product or service.
- Assist other discussion group members by answering their questions or pointing them to information.
- Include a few lines of advertising information (such as a brief description of your business or the price of an annual subscription to your newsletter) in the signature file at the bottom of your posting.

Here's an example of a posting on the subject of Internet trademark searches. The author is a Washington lawyer looking to snag some clients.

```
While I obviously have a built in bias, there is no substitute for having a l
awyer do a full trademark search for you. The following is not meant to be an
ad but for information purposes. At my firm, we can do a database search inex
pensively (approx. $35 per name) to identify any obvious problems. Once a cli
ent has narrowed down the list of possible names to a few, we usually hire a
tm search firm to do a full search. These pick up federal registrations, stat
e registrations, and common law usages. The fee depends on how fast you want
the results, but $250 is average. We do not mark up our costs for these servi
ces. Rather, we charge our regular hourly rates to review the results and adv
ise the client about whether they can safely use a mark.
Is this more expensive than CompuServe? Sure. Will it be cheaper in the long
run? I think so. Intellectual property is an asset; sometimes the value of a
mark is a company's most valuable asset. You should treat it as such.
I expect the usual flames, lawyer jokes etc. about how expensive lawyers can
be. My experience is quite the opposite. You need to look for a lawyer that
is a little hungry and values long term relationships.
```

```
Lewis Rose
Arent Fox Kintner Plotkin & Kahn
1050 Connecticut Avenue, N.W.
Washington, D.C.  20036-5339
(202) 857-6012 (voice)
(202) 857-6395 (fax)
lewrose@netcom.com (internet)
Expertise in Advertising and High Tech Marketing Law
```

As you can see, Rose keeps his posting brief and to the point. He discusses the advantages of hiring an attorney to handle a trademark search and then plugs his own firm's service and prices. He also attempts to ward off flames by publicly stating that he expects them. And finally, he includes a signature file that lists his name, firm's name, address, phone number, fax number, Internet address, and professional expertise. When we talked with Rose about his posting, he told us that not only hadn't his note generated any flames, but it prompted a request from a prospective client for a more detailed fee proposal.

"The name of the game is to increase your referral network," says Rose, who participates in a variety of newsgroups and mailing lists and spends several hours a day on the Internet. "The days when you say, 'I'm from XYZ law school' and you wait for the phone to ring are gone."

By contrast, here's an example of a posting, really more of a "chain letter," purportedly by a Dave Rhodes, that was re-posted to newsgroups all over the Internet last year in a none-too-flattering light.

```
Dear Friends,
My name is Dave Rhodes. In September 1988 my car was reposessed and the bill
collectors were hounding me like you wouldn't believe. I was laid off and my
unemployment checks had run out. The only escape I had from the pressure of f
ailure was my computer and my modem. I 3longed to turn my advocation into my
vocation.
This January 1989 my family and I went on a ten day cruise to the tropics.I
bought a Lincoln Town Car for CASH in Feburary 1989. I am currently building
a home on the West Coast of Florida, with a private pool, boat slip, and a be
autiful view of the bay from my breakfast room table and patio. I will never
have to work again. Today I am rich! I have earned over $400,000.00 (Four Hun
dred Thousand Dollars) to date and will become a millionaire within 4 or 5 mo
nths. Anyone can do the same. This money making program works perfectly every
time, 100% of the time. I have NEVER failed to earn $50,000.00 or more whenev
er I wanted. Best of all you never have to leave home except to go to your
mailbox or post office.
In October 1988, I received a letter in the mail telling me how I could earn
$50,000 dollars or more whenever I wanted. I was naturally very skeptical and
threw the letter on the desk next to my computer. It's funny though, when you
are desperate, backed into a corner, your mind does crazy things. I spent a f
rustating day looking through the want ads for a job with a future. The picki
ngs were sparse at best. That night I tried to unwind by booting up my comput
er and calling several bulletin boards. I read several of the message posts a
nd than glanced at the letter next to the computer. All at once it came to
```

me, I now had the key to my dreams. I realized that with the power of the computer I could expand and enhance this money making formula into the most unbelievable cash flow generator that has ever been created. I substituted the computer bulletin boards in place of the post office and electronically did by computer what others were doing 100% by mail. Now only a few letters are mailed manually. Most of the hard work is speedily downloaded to other bulletin boards throughout the world. If you believe that someday you deserve that lucky break that you have waited for all your life, simply follow the easy instructions below. Your dreams will come true.

Company name: West American T-shirt Company

Type of business: T-shirt Marketing Company

Location: Modesto, California

Owners: David Asprey and Robert Thomas

URL (or e-mail address): cyboman@cris.com and http://www.cris.com/~cyboman/

Internet tools: Netscape, Infoseek, Inet-marketing mailing list, e-mail

Length of time doing business on the Internet: About 2 years.

Reason for going on the Internet: I was intimately familiar with newsgroups and e-mail because of my job. I realized that my marketing could work on the Net— if I didn't step on any toes. I was successful because I knew the culture of the Net.

Internet business strategy: Find groups of people on Usenet and create a product to appeal to them.

Time and money invested: From ten to 40 hours a week.

Net results: I profitted about $2,000 in 3 months working part-time. Now that I spend less time, I cover costs and still turn a profit.

Future plans: Promote my web site more heavily and use online forms.

Lessons learned/Net philosophy: If you exploit it, it's gone. NEVER abuse the Net—it's a changing community of people, but it IS a community. Advertising and business on the Net is here to stay, but those advertisers who abuse the Net hurt the vast majority of the advertisers who are using the Net wisely. The biggest lesson I've learned from the Net (and from life) is "Being nice to people pays." By personally e-mailing each customer, I created happier customers and headed off problems before they started. (I also boosted sales!)

Contact address: cyboman@cris.com

Trend-Surfing on the Net

Thanks to the Internet, you don't have to spend time and money subscribing to industry trade publications to keep track of what's going on in your industry—though you will have to sort through a daily stack of e-mail. Two of the most widely followed business-oriented lists are com-priv, which focuses on the commercialization and privatization of the Internet, and Net-happenings, which distributes notices of interest to the Internet community—conference announcements, calls for papers, publications, newsletters, network tools updates, and network resources.

Here's an excerpt from an announcement that was posted recently to the Kidsphere educational mailing list and then re-posted to the Net-happenings newsgroup. The message announces a Web site that offers stock quotes without charge:

```
Date: Fri, 21 Apr 95 13:43:01 CDT
From: brian@spacecom.com
Subject: Re: Financial Site - new

PC Quote offers unlimited free stock quotes.....

A premier provider of real-time and delayed securities, quotations, and news.
The company's data is used to prepare the daily stock tables that appear in T
he New York Times, The Chicago Tribune, and dozens of other major newspapers
across the country. Also, most of the nation's on-line services,such as Compu
Serve and America On-Line, use PC Quote data.

The server can be located on the WWW at
<URL:http://www.spacecom.com/Participants/pcquote>

Future enhancements will include Market updates, exportability to financial s
oftware, and more.

Brian Boyd
brian@spacecom.com
SpaceCom Systems, Inc.
http://www.spacecom.com
```

Industry announcements are frequently posted to newsgroups as well. There's even a newsgroup for conference announcements: news.announce.conferences (originally this group was created by co-author Dave Taylor for those trivia buffs reading this!). Announcements can show up anywhere, however, though they're usually also posted in the news.announce.conferences newsgroup:

```
Announcement:  Call for participation.
Event:  Conference for Management Consultants
Name:  Institute of Management Consultants 1995 National Annual Conference "C
onsulting In The Virtual Future"
Dates:  4 May 1995, 5 May 1995, 6 May 1995.
```

```
Location:  Marriott Pavilion Downtown, St. Louis, Missouri
Organizer: Institute of Management Consultants,
Contact: Claire Rosenzweig,CAE, Executive Director
Keywords:  Management Consulting, Education, Information Technology
Language: English
Abstract:  The theme is "Consulting In The Virtual Future" This premier event
is focused on helping management consultants learn about the information supe
rhighway, virtual offices, virtual information, virtual employees. big firm i
ssues, small firm and solo issues, and more.  Dr. Marvin Schiller, former dir
ector of A.T. Kearney and John A. Byrne, senior writer for Business Week are
just two of the speakers.

For more information contact:
Claire Rosenzweig CAE
Executive Director
Institute of Management Consultants
521 Fifth Avenue - 35th Floor
New York, NY  10175
212-697-8262
```

The real value of Internet discussion groups for businesses is not only to read news releases, many of which, in fact, you can also read about in *The Wall Street Journal, The New York Times,* or your industry trade journal, but to ask questions to a worldwide group of high-level professionals in your field. Especially if your work involves computers or technology, the Internet can be a treasure chest of free information. And because Internet discussion groups tend to be more specialized than those on commercial online services, you can go straight to the experts instead of hoping that someone knowledgeable happens to drop by.

How specific can your questions get? Consider this example from the computer programming group `comp.lang.asm370`, focusing on assembly language for the IBM 370 computer system:

```
hi all,

a friend of mine is working for a large company. he has to deal with very ugl
y assembler programs (e.g., self-modifying), developed since about 1970. it w
ould be extremely helpful to use tools which help to analyse, restructure and
redesign such applications. i only found some tools which handle fortran or c
obol sources (e.g., Delta). any hints to assembler level tools are welcome.

thanks in advance
        timo
```

Customer Support

Businesses also use Internet discussion groups to offer customer support. Sometimes the companies drop in on groups discussing topics of interest to their customers (for example, tech support staffers at a financial-software company might hang around a discussion group about investments or personal finance); other companies set up their own discussion groups and invite customers in. We'll talk more about how to start your own discussion group later in the chapter.

Providing customer support online is an inexpensive way to provide a customer support while getting your company's name out in a positive way. This can take the form of responding to customers' questions or posting useful information such as the following FAQ posted by Digital Equipment Corp. on the `comp.sys.dec` newsgroup focused on the equipment and products released by DEC:

```
D3. How can I make an RZxx disk spinup on power-on?

In order to conserve power, the builtin disks on VAXstations, DECstations, an
d Alpha workstations do not spinup when the power is turned on, but do so und
er software control.  If you need to change this to use an RZxx disk on anoth
er system, there are several ways to do it:

1) On ULTRIX, use "rzdisk -c ask"
2) Move a jumper.  The location of this varies from drive to drive.
3) Use the SCSI console diagnostics on a DECstation.
4) Use the VAXstation service diagnostics (tricky)
5) On a Macintosh, use the "Silverlining" program.
6) On a DOS PC, use the shareware program SPINUP.

The drives do respond to the START UNIT command.
                              [William Jackson,
jackson@pravda.enet.dec.com]

                          [David Burren, davidb@otto.bf.rmit.oz.au]
```

Employee Recruitment

Many businesses find Internet discussion groups useful for another reason: They provide a quick and effective way to recruit employees without paying a headhunting fee. That said, there are plenty of recruiters who place ads on discussion groups as well. Internet users don't usually object to such postings because, after all, the advertiser is offering them money, not asking for it. In fact, there are a number of newsgroups, including `misc.jobs.wanted`, `misc.jobs.announce`, `misc.jobs.resume`, and `misc.jobs.contract` in the mainstream Usenet hierarchy, and `biz.jobs.offered` in the biz hierarchy, consisting of job listings, resumes, and discussion about finding a job.

Here's a recent posting on `misc.jobs.offered` from recruiting company Bluestone Inc. of New Jersey:

```
From: <DNASTASZ@ESOC.BITNET>
Organization: ESOC European Space Operations Centre
Date: Mon, 29 May 1995 19:44:47 EST
Newsgroups: comp.jobs,misc.jobs.offered,
Subject: Germany: Communications engineer/consultant
```

```
We have a position (permanent) for an Engineer/Consultant working in a team o
f 5, located in Darmstadt, Germany.

Mandatory Experience:
        Hands-on experience with Routers (Cisco preferred), Bridges, Hubs

Desired Experience:
        Good knowledge of protocol routing (BGP/IGRP preferred)
        SNMP/Network Management Platforms
        Ethernet, FDDI
        TCP/IP, Decnet IV and V
        Structured Cabling Systems

General Consultancy Skills required:
        Requirements gathering/analysis
        Network design
        Presentation ability
        Document writing
        Self discipline/Time management
        Ability to learn quickly without external support

Qualifications required:
        Degree (or equivalent) in Computing/Electronics/Communications

Language environment:
        All work is conducted in English.

Nationality requirements:
        In the first instance, the position is open to citizens of European
        Union countries.

For further details, contact dnastasz@ecnod.esoc.esa.de.
If you are interested in this vacancy, please email a copy of your CV/resume
to the above address or indicate an HTTP link to your CV/resume.

------------------------------------------------------------------------------
Dave Nastaszczuk.      Cray Systems at the European Space Operations Centre,
dnastasz@ecnod.esoc.esa.de                        64293 Darmstadt, Germany.
```

Here's an Internet "want ad" posted in `biz.jobs.offered` by PRT Corp. of America, a New York technology consulting firm:

```
From: p0064@psilink.com (Edward D. Lawler)
Subject: SYBASE, UNIX C DEVELOPER WANTED
Newsgroup: biz.jobs.offered
Date: Tue, 12 Apr 94 17:41

PRT Corp. of America, one of the countries fastest growing technology consult
ing firms, specializing in the emerging technologies, has an opening for:

A person to develop and build a Unix C Compliance Procedure System.
SYBASE, UNIX C, and SUN systems with financial background required.
Experience with General Counsel, Legal or regulation issues preferred.

Long term position in Greater New York Metropolitan Area.
```

```
Respond to:

Edward Lawler
PRT Corp. of America
342 Madison Avenue, Suite 1104
New York, NY 10173

TEL (800) 853-JOBS
FAX (212) 922-0806
INTERNET p0064@psilink.com
```

Just how effective are these Internet job listings? Last year, we asked Edward Lawler, the account manager at PRT, who told us that his company had been receiving two to three resumes a day since posting its first job notice on the Internet a month previous. Seventy percent of the responses, Lawler told us, "have come from very skilled people." In the past, he said, PRT had filled jobs through traditional methods such as word-of-mouth, networking, computer user groups, and unsolicited resumes. By advertising on the Internet, PRT doesn't have to spend money to take out a classified ad in a newspaper or to pay a recruiter a finder's fee. The company also can use the Internet to advertise its positions to programmers around the world at no extra cost, an important capability now that PRT is expanding its operations overseas.

"The Internet gives us access to untapped talent both at home and abroad," Lawler said. At the same time, he cautioned, "You have to be careful how much you disclose so that you don't give away your plans to your competitors."

Tip: There are also some great employment services available on the World Wide Web. We recommend exploring Employment Edge at `http://sensemedia.net/employment.edge`, Career Magazine at `http://www.careermag.com/careermag`, and SkillSearch, at `http://www.internet-is.com/skillsearch/imall.html`.

Creating Your Own Discussion Group

As we've already observed, there are thousands of different discussion groups on the Internet, with topics ranging far and wide. Nonetheless, there's a chance that none of them will meet your company's needs. That's why some businesses start their own discussion groups. On the Internet, unlike most commercial online services, you don't need anyone's permission to start a new group—you just do it. By creating your own discussion area, filtering out irrelevant or inflammatory postings, and providing leading-edge information about your products and your area of expertise, you can establish a relationship with current and potential customers without risking getting tarred with the "advertiser" tag.

For example, a Palo Alto, California, restaurant called Country Fare uses an Internet mailing list to distribute Menu Mailers, an electronic newsletter that informs subscribers of upcoming daily specials. (You can sign up by sending a message to `listserv@country-fare.com` with the message `subscribe menu your name`.) The idea is to whet customers' appetites for the restaurant's food and beverages.

We recommend that you create an electronic mailing list and then once it's set up, circulate an announcement about the group to a wide variety of different forums that your customers might read, inviting them to sign up. Don't forget to include information about the forum in your other promotions, too. If there's a high demand for the group and it becomes quite active, you can apply to have it changed into a Usenet newsgroup; we include details of how to create a group in the appendix "Tools and Resources," but we recommend against creating a group right away.

Once you set up your own discussion group, you can send all the promotional material you want, and instead of being viewed as an Internet despoiler, you'll be viewed as a welcome builder of the Internet community. Remember, however, that if there's nothing of value to the subscribers—your potential customers—everyone will rapidly leave your group. Again, remember the information-to-hype ratio that applies to all postings on the Internet.

If you have taken the step of creating either an open mailing list where all submissions are forwarded to all users (a strategy we recommend) or a Usenet newsgroup, remember that the entire world will know about it when a customer posts a complaint online.

Once customers find out that a vendor is actively involved in a discussion group, some may be tempted to post some fairly polemic notes. Here's an example from the Usenet discussion forum `biz.zeos.general`, a general discussion group for users of ZEOS PC-compatible laptop and personal computers:

```
From: faust@access.digex.net (Doug Linder)
Subject: Why I am returning my Pantera
Newsgroup: biz.zeos.general

Fernando Medrano (medrano@fraser.sfu.ca) wrote:

: My god, this place is starting to read more like the Gateway
: newsgroup. Though I am fairly satisfied with my Zeos so far,
: this story does not bode well for what could happen in the
: future. Does any out there have any recommendations for good,

This seems to be the way things work in mail-order.  They start small, then g
et huge by providing great customer service and beating out the Big Guy.
Then, when they get big themselves, one day they wake up to find they've lost
their coveted high honors in PC Magazine's readers survey. In the next issue,
you see a letter from them apologizing, and promising to do better.  After th
at, they slide into mediocrity.  Zeos will soon take its place next to Dell a
```

```
nd Gateway, and some up-and-coming young turk will take their place for a whi
le with lower prices and better support.

....................................................................
Doug Linder                             Beware the man of one book.
faust@access.digex.net                     Proud to be an atheist.
........ It's not illegal to be a straight, white male...yet. ........
```

As you might expect, computer and technology companies have been in the fore-front of launching Internet discussion groups, but other companies are starting them now as well. For example, in 1993, *The Seattle Times* set up a local Seattle newsgroup called seatimes.ptech where the newspaper's editors, reporters, and readers can interact. In its announcement, the paper said it plans to use the newsgroup to solicit reader responses that will run in the paper's weekly Personal Technology section as part of a regular feature called The Electronic Neighbor-hood.

"The idea is to allow readers to more than send us 'letters,' but also to exchange ideas and viewpoints among themselves, just as they would in any neighbor-hood," says Mark Watanabe, the technology section's editor.

Other companies are starting by creating mailing lists. Ted Kraus, president of TKO Real Estate Advisory Group in Mercerville, New Jersey, manages two Internet mailing lists, one about commercial real estate, the other about residen-tial properties. On Kraus' lists, brokers are allowed—even encouraged—to tack up offers to buy and sell properties without paying to post their listings.

Kraus acknowledges that selling advertising may prove controversial, but, he reasons, it's his list and he can do with it as he pleases. Subscribers who don't like getting ads in their e-mail boxes can simply cancel their subscriptions and leave the list.

Kraus wrote the following in a posting to the HTMARCOM high-tech marketing communications discussion group:

> Before everyone starts flaming, let me say this. I run the list, I pro-mote the list, I pay for the list, I'm the owner of the list. Nothing complicated to understand about that. No one is forced to receive the list. If they want to continue to receive the benefits of the lists, they accept the ads. If they don't want to see the ads, they can unsubscribe.

Another mailing list owner is Steve Outing, an El Cerrito, California, electronic publishing entrepreneur who runs the online-news and online-newspapers mail-ing lists. Outing's list began as a spinoff of the CARR-L computer-assisted journalism list and now has attracted more than 1,500 subscribers from all over the world. Though he doesn't make money from running the list, Outing says it's a good way to stay on top of developments in the electronic publishing industry and a valuable way to get his name before the media.

Outing says,

> My business requires that I stay on top of developments in electronic newspapers. The list is my best source of what's going on in my field. Often, I'll hear about something important on the list before it hits *The Wall Street Journal* or the trade press. It's my most valuable source of news for electronic newspaper developments.

Outing says his expenses are minimal because his lists are kept on a server operated by his partners at Cyberspace Development, a Boulder, Colorado, company that sets up Internet storefronts. Most of the time he's invested in the project occurred at the beginning when he was signing up his initial subscribers, and there have been many, sometimes surprising, positive results produced through his efforts. He says,

> Within the first couple months of running the list, I got several requests for interviews from reporters doing stories on electronic newspapers. By virtue of being the owner of these lists, all of a sudden I was perceived as an expert in this field. The downside is that owning a list can take up a lot of your time. I often have to spend an hour a day plowing through and answering my e-mail. I get upward of 100 messages a day during the week. The online lists account for about half of that, including lots of failed-delivery reports. I use the delete key a lot.

We encourage all potential mailing-list owners to keep two things in mind: Don't assume that you're able to dump anything you want to the list, and keep the discussion public so that you can work through any problems with customers in public, letting other customers (and potential customers) see how your firm works and resolves problems.

How to Start Your Own Mailing List

Starting a mailing list doesn't require any special permission or authorization, though you will need to work with the system administrator at your local Internet access provider if that's how you're connected to the Internet. Any individual or company with free time, a computer connected to the Internet (or account on an Internet system), and the storage capacity to handle a mailing list can set one up at any time. To find out whether your system can handle a mailing list, check first with your system administrator. We also recommend that you set up your list with the Listserv or majordomo packages; they offer similar capabilities. You can obtain both of these software packages for free through the Internet, too. Listserv software is available via anonymous ftp in the `/pub/listserv` directory on `cs.bu.edu`. Majordomo software is available via anonymous ftp at `pub/majordomo.tar.Z` from `ftp.GreatCircle.com`.

Before you actually create a list or grab any of the software listed previously, however, you need to spend some time thinking about the topic of your new discussion forum. What will be the central topic of discussion? Will you moderate the list or allow discussion to flow freely? Do you want to use a digest format (a list in which messages are gathered by the moderator and then sent out as a group)? Do you want to maintain archives of the discussions so that you or your subscribers can access them for future reference? (Two mailing list digest programs are DIGEST and DLIST, which are both available via anonymous ftp from `Simtel20.Army.Mil`. RFC 1153.)

Once you've decided what kind of list you want to create, the next step is to write a mission statement that includes a description of the topics your list will cover, the policy guidelines for the types of messages that are appropriate for the list, and whether you plan to keep archives or an FAQ for the list, and where and how subscribers can retrieve them. Once everything is in place, you can announce your list's existence to the Internet community by sending a message containing the list's description to `interest-groups-request@sri.com` and to `new-list@vmi.nodak.edu`.

BUSINESS NETIQUETTE

Whether you're creating a Web site, participating in a Usenet discussion group, or just hooking up an e-mail autoresponder, the ins and outs of joining the Internet are pretty straightforward. And, if you aren't comfortable doing it yourself, you can always hire a consultant to help you.

Network etiquette, or *netiquette,* as it's known, can be far trickier.

Netiquette is the unwritten code of conduct that every good Internet citizen is expected to follow. In the offline world it's considered bad manners to talk with food in your mouth or to interrupt someone in the middle of a sentence, and there's a whole list of things that are widely held to be unacceptable on the Internet, everything from typing your postings in all capital letters (that's considered shouting) to posting a reply that says, "Me, too!" (that's considered to be a waste of bandwidth). If you're a business owner trying to win acceptance for your company and its products on the Net, you'll want to be doubly sure to follow these guidelines.

Here are ten rules of Netiquette to keep in mind when posting or replying to an Internet discussion group:

If you don't have something interesting to say, don't say it. There's no better way to turn off fellow discussion group members than to gain a reputation as being a "me-too" kind of poster. Remember: Talk is cheap, bandwidth is not.

Brevity is the soul of wit, so be brief. The Internet is not a courtroom, a soap box, or a podium. If you can't say what you want in less than 100 lines, condense it. Though many Internet news and mail reader programs give you the ability to "capture" the text of the posting you're responding to and include it with your follow-up note, it's rarely necessary to include more than a few lines of the previous posting in your new note.

Don't post anything you wouldn't want seen around the world. The Internet may seem like a cozy, little place when you're typing on your home PC at two o'clock in the morning, but it's important to recognize that your little posting may well be excerpted, re-posted, archived, stored on CD-ROM, and published in a newspaper and read by millions of people all around the world today, tomorrow, and years after you posted it. Although private e-mail is confidential, mailing list and Usenet postings are considered by many journalists to be fair game.

Be considerate. No matter how angry that other discussion group member has made you or how inaccurate you think (or know) his or her posting to be, remember that the person on the other side of the computer screen is a human being. Stick to the issue at hand. Don't stoop to personal attacks. If you would rather not be flamed, don't light a match under somebody else.

Post your message once and only once. Don't send a follow-up message to make sure that everybody got your first one.

Title your posting clearly. Label your posting with a header that describes in a couple of words the contents of your message. There are few things more annoying than getting a posting entitled `Your Message` or `Hello`.

Respect others' privacy. Re-posting a private e-mail message to a public discussion group without the sender's permission is inappropriate and rude. Some lawyers also suggest that it may be a violation of U.S. copyright law.

Post only relevant material. If you're participating in a group for IBM PC users, don't launch into a discussion about the Macintosh. If you're not sure what's appropriate to post, take a look at the group's FAQ (Frequently Asked Questions) list.

Say what you mean. Online, nobody can see you smile and it's hard to tell if somebody's joking. As a result, what you may consider to be wry wit can frequently come across as obnoxious and offensive. If you want to convey humor or ironic intention, flag it with a "smiley," a sideways smile :-) or :) or a "grin" <g>.

Keep your signature short. Many Internet mail and news readers enable you to set up online "signatures" that are included at the bottom of any message you send. Typically, these "sig files" contain your name, address, company, and a line or two of other pertinent information. However, some people have turned them into a minor art form complete with "sketches," sayings, witticisms, and other electronic graffiti.

Here's our succinct summary of all of these rules: Be polite on the Net and keep it a pleasant place.

For a business user, here's a pithier guideline.

> **Rosalind and Dave's Golden Rule of Business Netiquette**
> Market and advertise unto others as you would have them market unto you.

The Miss Manners of Netiquette

If you keep these points in mind, you will find it easy to participate in Internet discussions. But just to give you an idea of what not to do, we've included some excerpts from a funny piece called "Emily Postnews" that was written by Brad Templeton. Besides being a witty guy, Templeton is president of the ClariNet Communications Corporation of San Jose, California, an Internet wire service that carries news and features ranging from Reuters to Dave Barry. The full Emily Postnews document is regularly posted on the news.newusers.questions newsgroup.

```
"Dear Emily Postnews"

        Emily Postnews, foremost authority on proper net behaviour, gives her ad
vice on how to act on the net.


Dear Miss Postnews: How long should my signature be? — verbose@noisy

A: Dear Verbose: Please try and make your signature as long as you can. It's muc
h more important than your article, of course, so try to have more lines of sign
ature than actual text.
```

Try to include a large graphic made of ASCII characters, plus lots of cute quote
s and slogans. People will never tire of reading these pearls of wisdom again an
d again, and you will soon become personally associated with the joy each reader
 feels at seeing yet another delightful repeat of your signature.

Be sure as well to include a complete map of USENET with each signature, to show
how anybody can get mail to you from any site in the world. Be sure to include In
ternet gateways as well. Also tell people on your own site how to mail to you. G
ive independent addresses for Internet, UUCP, and BITNET, even if they're all the
same.

Aside from your reply address, include your full name, company and organization.
It's just common courtesy — after all, in some newsreaders people have to type a
n entire keystroke to go back to the top of your article to see this information
in the header.

By all means include your phone number and street address in every single articl
e. People are always responding to Usenet articles with phone calls and letters.
 It would be silly to go to the extra trouble of including this information only
 in articles that need a response by conventional channels!

Q: How can I choose what groups to post in?

A: Pick as many as you can, so that you get the widest audience. After all, the
net exists to give you an audience. Ignore those who suggest you should only use
groups where you think the article is highly appropriate. Pick all groups where
anybody might even be slightly interested.

Always make sure follow-ups go to all the groups. In the rare event that you pos
t a followup which contains something original, make sure you expand the list of
groups. Never include a "Followup-to:" line in the header, since some people mig
ht miss part of the valuable discussion in the fringe groups.

Q: How should I pick a subject for my articles?

A: Keep it short and meaningless. That way people will be forced to actually read
your article to find out what's in it. This means a bigger audience for you, and
we all know that's what the net is for. If you do a followup, be sure and keep the
same subject, even if it's totally meaningless and not part of the same discussio
n. If you don't, you won't catch all the people who are looking for stuff on the
original topic, and that means less audience for you.

Q: What sort of tone should I take in my article?

A: Be as outrageous as possible. If you don't say outlandish things and fill your
article with libelous insults of net people, you may not stick out enough in the
flood of articles to get a response. The more insane your posting looks, the more
likely it is that you'll get lots of followups. The net is here, after all, so th
at you can get lots of attention.

```
Q: What is the measure of a worthwhile group?

A: Why, it's Volume, Volume, Volume. Any group that has lots of noise in it must
be good. Remember, the higher the volume of material in a group, the higher perc
entage of useful, factual and insightful articles you will find. In fact, if a g
roup can't demonstrate a high enough volume, it should be deleted from the net.
```

Netiquette for Web and Gopher Sites

Be aware, however, that the rules of netiquette don't apply to newsgroup postings only; they also apply to information you distribute through Web and Gopher sites. Although certain rules, such as the prohibition against quoting long passages of text obviously don't apply, there are additional sensibilities to respect and guidelines to follow.

Chief among these is to respect your visitors. Don't mislead them into spending time on your server looking for something that isn't available. Ultimately, the rules of Web netiquette really boil down to common courtesy. Here's our list of key business Netiquette guidelines to remember when creating your company's Web site:

Show clearly what information is at your site.

Offer easy and understandable navigational cues, even for those users who don't—or can't—load the graphics.

Include graphics and other elements only where appropriate and remember that not everyone who visits your site will be able to view them.

Don't mislead customers with false claims about your products or those of your competitors. Those claims will come back to haunt you.

Remember that Web pages and other Internet information are often duplicated in books, magazines, newspapers, and classrooms throughout the world, so make sure that the image conveyed by your site is appropriate for your business.

Be up-front about the information that you collect from users who visit your site and use the data judiciously. If you have a guest book, for example, don't put everybody who signs it on a mailing list and start blitzing them with unsolicited e-mail!

Include links, where appropriate, to your associates' or competitors' sites and invite them to do the same with your site.

Don't require a specific Web browser for visitors to access the information on your site. In particular, don't design pages for Netscape that are confusing when viewed within other browsers.

Web etiquette is evolving so quickly that it's difficult to pin down specifics. Our recommendation is to try to keep our ideas in mind as you build your Web or Gopher site and give visitors the opportunity to send you feedback. If anything that you've posted on your site could be considered rude, inappropriate, or a violation of Net culture, your visitors will quickly let you know!

Summary

How concerned should you be about Netiquette? It all depends on whether you view the Internet as a place to jump in and make a quick buck or as a virtual community to build and nurture. If you select the latter course, we believe that the effort you make to be a good network citizen will reap hefty dividends. We believe that those companies that work *with* the Internet community and make a concerted effort to improve it will be the big winners in the years to come.

MARKETING ON THE NET

MARKETING DO'S AND DON'TS

With more than 30,000,000 worldwide users connected to the Net and its population growing at a rate of 15% a month, selling products on the Internet ought to be as easy as shooting fish in a barrel. If traditional direct-mail marketing typically yields a positive response rate of 2% to 3%, blanketing cyberspace with e-mail should result in hundreds of thousands of new prospects.

Unfortunately for sales-hungry businesses, it doesn't work that way—though that hasn't stopped some entrepreneurs from trying. On the Internet, the traditional rules of sales and marketing are turned upside down. Not only does junk mail fall on deaf ears on the global network, but it often drives away the customers it was meant to attract. Slick ad copy with little or no informational content just doesn't fly, and businesses that send unsolicited advertisements to Internet users are more likely to generate a negative response than any interest in the product. Companies that don't take the hint even risk attack by angry hackers hurling huge payloads of system-clogging data.

The bottom line: *Caveat vendor* (Let the seller beware).

On a service like America Online, most groups tend to be fairly autonomous: If you alienate people in one forum by violating a guideline, others on the service are unlikely to hear about it. On the Internet, by contrast, users jealously guard what they view as the last bastion of non-commercial, non-advertising computer space, and a violation in one newsgroup, or even on a single mailing list, can often have far-reaching consequences. Worse, you need to be doubly careful because, once you alienate users on the Internet, it can be difficult to return to their good graces. Like the proverbial elephant, Internet users have long memories. (Though the Internet community's anti-business attitude is changing with the influx of subscribers from commercial online services, there's still plenty of resentment from the old guard—and anybody who tries to *spam the Net* will likely have his messages blotted out by the infamous *Cancelmoose*.)

On the other hand, no matter how lightly you tread and how religiously you adhere to the tenets of Internet culture, even the most subtly worded commercial message is bound to offend somebody on the Internet. *Netrepreneurs* who tell you they've never been flamed—attacked by hostile e-mail—are probably lying.

Profile: The first time that Rosalind posted a press release on the Internet about her consulting service for online publishers, she received nothing but positive responses for the first few days. Then, unbeknownst to her, someone forwarded her announcement to a mailing list about computer-assisted journalism. When she joined the list about a week later, she discovered to her horror that her announcement had become Topic A of the discussion and that list members were attacking not only her press release but her credentials and character.

Once the flame war died down, Rosalind began tacking up monthly press releases about her new newsletter, *Interactive Publishing Alert*, on the same list where she'd been attacked—and other lists as well. Though she has received a few flames, she has also received subscription orders from the *New York Times*, the *Washington Post*, *People*, America Online, *U.S. News & World Report*, Apple Computer, Inc., the *Los Angeles Times*, Ziff-Davis, and over 100 other major media and technology companies around the world.

When Dave's last book—*Teach Yourself UNIX in a Week*—was published, he posted a low-key press release explaining the book and how it differed from others with similar titles, and indicated that he was interested in hearing from journalists and other reviewers who would be interested in receiving a review copy. Within 72 hours, he heard from more than 50 journalists, including writers from *U.S. News & World Report,* the *Library of Congress,* a German public TV program, *Dallas Morning News,* and the *Charlotte Observer.* Though he posted his message to more than 15 different forums, he never received a single flame.

Without a doubt, posting press releases to Internet discussion groups has proved an important element in marketing Dave's book and Rosalind's newsletter and consulting firm.

The purpose of this chapter is to show you what works and what doesn't in the wild, woolly, and always unpredictable world of Internet marketing.

You'll find out why the Internet can be a direct marketer's dream come true—and how it can turn just as easily into a nightmare.

You'll also hear from top marketing gurus and professionals and learn about new marketing strategies and techniques.

You'll get tips on how to avoid getting flamed plus a glimpse of where Internet marketing is headed in the future.

Internet Marketing: Almost Ready for Prime Time?

An analysis of any market begins with its size and demographics. Unfortunately, the Internet is unlike any other online community, and quite unlike more traditional marketing venues, in that there is no scientific way to track the number of individuals and organizations that join. Best estimates suggest that more than 30,000,000 people have some level of access to the Internet, ranging from only e-mail to a high-speed connection with access to the World Wide Web.

According to The Internet Society, an international organization that promotes cooperation among Internet networks worldwide, the Internet currently reaches more than 5,000,000 host computers around the globe. Fifty-five percent of the Internet's smaller "internetworks" are commercial, 35% are educational, and 10% are government networks. Currently, more than 200 countries are connected to the Internet.

How fast is the Internet growing? Because the Internet does not register users the way commercial online services do, no one really knows and estimates vary widely, though many experts believe that the Internet is adding more than 1,000,000 new users a month and doubling each year.

Then there's the big-picture question: "Will the Internet become the information superhighway of the future?" Should a company invest in mastering the cultural and technological intricacies of this medium when it might be made obsolete by another communications technology?

Of course, many concerns about Internet marketing could vanish as more companies achieve commercial successes on the Internet. Think back to the fight that the Home Shopping Channel had in achieving legitimacy; advertising gurus initially ridiculed the idea as appealing only to poorly educated couch potatoes and doubted it would succeed. Then, one night, designer Diane Von Furstenberg went on and sold several million dollars worth of clothes in just a few hours.

Is Internet marketing ready for prime time? Well, it's getting there—and, with more than 7,000,000 Prodigy, CompuServe, and America Online users coming on board by the end of the year, we believe that the time to set up an Internet presence is now. With the cost of Internet advertising so low and the size of the potential market so huge, it pays to jump in and get your feet wet today.

Rules and Regulations

Before you attempt to market your products or services on the Internet, it's important to understand the rules of Internet commerce.

Unlike TV or radio, no government agency regulates what can and cannot be said or sold on the Internet (though the Federal Trade Commission is considering a rule that would extend controls on telemarketers to online advertising). In fact, four-letter words are zapped around the network every day with impunity (though there's a move in Congress to crack down on online obscenity, too). Nonetheless, there are still parts of the Internet—specifically, the National Science Foundation (NSFnet) backbone—that ban commercial traffic entirely. The NSFnet's acceptable use policy (AUP), which applies to all systems connecting to the Internet through the NSFnet, reads, in part, as follows:

```
NSFNet Backbone services are provided to support open research and education
in and among U.S. research and instructional institutions, plus research arms
of for-profit firms when engaged in open scholarly communication and research.
Use for other purposes is not acceptable.
```

Elsewhere on the Internet, this commercial ban doesn't apply—though people connecting through university accounts or community free-nets are also likely barred from using the Internet for commerce.

Although many Internet access providers and discussion groups have their own rules governing what's acceptable and what isn't, there's usually considerable leeway for commercial messages—especially if they combine promotional material with a generous dose of informational content.

> **Tip:** Ask your Internet access provider for a copy of his or her AUP and compare it to the NSFnet policy shown previously. Make sure that your intended use of the Internet is acceptable before signing up for an account.

Despite the changes of the last few years, however, the myth that the Internet is a business-averse environment remains prevalent. Now, more than 50% of the computer systems that comprise the Internet are commercial organizations and the commercial Internet—companies hooking their own networks up to the "network of networks"—is the fastest growing corner of the network. Tally the numbers and you'll see that more business users are on the Internet than all the commercial online services combined.

As long as you're not bound by academic or non-profit AUPs, the only real restrictions that you'll face are those imposed by the Internet community itself. That's why it's so vitally important that advertisers take the time to learn about the Internet culture and community, to find out what is and isn't considered acceptable practice, and only then begin to market their products and services.

A Direct Marketer's Dream Come True

Direct marketers are now discovering what technologically advanced users have known for years: Hop aboard the Internet and watch your printing and postage costs disappear. On the Internet, your flat monthly fee enables you to blast out all the mail you want to whomever you want without paying a penny extra.

What's more, there's no need to pay thousands of dollars to rent a targeted mailing list. Internet users have already organized themselves into mailing lists and discussion groups focused on a variety of topics ranging from Star Trek to medieval literature, imported cars to cooking, investments to education.

For small businesses, the Internet can be a powerful tool for achieving market equity with larger competitors and even for breaking into expensive—but potentially lucrative—foreign markets, markets traditionally reached through personal visits, attendance at international trade shows, or expensive worldwide advertising campaigns.

Thanks to the Internet, you can dial up your local Internet access provider and post a message that potential customers throughout the world will see. Take Rosalind's newsletter as an example. *Interactive Publishing Alert* now boasts subscribers from Canada, Britain, South Africa, Brazil, Argentina, Sweden, and

Israel, most of whom learned about her publication through the Internet, an advertising medium that costs Rosalind nothing.

Just as important as the Internet's international aspects is its capability of leveling the playing field in the domestic market. On the Internet, no one knows how large your company is, so one-person shops can create an advertising and marketing presence in cyberspace that rivals that of much larger competitors. If you want to compete with a large multinational in cyberspace, you need merely make your presence known and offer your customers an irresistible product or service.

Caveat Vendor: Let the Seller Beware

Despite the Internet's enormous potential as a launching pad for grass-roots advertising, marketing efforts face considerable resistance from much of the Internet population.

One barrier is cultural; many Internet users come from academia, the government, and other non-profit environments and vehemently oppose the idea of the Internet being "exploited" for commercial purposes.

Another barrier that's just as important is financial: Not only does Internet "junk mail" sent to users waste their time, but in some cases, it also costs the user money. CompuServe, for example, charges subscribers 10 cents for every Internet message they receive—whether it's a come-on for a get-rich-quick scheme or a letter from your daughter at college. Internet services that charge by the minute also penalize users who receive unsolicited commercial messages—the more mail they receive, the more time it takes to retrieve it.

Imagine how well advertising on television would be received if everyone watching a show was required to pay a dime for every commercial they viewed!

The fact that Internet mailings cost the recipients money and transgress the implicit privacy of individual e-mail mailboxes is a big reason why companies that violate the cultural restrictions on Internet commerce can face the wrath of the entire community. Although few people bother to fire off a letter of complaint to an advertiser sending a glossy flier into their home mailbox, many Internet users are quick to flame any business they view as an Internet intruder.

Profile: Consider what happened to San Diego-based Magma, a small computer board manufacturer. In 1993, the company sent an advertising blurb to an electronic mailing list, a list with 3,000 subscribers. Though Mesa's direct mail blitz brought in over $30,000 in new business, says Michael Seidel, vice president of sales and marketing, the company was inundated with hate mail from almost 100 Internet users who were outraged that the network was being used for such a blatantly commercial purpose.

"It was as if we had molested their daughters," Seidel noted wryly.

The negative reaction, Seidel says, has not deterred Magma from sending out additional mass mailings, however. Now, the company removes from the list anyone who objects to being on it.

Profile: Last year, a Phoenix, Arizona, law firm called Canter & Siegel violated the cultural mores of the network in a much more blatant fashion, posting an advertisement for their immigration services to 9,000 Usenet discussion groups, most of which had nothing to do with the topic of the firm's posting. Paying nothing beyond their $30 monthly Internet connection fee, the firm offered to provide legal services to people worldwide who wished to participate in the planned U.S. immigration "green card" lottery.

Although Canter & Siegel may have reached millions of people by spraying electronic graffiti on thousands of cyberspace walls, the Internet community was outraged that the firm had violated the unwritten rules of the global electronic community.

The results of the poorly considered attempt were fast and furious: Not only was Canter & Siegel attacked by thousands of "flames," but the firm immediately lost its Internet access account (and subsequently other accounts with other access providers) and Internet community members quickly spread unflattering information about the firm throughout the network.

When asked about its marketing tactics, the firm told *The Wall Street Journal* that it has received thousands of inquiries as a result of its posting and $100,000 worth of business. The firm's partners say they've been encouraged by the response and plan to send additional mailings in the future from new accounts on different Internet access providers. Emboldened by their newfound notoriety, partners Canter & Siegel have launched their own Internet marketing service, Cybersell, and have written a book called *How to Make a Fortune on the Information Superhighway* (HarperCollins, 1994).

All this raises an interesting question: How important is the good will of the Internet community if in-your-face advertising rings up sales? Canter & Siegel is certainly not the first company to flout cultural mores to make a buck—advertisements featuring barely clad women in computer magazines demonstrate this, too.

For Canter & Siegel, the good will of the entire Internet community may not be too important.

On the other hand, as we've noted before, the Internet community has a long memory and because the distribution system is based on electronic communication, some Internet sites have already taken the violation as a call to arms and added safeguards, or filters, intended to block similar advertising blitzes from entering their systems.

Blitzing the Internet with junk mail isn't the only mistake that marketers can make on the Internet, however. Here are four more to keep in mind before you launch your marketing campaign:

- **Lumping all Internet users together**—With a population of more than 30,000,000 users, the Internet is larger than any city in the world and more populous than many states. Although many users are highly educated technological professionals, the Internet also attracts college students, senior citizens, history buffs, sports fans, and just about any other socio-demographic group you can imagine. On the Internet, mass mailings just don't work.

    Instead, think of the Internet as a diverse set of specific markets, small online communities that have distinct histories, posting guidelines, rules, and discussion topics. Directed mailings are much more likely to succeed in this environment: Identify the target subpopulations, learn how the participants interact with one another and how they react to marketing and advertising material, and only then begin to use the group as a channel for your marketing efforts.

- **Tacking up a press release and walking away**—To win credibility on the Internet, you'll do best to join a discussion group and actively participate in the exchange of ideas. It's rarely enough to post a press release or product announcement online and never log on again.

- **Doling out information stingily**—To get something from the Internet, you should give something, too, preferably for free. Because many users get their Internet accounts at no charge through their university or research institution, the idea of paying for information—something that's taken for granted on commercial online services such as CompuServe,

Prodigy, and America Online—is often foreign. Supplying a free taste of what you're offering can whet Internet users' appetites for a product or service they'll be willing to pay for later.

- **Ignoring the Internet culture**—Treating the Internet as just another online service or computer bulletin board limits your chance for marketing success. Time invested in reading books about the Internet and browsing messages posted on Internet discussion groups can teach you how to work with the community and make you friends and win allies. If you're planning to include the Internet in your long-term marketing plans, make sure you start as a virtual tourist before you settle in for keeps.

Marketing Strategies that Work

So far, we've talked about the Internet market as it exists today. But it's important to recognize that the Internet culture is in a state of flux. What works with today's Internet users may not apply tomorrow.

As more private companies pour in and more users join the Internet from commercial online services, the community is rapidly assuming the characteristics of the online world as a whole—less technologically elite and more receptive to business.

For now, however, those who seek to market their products and services on the Internet must still tread cautiously and spend some time learning the *ins* and *outs* of this virtual marketplace. It may be better to miss out on a few sales now than to gain a reputation as a virtual carpetbagger, a reputation that could linger for years to come.

This doesn't mean, of course, that direct marketing is a dead letter on the Internet— especially not if it generates sales. Seidel, vice president of the circuit board company that drew scores of flames with its direct mail blitz, told us he doesn't care if he tramples a few electronic toes along the way. The bottom line, he says, is that his company rang up sales of $30,000 from its first mailing without spending a dime to do it.

Although there are as many different ways to market products on the Internet as there are products to market, they tend to fall into a number of basic categories.

We've already looked at passive techniques that respect the culture of the Internet, but there are other effective approaches to selling products on the network, too.

Direct Mail

Because each Internet posting contains the "return address" of the sender, it's easy for an advertiser to join a discussion group and build a database of sales leads.

For example, a bicycle manufacturing company could hang out in the `rec.bicycles` newsgroup for a few days, scoop up several hundred names and e-mail addresses, and then send pitch letters promoting its new mountain bike.

Although direct mail may be the most straightforward way to reach Internet users, it's also the most risky—and the fastest way to receive hostile e-mail, faxes, and other feedback from the very community you seek to sell. Nevertheless, that hasn't stopped some companies from trying it with greater and lesser degrees of success.

Press Release Postings

Another less offensive technique is to tack up a press release about your product, service, or company on an Internet "bulletin board" (that is, a mailing list or newsgroup).

Mailing lists can be especially effective. By posting a press release to a mailing list—that is, a discussion group about a particular topic or issue—you can broadcast your message to all of the list's subscribers while posting it only once. That's because anyone who subscribes to that mailing list automatically receives a copy of anything that's posted to the group.

The downside, of course, is that, if the members of the list find your posting offensive, you've turned off your entire target market in one fell swoop.

When posting a press release on the Internet, keep two things in mind: The rules (both written and unwritten) of the group you're posting to and the ratio of information to hype that your press release contains.

After you subscribe to a mailing list, you'll sometimes receive a "form letter" containing information about what should and should not be posted there; some groups make frequently asked questions (FAQ) documents available through e-mail. Read these files carefully to determine the nature of the forum and acceptable use policies.

Don't forget to spend a week or two as a cybertourist, watching what kind of topics are discussed and how participants react. If you're not sure whether your posting is appropriate, we recommend sending a brief note to the list moderator, or discussion host, and asking for advice.

Some lists, such as `net-happenings` and `com-priv`, are very receptive to new product announcements, conference announcements, and the like concerning Internet-related products and services. Newsgroups that welcome commercial announcements include `news.announce.net-happenings` (the newsgroup version of the net-happenings list), `alt.internet.services` (for Internet-related announcements), `biz.misc` (miscellaneous postings of a commercial nature) and `comp.infosystems.announce` (for announcements of new Gopher and Web sites). You can also post notices about your site on discussion groups related to your industry; for example, Rosalind posts periodic press releases about her newsletter, *Interactive Publishing Alert,* to the `online-news` mailing list with nary a flame.

Tip: As a general rule, we suggest waiting at least a week after joining an Internet discussion group before posting a press release there. We've seen too many people who instantly wore out their welcome by blundering into an existing discussion or immediately subverting an existing group for a new purpose.

Wherever you post your release, it's crucial to keep the informational content high. Although there's no hard-and-fast rule, we suggest that the information/promotion ratio should be around 80/20.

Here's a copy of the press release that we posted to the `net-happenings`, `com-priv`, and other mailing lists to promote the first edition of our book:

```
The Internet Business Guide: Riding the Information Superhighway to Profit is now
available from Sams. The Internet Business Guide goes beyond B-school case studie
s and descriptions of Internet tools to teach readers how to effectively use the
Internet to boost sales and cut costs. Through real world examples and expert adv
ice, you'll learn how to use the Internet to build market share, track down busin
ess leads, communicate with colleagues, search online databases, provide cost-eff
ective customer support, and access time-critical information. You'll also explor
e the many business opportunities now available on the Internet and get tips on s
hopping for the best deal on Internet access and "cybermall" space.

The Internet Business Guide also contains detailed descriptions of the authors' f
irst-hand experience in doing business on the Internet. Co-author Rosalind Resnic
k is a veteran business and technology writer and publisher of Interactive Publis
hing Alert, a newsletter that tracks trends and developments in electronic newspa
per and magazine publishing. Co-author Dave Taylor is the owner of The Internet M
all, an electronic listing of products available through the Internet, and the au
thor of the ELM e-mail program.

Here's the basic information:

Resnick, Rosalind & Taylor, Dave, The Internet Business Guide: Riding the
Information Superhighway to Profit, SAMS Publishing, 1994. 418 pages. $25.00
USD, $34.95 CAN.
```

```
Table of Contents:

  1.  Putting the Internet to Work for You

  2.  Getting Connected

  3.  Risks and Realities

  4.  Doing Business on the Internet

  5.  Marketing Do's and Don'ts

  6.  The Electronic Schmooze

  7.  Dialing for Data

  8.  Connecting the World with Internet E-mail

  9.  Customer Support

 10.  The Virtual Corporation

 11.  Internet Cybermalls

 12.  The Commercial Online Services

 13.  The Future of Internet Business

Appendices:

  A:  Internet On-Ramps

  B.  How to Start your own Usenet Group

  C.  The World According to the Internet

  D.  Working with the World Wide Web

  E.  The Full Scoop on Gopher

      To order the book from the publisher,
      * Send e-mail to Jordan Gold at jordan@use.com
      * Call 1-800-428-5331 during regular business hours or
      * Send a fax to Jordan Gold at 1-317-581-4669

      Mention the code, IBG, and get $5 off the cover price. There's a $4 shipping
      charge for orders delivered within the United States; international shipping
      charges vary.

      Rosalind Resnick
      Co-author, The Internet Business Guide: Riding the Information Superhighway
      to Profit

      305-920-5326 (voice)
```

Internet press releases can also be succinct pointers to more extensive information available through the Web, FTP, or even an automatic e-mail responder. The latter is a strategy we recommend because every one of the millions of Internet users has access to electronic mail, whereas few people can access more sophisticated systems like the Web.

Many Internet shopping mall services offer this service along with their Gopher and World Wide Web sites. This way, you can neatly sidestep the risk of a *flame war*—a flare-up of hostile messages from angry users—by keeping the promotional information out of the press release. Even better, most of the popular automatic e-mail response systems (filter, procmail, Majordomo) keep track of who requested information, offering a ready database for future direct mailings.

Billboards on the Net

A very low-key way to promote your business or service on the Internet is through the signature portion at the end of each message that you send to discussion groups or mailing lists. Think of these "signature files" as bumper stickers—or perhaps even vanity license plates—that tell passing cars about your firm, and you'll start to get the idea. Rosalind calls these "mini-billboards."

We should caution you, however, that blatant or extensive blurbs like "Make Money Fast: Send e-mail!" are sure to raise hackles in any Internet discussion group (except for those devoted to that sort of thing). Internet users consider it perfectly acceptable, however, to include in the signature portion at the end of your message a line or two about your company and what it does.

It's also perfectly acceptable to include your phone number, fax number, and postal address on business postings. This way, people who see your posting and like what you have to say can call or write if they're interested in learning more about your business.

Here's a good example of what we're talking about from Gordon Cook, publisher of the COOK Report on the Internet. All articles or messages that Gordon sends to mailing lists or Usenet discussion groups include the following few lines at the bottom:

```
Gordon Cook, Editor Publisher:  COOK Report on Internet -> NREN
431 Greenway Ave, Ewing, NJ 08618
cook@path.net                                 (609) 882-2572
COOK Report Subscriptions Range in price from $85 to $500.
```

Another type of Internet billboard is associated with the Internet *finger* service, a simple way to ascertain whether a user is logged onto a system and learn more about that user.

Profile: Jeff Freeman of Front Porch Computers, a mail-order computer retailer in rural Chatsworth, Georgia, says he uses his "signature file" to rake in roughly 60% of the company's $4,000,000 annual sales to customers all over the world. Whenever Freeman responds to an Internet user's question, anyone who reads the messages on that board can see the note and contact Freeman if they're interested in what he has to sell. Though Freeman admits he got flamed a few times when he first ventured onto the Internet last year, he says, "Now, we don't get any flames at all, probably because there are so many new people who have come on, and they have been much more offensive than we have."

All public access Internet services support finger, and the key file to create is either called `.plan` in UNIX or `plan.txt` on PCs. Your plan file can contain just about anything you would like, including information about your company's products or services or your personal credentials; it can even include a price list and other detailed sales and marketing information.

What makes a commercial plan file acceptable on the Internet is that it remains invisible until other users request it using the finger utility. And how does the Internet user know what account to *finger?* Because you've advertised it in your signature. With a plan file, you can be as promotional as you want to be because the Internet user is seeking information from you; therefore, it's not considered unsolicited advertising.

Relationship Marketing

Another highly effective Internet marketing technique is what MBA programs call *relationship marketing.* Instead of—or in addition to—posting a press release about your company's products or services, you join a discussion group focused on a topic related to your company or industry and then post messages, answer questions, and contribute to the general discussion. Although it's hard to market a specific product this way, it's a good way to boost your visibility among customers you want to reach.

If you read trade or industry magazines, you've already encountered this sort of marketing strategy—for example, articles about engine design written by an engineer at an automobile company or a story about new printing technologies from a consultant who works in the printing industry.

Silicon Graphics Daily demonstrates this by encouraging its engineers to participate in SGI-related Usenet newsgroups. Freelance writer Kevin Savetz also uses relationship marketing by managing and maintaining the Internet Book List.

Both Rosalind and Dave use relationship marketing, too. Dave specializes in helping companies exploit the Internet to sell products or services in an Internet-friendly manner. To accomplish this, he maintains the Internet Mall, the only free storefront in cyberspace. He accomplishes a number of goals through this project, including an opportunity to interact with most businesses using the Internet for commerce.

More subtle gains result from this strategy, too: Through maintaining the Mall, he learns more about which companies are finding the Internet a friendly, lucrative environment and how they use the various services available. The Mall also serves as an extensive database of companies and services for market analysis. Since launching the Internet Mall in early 1994, Dave has been interviewed by a variety of magazines, most recently *Business Week.*

This approach has also worked quite well for Rosalind. In addition to posting notices about her newsletter on the various journalism and business discussion groups, she also contributes her proverbial two cents on topics being discussed in the various forums. As a result of her high visibility there, she has been interviewed in her capacity as an online publishing expert by *U.S. News & World Report,* the *Los Angeles Times, The Seybold Report on Desktop Publishing,* and dozens of other newspapers and magazines around the world. She also has received numerous invitations to speak at industry conferences.

Relationship marketing comes naturally to small companies where the president often answers his or her own phone and e-mail, but larger companies accustomed to paying large fees for slick advertising messages broadcast to mass markets may find it more difficult to interact with customers one-on-one.

This requirement of interacting with the community, of bringing some value to the network, is crucial to success on any long-term venture on the Internet. Though some companies have tried to use the Internet as a blanket advertising medium without any interest in contributing to the discussion, we strongly advise against doing that and instead encourage you to think of ways in which you and your employees can help make cyberspace a better place to do business. If you're spending the time, of course, make sure you focus on topics relevant to your business and participate for a while before you look for sales and marketing results.

Display Advertising (World Wide Web)

Despite the many marketing opportunities available on the Internet today, the Holy Grail of Internet marketing is the World Wide Web.

The Web, a hypermedia information retrieval system that courses throughout the Internet, has captured the fancy of businesses, publishers, and advertising agencies around the world.

Now that the Web is becoming universally available to the Internet community, advertisers have the power to lure Internet users to their own colorful, graphical, easy-to-use shopping malls and then present whatever information they desire to an eager audience.

Once a backwater on the Internet, the Web has exploded to nearly 14% of all Internet traffic over the NSFnet backbone. If Web growth continues at its current 30%-a-month clip, Web traffic will surpass that of all other Internet applications this year.

Here's how the Web works: By creating a *home page* on the Web, companies can flash their message to the world as on a giant information superhighway billboard. Potential customers who stop and look can access a rich marketing message and use it to sift through layer upon layer of information to find out more about the company's products and services.

Since 1984, the Spindler family has run a retail candy store in the rolling hills of Bucks County, Pennsylvania. Business has been good at The Chocolate Factory—for a small confectioner, that is.

Then, last September, the Spindlers made the leap into cyberspace—setting up shop on the Internet's World Wide Web hypermedia system with the aim of reaching millions of customers around the globe. The company's Web site (`http://mmink.com/mmink/dossiers/choco.html`) features clever descriptions of the company's delicious products and mouth-watering pictures, too. Customers who like what they see can place their orders online or call a toll-free number.

Karen Spindler, who manages the store and wrote the ad copy for the site, says the company has received several hundred orders from the Internet so far. Though Internet orders are still a small part of the company's annual sales, that's not a bad return on a $40-a-month investment to rent space on an Internet-connected computer.

"We've shipped chocolate all over the world—even to the outback in Australia," Spindler says. "We'd never be able to afford this kind of international distribution without the Internet."

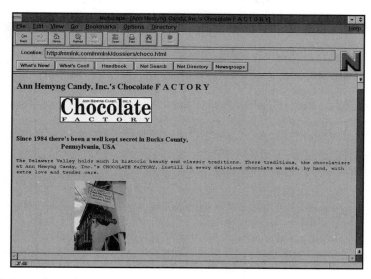

Figure 11.1. A small candy company uses the Chocolate Factory home page to market its products worldwide.

Then there's a Washington, D.C., restaurant called The Red Sage. The restaurant treats Internet users who click on a bright red chili pepper icon that reads "Greet the Hostess" to strains of classical violin music followed by a woman's voice saying, "Welcome to Red Sage." Click on another chili pepper to view Red Sage's illustrated menu, which features mouth-watering photographs of dishes such as roasted boneless trout stuffed with potato-apple hash and cowboy ribeye steak with barbecue black-beans chile onion rings. Red Sage customers can even make reservations by e-mail.

Combined with print, radio, television, direct mail, and telemarketing, the Web can be a powerful tool to get your message out to a worldwide audience. By posting your brochure and other marketing information on the Web, you can show potential customers much more about your company and its products than you can in a quarter-page newspaper ad or a 30-second TV spot.

For information about setting up a Web site and ringing up sales in storefronts and cybermalls, check out Chapter 12, "Setting Up a Web Site," and Chapter 15, "Internet Cybermalls."

Figure 11.2. Red Sage's home page helps lure diners to the Washington, D.C., restaurant.

Tips on Avoiding Flame Wars

The best way to avoid Internet flame wars—apart from never posting a commercial message—is to spend some time getting to know your target market instead of just diving in with a direct-mail pitch. Monitor the current conversations, paying particular attention to what your potential customers want, how they like to interact, and what level of seriousness, professionalism, or information is most apt.

It's a good idea to keep your message short. Otherwise, you'll almost certainly be accused of chewing up valuable bandwidth and wasting Internet users' time and money. We recommend postings no longer than 45 lines of text.

Remember that you can always end the message with "for more details, send e-mail to" or some other pointer to further information.

Perhaps the most common problem with Internet advertising is the tendency of marketing types to sensationalize their message. Because the Internet community prefers information to hype and many Internet users still experience the Internet as streams of plain text rather than full-color pages on the World Wide Web, ad copy that lays it on thick is likely to fall flat.

Future of Internet Marketing

What does the future hold for marketing products and services through the Internet?

One indisputable fact is that there will be more of it; there's clearly no going back. The Internet's high-income demographics, its low cost, and its huge size and fast growth makes the Internet irresistible to any marketer. In the future, marketing experts predict, the question won't be whether to market products on the Internet but how. We expect that more and more mechanisms for advertising will appear, ranging from targeted direct mail to mailing lists to interactive billboards on the Web. Rosalind believes that, for now, Internet marketing is more effective as a marketing channel—along the lines of TV, newspapers, and radio—than as a way to sell products and services. Currently, companies such as Ziff-Davis, Wired, Prodigy, and Netscape are raking in $10,000 a month or more for ads on their Web sites.

It's impossible to say what will happen in five years, of course. However, we believe it's safe to bet that commercial activity will continue on the Internet, that soon entrepreneurs will start making serious money in cyberspace, and that larger businesses will play a bigger role in the network. As with any new marketing opportunity, take any sales pitch you hear with a grain of salt and make sure you work with the Internet community to achieve the best possible results.

SETTING UP A WEB SITE

If you've picked up a newspaper or magazine lately, you've probably read about the many ways in which the World Wide Web, and the Mosaic-style browsers used to surf it, can help you market your business and ring up new sales. And it's true—these days, companies are using Web sites to market everything from new stock issues to lobsters to gourmet popcorn. But although the Web's sales and marketing potential has garnered the most media attention, Web sites are also ideal for customer support, investor relations, directory listings, and more.

The purpose of this chapter is to show you how to set up a Web site that will help your company boost sales, cut costs, and gain exposure worldwide. We'll also walk you through the many steps involved in designing, housing, maintaining, and promoting your site and help you choose a Web designer, graphic artist, and programmer who can help you put your site together. Then we'll take a detailed look at the costs involved in running your own server and help you decide if you want to make that investment or rent space elsewhere.

How the Web Came to Be

Created by the European Particle Physics Laboratory (CERN) in Geneva as a way for European scientists to share documents, the World Wide Web is a hypermedia system that offers hyperlinked words, phrases, and pictures for you to use to jump to documents, pictures and audio, and video clips on Internet-connected computers anywhere in the world. Back in 1991, the Web was text-based; that is, you couldn't see pictures, listen to audio clips, or watch a video unless you first downloaded them and viewed them offline.

Two years later, the National Center for Supercomputing Applications (NCSA) at the University of Illinois released Mosaic—an easy-to-use graphical interface for the Web that offered pop-up windows, pull-down menus, and point-and-click navigation. Today, there are dozens of Mosaic-style browsers on the market—Netscape, Spyglass, Netcruiser, and Pipeline—just to name a few. What's more, all three major commercial online services have released Web browsers for their members.

Now that surfing the Web is getting to be as easy as zapping a remote control, millions of computer users—13,500,000 at last count—are discovering the Web and making Net-surfing a national pastime. And publishers, retailers, software developers, restaurants, and scores of other businesses are using the Web for brochures, storefronts, catalog showrooms, and interactive billboards.

How the Web Works

If you're used to accessing the Internet through a text-based UNIX shell, you're in for a surprise the first time you access the Web through a graphical browser such as Netscape or NCSA Mosaic. Seen through a graphical browser, the Internet becomes colorful and exciting, its virtual thoroughfares dotted with storefronts and cybermalls that you can surf with a click of your mouse.

But there's more to the Web than a pretty interface. Because Web software provides hypertext and hypermedia links to other document sources throughout the network, Internet users can click a word or a picture on a Web page to access product information housed on a computer thousands of miles away.

Note: Hypertext works as does a footnote—a pointer to other text within the same or another document. Hypermedia works the same way except that, instead of pointing to words, it points to images, sound, or even animation. Through these hyperlinks, documents can be linked to other documents on other computers anywhere on the Internet, transforming the Internet into a giant relational database that's transparent to the user.

The Web embraces more than just words and graphics, however. Inventive programmers have designed interfaces for a wide variety of information services on the Internet. Here's a list of the types of information available through the Web in addition to hypermedia documents:

Anything served through Gopher
Anything served through WAIS
Anything on an FTP site
Anything on Usenet
Anything accessible through telnet
Anything in Hytelnet

Web sites are typically referred to by their Uniform Resource Locator (URL) address, an awkward but useful format for specifying an information object on the Internet, such as a file or newsgroup. All URLs indicate the type of object, a colon, and then the address of the object and any further information required. All Web documents are accessed through a protocol called the *hypertext transfer protocol*, so Web server URLs all begin with `http:`.

Here are some examples of URL addresses:

```
http://info.cern.ch:80/default.html
news:alt.hypertext
gopher://tyrell.net
telnet://dra.com
```

The first address is a hypertext pointer to the CERN Web server in Switzerland, the second is a Usenet newsgroup URL, the third points to the Gopher server at Tyrell Corporation of Kansas City, MO, and the last denotes a telnet connection to the Data Research Associates in St. Louis, MO.

Using the Web for Business

Think of the Web as your own private printing press—or your own television station for that matter. On the Web, you control the content and the programming; there's no editorial board, Federal Communications Commission, or other authority to tell you what you can or can't say (though some federal lawmakers are certainly trying). Remember, however, that even in cyberspace, the laws of copyright, trademark, and libel still apply.

Typically, the Web can be used for business in the following six ways:

Displaying a brochure
Operating a store
Publishing a newspaper, magazine or newsletter

Providing customer support
Communicating with company investors and shareholders
Setting up a yellow pages-style directory service

For more information about ways in which you can use the Web in your business, check out Chapter 15, "Storefronts and Cybermalls."

Does the Web Make Sense for Your Business?

These days, many businesses are setting up Web sites simply because everybody else seems to be doing it. Although we certainly understand the need to keep pace with the competition, we also think it's important for you to ask yourself if establishing a presence on the Web really makes sense for your company.

As is the Internet itself, the Web is a far more effective tool for businesses that want to market their products and services nationally and internationally than it is for a local dry cleaner or hairdresser—unless that local hairdresser is located in Silicon Valley or some other Net-saturated market!

How Much Does It Cost?

Before you decide to put your business on the Web, you'll need to consider the costs.

Unlike direct mail or retail space in suburban malls, the cost of putting up a Web site varies all over the map. You can rent Web space at a cybermall for less than $1,000 a year for a single Web page or spend as much as $25,000 for a full-blown product catalog consisting of hundreds of pages. Some Web site operators will reduce their fees in return for a percentage of the merchant's online sales; others are willing to work on a commission-only basis with no setup charge.

Another option is to build your own Web site and buy your own server, or Internet-connected computer, though if you've ever tried your hand at home repair, you know the do-it-yourself route is never as cheap or as easy as it first appears. Tally the cost of buying a high-powered UNIX workstation; leasing a high-speed Internet access line, phone connection, and routers, and employing a part- or full-time programmer to translate your text and graphics into the hypertext format that makes it accessible through the Web, and you're looking at shelling out $50,000 or more.

Essentially, the costs involved in setting up a Web site can be divided into three categories:

Page design and creation
Site hosting
Advertising

Page Design and Creation

To display documents and pictures that everyone on the Web can see, it's necessary to code your materials in HyperText Markup Language (HTML). This means marking up your text with special formatting codes called *tags* to create headers, line breaks, paragraphs, boldface characters, lists, and other features. For example, inserting the coding, `<H1>ABC Exports</h1>`, around your company's name displays it in the largest possible HTML header size when the text is viewed through a Web browser. You can also use special codes called *anchors* to link to information within your own Web documents and to documents, images, and audio and video clips created by somebody else and stored on another Web server.

Putting up a basic home page isn't rocket science, and you don't need to be a computer programmer to do it. You can either pick up a book on HTML, get a copy of an HTML conversion program such as Microsoft's Internet Assistant, or hire a college student to do it for as little as $15 a page. If, on the other hand, you want to put up something better designed and more sophisticated with, say, an online order form, a search engine, an interactive game, or a virtual tour of your production plant, you'll probably want to turn things over to the professionals. NetCreations, the Web design company run by Rosalind and her partner, Ryan Scott, charges $950 for creating up to six pages, plus $200 for each additional page. Large corporations typically pay $10,000 or more for elaborate Web sites with all the bells and whistles.

> **Tip:** Web page creation doesn't end the moment your site goes live on the Net. You'll need to keep updating it with fresh information if you want people to keep coming back. This means paying a college student or Web designer to gather the information, convert it to HTML, and post it to your site. If you're planning to make lots of changes, it may be worth your while to bring the work in-house, either by hiring someone to handle it or by training an employee and making it part of that person's job.

Site Hosting

In the past, many Internet access providers would host companies' Web sites on their servers for free. No longer. Providers aren't blind to the phenomenal growth of the Web or the money to be made by hosting companies' pages on their servers. As with Web page design and creation, hosting prices run the gamut from less than $50 a month to several thousand dollars a month depending on the site's size, the amount of traffic it gets, and other factors. NetCreations, for example, charges $100 a month to host six pages on the server operated by SatelNet Communications, a South Florida Internet access provider, and $10 a month for each additional page.

Tip: Beware cheap server space! Rock-bottom prices typically attract lots of Web sites to a server, slowing access speeds to a crawl and making Net surfers hit the "stop" button in frustration before your page can load.

Generally, hosting fees are calculated one of four ways (or some combination of all four):

By the number of pages hosted

By the amount of data you store (number of megabytes)

By the number of "hits," or accesses, your site receives

By the amount of data transferred from your site to Internet users' computers

Note: Paying by the hit could leave you with a bad case of sticker shock when you get your hosting bill at the end of the month. If your site is chosen as a "cool site of the day" by a popular online magazine or listing service, you could end up paying a small fortune if you're getting billed by the hit. Paying by the hit not only penalizes you for being popular, it also penalizes you for using graphics and buttons—each of which counts a separate hit even if the page itself is accessed only once.

Advertising

Advertising your page is almost as important as creating the page itself—if not more so. As we note in Chapter 13, "Getting Your Business Noticed," there are so many Web sites out there that simply getting anyone to find your site, much less visit it or buy from it, can be a real challenge. The good news is that there are dozens of newsgroups, mailing lists, and Web sites where you can advertise your site for free. You'll find a list of these places in Chapter 13.

Creating Your Web Site

Creating a Web site requires three basic elements:

Content
Design
Programming

As you do when working with an advertising agency to launch an ad campaign, you'll first need to figure out what you want your pages to communicate and how you want to express that message through words, pictures, and, in this case, audio and video clips. It's a good idea to meet with your Web designer and possibly a graphic artist at the project's outset and rough out a storyboard that will tell your company's story on the Web.

Typically, you can take text and artwork that you've used in your print ads and use them as the foundation of your Web site; you can also scan pictures from your mail order catalog. However, it's also important to create content that's compelling enough to keep Internet users coming back to your site again and again. This can mean creating hyperlinks to related information resources on the Net; for example, an ostrich-breeding farm can create the definitive site that tells Internet users everything they ever wanted to know about ostriches. Companies with bigger budgets can hire a team of writers, graphic designers, and programmers to create a content-rich site such as HotWired or Virtual Vineyards, complete with message boards, online tours, and interactive games.

You may also need to hire a programmer to create the back-end scripts to create searchable databases, and to activate your site's online order forms. Hiring a programmer to write Common Gateway Interface (CGI) scripts generally will run $15 to $100 an hour depending on the complexity of the job and the programmer's experience. If you want to save some money, try to find prewritten scripts by searching through Internet catalogs. One good place to look is the Yahoo directory's Computers/World Wide Web section (http://www.yahoo.com/).

Making Your Page Interactive

Most computer users like to play games—and Internet users are no exception. One of the best ways to draw crowds to your site is to give visitors something to do. For example, South Carolina's Wild Dunes resort (http://www.persimmon.com/WildDunes/) offers visitors to its home page the chance to play a round of interactive golf (on an online course that simulates the resort's own), the chance to sign up for special promotions, and the chance to take a virtual "tour" of the clubhouse. Visitors can also book reservations online.

J.P. Morgan, the investment banking firm, hosts RiskMetrics, a risk-measurement service that provides complex mathematical formulas to help institutional investors measure the potential risks of various investments. In December 1994, the firm added a government bond index, a mortgage refinance index, and a mortgage purchase index to its regular Web postings. Check out its home page at http://www.jpmorgan.com/.

At the Stolichnaya vodka site (http://www.stoli.com), you mix your own drinks and color your own label. The Ragu spaghetti sauce site (http://www.eat.com/) teaches you Italian and gives you a chance to win a free trip to Italy.

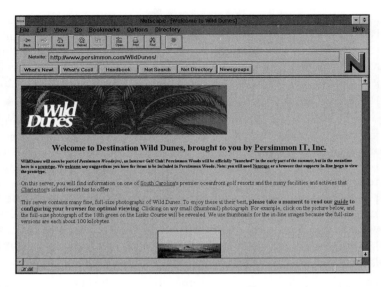

Figure 12.1. The Wild Dunes resort uses an interactive golf game to draw visitors to its site.

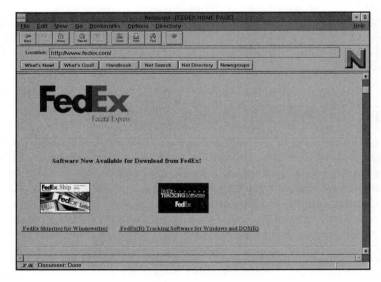

Figure 12.2. One of the most popular commercial sites on the Web is the Federal Express site (`http://www.fedex.com/`) where visitors track their packages!

Page Design Tips

There are plenty of books that can help you design good-looking Web pages, including Dave's newly published *Creating Cool Web Pages with HTML* (and *MacWorld's Creating Cool Web Pages with HTML* for the Macintosh audience), so we won't attempt to cover it in a few short paragraphs here.

However, here are some helpful design tips to keep in mind when creating your site:

> Try to put all your company's key information on the first screen that appears on the visitor's computer. This way, potential customers won't have to wait until all your information loads to find out what your company is all about—or worse, click the Stop button before they get to your company's e-mail address or toll-free number.
>
> Don't overdose on graphics, again for the same reasons. Not everybody has T1 connectivity to the desktop.
>
> Don't create a site that's more than three or four levels deep. Internet users love to surf, but they also get bored when they can't find the information they're looking for right away.
>
> Use icons and button bars to create clear navigational paths. Most well-designed sites feature a button at the bottom of each subpage that instantly transports the visitor back to the site's home page.
>
> Don't forget to put your company's e-mail address and phone number on your Web site. Otherwise, potential customers won't have any way to reach you. It's also a good idea to hyperlink your e-mail address; this way, visitors can simply point and click to open a message blank and send you a note.
>
> Don't ignore text-based Web users. If your site features an image map (a large graphic containing hyperlinked pictures), make sure to include text-based links underneath it so that Internet users with text-based browsers such as lynx can surf your site, too.
>
> If you're setting up a storefront, give your customers a way to pay you—an online order form, a toll-free phone number, or a fax line.

Note: Recently, there's been some controversy among Web designers about whether to use "extensions," or special coding, that can be viewed only by those using Netscape's Web browser. Web designers use these extensions to dress up pages with colored text, background fills, tables, and animation and to employ dynamic document updating so that users can view continuously changing data such as stock quotes and weather maps. Trouble is, Net-surfers using other browsers such as NCSA Mosaic, Spyglass, and browsers provided by the commercial online services can't see the Netscape extensions—and in the case of tables, see a jumble of text instead. Although we don't want to warn you away from using Netscape extensions (after all, Netscape controls more than 50% of the browser market), we do want to caution you against relying on them too heavily.

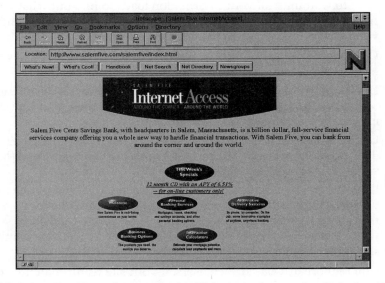

Figure 12.3. Salem Five Cents Savings Bank's Web site is clean and well-designed, communicating its key information at the top of the screen.

Should You Do It Yourself?

Some business owners, faced with the not inconsiderable cost of hiring a Web designer and/or programmer to create their company's Web site, opt to go it alone. Although you may or may not have the technical ability to evaluate the tradeoff between your money and your time, it's important that you do so.

Here's a checklist of factors to consider in making your decision:

Do you have the time to learn HTML? (It does take more than 10 minutes to master the nuances, despite what many books would have you believe.)

Do you know how to create the CGI scripts necessary to process online order forms? If not, how quickly can you learn?

Do you have a scanner and a graphics software program that you can use to convert pictures to digital format and manipulate their size and resolution?

Do you know how to use file-transfer protocol (FTP) to upload your pages to a server?

Do you really have the time to do all this yourself?

Questions to Ask a Web Designer

If, after carefully assessing your available time and technical ability, you decide to hire a team of professionals to create your site, you still need to satisfy yourself that the person or firm you hire can handle the job.

Here are some key questions to ask:

Have you ever created a Web site before?

Can we see some samples of your work? (Many Web designers post links on their home page to clients' sites that they've created.)

Do you know CGI programming? Do you know how to create databases?

How much do you charge? Do you charge by the hour, by the page, or by the project? Specify in your contract that your pages belong to your company so that you can move your pages to another server if you want to.

Are there any other clients we can talk to?

Housing Your Pages

When it comes to housing your Web site, you have two options—buying and renting. Although new Web servers are going up every day and the cost of renting Web space is dropping, you need to consider a technical and a business issue in making your decision. First, does your company have a technical staff capable of setting up and maintaining the server? Second, do the potential sales and marketing benefits justify the expense of setting up your own?

How much does it cost to set up your own Web server? Here's how the first-year costs typically break down:

UNIX Workstation (server):	$5,000
Internet Access (T1, including setup fee):	$23,600
Dedicated telephone circuit:	$3,350
Router:	$3,875
Full-time programmer:	$30,000 a year
	(benefits included)
TOTAL =	$65,825

(This does not include the cost of encryption or authoring software, which can easily add another $10,000 to your bill.)

Of course, there are more modestly priced solutions as well. We estimate that you can get your own Web server up and running for roughly $4,500 in setup fees and $350 a month in operating costs. Here's how much you'll pay: $2,000 for a Pentium PC or Macintosh computer, $1,500 for a router, $250 a month for a 64Kbps Internet connection, $100 a month for an ISDN line from your local phone company, and roughly $1,000 for a consultant to help you set it up.

Here are the *pros* and *cons* of renting versus buying as we see it.

Renting

Pros: It's cheaper, less labor-intensive, and you can get your pages on the Web much faster.

Cons: You have to pay a hosting fee, rely on somebody else's server, and share that server with other customers. Also, your connection may turn out to be slower than you need, and your server may lack the bandwidth to serve up graphics as quickly as you would like. If the server isn't secure, you'll have to find your own security solution or do without.

Buying

Pros: You get total control over your server plus as much speed and bandwidth as you pay for. You can also generate revenue by renting space to other companies who need Web sites.

Cons: There's a big upfront expense for computer hardware and phone and Internet connectivity. You'll also need to hire someone to run it.

Questions to Ask a Server Operator

As you would when interviewing a Web designer, it's essential to make sure that your server operator can give you what you need. A server with a slow Internet connection can get bogged down if too many people try to access it at once.

Here are the questions you'll need to ask:

How fast is your connection?

How powerful is your computer?

Is your server secure?

Do you have the resources to keep up with Web traffic if your server gets overloaded? If not, can you move your site to another server?

What other companies are on your server?

Do you have someone accessible 24 hours a day in the event of problems?

Does your server support CGI scripts and image maps?

Are there any customers I can talk to?

Measuring Traffic at Your Site

Whether you buy your own server or rent space on someone else's, it's important to be able to measure the traffic at your site. Otherwise, you'll have no idea how many people check out your pages. One way to measure site traffic is by the number of "hits," or accesses, your site receives. However, that's a misleading number because, as we noted above, a page with, say, 17 graphical buttons will register 18 hits when a single user accesses your page. For example, the Netscape Web site receives approximately 5,000,000 hits a day but only around 400,000 visitors.

A more sensible way to keep score, we believe, is to measure the number of visitors—that is, the number of visits your site's home page receives on a daily basis. Of course, that's similar to McDonald's boasting about the billions of hamburgers served—fact is, the same small group of people may be checking out your site multiple times. One way to get a better handle on the number of actual visitors you get is to do what HotWired does, and require your visitors to register.

Tip: If you are renting space on somebody else's server, ask your server operator to e-mail you daily reports on the number of accesses your site receives.

Internet Auditing Services

These days, a number of companies are springing up to track Web traffic and to help businesses measure the results they're getting from their sites. Internet Profiles (I/Pro) of Palo Alto, California, is launching a service to track usage of Web sites for both publishers and advertisers who want to know the demographics of their visitors. Check out the company's Web site at `http://ipro.com/`. Another company, Interactive Information Index, will compile information on consumers who use all kinds of interactive media, not just the Internet. The New York company, a partnership of Arbitron New Media, ASI Market Research, and Next Century Media, has already coined the term *clickstream* to gauge how consumers interact with the new electronic media.

Here's how I/Pro works: I/Pro's first product, I/Count, will track Web site visitors (not just hits) plus the length of time visitors spend on each page, how many pages they view per session and how they navigate through the site. Every night, each I/Count customer's server will send data securely to I/Pro's server, where it will be analyzed and put into a database so that customers can analyze their own data through the Web. Then that data is checked against a database of Internet addresses to identify the user's domain, SIC industry code, and geographic location but not addresses or demographic data about individual users (which would be a breach of Netiquette).

But don't expect to get this valuable information free. Set for release this fall, I/Pro's I/Count service will cost $250 to $3,000 a month depending on server size.

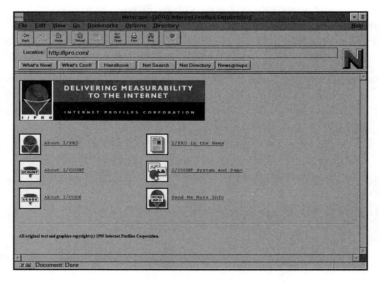

Figure 12.4. New traffic-tracking services such as I/Pro gather key data about Internet users—at a price.

The Last Word on Web Sites

Remember when you build your Web site that it's not a monument cast in stone but rather a work in progress. By inviting and encouraging feedback from your visitors, by opening a two-way dialog rather than broadcasting your message from on high, you can reach a new audience in a way that you've never done before. Use your Web site to convey your company's unique personality, and soon you'll have customers beating a path to your door.

GETTING YOUR BUSINESS NOTICED

No matter how small or obscure your company might be, it can be a star on the Internet. Simply by posting a press release to a newsgroup or putting up a home page on the World Wide Web, you can announce your presence to millions of people all over the world. On the Internet, it doesn't matter whether your company is Pizza Hut or Joe's Pizza and Dry Cleaning. Just zap out a note or build a cool site, and the Internet population will surf a path to your door.

At least, that's the theory. The problem is that with over 27,000 Web servers on the Net—and the number doubles every 53 days—getting anybody to *find* your home page is about as easy as getting a baby-sitter on New Year's Eve. As for postings to newsgroups and mailing lists, the attention you get will be fleeting at best—and if you keep posting the same press release, you're certain to get flamed.

The goal of this chapter is to teach you how to increase the odds of getting your business noticed on the Internet without getting scorched in the process. You'll get specific recommendations regarding relevant newsgroups, mailing lists, and Web and Gopher sites that are prime venues for your advertisements. What's more, many of these marketing channels are free.

Getting the Word Out on the Internet

There are probably as many ways to get the word out on the Internet as there are people, but they all have some basics in common. They communicate your message intelligently, sensitively, and concisely. You should

- Spread the word to a few industry-appropriate forums instead of blitzing every mailing list and discussion group.

- Be succinct in your postings. Remember that many Internet users pay by the minute, byte, or packet.

- Avoid flouting Internet culture. By this, we mean not only the overall culture of the network but also the subcultures found in the thousands of discussion groups. Remember that a posting that might generate a positive response in one group could raise hackles in another. Know your audience.

- Present information, not hype. With traditional mass media such as newspapers and television, you're forced to shoehorn your commercial message into a limited amount of time or space. On the Internet, by contrast, you can broadcast all the information you want 24 hours a day, enabling you to go beyond hype and provide potential customers with meaningful information about the product or service you're selling.

- Get involved. A music store whose employees actively participate in music-related discussion groups is more likely to succeed on the Internet than a shop that uses the Internet just to blast out commercial messages.

- Offer a free product or service. If you sell modems, for example, offer a set of free technical notes that shows how to configure a variety of modems to work with common software and hardware. If you publish an electronic newsletter, give away a free trial issue to potential subscribers. When all else fails, give away a free T-shirt.

All of these guidelines can be summed up in what we advised in the first edition of *The Internet Business Guide*. We call it the Golden Rule of Internet marketing: Advertise unto others as you would like advertised unto you.

On the Internet, the rule of thumb is this: Err on the side of caution. Respect the existing Internet community, and you'll find it a profitable place to do business—as many companies have discovered already.

Company name: Salsas, Etc!

Type of business: International retailer of hot and spicy food products

Location: Milpitas, California

Owners: Rob and Joni Rayment

URL or e-mail address: `CarlD95148@aol.com` or `rrayment@InterServ.com`

Internet tools: We currently use e-mail almost exclusively. However, we are in the design stages for a Web site.

Length of time doing business on the Internet: Since November, 1994

Reason for going on the Net: We feel that the Internet offers one of the largest untapped markets available and that entry into this market at this early stage is essential to companies who plan on being around in the future.

Internet business strategy: Because the Internet culture is essentially that of an information service, we make our sales campaigns informational in nature and offer the opportunity to purchase items about which we provide information. For example, we publish a monthly newsletter that contains news about hot and spicy food products, information on peppers and spices, and recipes. We distribute the newsletter via Internet e-mail to people who have requested it. As far as we know, it is the first and only newsletter on the Internet that is devoted to hot and spicy food. As the Internet changes, our strategy will also have to change. Until trends change, though, we will stick with our informational approach to Internet marketing.

Time and money invested: Cash outlay to date has been minimal. As for time, we spend about two hours every day reading and answering e-mail and writing the newsletter.

Net results: In the short period of time that we have been on the Internet, we have received several hundred inquiries. Sales to date have been minimal. Nonetheless, we are encouraged by the fact that we are learning more everyday about what is essentially an unknown market. What we are learning and the name recognition we are generating places us in a good position to make many sales in the future.

Future plans: Our immediate plans include a Web site so that potential customers can view our catalog online and easily make purchases from it. We hope to link our home page with other home pages such as the Internet Mall, Chile-Heads, Cajun Pages, and Chile Pepper Magazine.

> **Lessons learned/Net philosophy:** Our philosophy is that our marketing efforts on the Internet shouldn't clash with the Internet culture. Therefore, we take the approach that we are offering information on a product that we also happen to sell. This is a low-key approach, but it fits the Internet culture as it currently exists. The most important lesson learned to date is that there is no one single approach that is likely to work by itself. You need as much exposure as you can get. The more closely you target your audience, the more successful you are. For example, although we have an Internet Mall listing and have tried advertising with one of the more responsible Internet advertising firms, our most successful contacts have come from special interest groups such as Chile Heads. We monitor that list; when someone asks for information relative to products that we sell, we answer by means of private e-mail. We think that this approach will continue to be an important part of our way of doing business on the Internet even though we expect the Internet Mall to become increasingly important, especially when we link a home page to the Mall.
>
> **Contact address:** `CarlD95148@aol.com`

Low-Cost Advertising Techniques

One of the best things about advertising on the Internet is that you don't have to spend a lot of money to get noticed. A 30-second spot on network television can cost hundreds of thousands of dollars. On the Internet, however, a tiny record company can put up its own Web site at minimal cost, promote it for free through newsgroup postings, and generate as much traffic as a site operated by Warner Brothers.

Here are five low-cost ways to get Internet users to sit up and take notice:

- **Have something to say.** The best Web sites are those that inform, educate, and even make people laugh. Simply putting up the Net equivalent of a brochure or newspaper ad usually isn't enough. Think about it: Would you watch a cable channel that aired nothing but commercials? That is why it's important to treat visitors to free information packaged in an entertaining way. For example, Whistling Wing Farm Products, a berry grower in Maine that sells mail order gift baskets and other products, has created a Web site, shown in Figure 13.1, that is jam-packed with Berry News and Views, a raspberry research page, a raspberry FAQ, and Mother Goosbry's Berry Recipes. It even includes celebrity endorsements—George and Barbara Bush are fans. You can check out the company's home page at `http://www.biddeford.com/~dtaylor//ww/ww1a.html`.

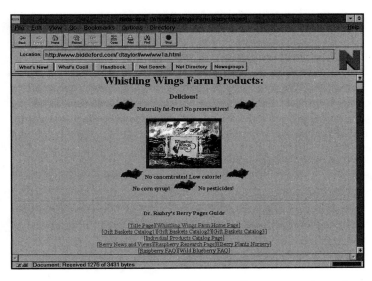

Figure 13.1. Whistling Wings Farm Products' Web site tells you everything that you ever wanted to know about berries.

- **Say it with style.** Besides being packed with information, your Web site should be well designed. Like a well-laid out newspaper or magazine, your home page should lead off with a catchy headline and display a table of contents for the pages that follow. Crowding all your information onto a single page is a mistake; the same is true for clogging your page with photos and graphics that take a long time for users to download at standard modem speeds. It is also a good idea for your site to have a unified theme. For example, the Whistling Wing home page features tiny raspberry icons.

  You can also get fancy if you want. The latest version of Netscape Navigator, the Web's most popular browser software, enables you to change the color of your page, text, and hyperlinks. You can create background "wallpaper," include tables and animation, or give users a guided tour of your site. One exquisitely designed site, shown in Figure 13.2, is Enzian— http://www.magicnet.net/enzian/. It is a collection of resources for film makers and film buffs that is hosted by Enzian Theater, an alternative cinema in central Florida.

  Check out Chapter 12, "Setting Up a Web Site," for detailed information on building a presence on the Web.

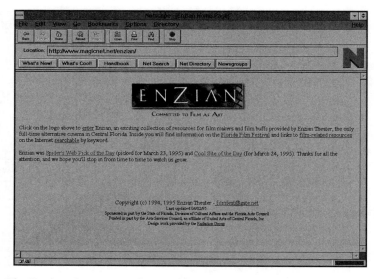

Figure 13.2. The Enzian site uses an elegant design to attract visitors to its site.

- **Stick your URL wherever you can.** URL—short for Uniform Resource Locator—is the sequence of letters that spells out the address of a Web site. For example, `http://www.pizzahut.com/` is the URL for Pizza Hut's home page, which is shown in Figure 13.3. If you want people to check you out, slap your URL on business cards, letterhead, bumper stickers, company T-shirts, and ads you run in newspapers and magazines. Don't forget to put your URL in the signature file you put at the bottom of e-mail messages that you send to customers and colleagues and the postings that you make to Internet newsgroups and mailing lists.

- **Announce your Web site on the Net.** Although the Internet community generally frowns on unsolicited e-mailings and newsgroup postings, there are a large number of Internet discussion groups that actually invite commercial messages. One of the best-known is Net-happenings, a mailing list run by Gleason Sackman and InterNIC Information Services. The purpose of the list is to distribute notices of interest to the Internet community, such as conference announcements, calls for papers, publications, newsletters, network tools updates, and network resources. To post a message to Net-happenings, send it to `net-happenings@is.internic.net`. To subscribe to the list, send e-mail to `listserv@is.internic.net`. Type `subscribe net-happenings` *yourname*, where *yourname* is your full name.

  Newsgroups that welcome commercial announcements include `news.announce.net-happenings`—the newsgroup version of the Net-happenings list `alt.internet.services`—for Internet-related announcements

`biz.misc`—for miscellaneous commercial postings

`comp.infosystems.announce`—for announcements of new Gopher and Web sites

You can also post notices about your site on discussion groups related to your industry. For example, Rosalind posts periodic press releases about her newsletter, Interactive Publishing Alert, to the online-news list, the inet-marketing list and the `alt.journalism` newsgroup. Together with her partner, Ryan, she recently revamped the IPA Web site and posted notices to the Net-happenings newsgroup, the `comp.infosystems.www.announce` newsgroup, and several dozen other places on the Net.

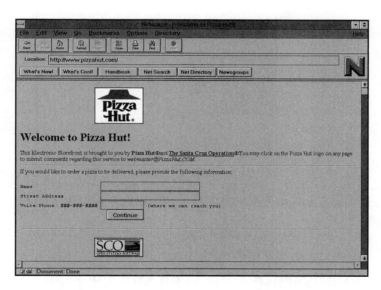

Figure 13.3. Pizza Hut's URL is one of the best-known addresses on the Web.

- **Get your site listed in Internet directories.** Another excellent way to publicize your Web site is to get it listed in the Internet's electronic directories, some of which are hosted on Web sites themselves. Usually, no charge applies, but some enable you to buy the online equivalent of display ads if you want additional visibility. The hottest directory right now is the Yahoo site—`http://www.yahoo.com/`—as shown in Figure 13.4, which several Stanford students operate. It lists thousands of Web sites by topic, such as business, politics, and entertainment. There is also the

What's New page of the National Center for Supercomputing Applications—http://nearnet.gnn.com/gnn/wn/whats-new.html—and Open Market's Commercial Sites Index—http://www.directory.net/. Another free place to get your site listed is the Internet Mall—http://www.mecklerweb.com/imall—which Dave Taylor runs. For details on getting your company listed, visit http://www.mecklerweb.com/imall/howto.htm or send e-mail to taylor@netcom.com with the subject send addme.

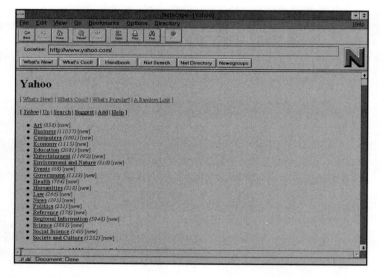

Figure 13.4. The Yahoo directory is a popular place to post free announcements about new Web sites.

Places to Advertise Your Web Site for Free

For a list of over three dozen places on which to advertise your Web site for free, check out HomeCom's Pointers to Pointers page at http://www.homecom.com/global/pointers.html.

The following newsgroups invite commercial announcements:

comp.infosystems.www.announce

alt.internet.services

comp.internet.net-happenings

comp.infosystems.www.users

```
comp.infosystems.www.misc

comp.infosystems.www.providers

bionet.software.www

fj.net.infosystems.www

cern.www.talk

bit.listserv.www-vm

swnet.infosystems.www

tnn.internet.www

demon.ip.www

umn.local-lists.umn-www

hannet.ml.www.netscape

imsi.mail.www-talk
```

These Web sites enable you to register your site and provide back-pointers to you at no charge:

```
http://www.yahoo.com/

http://www.homecom.com/global/gc_entry.html

http://www.digimark.net/wow/

http://newtoo.manifest.com/WhatsNewToo/index.html

http://www.cs.colorado.edu/homes/mcbryan/public_html/bb/summary.html

http://www.ncsa.uiuc.edu/SDG/Software/Mosaic/Docs/whats-new-form.html

http://www.mecklerweb.com/imall

http://www.yellow.com/

http://www.directory.net/dir/submit.cgi

http://www.stpt.com

http://www.city.net

http://schiller.wustl.edu/DACLOD/daclod/

http://galaxy.einet.net/galaxy.html

http://www.w3.org/hypertext/DataSources/WWW/Geographical_generation/
new.html

http://www.stir.ac.uk/jsbin/jsii

http://netcenter.com/

http://www.cc.emory.edu/GaCern/GA.html

http://www.llnl.gov/llnl/lists/listsl.html

http://www.llnl.gov/atp/companies.html
```

```
http://www.bizweb.com/InfoForm/infoform.html
http://www.thomasregister.com/listyou.html
http://www.cen.uiuc.edu/~banister/submit-it/
http://webnotes.ostech.com/web_sites
http://www.mid.net/NET/
http://www.mecklerweb.com:80/imall/howto.htm
http://lycos.cs.cmu.edu
http://www.demon.co.uk/cybergte
http://mfginfo.com/home.htm
http://www.theworld.com/default.htm
http://www.ais.net/netsearch
http://home.netscape.com/escapes/submit_new.html
```

You can also list your site on a variety of special interest and regional Web sites.
Table 13.1 describes some of them.

Table 13.1. Special-interest and regional Web sites.

Web Site	Topic
`http://www.cyberspace.com/bobk`	Washington State Internet resources
`http://www_wwrc.uwyo.edu/wwrc.htm`	Wyoming Water Resources Center
`http://www.netview.com/servreg/`	Silicon Valley and northern California
`http://www.lm.com/concierge.html`	Pittsburgh and western Pennsylvania
`http://www-hpcc.astro.washington.edu/k12/astroindex.html`	Science and math education
`http://www.rpi.edu/Internet/cwis.html`	Campus Wide Information Systems
`http://www.frontier.net/MEDMarket/indexes/indexmfr.html`	Healthcare and biotechnology companies
`http://www.fractals.com/museums.html`	Online museums
`http://www.nas.nasa.gov/HPCC/K12/edures.html`	Online educational resources
`http://wcl-rs.bham.ac.uk/GamesDomain`	Game-related sites

Note: As with most things in business, promoting your Internet site comes down to a choice between your money and your time. Even though posting announcements on the Net entails no monetary cost, you can spend hours posting to all the right places. Therefore, we suggest that you write a short announcement about your site and hire a Net-savvy college student to do the work for you. A number of Internet posting services are also springing up. One company, Net Post, charges $150 to put announcements about your site on 20 popular places, including Yahoo, Lycos, Open Market, the NCSA What's New page, `comp.infosystems.www.announce`, `net-happenings`, and the Internet Mall. For more information, send e-mail to `netpost@netpost.com`.

Tip: Don't expect your announcements to appear on the Net immediately after you post them. Whereas newsgroup and mailing list postings typically appear within hours—or even minutes—some popular Web sites, such as the NCSA What's New page, can take as long as two weeks to put up your listing. That is because many listing services reject postings by adult-oriented sites and process each request manually.

Company name: Lighthouse Marina, Salmon River Anglers Lodge

Type of business: Boat rental and repair, charter fleet management, and tourist lodging. "I'm the first actual lighthouse keeper on the Net."

Location: Port Ontario, New York

Owner: Jim Walker

URL and e-mail addresses: `http://www.maine.com/fish-ny` and `jrwalker@ix.netcom.com`

Internet tools: Netcom's Netcruiser graphical interface, Microsoft's HTML Assistant, and WinWeb

Length of time doing business on the Internet: Since December 1994

Reason for going on the Net: I decided to give it a try based on the groundswell of articles in *PC Magazine, Windows Magazine,* and special sections in the Syracuse and Portland, Maine, Sunday papers. I bought a few books, tucked in for a weekend, and came out on Netcom two days later.

Internet business strategy: It's kind of like this and in approximately this order: I get off my duff, learn the basic philosophy, get online, wander around the candy store developing a comfort level, develop more enthusiasm, and collect ideas. Next, I establish a basic presence and mentor with a few pros. I find out what locations—Web sites, Usenet, mailing lists, and so on—I have personal and business interests in, and I monitor the traffic for a while. Gradually I contribute to get some recognition and to determine the character of each forum and its suitability for much, some, or no commercialism.

Then I start building .sig files to give information that would offer credibility and to solicit questions from readers. I put small ads in the Internet Mall and Apollo, along with bits in `rec.travel.marketplace`. I place e-mail address on our literature and advertising materials.

I also send press releases to the newspapers and magazines, to spotlight Net development. I've notified them that Lighthouse Marina is relatively new to the Net, and I credit them with having pushed us into it. This has yielded five whopping feature articles in less than a month's time.

I contribute to other folks' collections and interests by continuing to forward them juicy bits that I've found along the way. I survey Usenet and other readers to determine whether our monthly copy written for a New England sporting journal would be of interest to others. The positive response has been overwhelming.

I package up articles, wrap them in HTML, and put them on the Web without a clue as to eventual direction. The emphasis is 98 percent content, 2 percent commercialism. Readers suggest possible directions for future evolutions. I also contact Web catalog maintainers, Yahoo, Yanoff, and others, encouraging them to include pointers to us. Many readers add pointers to us to their pages automatically.

The Web server provides us with daily reader statistics, which we analyze to identify who our readers are and to monitor the general volume of readers. I build e-mailing lists of the most enthusiastic readers—with their permission, of course. At least once a week, I look around on the Net for new ideas and possible competitors.

Time and money invested: Approximately $100 in reference books, $20 per month for Netcom, and $10 per month for Web space

Net results: We expand gradually as we gain experience and have the time. Currently, we process five to eight inquiries weekly and book two to three parties weekly.

Future plans: I'm trying to figure out just how much time I can afford to spend on this, relative to day-to-day responsibilities and customer contact through traditional channels. I have just ordered, however, a full-blown multimedia Pentium 120 to help balance the load and in anticipation of establishing my own Web server. I have at least three additional Web packages in development, and a major rewrite of the initial one is pending. They all need to be refreshed periodically, because static presentations grow stale quickly.

Lessons learned/Net philosophy: Because Lighthouse Marina is a small business and I'm the only technical person, I have to gauge just how much I can do personally and how much can be delegated. Obviously, this will soon become a major channel for our business, and it offers the prospects of expanding into entirely new arenas.

Contact address: `jrwalker@ix.netcom.com`

Should You Pay to Advertise?

Despite all the opportunities on the Net to advertise your business for free, you might want to consider taking out an ad. Dozens of Internet newspapers, magazines, and Web sites are ready and eager to sell you one. Here are three reasons why you might want to consider buying an ad:

- **Greater visibility.** Instead of being one of a thousand Web sites on a list, you can stand out from the rest of the pack by waving your sponsorship banner for all to see.

- **Greater exposure.** By obtaining a link from a popular online publication such as HotWired (`www.hotwired.com`), you can draw more visitors to your site.

- **Better placement.** When you post an announcement on a free listing service, you have no control over where on the list your site appears or how long it will stay there. When you buy an ad, your ad appears as long as you keep paying your bill.

What the Top Sites Charge

How much does it cost to place an ad on the Net? With the mass-media concept of cost-per-thousand almost meaningless in cyberspace, Web publishers and site operators are charging rates ranging from a few hundred dollars a year to $15,000 a month. Typically, the more popular the site—as measured by the number of people who visit it—the more you pay to place an ad there.

Tip: When shopping for ad space on the Internet, don't be fooled by a site operator who boasts of the huge number of hits, or accesses, that his site receives. Because of the way Web servers measure traffic, a hit is recorded for every graphic that pops up when an Internet user accesses a page. The key number to find out is the number of visitors who come to the site—that is, the number of people who access the site's home page. That number is typically much smaller—and far more relevant—than the number of hits.

Here is what some of the top sites charge for ad space:

■ **HotWired,** the online edition of *Wired* magazine, attracts 16 advertisers ranging from AT&T to Volvo. Each advertiser pays $30,000 for the right to hoist its sponsorship banner over a HotWired editorial department for two months. (The rate was $30,000 for three months when the magazine launched in October.) Assuming that all 16 sponsors renew— not an unreasonable assumption considering that 12 of the publication's 14 sponsors have renewed already—HotWired, shown in Figure 13.5, will generate gross revenues of over $2 million this year. Currently, the online magazine has over 180,000 subscribers and its Web site (`http://www.hotwired.com`) gets over 250,000 hits a day.

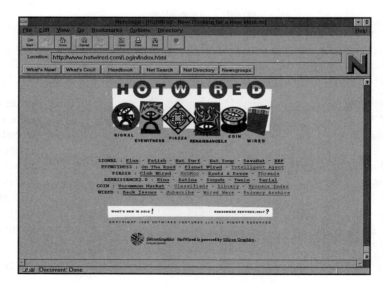

Figure 13.5. HotWired, the online edition of *Wired* magazine, charges $15,000 a month to place an ad.

- **O'Reilly & Associates**, publishers of the Global Network Navigator, charge $7,500 a week for a link on the NCSA What's New page. Currently, the page (`http://nearnet.gnn.com/gnn/wn/whats-new.html`) is sponsored by Zima Clearmalt, a product of the Coors Brewing Co. As many as two million readers visit the What's New page—dubbed "the Super Bowl of the Web" by *Internet World* magazine—each month.
- **Ziff-Davis Publishing's Internet-based ZD Net** (`http://www.ziff.com`) charges rates of $10,000 to $25,000 for a three-month ad.
- **Merc Center Web** (`http://www.sjmercury.com`), the Internet edition of *The San Jose Mercury News*, charges $100 a day for display ads that run across the bottom of the screen. So far, seven advertisers have signed up. They include Netcom, IBM, and Coldwell Banker.
- **Netscape**, developer of the popular World Wide Web browser, charges $40,000 for three-month sponsorships on its Web site. Every day, the site draws 400,000 visits to the top level and 175,000 visits to its most popular level-two pages. Advertisers include General Motors, EDS, MasterCard, AT&T, Adobe, and Netcom Online Communications Services.
- **Prodigy**, the national online service, charges $4,000 a week for a premium listing on its home page.
- The **Internet Mall**, an online business directory created by Dave Taylor and hosted by the publisher Mecklermedia, charges $600 a month (or more, based on advert location in the Mall) to sponsor a department, floor, or the home page of the Mall.

Advertising for Less

Of course, not every business has $15,000 a month to blow on Internet advertising. The good news is that plenty of smaller publishers and Web site operators charge much less than HotWired and Netscape. For example, the publisher of Netsurfer Digest, Netsurfer Tools, and Netsurfer Focus, which are guides to news and resources available on the Internet, charges $350 to place an eight-line ad in a single biweekly issue. The Netsurfer site (`http://www.netsurf.com`) gets approximately 12,000 hits every day and has attracted a number of national advertisers, including Cray Research, First Virtual, Kauai Exotix, Network Computing Devices, NetManage, and Computer Express. For more information, send e-mail to `ad@netsurf.com`.

Note: To help media buyers figure out how much to pay for Internet advertising, Rosalind has set up an Online Advertising Index on the home page of her newsletter, Interactive Publishing Alert. The Index tracks ad rates charged by dozens of leading publishers and Web site operators, and it includes information about site traffic and the method of calculating advertising rates. Check it out at `http://www.netcreations.com/ipa/`.

What to Do if Your Net Advertising Campaign Bombs

You have no guarantee that any of these techniques will get your site noticed—much less ring up sales or bring in deals. The key is to be patient and persistent. As with any form of advertising, the only way to succeed on the Internet is through constant exposure. When Rosalind launched her newsletter last year, for example, she had to post notes all over the place just to get noticed. Now she posts to fewer places but receives one or two subscription orders a day from people who visit her Web site.

If you find yourself getting demoralized, keep in mind this little poem that Jim Sterne of Target Marketing (`jsterne@targeting.com`) contributed to the `inet-marketing` mailing list:

> Shout it from the roof tops
> Write it in the sky
> Promote until your budget pops
> Until they all surf by
>
> Announce in proper newsgroups
> Mail directly through the post
> Fire up the sales troops
> Televise the most
>
> A 1-800 number
> Won't get you any calls
> Unless you advertise it
> And paint it on the walls
>
> Put it on your letterhead
> Put it on your cards
> A Web site will be left for dead
> Unless it's known on Mars
>
> Your Web site can be funny, pretty, useful, crisp and clean
> But if you don't promote it, its message won't be seen

Advertising Your Net Site in Other Media

As we advised you earlier in the chapter, advertising your site only on the Internet is not enough. It is vital to promote it on your business cards and letterhead and in print, radio, and television ads. Plenty of magazines, newsletters, and newspapers focus on the Internet and online networks, so don't forget to send a press release to the appropriate editors. (In fact, many of these editors now have e-mail addresses.) Finally, don't forget word of mouth. The more people you tell about your new Internet site or service, the more people they will tell about it—and the more visitors and customers you will get.

Remember: The Internet is the cheapest form of mass-media advertising available today. To make it work for you and your business, you can't be shy about using it to get the word out. So long as you respect the tenets of Internet culture, you can be as promotional as you want without getting seared by the flame-throwers.

NET SALES

IS ANYBODY MAKING MONEY ON THE NET?

Despite the encouraging trends, few companies are making a fortune on the Internet right now—although, we think, many more will before the year is out. More bouquets are sold by Prodigy's PC Flowers shop every day than on all the Internet cybermalls combined—even though the Internet has 10 times as many users. Even Canter & Siegel, the notorious lawyers who covered the Net last year with advertisements about their immigration law services, raked in only $100,000 for their efforts—not exactly highway robbery.

As you saw in Chapter 13, "Getting Your Business Noticed," the companies earning the biggest bucks on the Internet these days are publishers and Web site operators selling advertising on their servers. That is because the main thing that the Internet has to offer is visibility. There is no shortage of people who want to surf around and see the sites.

The purpose of this chapter is to show you what sells and what doesn't on the Internet and to help you identify profitable niches for your company's products and services. We'll introduce you to companies that are making money on the Net today and give you a glimpse of those firms poised for profit in the future.

Why Internet Retailing Isn't Ready for Prime Time

Consider this: PC Gifts and Flowers, based in Stamford, Connecticut, rang up over $4 million in sales last year by peddling bouquets on Prodigy, a commercial online service with about 2,000,000 users. On the Internet's World Wide Web, however, President Bill Tobin has yet to taste what he considers to be success. Although his site (`http://www.pcgifts.ibm.com`) typically gets 25,000 to 30,000 accesses a day, PC Gifts and Flowers chalks up fewer than 200 orders a month—big volume by Internet standards, but only a small fraction of the more than 150,000 orders a year he gets from Prodigy.

Tobin has big plans for expanding his business on the Internet, but he says he won't consider it "a commercial environment" until his Web site, shown in Figure 14.1, generates $10,000,000 to $15,000,000 in annual sales. "Until then, it's an experiment."

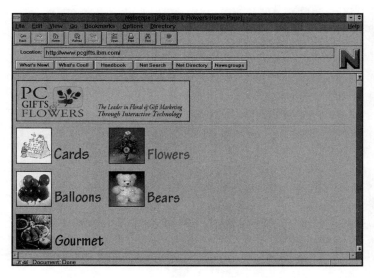

Figure 14.1. PC Flowers sells far fewer flowers on the Internet than it does on Prodigy, despite Prodigy's smaller user base.

For all the hype about Internet commerce, the reality is that Internet shopping is not ready for prime time—at least not yet. We're big believers in the Internet's commercial possibilities, but we think a reality check is overdue. The Internet is great for marketing—depending on the audience that you are trying to reach—but it is far less effective in generating actual sales.

Five Stumbling Blocks to Net Sales

The way we see it, there are five main reasons why Internet marketing still is not ready for prime time.

- There is no directory to the mall.

  Imagine walking into your local shopping mall and wandering around—without a map or directory to guide you—until you happen upon a store that has what you want. That's what shopping the Internet's cybermalls can be like if you don't know how to find what you're looking for. Even if you are fairly Net-savvy, it is still much easier to order a pizza by telephone than by logging on to the Internet and typing `http://www.pizzahut.com/`.

> **Tip:** Look for directory services to become the first "killer application" for Internet business.

  One of the reasons why PC Flowers is so successful on Prodigy is because Prodigy aggressively promotes the business on the welcome screen that members see when they log on. Click a colorful picture of a bouquet, and you are instantly transported to an online shopping area where placing your order is as easy as typing in your credit card number and hitting the Send button. On the Internet, by contrast, you must type in the name of an Internet flower shop, or you must do a keyword search with an Internet search utility, such as Lycos or Webcrawler. (Of course, you need to know how to find a search tool before you can use it.) Because the Internet is a computer cooperative, not a for-profit online service, there's no marketing manager who organizes all the storefronts and cybermalls into a single online marketplace.

- It is difficult to comparison shop.

  When Rosalind is in the market for a new computer or modem, she first scans the ads in a few computer magazines—yes, the paper kind. She might also log on to Prodigy and check out PC Catalog, an online shopping service that lists prices and features for thousands of makes and models. With a couple of mouse clicks, she can find out the name, location, and telephone number of the store that has the computer or modem she needs.

On the Internet, comparison shopping is difficult. Sure, plenty of computer stores are on the network, but there's no way to browse them all at once—or even find out where they all are without spending a lot of time searching. Internet merchants also seem hesitant to compete on price, a time-honored retailing tradition. At a recent Web World conference in Orlando, several Internet merchants actually even questioned whether they should publish their prices at all.

■ Mall security is lax.

On a commercial online service like Prodigy, where only paying subscribers are allowed to access the service, your credit card number is safe from thieves. This is not true on the free-wheeling Internet. Because it is an open network, hackers can easily break in and take whatever strikes their fancy. Few instances of Internet credit card robbery have been reported so far, and new encryption technologies are making online ordering safer, but it doesn't take too many Kevin Mitnicks to frighten shoppers away. Given the choice between shopping in a dangerous neighborhood and a place with round-the-clock police protection and brightly lit parking lots, most people choose the safer one—unless they think that it's worth the risk to scoop up the deal of the century.

■ There are not enough shoppers.

Even though the Internet's population is estimated at 20,000,000 to 30,000,000, bona fide shoppers are still in scarce supply on the Net. Many Internet users are college students, university professors, and government bureaucrats who get their Internet access for free and who tend to be less willing than people who pay to subscribe to Prodigy, CompuServe, and America Online to plunk down their money for goods and services. Moreover, only around 4 million Internet users can access the Web's multimedia cybermalls in graphical format, and over half the Internet population has access only to e-mail. All this is changing now that the three big commercial services are starting to roll out Web access to their members. For now, though, the ratio of Internet shops to Internet shoppers remains high.

■ It's not much fun.

Despite its cool hyperlinks and flashy graphics, the Internet is not a cozy place to browse. There are no benches, fountains, ice cream stands, or espresso bars as in real-world shopping areas. California marketer Jim Redfield summed up the problem in a recent posting to the Internet's inet-marketing discussion group: "Internet providers haven't yet realized that for most people, shopping is not considered a nuisance activity from which the Net offers electronic respite. Sellers of mainstream goods who think that they will succeed on the Net simply because they're making purchasing more convenient miss the point. Shopping at their sites must be fun to attract customers."

You Can Make Money on the Internet!

Despite everything we have just told you, companies are streaming on to the Internet in record numbers to cash in on what they see as one of the world's largest and fastest growing markets. They sell tennis rackets, peddle rare books, and hawk lobsters, but only a few of them make big money.

So does this mean that Internet business is just a flash in the pan? Are thousands of entrepreneurs all over the world just spinning their wheels?

We believe that the answer is no—otherwise, we would not be writing this book. On the other hand, if we knew the secret to Internet riches, we would be cooling our heels on a tropical island, downing Margaritas instead of slaving away at our computers. (Well, we might bring Dave's Powerbook along…)

We also believe that Internet retailing is still in its infancy. It is too early to tell for certain how to make a fortune on the Internet.

As we see it, there are four principal ways to make money on the Net today.

- Sell Internet-related products and services
- Sell advertising on a Web site
- Sell unique or hard-to-find items
- Sell to a local market with a heavy concentration of Internet users

Of the more than 100 businesses that replied to a survey we sent out in the course of updating this book, the company that reported the highest revenues was Ceram, Inc., an electronics firm in Colorado Springs that specializes in equipment for Internet service providers. Over the last 12 months, Ceram has racked up roughly $4 million in sales on a $100,000 investment. The company hopes to increase its sales to $10 million over the next year. Figure 14.2 shows Ceram's Web site (`http://www.ceram.com`).

Other companies, meanwhile, have invested months of effort and thousands of hours only to reap disappointing results. Take Prima Travel Centre, a travel agency in Absecon, New Jersey. Early last year, owner Paula Jerome decided to hop aboard the Internet as a way to get a leg up on the local competition. After spending countless hours responding to e-mail inquiries and putting up her own Web site (`http://www.explore.com/prima.html`), shown in Figure 14.3, she has made only one sale.

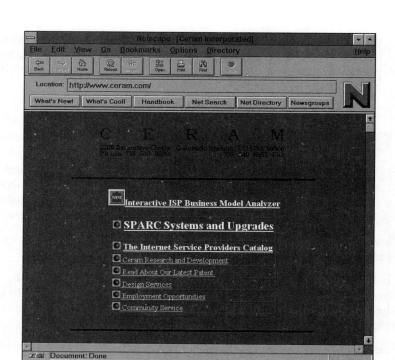

Figure 14.2. Ceram, Inc., has rung up $4,000,000 in revenues by selling Internet-related equipment over the Net.

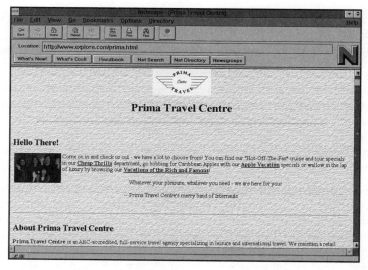

Figure 14.3. Prima Travel Centre has experienced slow going on the Net so far despite major efforts.

"I wanted to sell big-time on the Net, but the Net dictates what you will do," Jerome says. "The people who surf the Net are too busy surfing to buy services. A company on the Net has to prove longevity in the form of name recognition and goodwill and to pay its dues before consumer confidence takes hold and people buy." Nevertheless, Jerome vows to continue her efforts on the Internet.

In fact, even companies doing fairly well on the Internet, such as ModulaWare, a software company in La Chanenche, France, warn not to expect too much from Internet sales channels. According to ModulaWare owner Guenter Dotzel, customers who ask the most questions produce the least profit. Customers who do not follow up quickly are not interested in your products or services. In most cases, they think the price is too high. "The Internet makes less turnover in one year than the supermarket around the corner in one afternoon. The more information people gather, the more likely it is that they don't want to spend money to buy something. They spend their time on the Internet to find something cheaper or for free."

What's Hot, What's Not

To get a basic idea of what sells and what doesn't on the Internet right now, look at the chart below. Even though we wrote it tongue-in-cheek, there is more than a grain of truth to it.

Hot	Not
Computer books	Children's books
Pizza	Lobster
DOOM	Squash
Routers	Teddy bears
Software	T-shirts

You get the picture. High tech sells better than high touch, and anything that appeals to a twenty-something computer guy who lives life on the Net is probably going to do better than a warm and fuzzy product designed for family fun.

Internet Success Stories

Despite the odds, a handful of companies are making money on the Internet. All of them fall into one of the hot categories mentioned previously. Each company either sells an Internet-related product or service, offers advertising space on its site, supplies unique or hard-to-find items, or sells to a local market with a large population of Internet users.

Internet Distribution Services

With companies large and small racing to get on to the Web, it's no surprise that Internet Distribution Services has seen its business boom.

IDS, owned by Palo Alto programmer and graphic designer Marc Fleischmann, designs and builds Web sites and operates its own Web, Gopher, WAIS, ftp, and list server. Clients range from Country Fare, a local restaurant, to CareerMosaic, a nationwide employment service. IDS, as you might recall from the first edition of *The Internet Business Guide,* was the company that put *The Palo Alto Weekly* on the Web, making it one of the first commercial newspapers on the Net.

Fleischmann's strategy is to create eye-catching Web sites by fusing design, technology, and marketing and to provide the best possible service to his dozens of business clients. Last year IDS set up approximately 70 Web sites. This year it expects to set up 100. Check out the IDS home page, shown in Figure 14.4, at `http://www.service.com/`.

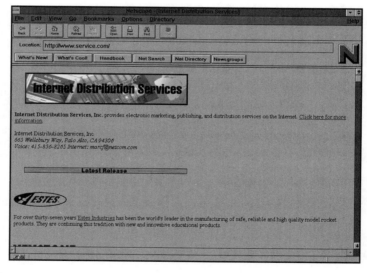

Figure 14.4. Internet Distribution Services, a Web site designer and operator, expects to set up 100 sites this year.

"Our strategy is to provide the best value to our customers," Fleischmann says. "We do not compete on price. We solve customer problems that competitors can't even identify."

Fleischmann is not worried about the growing number of competitors that have entered the field over the last year. Few of them, he says, have the experience that he does in creating sites on the Web. "The large network organizations don't understand that this is a service business—not technology—and the smaller companies don't have the expertise."

HotWired

HotWired, the online edition of *Wired* magazine, doesn't making money by peddling thousands of copies at a couple bucks apiece. It makes money the old-fashioned way—selling high-priced advertising to deep-pocketed sponsors.

The Web-based magazine debuted in October 1994 and has attracted 16 advertisers ranging from AT&T to Volvo. Each advertiser pays $30,000 for the right to hoist its sponsorship banner over a HotWired editorial department for two months. Assuming that all 16 sponsors renew— not an unreasonable bet considering that 12 of the publication's 14 sponsors have renewed already—HotWired will generate gross revenues of well over $2 million this year.

How does HotWired do it?

By combining "content and community"—that is, gathering talented writers and artists and techno-savvy readers around the "information campfire" and giving them a place to hang out on the Net—says Jonathan Steuer, one of HotWired's developers. This means hiring 25 online staffers to interact with readers and a top design firm to create a signature look and feel, creating custom editorial content (as opposed to "shovelware" from its print edition), and using the online medium to display multimedia artwork and all kinds of other cool stuff.

HotWired's marketing strategy clearly works. According to Steuer, HotWired attracted 12,000 subscribers in its first five days, signing up new members at a rate of 100 an hour. Currently, HotWired has over 90,000 subscribers, and its Web site gets 250,000 hits every day. Check it out at `http://www.hotwired.com/`.

Aunt Agatha's

Aunt Agatha's uses leading-edge technology to market some very old products, and it's off to a promising start. The company, located in Coquitlam, British Columbia, sells metaphysical, occult, and pagan supplies by mail order.

Earlier this year, owner Lisa Forryan (`aunt@agatha.com`) decided to tap into what she perceived was "a large crossover between the mystical and the electronic." After a minimal investment of $600 and 60 hours on the Internet, Forryan's company has seen requests for catalogs triple. Now she plans to put up a Web site that will offer a catalog, a newsletter, an events calendar, listings of related magazines and periodicals, and a business directory. "As long as you have a sure idea that people interested in your product use the Internet, there's no better way to reach them," Forryan says.

Waiters on Wheels

Waiters on Wheels bills itself as "the world's only online restaurant delivery network." The company's promise: Fast, hot delivery of great food within an hour from your favorite local restaurants.

With locations in San Francisco, San Jose, Palo Alto, San Mateo, and Redwood City in California and in Seattle and Spokane in Washington, Waiters on Wheels, shown in Figure 14.5, enables Internet users to browse through hundreds of complete, up-to-date menus displayed on the company's Web site and to place their orders by typing their credit card number into their Web browser or by calling Waiters on Wheels directly. For every order, the company collects a $5 delivery charge from the customer and a $6 fee from the restaurant.

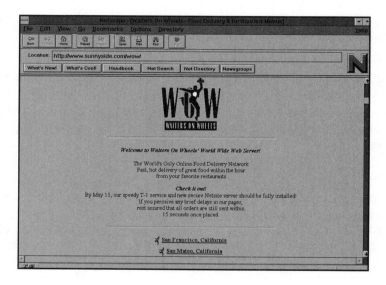

Figure 14.5. Waiters on Wheels, an online restaurant delivery service, rakes in $15,000 a month by selling convenience to a high-tech customer base.

Owner Constantine Stathopolous describes his Internet business strategy like this: Develop a unique service that sells itself, target a high-tech customer base, and offer an interactive service—not a billboard. Check it out at http://www.sunnyside.com/wow/.

Stathopolous' strategy is paying off. After only five months on the Internet and an investment of $2,000, Waiters on Wheels has seen its sales shoot up to $15,000 with no end in sight. In fact, Stathopolous plans to expand his business and launch what he calls the Internet Restaurant Network. He is upgrading to a high-speed T1 line and installing a copy of Netscape's Netsite server to make credit card entry safe for his customers.

Sex Sells—or Does It?

One of the oldest adages of business is that sex sells. Does it sell on the Internet? We're not so sure. Although the *Playboy* and *Penthouse* Web sites attract hundreds of thousands of visitors a day, adult-oriented shops selling books, videos, and sex toys don't seem to make many sales—though they do get lots of window shoppers.

On the other hand, David Levine, who runs the Wicked Cool Mall (`http://www.wcool.com/`), says that he does a bang-up business selling vibrators, lotions, condoms, and love dolls. He soon plans to add lingerie, CD-ROMs, videos, games, and books. Because he has no retail shop and does no direct mailings, he has very little overhead.

"I am making a living," says Levine, who won't disclose his financial data. "It should be a nice living within a couple of months."

Making Money on the Internet Tomorrow

Who will be making money on the Internet when we update this book next year? It is impossible to know, but we believe that the next hot business opportunity on the Net will be selling interactive services via online order forms. Now that encryption technology is making it safe to enter credit card information through a Web browser, the Internet might turn into one big ATM machine that dispenses all manner of products and services.

One company pointing the way is Shrink-Link. A Web-based advice service, it invites people to submit questions via e-mail to a panel of seven psychiatrists and psychologists.

To use Shrink-Link, you access the Shrink-Link home page, shown in Figure 14.6, at `http://www.westnet.com/shrink`. Click the hyperlinked words `Compose a query!`. Instantly, you are transported to another page that enables you to type in a 200-word question about your fears, anxieties, marital troubles, sexual problems, or anything else on your mind. Depending on the nature of your question, you can route your question to a panelist specializing in family issues, relationships, depression, alcohol and drug use, eating disorders, sex and gender issues, obsessions, compulsions and eating disorders, women's issues, or psychiatry and medication.

Once you have typed your query, fill in the online order form with your name and credit card number with expiration date. Click the Submit Query button. Within about 24 hours, you receive a response via e-mail, and your credit card is billed $20.

According to Daniel Litwin, a former Coopers & Lybrand consultant who launched the service together with his wife, Georgia Chu, who handled public relations for Northern Telecom, Shrink-Link gets 500 to 1,500 hits a day and rings up 10 to 30 daily sales. The bottom line: 450 paid users and $9,000 in revenue in February alone, the company's first month in business. That is not a bad return on an investment whose startup costs were under $2,000.

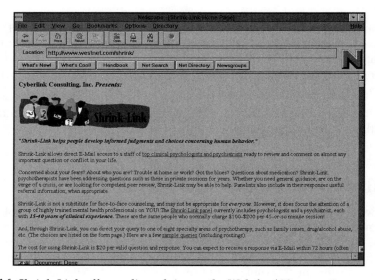

Figure 14.6. Shrink-Link offers online advice on the Web for $20 a question.

Why has Shrink-Link gotten off to such an impressive start whereas other Internet retailers have lagged behind? Unlike flowers and sweaters that shoppers prefer to see, touch, or try on, mental health advice is a service that can be delivered online even more effectively, in some cases, than face-to-face or by telephone. Many people grappling with psychological issues are reluctant to seek out professional help for fear of embarrassment, so typing a question online offers the ultimate in privacy and anonymity. Moreover, the $20 fee is cheaper than an hour of psychotherapy at $100.

Finally, Shrink-Link delivers faster and more personal service than writing to a newspaper advice columnist or calling in to a radio show because the service answers all queries rather than just newsworthy ones, and it does so more quickly than Ann Landers ever could. Thanks to the Internet's dirt-cheap e-mail distribution system, the cost to operate a service like this is minuscule except for the expense of paying the panelists.

Despite its quick start, however, Shrink-Link's success is not guaranteed. Like other forms of online professional interaction, its future is clouded by the prospect of regulation and the risk of malpractice litigation. The ethics code of the

American Psychological Association does not specifically address online therapy because the field is so new, but Litwin concedes that it would probably be considered unethical to offer a service that mimics one usually provided face-to-face. Unlike traditional therapy, online therapy cannot rely on body language and other visual clues to a patient's psychological state. Moreover, it is hard to develop a patient-therapist relationship in cyberspace.

To get around these problems, Shrink-Link makes it clear that it is not providing online therapy but rather a question-and-answer service staffed by mental health professionals. If a patient begins to rely on the service too heavily—that is, keeps coming back every day with questions—Shrink-Link attempts to steer the patient to a face-to-face therapist or clinic. Once the first disgruntled client files a malpractice suit against an operation like Shrink-Link, however, it is a safe bet that state regulators will be swarming all over the place before you can say, "cyberspace."

No matter what you might think of the ethics of online therapy, you cannot deny that this kind of information sells on the Internet. Selling professional advice to bewildered Net surfers is emerging as one of the first breakthrough products and services that makes Internet retailing a reality.

Dave and Rosalind Do the Net

Now that we have told you about other people's successes and failures on the Net, we feel it's only fair that we tell you ours. When we wrote this book last year, Rosalind had just launched Interactive Publishing Alert and Dave was in the middle of building the Internet Mall.

Since posting her first press release about Interactive Publishing Alert, shown in Figure 14.7, on the Net-happenings list in February 1994—and getting flamed for it—Rosalind has built up her circulation base to approximately 150 subscribers, from *The New York Times* and *The Financial Times* of London to Microsoft, Apple, and America Online. She has raised the yearly subscription price from $149 to $295 and doubled the frequency of publication from once a month to twice a month.

She has also licensed Interactive Newspapers, Inc., a joint venture with the Kelsey Group consulting firm and *Editor & Publisher* magazine to market a hard copy edition of IPA for $345 a year through traditional direct mail and telemarketing channels. Finally, she has brought on an assistant, Heidi Anderson, to help her produce periodic research reports, such as IPA's *Directory of Online Publications*, and to help gather information for her newsletter.

Technologically, Rosalind has made strides. She still distributes the e-mail edition of her newsletter as a plain ASCII text file so that all of her subscribers can read it without special software, but she now has a mailing list that she uses to foster interactive discussions with subscribers about online publishing topics. Thanks to programmer Ryan Scott, a partner in her new company, NetCreations, which designs Web sites for businesses, Rosalind now has an IPA Web site and makes the full text of her newsletter available on the site to subscribers by distributing user IDs and passwords.

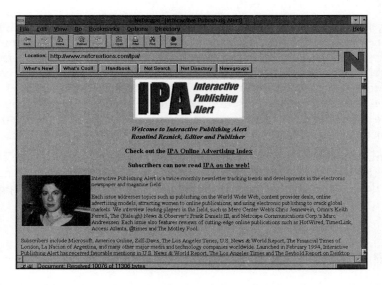

Figure 14.7. Interactive Publishing Alert now has about 150 subscribers, a hard copy edition and, yes, its own Web site.

The bottom line: Since its launch in February 1994, Rosalind's newsletter has generated more than $50,000 in revenues; costs have been minimal, apart from paying Heidi. That does not count all the consulting jobs, writing assignments, and other money-making opportunities that have sprung from it. For Rosalind, the greatest reward of publishing her own newsletter has not been money alone—it is the joy and pride that come with creating her own publications and controlling her own professional destiny.

Meanwhile, the Internet Mall, as shown in Figure 14.8, is exploding in popularity and has grown far beyond the wildest expectations Dave had 18 months ago when he started what was essentially a Frequently Asked Questions file about what shops were accessible online. As of this writing, the Internet Mall contains more than 2,500 stores, divided into eight separate floors (including clothes, personal goods, business to business, media, and computer-related goods and services) and is growing by about 100 new shops each week.

There are a few key decisions that Dave made early on which have proven pivotal in the growth of the Mall; to offer all store listings free of charge and to let any electronic shop into the Mall, whether that shop had a fancy Web page or just an e-mail address. In the same way, the Mall is not only an exciting Web page (`http://www.mecklerweb.com/imall`) but it's also available through e-mail (send mail to `taylor@netcom.com` with the subject line `send mall`), anonymous FTP, or Gopher. The Mall is also posted to about a half-dozen Usenet groups bi-weekly, and it's also uploaded to CompuServe, America Online, ZiffNet, and eWorld. All told, Dave estimates that more than 7,500 people visit the Mall each day.

Revenue from the Internet Mall comes from corporate sponsors of the entire Mall or any of the eight floors or more than 200 departments. If you sell flowers, for example, a sponsorship fee of only $600 per month gives you top billing in the floral department of the Mall and results in your graphics image being the only graphics image in that department of the Mall's Web-based version. Further, sponsor information appears at the top of the relevant section, so you're guaranteed that everyone visiting the floor or department sees your advertisement. With a total visitor count of more than 225,000 people each month, the Mall is a smart place to advertise online.

Has it been profitable? Yes, but the profits have been starting to show up only recently. Earlier in 1995, Dave signed a partnership agreement with Mecklermedia, publishers of Internet World and WebWEEK, and maintainers of MecklerWeb (`http://www.mecklerweb.com/`). Meckler will offer its advertising sales expertise in return for a slice of the revenue stream. Since then, six large companies have signed up to sponsor various sections of the Internet Mall, and there are negotiations under way with at least 20 more firms. In specific, tangible revenue terms, the Mall has netted Dave about $15,000 so far, but the intangible returns are immense: speaking opportunities, invitations to contribute to Internet books, interviews on radio and television, and much more.

Ultimately, our experiences lead us to believe that a major enterprise on the Internet is quite likely to generate positive marketing results, improve corporate image, and help grow your business, often in ways you never expected. To expect a direct, cash-on-the-barrel profit line within a short period of time, however, is premature. Today people are browsing and exploring the network, not buying products.

Even the Best Laid Plans Can Go Awry

But don't let our modest successes lead you to believe that it is possible to reduce Internet business to some sort of predictable science. Despite its rapid evolution as a commercial marketplace since we wrote this book last year, the Internet still has a long way to go before it is a reliable place to do business. To see what we mean, consider the following story about one of Rosalind's Internet publishing ventures that encountered some bumps along the way.

Last fall, Rosalind decided to launch a monthly electronic newsletter called Interactive Marketing Alert and to distribute it through an Internet mailing list. Her plan was to post monthly press releases on business-related Internet discussion groups, offering free subscriptions to anybody who wanted to sign up. Once her circulation reached 1,000 subscribers, she would start selling ads to companies that wanted to reach her readers. Essentially, she was trying to create the Internet equivalent of a controlled circulation magazine—a technique that has worked extremely well for other online publications.

Figure 14.8. the Internet Mall contains more than 2,500 stores and is growing at about 100 new shops each week.

At first, her little publishing venture seemed to go well. Her press releases quickly generated hundreds of subscriptions. Her readers liked what she had to say, and hardly anybody flamed her for using the Internet to publicize her commercial venture. After all, she was giving away the newsletter for free.

Then, in early March, shortly after posting the February issue of her newsletter to the mailing list, she found a strange note in her e-mail box. It was an unsolicited pitch letter from a Tennessee company trying to interest her in what it described as a "business opportunity." She was puzzled at first—how did this company from which she had never requested information get her name?

Soon afterward, Rosalind began getting angry e-mail from subscribers accusing her of committing the ultimate Internet business crime: spamming—or, in this case, renting out her list to a company that went out and spammed. That is when she realized that the company had not simply sent the pitch letter to her but had piggybacked on her list to send junk mail to all her subscribers.

After sending out a few apologetic notes to the handful of subscribers who had complained, Rosalind decided it was time for some serious damage control. She posted a note to the list apologizing for the junk mailer's actions—the company in question insisted that it did not know that her list was not supposed to be used for that purpose—and assuring her subscribers that the folks at Cyberspace Development, the Colorado company that manages her list, were trying to get to the bottom of what was happening.

Rosalind thought that would nip the problem in the bud, but she was wrong. The folks in Colorado had inadvertently set up her list so that anybody could post to it—not just the list owner. As a result, subscribers started replying to her posting, and other subscribers began replying to their postings. Everybody's postings got posted to everybody on the list. Rosalind pleaded with everybody to stop posting to the list until her list operator could fix it. But it was no use. It was as if Rosalind was trapped in the Internet version of *The Sorcerer's Apprentice*. No matter how many times she tried to stop those postings, even more postings would pop up to take their place.

Then things got even worse. At first, a few people had unsubscribed—Internet lingo for getting off a mailing list—because of the spamming. Now dozens of people canceled their subscriptions because their mailboxes were getting flooded with e-mail from other subscribers discussing the spamming incident. Months of hard work seemed to be slipping down the drain. Chagrined, Rosalind posted a note to the list telling her readers that she might have to pull the plug on her list if this craziness didn't stop soon.

Then the tide started turning. Readers started sending her letters of support, urging her to keep the newsletter alive. Before long, the e-mail slowed to a trickle. A few months later, Rosalind decided to pull the plug on her mailing list and post the articles on her Web site.

The moral of the story: Whatever commercial venture you try on the Internet, expect the unexpected. That way, you will never be surprised.

Don't Expect to Get Rich Quickly

The next time you read an article in a newspaper or a magazine about the money-making opportunities on the Internet, take it with a grain of salt. Divide any numbers you see by a factor of at least two. As you saw in this chapter, there are real opportunities to make money on the Internet, but you need to pick your niches carefully. Don't expect an immediate payoff.

At the same time, don't be discouraged if you don't get rich quickly. By this time next year, we hope to have many more success stories to report. One of them might be yours.

INTERNET
CYBERMALLS

Whenever a new highway comes to an area, retail shops and malls spring up to provide goods and services to the burgeoning population. The information superhighway is no exception.

These days, retailing is becoming big business on the Internet, and storefronts, shopping centers, and cybermalls are springing up on virtually every electronic street corner. Bookstores, software companies, incorporation services, auction houses, florists, newspaper publishers, law firms, and even restaurants display their goods and services on the Internet, and customers are making their purchases online. Few merchants have made big money, as you saw in Chapter 14, but that has not stopped thousands from trying their luck.

The driving force behind this retailing boom is Mosaic-World Wide Web technology, which enables merchants to create full-color displays through which shoppers can browse for products with the click of a mouse. Through the Web, Internet shoppers can use hyperlinks to access information and product descriptions located elsewhere on the network.

The goal of this chapter is to give you an overview of the Internet retailing options now available. You will learn how companies successfully use the Internet to attract new customers, ring up sales, and deliver electronic merchandise directly to a customer's computer.

Internet Shopping Malls

Internet stores run the gamut from tiny boutiques to sprawling retail complexes. On the Internet, a storefront can be as simple as an e-mail box or a brochure on the Web. Using a mail responder, companies can automatically blast out a price list or a catalog to anyone who requests one—without hiring staff to stuff envelopes. On the Web, a company can put up everything from a modest brochure to a multimedia specialty store that displays products, takes customer orders, and in the case of software programs and electronic publications, fulfills the orders online. There also are Web-based *cybermalls,* which house dozens of online shops and attract hundreds of thousands of shoppers a day.

Four kinds of retail establishments exist on the Internet today:

- The brochure
- The company mailbox
- The specialty store
- The cybermall

The Brochure

The first step for many companies is a home page on the Web that tells the company's story in text and pictures. This sort of online brochure is often a hypermedia version of the print brochure that the company passes out to its clients or of an ad that it runs in a magazine. Web brochures can be as simple as a single page with no hypermedia links or as complex as a full-blown multimedia production with all the bells and whistles. Companies that put up a Web home page include Fidelity Investments and Southwest Airlines.

Fidelity Investments

Fidelity Investments, the big mutual fund company, recently put up a Web site to "deliver on our commitment to provide investors with the information and assistance they need to make more informed choices." The company's Web-based Fidelity Investments Information Center (`http://www.fid-inv.com/`) is shown in Figure 15.1. It offers information about mutual funds, brokerage services, and new products. Visitors can enter contests and play interactive games. For example, Internet users who enter Fidelity's Guess the Dow contest can win a NEC triple-speed CD-ROM drive and take a quiz to find out their savings personality. The Center hosts a variety of informational and educational events.

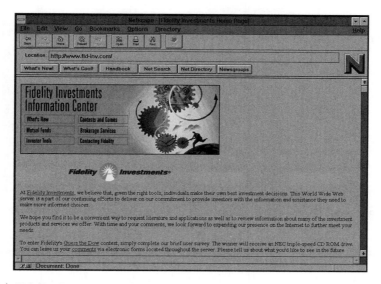

Figure 15.1. Fidelity Investments draws users to its site through games and contests.

Southwest Airlines

Southwest Airlines, with 200 planes serving 45 cities and $2.5 billion in revenues, has made a name for itself as a no-frills airline that sells bargain-basement tickets on ticketless flights. On the Internet, the company has continued its maverick tradition. Its home page (`http://www.iflyswa.com/`), called Southwest Airlines Home Gate and shown in Figure 15.2, features an online reservations system that enables you to check flights and fares. (You still need to call the voice registration line to book a flight or buy a ticket, though.) The site contains press releases about the company, financial statements, fact sheets on each of the cities to which the airline flies, lists of rental car agencies in and around the airport, and even photographs of Southwest Airlines planes.

Tip: There's nothing like a contest or giveaway to draw people to your Web site—even if it offers the chance to win only a T-shirt or a coffee mug. Internet users will gladly visit your site and fill out a registration form if you dangle a prize in front of them.

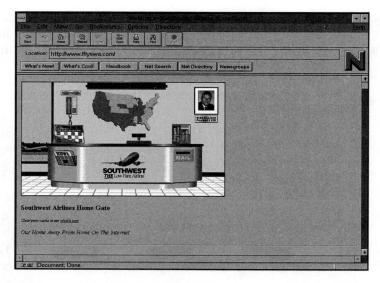

Figure 15.2. Southwest Airlines' home page enables you to check flight information online, although you still need to telephone in a reservation.

Company name: Arent Fox Kintner Plotkin & Kahn (see Figure 15.3)

Type of business: Law firm

Location: Washington, D.C.

Owner: 100 Partners

URL: `http://www.webcom.com/~lewrose/home.html` (advertising law Internet site) and `http://www.arentfox.com` (Arent Fox home page). Also on the `net-lawyers` mailing list at `net-lawyers@webcom.com`.

Internet tools: Web and mailing list

Length of time doing business on the Internet: Since August 1994

Reason for going on the Internet: It's a growth industry. Lots of startup businesses and Fortune 500 companies use it, but relatively few lawyers do. This makes it an ideal marketing opportunity for lawyers, at least in the short run. By being there at the start, we get to establish ourselves as experts right out of the box. The Internet is a cost-effective mechanism for accomplishing this.

Internet business strategy: To use the Internet to increase our visibility and recognition as the law firm that can assist businesses seeking to do business on the Internet.

Time and money you have invested: More than 200 hours and less than $500.

Net results: We have more than recouped our costs by revenues generated through contacts made on the Internet. In addition, the publicity and name recognition that we have gained is invaluable. Virtually every computer and law publication has written up our site and our efforts to date. All have been extremely positive.

Future plans: To offer more and more specialized home pages on specific topics of law. To move away from typical law firm PR marketing materials and provide clients with substantive information via the Internet.

Lessons learned/Net philosophy: The hardest part is separating out the folks seeking legal advice who cannot afford to pay for it from those who have significant capital.

Contact address: Lew Rose at `lewrose@netcom.com`

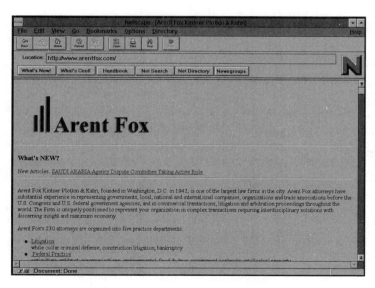

Figure 15.3. Arent Fox's information-packed Web site has already begun bringing the firm clients.

The Company Mailbox

A less flashy but highly effective way to sell products and services on the Internet is to set up a company e-mail box. By this, we mean an automated mail responder that zaps out a copy of your company brochure or catalog to anyone who requests it by e-mail.

Information Researchers, a company working out of the University of Illinois at Champaign-Urbana, has years of experience working on the Internet. The company knows that when customers seek specific pieces of information, the right tools do not necessarily help them find what they want. That is why the company offers a broad range of custom research tools, including company and industry profiles, literature and database searches, and bibliographies. Through the Internet, the company electronically delivers the results of queries and searches.

Here is what you get when you send e-mail to the company's mail responder at info@uiuc.edu:

```
INFORMATION RESEARCHERS (IR) is a full-service, professional information broker
  offering custom research, online database searching, and document delivery. IR
  has been in operation since 1976 as a cost recovery unit of the Graduate Schoo
l of Library and Information Science at the University of Illinois at Champaign
  -Urbana.

Products and Services

Information Researchers offers rapid, convenient document delivery from a wide
variety of sources, and provides a broad range of custom research on any topic,
  including: retrieval of specific facts and statistics; literature and online d
atabase searches; custom bibliographies; company and industry profiles; written
  reports, from brief summaries to extensive papers; custom mailing lists; and c
ustom-designed projects.

Clients

Information Researchers serves individuals and organizations in business, indus
try, education, and government, in fields such as manufacturing, law, environme
nt, health sciences, and small business.

Resources

IR provides copies of almost any published documents, from the collections of t
he University of Illinois (the third largest academic library in the nation), a
s well as most other libraries in the United States, the British Library, comme
rcial document suppliers, publishers, and government agencies.

Information Researchers also subscribes to the major database vendors, such as
DIALOG, NewsNet, OCLC and LEXIS/NEXIS, which allows access to thousands of data
bases. In-house CD-ROM and other databases are also available.

IR staff includes professional information specialists with Master's degrees as
  well as college-educated writers and researchers.
```

For more information, or a free initial consultation and estimate, contact Info
rmation Researchers at: University of Illinois, 501 East Daniel Street #215, Ch
ampaign, IL 61820-6212. Telephone: 800-643-2807, 217-333-6202; Fax 217-333-9361.

The company's electronic brochure also includes a price list.

```
***********************************************************************
                      INFORMATION RESEARCHERS
                        PRICING SCHEDULE
                          July 1994

RESEARCH HOURLY RATE:
1 hour minimum                         $ 70 per hour, plus costs
Rush Research Rate                     $ 90 per hour, plus costs
COSTS:
Photocopies                            $   .10 per page
Microform Copies                       $   .25 per page
Fax Delivery                           $  1.00 per page
Copyright Royalty Fees                 $  at cost
Express Courier Delivery               $  at cost
Online Database Fees                   $  at cost
JOURNAL ARTICLES AND BOOK LOANS:
Provided from the University
of Illinois Libraries.                 $ 12 per title, plus copyright
  Loan period for books is three weeks.
Documents provided from outside        $ 12 per title, plus supplier's cost
  the University of Illinois Libraries.
  Loan period for books may vary.
The document fee of $12 includes up to 20 pages of photocopies per title and de
livery by 1st class mail. The applicable copyright royalty fee is in addition t
o the $12 fee.
RUSH DOCUMENT SERVICE:
Next Day Rush - shipped next working day  $  5 additional per title
Same Day Rush - shipped same working day  $ 10 additional per title
Request received by noon, fax delivery not included.
REFERRALS:                             $  8 per title
Names of suppliers which may hold documents not available from the University o
f Illinois Libraries.
CITATION VERIFICATION:                 $ 10 per title
Documents with incorrect or incomplete citations, or which are otherwise diffic
ult to locate.
LOST BOOK FEE:                         $100 per title
BILLING:
Receive a monthly bill, use VISA/MasterCard, or establish a deposit account fro

m $100. Clients outside the United States may use VISA/MasterCard,or pre-pay wi
th a check in US dollars.
***********************************************************************
```

The Specialty Store

Thanks to the Web's soaring popularity, many businesses take advantage of hypermedia technology to create online storefronts to advertise and sell their products and services. Stores like these function as both a retail outlet and a direct-mail catalog—without the need to pay for rent, printing, or postage. The typical specialty store features a product catalog that includes text and pictures plus an online order form or a toll-free telephone number. It might also contain links to related sites, detailed information about the company, and special features such as a searchable database, an online tour, an interactive bulletin board, or an advice service.

> **Tip:** Stock your online store with information about your company, as well as your products and prices. On the Internet, shoppers want to know who you are—not just what you sell.

The Gadget Page and Virtual Vineyards are two specialty stores on the Web.

The Gadget Page

A good example of a specialty store is The Gadget Page, a Web site that Rosalind and Ryan put up for New Tech Industries, a Davie, Florida, importer, exporter, and wholesaler of novelty telephones and other telecommunications devices. The Gadget Page store, shown in Figure 15.4, is stocked with jukebox-shaped radios, Star Trek gizmos, novelty phones, and phone-related gadgets and switches. Shoppers place their orders by clicking the box next to the item they want and by typing their name, address, and credit-card information into an online order form.

The Gadget Page is more than just an online catalog, though. The site includes links to gadget-related information elsewhere on the Net, such as HotWired's Fetish department and the Weird Science site, which features "weird research, anomalous physics, free energy devices, and more strangeness!"

The Gadget Page invites shopper feedback—another essential part of Web-based retailing. "We want to make this the site for cool gadgets, strange devices, or useful bits of electronic parts. But we need your help!" the company writes on its home page. "If you have a gadget or a site you think rates a mention, send it to GURUGADGET@aol.com."

> **Tip:** Display a picture of every item in your catalog if you can. Like shoppers everywhere, shoppers on the Web want to see what they are buying.

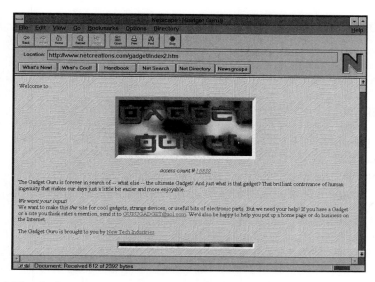

Figure 15.4. The Gadget Page's Web-based specialty store sells everything from Barbie telephones to remote controls shaped like Star Trek phasers.

Virtual Vineyards

A larger, more elaborate specialty store is Virtual Vineyards, shown in Figure 15.5. Created by California wine expert Peter Granoff, Virtual Vineyards not only sells wine, but it entices wine buffs into an elegant, interactive world where they can do everything from tour the site to pose questions to the Cork Dork (a.k.a. Peter Granoff). There is a tasting chart for every wine from every winery listed—so far, there are 22. The chart features sliding indicators of the wine's vital statistics—intensity, dryness, body, acidity, tanning, oak flavors, and complexity. Each wine and winery features a little JPEG image of the label plus a write-up by the Cork Dork himself. Next to each wine is a Remember This Wine button that you can click to order later. Virtual Vineyards comes with a glossary of terms, articles from *Wine and Spirits* magazine, and recipes for meals to go with the wines advertised.

Virtual Vineyards' online order form, shown in Figure 15.6, is a standout. When you access the area, you find a list containing every wine you "remembered" along with its price and a box that enables you to enter the number of bottles you want to order. Virtual Vineyards offers a 10% discount on cases, which can be mixed, and second-day air or ground shipping. Moreover, Virtual Vineyards safeguards its shoppers' online credit card transactions with Netscape's Secure Sockets Layer encryption technology. Shoppers can dial a toll-free telephone number or use CyberCash's Secure Internet Payment Service. (See Chapter 16 for more information about CyberCash and other secure payment systems.)

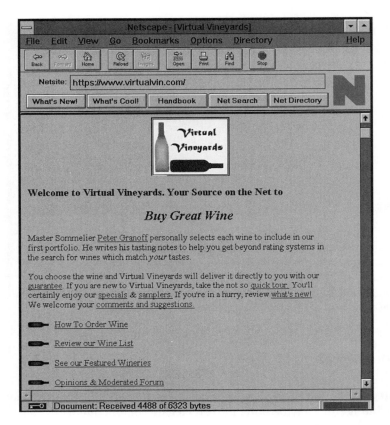

Figure 15.5. Virtual Vineyards entices visitors with wine lists, an online tour, a moderated discussion group, and a chance to get their questions answered by the Cork Dork.

Unlike other Web-based retailers, Virtual Vineyards doesn't market any old wine made by a winery that pays Virtual Wineyards a setup fee. Granoff, a former restaurant beverage manager who has traveled the world tasting wines and earned the rarefied designation of "master sommelier," stocks only those wines that meet his exacting standards.

When the 22 wineries that sell wines through Virtual Vineyards send over bottles for him to try, "I taste the samples and compile my notes and then I'll say, 'I'm interested in this, this and this,'" Granoff says. "Sometimes, I take all of them, sometimes I take some of them, sometimes I take none of them."

Virtual Vineyards doesn't charge a setup fee to create Web pages for the wineries whose wines it sells. Rather, the store makes its money the old-fashioned way— by clipping a percentage of each transaction.

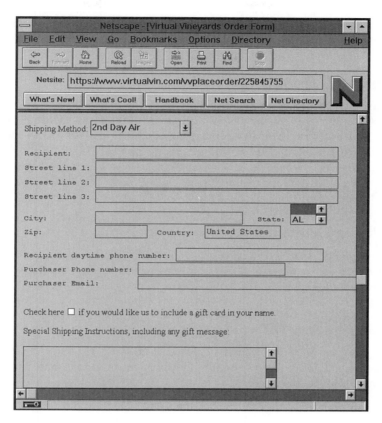

Figure 15.6. Virtual Vineyards' online order form enables shoppers to purchase wines that they "remembered" while browsing.

The Cybermall

The Internet is quickly becoming crowded with cybermalls—Web-based retail complexes that house dozens of specialty stores that sell everything from computer software to gourmet chocolates. One advantage to setting up shop in a cybermall is walk-in traffic. Shoppers who come to the mall looking for a new CD might wander over to your shoe store—at least, that is the idea. Another advantage is that you do not have to worry about hiring a programmer to create your Web pages or finding a server to house them. Typically, the mall operator does all of that for you.

It costs more to rent space in a mall than it does to put up a specialty store on your own. The following is a list of some cybermall operators.

Internet Distribution Services

Services include design, marketing, World Wide Web, Gopher, online ordering, Wide Area Information Servers (WAIS), and mailing lists. Marc Fleischmann is the landlord. Contact him at `marcf@netcom.com`. Monthly fees are all-inclusive and range from $1,000 to $2,500. Setup fees range from $10,000 to $25,000.

Branch Mall

Services include World Wide Web, Gopher, e-mail, ftp, and virtual hosts. Jon Zeeff is the landlord. Contact him at `branch-info@branch.com`.

Single-page Web listings cost $960 per year, which includes production and maintenance fees. Extra pages cost $500. Online order forms are available for $600 per year, and catalogs cost $2,900 plus $40 per item.

The Global Shopping Mall

Louis Marcus is the landlord. Contact him at `sysadm@magibox.net` or `admgsm@magibox.net`. Services include Gopher, automated e-mail brochures, list-serv, and online ordering.

Annual storage fees range from $500 for up to 125MB of data storage; additional storage costs range from $3.50 to $2.50 per megabyte plus 3% of gross sales. There are additional fees for toll-free order lines, credit-card processing, and other services.

Shopping at Branch Mall

Branch Mall is one of the Internet's oldest and largest shopping plazas. It features hundreds of shops peddling sunglasses, T-shirts, coffee, bonsai trees, and everything in-between. Branch Mall organizes its shops by topic to make them easy to find. Each store's name is hyperlinked, which enables shoppers to go directly to it (see Figure 15.7).

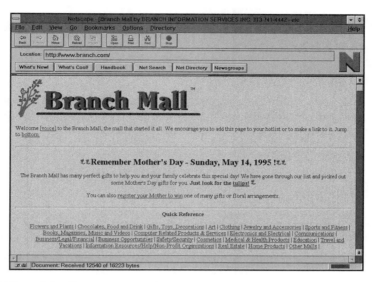

Figure 15.7. Branch Mall organizes its shops by topic to make them easy to find.

Here is a partial listing of Branch Mall's tenants:

```
Flowers and Plants
     Grant's Flowers
     A White Dove Flower and Gift Shop
     Flowers on Lexington
     Mayflower Florists, Inc - An FTD Florist
     Flowerstop - Your Online Fresh Flower Market
     Exotic Flowers of Hawaii
     Miniature Wine Grapevines of California - For Wine Lovers and Others
     Bonsai Boy of New York
Chocolates, Food and Drink
     Chocolate Strawberries by Sophisticated Chocolates
     Toucan Chocolates - Fine Chocolates
     Griffin Chocolates
     Goodies from Goodman - Food Gifts by Mail!
     Unique Concepts - Treat of the Month Club for Cats and Dogs
     Lobsternet - Live Maine Lobsters
     Lobster Direct - Fresh Nova Scotia lobster and lox overnight
     Food by Phone! Ann Arbor, Michigan
     Forest Hill Vineyard - Chardonnay
     Orfila Vineyards - Fine Wines and More
     American Homebrewers Association
     Hawaii's Best Espresso Company
     Todd & Holland - Tea Merchants
Art
     Muscovy Imports - Contemporary Russian Fine Art
     Gallery of Artists - Features Weekly Artwork
     Artworking - Gargoyles and Sculptures with a Byte
Gifts, Toys, Decorations
     The Grandparent's Book by Milton Kamen
```

```
Gift Connection - Corporate and Personal Gifts
Fabulous Flags from Ember'Glo Gifts
The USS Enterprise NCC-1701 Cutaway Poster
Discovery Toys
1950's Fun - The Original Burp Gun
Lazyciser - Easy to Use Exercise Device
The Commuter CoverUp (tm) - Protection Against Spills While Driving
The Golden Rose by Silvercraft
```

Grant's Flowers is one of Branch Mall's most successful tenants.

In December 1993, Larry Grant, a florist in Ann Arbor, Michigan, was approached by local cybermall operator Jon Zeeff about setting up shop on Zeeff's Branch Mall. Although Grant did not know much about the Internet, the florist's eyes lit up when Zeeff described the size of the market. "He told me there were 20 million users on the Internet," Grant recalls. "That's a lot of people."

Grant's Flowers gets two to eight orders each day from his Branch Mall cybershop and as many as 40 a day during holidays. On Mother's Day 1994, he says, he received 40 orders for Mother's Day bouquets through the Internet, versus 45 from the international FTD network. Internet orders are still a relatively small part of his total sales, but their importance is steadily growing.

"A lot of it is people looking to see what's out there," Grant says. "Once they visit they know where we're at. A consumer can shop 24 hours around the clock; orders come in 24 hours around the clock… We've changed from being a hometown business to an international business."

Interestingly, Grant does not have an Internet e-mail address; he does not need one. Branch's Zeeff compares the arrangement to advertising in a publication that you do not read. "You don't have to be a subscriber to advertise," he notes.

To shop at Grant's cyberstore, a customer clicks the Grant's Flowers menu item on the Branch Mall's home page and jumps to Grant's home page to browse through a listing of bouquets and floral arrangements (see Figure 15.7). A shopper who clicks order code BFL033, for example, sees a color photograph of a dozen red long-stemmed roses. Clicking the hyperlinked words Press here to order brings up an order screen on which the customer types his credit-card number, the delivery address, and how he wants the card to read. Clicking the Send button at the bottom of the form instantly transmits the order to Branch Mall's computer system, which in turn sends it by fax to Grant's real-world location.

Recently, Grant's success has prompted him to try his hand at other Internet business ventures. Last November, he launched a new service called Exotic Flowers of Hawaii, also on Branch Mall, to market flowers grown in Maui and typically receives two to three orders a week for these higher-ticket items. He says that the Hawaiian grower contacted him after learning of his success selling flowers on the Internet. Grant also has become an independent distributor for the Fuller Brush company and started selling subdistributorships for $14.95 a year. He has sold 119 of them so far.

Despite his growing involvement in cybersales, though, Grant has no plans to go online as an Internet user. "I'm not a computer person, so I really don't get into that stuff."

marketplaceMCI

Since we wrote our book last year, many major corporations that had been taking a wait-and-see approach toward Internet commerce have jumped into the retailing fray. IBM, for example, has gone into the Web hosting business, offering merchants high-speed leased lines and firewall security protection through its IBM Global Network. Tenants include NationsBank, PC Flowers, and Mecklermedia (publisher of *Internet World* magazine).

MCI, the international long-distance carrier, recently launched marketplaceMCI as part of its internetMCI initiative (`http://www.internetmci.com/`), shown in Figure 15.8. Tenants include Art Access, Covey Leadership Center, Damark Electronics, Doneckers, Dun & Bradstreet Information Services, FTP Software, Hammacher Schlemmer, Intercontinental Florist, The Mac Zone and The PC Zone, OfficeMax OnLine, Proxima, QUALCOMM (developers of the popular Eudora e-mail software), Reiter's Scientific & Professional Books, and Reveal Computer Products. Because MCI runs Netscape's SSL software on its server, marketplaceMCI merchants can offer their shoppers credit-card security—an advantage that many other Internet malls cannot.

Tip: Expect to pay a premium for renting space on a cybermall run by a big corporation like IBM or MCI. IBM charges $800 to $6,000 a month to host a merchant's Web site on its cybermall, and that does not include the cost of site creation. On the other hand, Big Blue offers lightning-fast T3 (44.7 megabits per second) connections and high-performance computing power.

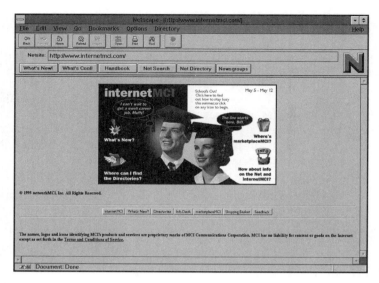

Figure 15.8. Major corporations such as MCI are opening cybermalls in an effort to crack the Internet market.

Should You Have a Home Page of Your Own?

These days, thousands of Internet users from college students to grandmothers are putting up personal home pages on the Web, filling them with family photos, samples of their favorite songs, and even short clips from home videos. If you decide to put up a home page for your business, we advise you to put up also a personal home page to tell potential customers about yourself. Don't hesitate on account of modesty. Remember: On the Internet, the more people know about you, the more willing they are to trust you—and buy from you, too.

> **Tip:** When you create your personal page, let your imagination run wild. A little silliness goes a long way on the Internet.

Rosalind's home page, shown in Figure 15.9, features a FAQ about her life, a list of favorite books and movies, a hyperlinked poem that she wrote, and a collection of family photos.

Figure 15.9. Rosalind's home page.

Dave's home page, shown in Figure 15.10, contains chapters from his books and pictures of his dogs.

Figure 15.10. Dave's home page.

The Future of Internet Retailing

What is the future of Internet retailing? Last year, we summed it up in three words: World Wide Web. Since then, Gopher, the text-based cataloguing software that was a popular Internet retailing platform back, has all but disappeared from view.

While only about 4,000,000 to 5,000,000 of the Internet's close to 30 million users have Web access today, that number is surging rapidly—making graphical Web access for the majority of Internet users a strong possibility within a year's time.

We recognize, of course, that savvy retailers operate in the present, not the future, so we strongly encourage businesses selling products on the Internet to offer multiple ways of distributing information to the Internet community. Although the Web is clearly the wave of the future, it's important for your company to provide the same information through text-based tools such as e-mail for those Internet users who lack access to graphical tools.

Looking ahead, however, we see Web-based storefronts and cybermalls as merely a harbinger of even better things to come. VRML—Virtual Reality Modeling Language—is on the way. It will enable shoppers to go beyond mere pointing and clicking so that they take guided tours of malls and catalogs instead. At the April 1995 Internet World show, Silicon Graphics, best known to the public for its role in creating the special-effects for the movie *Jurassic Park*, rolled out WebSpace, the first commercially available three-dimensional viewer for the World Wide Web. The WebSpace viewer is not itself a browser, but it works with popular Web browsers such as those from Netscape and Spyglass.

Our advice: Climb aboard and hang on for the ride!

GETTING PAID (SAFELY)

At this very moment, thousands of Internet shoppers are innocently typing their credit card numbers into e-mail messages and zapping them to online vendors, while others are entering their credit-card data into online forms at Internet cybermalls. Happy merchants, meanwhile, are ringing up sales in a virtual world.

But is it safe?

When we wrote our book last year, we contended that sending credit-card information through the Internet was an acceptable risk—but a significant risk just the same. In recent months, however, some important, new technological advances have emerged to make Internet commerce much safer. The biggest break-through occurred the day before the April Internet World show in San Jose, California when backers of two competing Internet security standards agreed to call a truce and to throw their support behind Terisa Systems, a Menlo Park, California, company that licenses and markets technologies that make secure transactions on the Internet possible. The new Terisa software, expected to be available by the time this book comes out, integrates both Enterprise Integration Technologies' Secure HTTP and Netscape's Secure Sockets Layer protocols—making it possible for almost anyone with a Web browser to order products and services safely.

In this chapter, we show you the Internet payment systems—from credit cards to digital cash—that exist today and explain the pros and cons of each. You will learn how to make your online store's transactions more secure and what questions to ask the vendors with whom you do business.

Danger Lurking in Every Wire

There is no shortage of places for merchants to peddle their wares on the Internet. The trouble is getting paid—safely, that is.

Unlike commercial online services such as CompuServe and Prodigy, the Internet is not a secure network, as recent incidents have shown all too plainly. Thieves and vandals who hang out on the network routinely hack their way into Internet-connected computers and filch passwords and other confidential data. For online merchants, that means the risk that precious customer credit-card data can be pilfered—a chilling prospect for buyers and sellers alike.

What makes the Internet so vulnerable to electronic mischief? Unlike centralized networks operated by commercial online services, the Internet is a decentralized system spread out across hundreds of thousands of computers worldwide. Each of these machines has its own passwords and security procedures, or lack thereof.

That's not all. One of the biggest stumbling blocks to commerce on the Internet is the lack of universally accepted legal tender—in other words, digital cash. Unlike the real world, where dollars, francs, lire, sterling, and even wampum beads are exchanged for goods and services, there are no equivalent "cyberbucks" that Internet shoppers can use to make their purchases. Moreover, the payment systems that do exist on the Internet are fraught with problems. Despite the slew of new security technologies to safeguard credit-card transactions, few cybermalls have implemented them. Setting up an account with an Internet merchant, meanwhile, remains troublesome and time-consuming.

Internet Payment Systems Today

Currently, business is transacted on the Internet in four main ways:

- Toll-free telephone numbers
- Shopping clubs
- Online credit-card entry
- Offline ordering

Many Internet merchants display their goods and services in cybermalls on the World Wide Web but post their toll-free numbers online so that Internet shoppers can order by telephone. One example is PC Flowers and Gifts, shown in

Figure 16.1, the Internet version of Prodigy's popular PC Flowers shopping service. Although not as convenient as enabling shoppers to type their credit-card information online, telephone ordering is more secure and more comfortable for the customer.

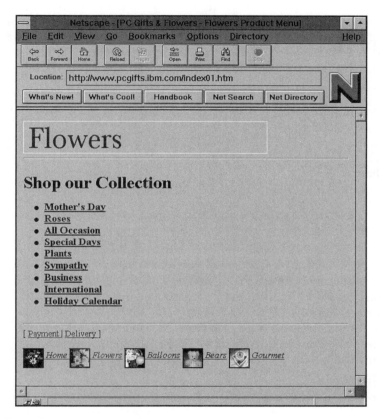

Figure 16.1. PC Flowers and Gifts, the Internet version of Prodigy's popular PC Flowers shopping service, takes orders via a toll-free telephone number because of the risk of credit-card theft on the Internet.

Another option is shopping clubs, which skirt the credit-card security issue in a different way. For example, Internet Shopping Network, a Web-based catalog retailer of computer hardware and software, requires new customers to join the club by submitting their credit-card information via fax. Purchases are charged to that card. A cybermall called Downtown Anywhere employs a Personal Payment system, which enables any shopper with a credit card and a touch-tone telephone to acquire a Personal Payment password that can be used for online purchases in Downtown Anywhere and at other participating sites. In seconds, information about online purchases of goods or services is transmitted by e-mail or fax to the merchants offering those products.

Many Internet merchants offer online order blanks for shoppers to type their credit- card numbers directly onto their Web sites—despite the risks involved. Even though server-based encryption programs such as Secure-HTTP protocol and Secure Sockets Layer are now available, relatively few storefronts or cybermalls have installed them. In the meantime, many merchants use on-the-fly security techniques such as PGP (Pretty Good Privacy), or they simply cross their fingers and take their chances. Another problem with credit cards is that they are not well suited to small transactions. On a 10-cent item, a bank or credit-card company would spend more money processing the transaction than the item costs.

Finally, some Internet merchants transact their sales offline by asking customers to send them checks. For example, some subscribers to Rosalind's electronic newsletter, Interactive Publishing Alert, pay by credit card, whereas others feel more comfortable paying by check. Checks work well for full-year $295 subscriptions, but it's a pain in the neck for her to handle $20 single-copy issues or $9.95 special supplements that way.

Battle of the Cards

Probably the most common way to pay for purchases on the Internet is by credit card, despite the safety risks involved. As we noted earlier, there are currently two main standards for credit-card security on the Internet—Secure Sockets Layer (SSL) and Secure HTTP (S-HTTP). Both protocols are based on public key encryption algorithms from RSA Data Security. SSL is a proprietary protocol that works only with the Netscape Navigator browser on cybermalls running Netscape's NetSite server software, whereas S-HTTP is an open protocol designed to work with any Mosaic-style browser.

Before the Terisa deal in April, the existence of two competing security systems raised potential interoperability problems because merchants and cybermall operators running NetSite could not guarantee the security of credit-card transactions initiated by shoppers using browsers other than Netscape's. Moreover, Netscape's SSL standard had gained an early lead by posting the SSL source code on its Web site and lining up the backing of big-name partners, including Apple Soft, Digital Equipment Corp., and MasterCard International. MCI, the international long-distance giant, gave SSL an extra boost by selecting it to provide data security for its new marketplaceMCI online shopping area (see Figure 16.2). According to Netscape, more than 3,000,000 people are already using SSL-enabled software.

S-HTTP, on the other hand, enjoys strong support from the Internet establishment—notably the Internet Engineering Task Force and the World Wide Web Consortium. In addition, Spry, Spyglass, Open Market, the CommerceNet consortium, and other key industry players have rallied behind the S-HTTP protocol and accused Netscape of developing its own proprietary protocol to maintain the market momentum generated by the widespread popularity of the Netscape browser.

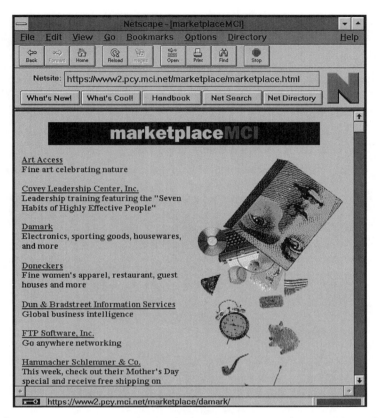

Figure 16.2. MCI chose Netscape's Secure Sockets Layer protocol to provide credit-card security for its new marketplaceMCI cybermall.

The good news for your company is that the two sides have come together to create a software standard that will accommodate both protocols. You don't have to risk placing your bet on the wrong horse.

Secure HTTP

With S-HTTP, an Internet shopper logs on to the network, accesses the merchant's Web site, and enters his credit-card number into his Web browser. S-HTTP encrypts the card number, and the encrypted file is transmitted to the merchant. Then S-HTTP decrypts the file and relays back to the browser to authenticate the shopper's digital signature. The transaction proceeds as soon as the signature is verified.

Tip: To see a demonstration of how S-HHTP works, check out the examples directory in CommerceNet's Web site (`http://www.commerce.net/information/examples/examples.html`). The first example shows how to use S-HTTP for online ordering. The second example shows how online checks are implemented. The third example shows how you can use S-HTTP to make information available only to those people who pay for it. CommerceNet's Web site is shown in Figure 16.3.

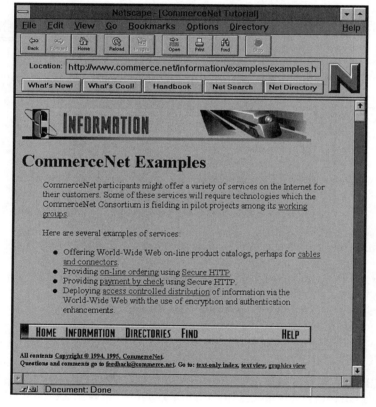

Figure 16.3. CommerceNet's Web site shows how S-HTTP makes credit-card ordering safer.

Secure Sockets Layer

With SSL, shown in Figure 16.4, an Internet shopper using the Netscape browser accesses the merchant's Web site, which must be running the NetSite server software—although this is soon to change—and enters his credit-card number. SSL encrypts the card number and sends the encrypted file to the merchant. The transaction proceeds as soon as SSL decrypts the file.

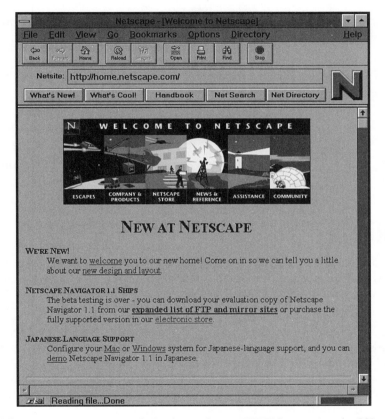

Figure 16.4. Netscape seized an early lead over Secure HTTP by posting the SSL source code on its Web site and lining up major backers.

Questions to Ask Your Vendors

Whether you're planning to rent space on a cybermall or to set up your own, it is important to find out the features of the security system and whether it's the best fit for your business.

You must decide what information needs to be protected—credit-card data, an electronic newsletter, market research statistics, and so on. How does that information enter the system? Who is going to need to see it? Explain to your vendor, in layman's terms, how you envision the information flow between you and your customer. Don't be bamboozled by jargon like "digital signature" and "public key cryptography."

Here are some questions that we recommend you ask your vendor:

- Can customers send me encrypted messages that only I can read?
- Can I send my customers encrypted messages that only they can read?
- Do I need both a secure browser and a secure server to send encrypted messages in both directions?
- If I use only a secure browser and not Secure HTTP, what additional security features am I not able to use?
- Does your software include a built-in solution for transferring credit-card data securely? Does this solution require the customer to use a secure browser?

Doing your homework ahead of time will save you lots of aggravation down the road.

The Rise of Digital Cash

An alternative to requiring customers to enter credit-card data on the Internet is digital cash—a system by which online shoppers swap real dollars for Internet scrip to pay for goods and services.

With digital cash—often called *e-cash*—you simply transfer money from your checking account to your digital cash account, converting real-world dollars or other currency into digital coins that you store on your hard drive. When you spend those coins on Internet goods or services, the transaction is credited to the merchant's account by the clearing bank and the proceeds are deposited into the merchant's bank account. Digital coins cannot be easily stolen or faked, which reduces the risk for both the buyer and seller.

Digital coins are perfect for handling micropayments, making it possible for all kinds of booklets, pamphlets, and other low-cost bits of information to be marketed worldwide.

"Famous writers and columnists might find it profitable to use this medium to write 10-cent and 20-cent articles," speculates Arnold Kling, formerly of the Federal Reserve, in an article about Internet banking recently posted on the Global

Network Navigator Internet site. "Nonfiction authors with only 20 pages of things to say would issue pithy $2 online pamphlets, rather than repetitive $20 books." Those small sums add up.

Let's take a look at four electronic cash systems vying to be top dollar:

- DigiCash
- First Virtual Holdings
- NetCash
- CyberCash

DigiCash

In May 1994, an Amsterdam-based company called DigiCash rolled out an electronic cash system that enables Internet users to pay for products and services without typing credit-card numbers or mailing checks. Founded by David Chaum, a bearded, ponytailed Los Angeles native who holds a doctorate in cryptography, DigiCash previously pioneered a similar system for automatic highway toll collection using what are known as smart cards.

Figure 16.5 shows the DigiCash system (http://www.digicash.com/). It is still in the testing phase, but approximately 500 customers and 25 online merchants around the world, including Encyclopedia Britannica and Massachusetts Institute of Technology, are already swapping play money for goods and services ranging from books to groceries. If the talks now underway between DigiCash and bankers are successful, real money will be able to be exchanged through the system.

"You can pay for access to a database, buy software or a newsletter by e-mail, play a computer game over the Net, receive $5 owed you by a friend, or just order a pizza," says Chaum, DigiCash's managing director. "The possibilities are truly unlimited."

Some of the online merchants accepting DigiCash money include

- Big Mac, which sells Monty Python scenes
- Bytown Electronic Marketplace, which offers electronic novelty items and has a Document Rack online
- Wane's Online Grocery Store
- MIT's IESL Bookstore
- The Weekly e-Mail, the electronic version of South Africa's *Weekly Mail and Guardian* newspaper

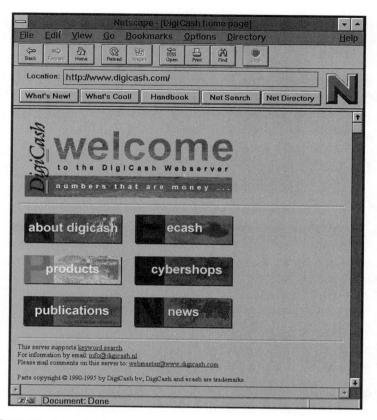

Figure 16.5. DigiCash, an Amsterdam-based electronic cash company, enables Internet shoppers to pay for products and services without typing credit-card numbers or mailing out checks.

Of the four e-cash systems, DigiCash most closely resembles real money. Here is how it works: Joe Sixpack downloads a free copy of the encryption software developed by DigiCash from any Web site that codes the company's electronic money. Then he goes to the DigiCash Bank (not a real place), where he deposits money using either a credit card or personal check and receives digital coins in exchange. When he sees a product on the Internet that he wants to buy, he e-mails his request to the bank, which checks Joe's digital signature against the signature on record.

Once the bank verifies that the signatures match, it replaces Joe's signature with the bank's signature, authorizes the transaction, and returns the money to Joe.

Joe sends the e-cash to an Internet merchant, which accepts the digital money because it has the bank's seal of approval.

Like real-world cash, DigiCash coins possess another important feature—anonymity. Because the merchant sees only the bank's signature and not Joe's, Joe remains anonymous throughout the entire process, enabling Joe to purchase anything he wants without fear of embarrassment.

Interestingly, the DigiCash system is not restricted to the Internet. In February 1995, DigiCash announced that it was nearing completion of a technology that enables e-cash to be used on a smart card, which are popular in Europe, where many currencies coexist. The technology, code-named Blue, uses a low-cost chip that takes advantage of DigiCash's encryption technology.

Of course, the DigiCash system is by no means foolproof. As with credit cards, it is possible for someone to steal your digital encryption key and use it for purchases that you might not find out about until it is too late.

First Virtual Holdings

Whereas DigiCash is experimenting with Internet money, First Virtual Holdings is pioneering Internet credit.

At First Virtual (`http://www.fv.com`), shown in Figure 16.6, Internet shoppers access the First Virtual Web server and set up an account by giving First Virtual their credit-card number. Instead of getting cyberbucks as they do with DigiCash, shoppers get online accounts. When a shopper sees something he wants to buy, he simply gives his account number to the merchant by typing it into the First Virtual server. Unlike DigiCash, there is no software to download and install.

The merchant, who pays First Virtual a $10 registration fee plus a 2% commission on each sale, ships the product to the customer. Every week, the merchant supplies a list of sales to First Virtual, which, in turn, sends e-mail to the customer confirming the order.

If the buyer wants to keep the product, he notifies First Virtual, which charges it to his credit card. If he decides to return it, no money changes hands.

To be sure, this system entails some serious drawbacks for participating merchants—it requires the seller to ship a product and trust the buyer to pay for it. Although First Virtual says that it will close the accounts of shoppers who consistently return products, the burden is clearly on the merchant.

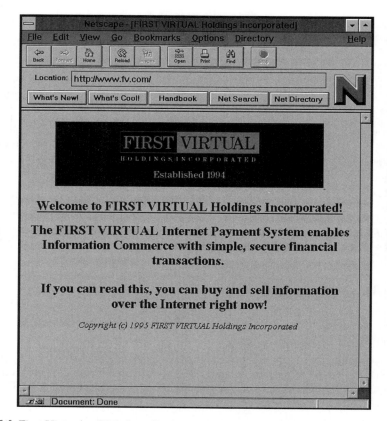

Figure 16.6. First Virtual, a Web-based cybermall that sells electronic information products, is pioneering Internet credit.

Another drawback is that the system is available only to vendors of information, not tangible goods. Although this fits well with the Internet's current demographic profile, less computer-savvy buyers who now are making their presence felt in cyberspace want products they can see and feel. The system also requires a large volume of e-mail. A buyer and seller cannot meet in real time and exchange cash for goods. Instead, a bank must act as a go-between.

Despite its faults, First Virtual has something that DigiCash doesn't—a real bank as a partner. By teaming up with FirstUSA, First Virtual can handle real transactions, rather than run as an experiment with funny money.

Profile: If Mike Walsh had a dollar for every time he has been mentioned in the media, he would be a rich man.

Actually, Walsh, the owner of Internet Info, a market research firm in Falls Church, Virginia, is not doing too badly—although not because of the lists of commercial domain names he peddles for $10 apiece on Internet cybermalls like Open Market and First Virtual. "Sales on the Internet have been insignificant," Walsh says, "but the contacts I made have been tremendous. Requests for consulting work have been more than I can handle."

Walsh's experience typifies that of many entrepreneurs trying to peddle information on the Internet—tons of publicity, yet relatively little in the way of direct sales.

"I continue to get sales from both the Open Market and First Virtual systems—more than I expected," Walsh says. "I also get a lot of calls from people who didn't want to put up with the mechanics of the purchasing process, but I suspect that my sales would be ten times higher if people felt confident and familiar with entering their credit card information into the system."

NetCash

Yet another digital cash experiment is NetCash, the Internet's answer to travelers' checks. The oldest of the payment systems profiled in this chapter, NetCash has been up and running via e-mail since May, 1994.

NetCash (`http://www.netbank.com/~netcash/`) was developed by Bob Houston, president of Software Technologies in Germantown, Maryland, and is both easy to use and fairly secure. It is shown in Figure 16.7.

To use NetCash, an Internet shopper enters his checking account or credit card number into an on-screen form and e-mails it to the NetCash system. This entitles the buyer to buy electronic coupons from NetCash for their face value plus a 2% commission. Each coupon is marked with a serial number.

Then the shopper browses NetCash's merchant list. Currently, shoppers must do this by e-mail, although soon they will be able to use a Web site. The shopper selects a product and sends the NetCash coupon to the merchant. The merchant redeems the coupon at the NetCash NetBank—a computer program, not a physical location—and NetCash takes 2% off the top as its fee. Currently, NetCash's most active merchant is *Boardwatch* magazine, which sells subscriptions. Other NetCash merchants include software companies and music and video stores.

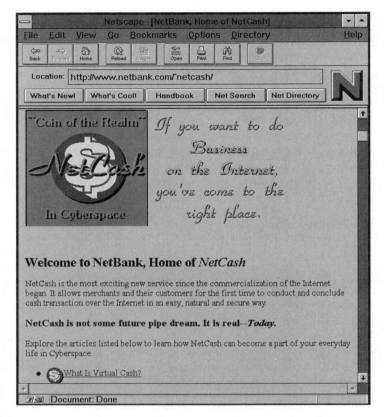

Figure 16.7. NetCash, which enables shoppers to purchase goods and services using electronic coupons, is the Internet's answer to travelers' checks.

Because there is no minimum transaction fee, the NetCash system is ideal for small sales. Because the system is not totally secure, though, NetCash is not such an ideal way to sell bigger-ticket items. In fact, NetCash places a $100 ceiling on vendors' offerings. "We prefer people to use existing systems for larger transaction items," Houston says. "We don't want them buying houses or cars online. One hundred dollars is the limit on any one item."

Despite the drawbacks of the low ceiling and lack of total security, the fact is that NetCash is up and running now—handling real transactions and helping Internet merchants make money. Houston won't release sales figures, but he says that several thousand people have registered to shop on the system.

Unlike First Virtual, NetCash vendors can sell tangible products, not just electronic information. Users can have products shipped by postal mail. They can also order by telephone so long as they give their NetCash serial number to the merchant. There is no minimum transaction.

CyberCash

Whereas many companies are creating cash substitutes that can be passed across the Internet, CyberCash is working on a way to enable Internet consumers to use something that they already think of as money—their credit cards. Although not exactly digital cash, CyberCash works much like a money order, guaranteeing payment to the merchant before the goods are shipped.

CyberCash (http://www.cybercash.com), launched in August, 1994, by Bill Melton and Dan Lynch, comes close to providing a secure solution for sending credit-card information across the Internet. The Reston, Virginia, company has teamed up with encryption experts Enterprise Integration Technologies, Trusted Information Systems, and RSA Data Security to create a way to encode credit-card data so that it can be sent through cyberspace safe from hackers (see Figure 16.8). Instead of acting as a bank that exchanges offline money for cash that can be spent online, CyberCash acts as an Internet postal service.

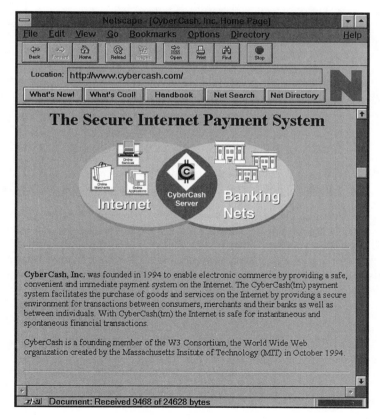

Figure 16.8. CyberCash provides a relatively secure way for Internet shoppers to use credit cards on the network.

To use CyberCash, a consumer downloads the free, graphical CyberCash interface, views the merchandise online, and hits the CyberCash Pay button. This automatically notifies the merchant to send an online invoice to the consumer, who fills in his name and credit-card information on the order blank. The credit-card information is encrypted and sent to the merchant, who in turn sends the invoice and identification information to the CyberCash server.

When this information hits the server, the CyberCash computer sends a standard credit card authorization to the merchant's bank and forwards the response to the merchant. The merchant ships the product or service. The entire process is conducted quickly and with little cost to the buyer—CyberCash compares it to the cost of a postage stamp. Processing fees are in line with those of systems now in place.

CyberCash's advantage to Internet shoppers is that it is cheap and easy to use. Buyers do not have to set up special accounts with a bank or with CyberCash as they do with NetCash; they just type credit-card data. The main advantage to the merchant is that payment is guaranteed before any product is shipped, unlike the First Virtual system. In theory, merchants can use the CyberCash system to sell any product online that they could offline—they are not restricted to nonphysical goods or services under $100.

The main drawback to the system is that it is still in the trial stage and has not yet proved its worth. CyberCash signed a deal with Wells Fargo Bank of San Francisco last December, enabling merchants with accounts at Wells Fargo to sell their products through the system. Merchants with other banks, however, cannot. To date, only a handful of merchants are participating in the test. A release date has not been announced, but the system is expected to be ready within the next few months. Another, minor disadvantage is that buyers must have credit cards, although most Internet consumers presumably have them or they probably could not have opened an online account.

The CyberCash system is expanding into other areas as well. For example, there are CyberCash accounts for organizations, with which an individual uses the organization's key to conduct a transaction. There are also electronic cash payments, which enable merchants to sell products that are too inexpensive to process cost-effectively, such as searchable databases.

The Future of Internet Payment Systems

As you read this chapter, you might have wondered which payment system—credit cards or digital cash—will ultimately emerge the winner. We believe that the storefronts and cybermalls of the future will accept both forms of payment, just as most real-world stores accept both credit cards and paper money. Recognize, too, that the four digital cash systems profiled in this chapter each have their limitations. In the end, none of them may emerge as the Internet's answer to universally accepted legal tender. It is also possible that all four systems will coexist in the future—together with shopping clubs and offline payment methods such as toll-free telephone ordering and checks sent by postal mail.

The key for Internet merchants is to show online shoppers that they have a choice in how they pay—a choice that is convenient, secure, and suited to their individual needs.

Bringing The Internet In-House

MINING FOR BUSINESS INFORMATION

What's the fastest growing city in the Pacific Northwest?

Which is the hottest foreign market for fax machines?

How many shares of stock have the officers and directors of Sun Microsystems sold this year?

Gathering up-to-the-minute market intelligence is vital for any business, and businesspeople hooked into the Internet know that it's available through the network—for free—any time they want it. Unlike commercial online services and database providers that charge as much as $200 an hour to tap into specialized business and financial databases, you can use the Internet to search and retrieve millions of files from libraries, universities, and government agencies worldwide for nothing more than the cost of an Internet account.

Of course, you don't get something for nothing. Finding information on the Internet is akin to finding a needle in a field of haystacks. Another problem is information overload; there's so much available on the Internet that trying to keep track of it can be overwhelming, especially if you're new to the network. And, although the Internet offers unparalleled access to government data, library card catalogs, and university research, many of the best sources of business information are still available only from commercial services such as Dialog, Mead Data Central, and CompuServe. If you're looking for real-time stock quotes or full-text articles from The Wall Street Journal, there's nowhere else to get them except Dow Jones News/Retrieval.

The good news is that there's more and more business and financial information becoming available on the Internet every day, and the Internet tools required to find it are becoming much easier to use. Another plus is that many leading commercial services are beginning to provide gateways for Internet users; you still have to pay to access their information but this way, you don't have to log on and off every time you want to search a database on CompuServe, Nexis, or Newsnet.

In this chapter, we teach you the basics of finding information on the Internet, searching through various Internet databases for information that can help your company grow and prosper. You'll get an overview of the government, university, business, and financial databases that can be accessed through the Internet—*Commerce Business Daily*, the Federal Register, the Library of Congress catalog, the U.S. Department of Commerce's Economic Bulletin Board, and many more—and learn the fastest and easiest ways to use them. We also revisit some of the Internet tools first introduced in Chapters 5, "Communications Tools," 6, "Marketing Tools," and 7, "Research Tools," including ftp, telnet, Gopher, Veronica, WAIS, and the World Wide Web.

Infomania on the Internet

Until online databases became popular, up-to-date business and financial information was difficult to find and frustratingly slow to retrieve. Gathering government export statistics, for example, often meant trekking to far-away libraries and sifting through huge volumes filled with tiny print. Compiling postal mailing lists required manually combing obscure trade association directories and other hard-to-find books. Doing market research to find out which part of the country buys the most cellular phones or which company is expected to emerge as the leader in the global aerospace industry by the year 2000 could take weeks—not to mention dozens of expensive long-distance phone calls.

These days, all you need is a computer and a modem to instantly access the kind of business and financial information once available only to Wall Street professionals and Fortune 500 companies. With ready access to everything from the number of chocolate truffles consumed in Peoria, Illinois, to the number of satellite dishes hooked up to households in Singapore, you can quickly and easily target new markets and boost business with customers you already have. You also can find out about trademark availability, credit information, and sometimes, your competition's marketing plans.

The trouble is, getting information from commercial services can cost a lot of money, especially if you aren't a professional information-hunter and if you've never searched a database before. On the Internet, much of the same data is available for free—if you know where to look.

Bargain-Hunting on the Internet

Consider this scenario: Two companies send you fliers advertising fax paper. One company's paper is free if you drive to their shop, about two hours out of town, to pick it up. The other company is a toll-free phone call away, with overnight delivery, but charges $20 for the same product. That afternoon you bump into a colleague at a local cafe, and she tells you that the free fax paper is great, but the proprietor of the store is a bit forgetful, sometimes isn't in the shop, and doesn't stock a lot of the paper, so sometimes she drives out to get some, and it is a wasted drive. Which route would you take? Seemingly free? A fixed cost with no hassles?

The Internet is like the free fax paper store of this analogy: There's a lot of information available, but you have to figure out where it is, and even then, it might not be quite what you were hoping for. On the other hand, it's free, and when compared to the expense of major commercial business data services, that can seem quite appealing. Although the two databases may be identical, many online users, especially time-pressed entrepreneurs and executives, prefer to pay a commercial service in return for greater ease and convenience.

Blake Gumprecht, in his forward to *Internet Sources of Government Information*, an electronic guide to Internet information available from local, state, federal, and international government agencies, writes

> Internet resources are often more up-to-date than their paper counterparts.
> Frequently they can be searched by keyword. Sometimes they provide
> information simply not available in more traditional formats. A word of
> warning is necessary, though. Internet resources are constantly changing.
> What is available one minute may not be available the next. System ad-
> dresses, source directories, and file names are often changed without notice.
> Sometimes a remote system may be temporarily unavailable.

> **Tip:** You can obtain your own copy of the *Internet Sources of Government Information* by using your Gopher software to connect to `una.hh.lib.umich.edu` and selecting `Inetdirs`, then `All Guides`, and then `Government Information`.
>
> If you have access to the World Wide Web, here are two excellent options: Federal Government Information on the Internet at `http://www.wcs-online.com/usgovdoc` and the InfoMine of Government Information Resources at `http://lib-www.ucr.edu/govpub/`.

Here's another scenario: You're head of a major corporation and are curious about the assets of a competitor. Indeed, you're wondering whether it would make sense to buy the company outright. If you had access to a commercial service, you might click an "investment forum" icon and immediately be able to choose among S&P data, Disclosure II, Dun's Market Identifiers, and more. Instead, you figure it's a great opportunity to explore the Internet to see what information you can glean from the public networks. On the Internet, you can find the same information, but what are the tradeoffs? The first is immediately obvious: There's no centralized Internet information manager to tell you where to find the information. Worse, you realize that unlike paid commercial services, there's no guarantee that the computer holding the information will be available, and even if it is, no guarantee that the information is timely and accurate.

Fortunately, finding information on the Internet is easier than it may seem from our scenarios! We'll show you proven strategies for tracking down and finding information on the Internet with a minimum of time and trouble. But before we get there, we want to whet your appetite with a sample of Internet information—two business and financial databases available for free on the Internet that you would otherwise have to pay big money to access through a commercial online service.

EDGAR

One of the best financial freebies on the Internet today is brought to you by the Securities & Exchange Commission, the federal agency with which every publicly traded company files financial results on an annual and quarterly basis. The SEC recently started an experimental electronic data-gathering, analysis, and retrieval system known by its acronym: EDGAR. Sponsored by a grant from the National Science Foundation to the New York University School of Business, the EDGAR database makes records of all SEC-required corporate filings available to Internet users for free.

The EDGAR database is huge—and so is the demand for the information it contains. Carl Malamud, an NSF subcontractor and president of the Internet Multicasting Service, another participant in the project, estimates that roughly 14GB of data—the equivalent of 14,000,000 pages of information—were sent out in a single month. Over 32,000 documents from thousands of different companies are available, each with a digital signature to guarantee authenticity.

To get similar information on a commercial service such as CompuServe, you would have to access the service's Disclosure database and pay $11 per report plus connect-time charges. To be fair, EDGAR is still a new system, with considerably less historical data than Disclosure. Although the commercial database offers historical financial data dating back years, EDGAR today offers only 1994 and 1995 electronic filings that are publicly available. Financial reports by companies that don't file electronically and filings that aren't available to the general public cannot be accessed through EDGAR. And because the project is experimental, the data is provided as-is with no guarantee as to its accuracy.

Tip: Access EDGAR yourself: Send an e-mail message to `mail@town.hall.org` with the body of the message containing the single word HELP. On the Web? Try `http://edgar.stern.nyu.edu/EDGAR.html`.

State Department Travel Advisories

Thinking of scouting the local market for tractor parts in Algeria? Better check with the State Department first. You'll want to know how safe it is before you get on that plane.

The State Department's Travel Advisories database provides the full text of U.S. Department of State reports that provide travel information and travel advisories for countries around the world. Arranged by country, the files include current conditions, country descriptions, entry requirements, embassy and consulate locations, information about registration, medical facilities, drug penalties, crime, and more. They can also be searched by keyword.

Tip: You can connect directly to the State Department database of travel advisories by typing `gopher gopher.stolaf.edu` from your Internet access account, or entering `gopher.stolaf.edu` to your Gopher program directly, or use a Web browser to check out `http://www.stolaf.edu/network/travel-advisories.html`.

Exploring the Internet with a Map

Now that you're beginning to get an idea of the information that's out there, press ahead. When you prepare for any expedition, it's a good idea to take a map. Because the Internet isn't a centralized system, you can't type GO INDEX and see a list of databases pop up on your screen. And because new computer systems are hooking up to the Internet every day and bringing their databases along with them, there's no way of knowing exactly what information is on the Internet at any given moment. In fact, even Internet experts are continually stumbling on rich repositories of data they didn't know were there.

Fortunately, a number of excellent Internet books and directories are available as are a number of comprehensive online resources. One of the most useful we've found is *Internet Sources of Government Information* compiled by Blake Gumprecht, former documents librarian at Temple University in Philadelphia. The latest edition lists hundreds of different sources, two-thirds of which weren't listed in the first edition, along with their Internet locations. The guide is available for free: Use your Gopher software to connect to una.hh.lib.umich.edu and select Inetdirs, then All Guides, and then Government Information.

Web users will find the Federal Government Information on the Internet document at http://www.webvertising.com/usgovdoc and the InfoMine of Government Information Resources at http://lib-www.ucr.edu/govpub/ to be terrific starting points for exploring Web-based government resources.

> **Tip:** Check out the wide range of Frequently Asked Questions (FAQ) documents directly on gopher at sol.csd.unb.ca or on the Web at http://www.lib.ox.ac.uk/internet/news/faq/by_category.index.html.

Another useful guide is *Business Sources on the Net*, compiled by Leslie Haas, business reference librarian at Kent State University Libraries and Media Services, with assistance from information-hunters throughout the Internet. The BSN guide is organized by subject and includes sections on finance, economics, management, personnel, and statistics. Each section is a separate file available via anonymous ftp from ksuvxa.kent.edu in the /library directory. BSN is also available via gopher at refmac.kent.edu.

There's a guide called *Government Sources of Business and Economic Information on the Internet* by Terese Austin and Kim Tsang, available at a variety of sites including Sam Houston State University in Texas. You can obtain your own copy by pointing your gopher program to Niord.SHSU.edu. The guide lists many of the same databases included in Gumprecht's guide plus a valuable list of business-related mailing lists and newsgroups.

Check out the Economics Bulletin Board, run by the U.S. Department of Commerce, Office of Business Analysis, via a Web browser at `gopher://una.hh.lib.umich.edu/11/ebb`. (That's also a gopher address: connect via gopher to `una.hh.lib.umich.edu`).

Once you know the name and location of the database you're seeking, the next step is to log onto the Internet and find it. Fortunately, a number of excellent search and retrieval tools are available, from straightforward e-mail to menu-driven Gopher to the hypertext-based World Wide Web. In fact, many Internet information sources may be searched using any number of different tools, such as e-mail, telnet, ftp, gopher, or some combination thereof.

Stock-Picking with EDGAR

Suppose that you're trying to track down the latest quarterly financial report filed by Sun Microsystems. You've just read an article about the company in *The Wall Street Journal* and think that now might be a good time to invest. You don't want to call your stockbroker, however, before you've had a chance to analyze the company's latest financials.

It's a perfect time to try EDGAR, the free SEC database you learned about earlier in the chapter. EDGAR can be accessed several different ways—e-mail, ftp, Gopher, and the World Wide Web—depending on what's most convenient for you. Assuming that you're like many Internet users these days, and all you have is e-mail access to the network, you can simply send an e-mail message to `mail@town.hall.org` and type the words SEARCH EDGAR Sun Microsystems in the body of the message. Within a few minutes, the system will respond with the results of your query:

```
=> Search: EDGAR Sun Microsystems

Partial Result(s) of EDGAR search

SUN MICROSYSTEMS INC
    10-K        (09/27/1994)      651572 Bytes
  edgar/data/709519/0000891618-94-000198.txt

SUN MICROSYSTEMS INC
    10-Q        (02/08/1994)       58659 Bytes
  edgar/data/709519/0000891618-94-000031.txt

SUN MICROSYSTEMS INC
    10-Q        (02/15/1995)       55005 Bytes
  edgar/data/709519/0000891618-95-000086.txt

SUN MICROSYSTEMS INC
    10-Q        (05/09/1995)       52038 Bytes
  edgar/data/709519/0000891618-95-000248.txt
```

```
SUN MICROSYSTEMS INC
   10-Q         (05/10/1994)       44294 Bytes
   edgar/data/709519/0000891618-94-000111.txt

SUN MICROSYSTEMS INC
   10-Q         (11/15/1994)      409147 Bytes
   edgar/data/709519/0000891618-94-000234.txt

SUN MICROSYSTEMS INC
   10-Q/A       (02/22/1995)        9715 Bytes
   edgar/data/709519/0000891618-95-000097.txt

SUN MICROSYSTEMS INC
   8-A12G/A     (11/17/1994)       25110 Bytes
   edgar/data/709519/0000891618-94-000236.txt

SUN MICROSYSTEMS INC
   8-K  (01/09/1995)        7332 Bytes
   edgar/data/709519/0000891618-95-000003.txt

SUN MICROSYSTEMS INC
   8-K  (04/01/1994)        6566 Bytes
   edgar/data/709519/0000891618-94-000092.txt

SUN MICROSYSTEMS INC
   8-K  (04/07/1994)        6860 Bytes
   edgar/data/709519/0000891618-94-000095.txt

SUN MICROSYSTEMS INC
   DEF 14A      (09/21/1994)      203063 Bytes
   edgar/data/709519/0000891618-94-000196.txt

SUN MICROSYSTEMS INC
   S-8  (11/23/1994)       94819 Bytes
   edgar/data/709519/0000891618-94-000239.txt

SUN MICROSYSTEMS INC
   SC 13G       (02/10/1994)        6122 Bytes
   edgar/data/729057/0000729057-94-000076.txt

SUN MICROSYSTEMS INC
   SC 13G       (02/11/1994)       12283 Bytes
   edgar/data/732812/0000950150-94-000300.txt

SUN MICROSYSTEMS INC
   SC 13G       (11/08/1994)       13214 Bytes
   edgar/data/315066/0000315066-94-001757.txt

SUN MICROSYSTEMS INC
   SC 13G/A     (02/10/1995)       14593 Bytes
   edgar/data/315066/0000315066-95-002075.txt
```

```
SUN MICROSYSTEMS INC
   SC 13G/A    (02/14/1994)      43756 Bytes
   edgar/data/888002/0000888002-94-000087.txt

SUN MICROSYSTEMS INC
   SC 13G/A    (10/06/1994)       9963 Bytes
   edgar/data/709519/0000732812-94-000014.txt

Your message has been processed.

Server general info:

  - Commands are case-insensitive, files are case-sensitive.  Be aware of this.

  - The files available through this mail server are the same files
    that can be retrieved via anonymous ftp to town.hall.org.

  - If you are looking for information on EDGAR, issue the following
    command:

      For example:  send edgar/general.txt

  - "help" will yield a document with more info on how to use
    the server.

Mail Server finished.
```

You can see from the bottom of the message how to retrieve the various documents available, but what if you don't want to wait and would like to be able to search interactively? After all, when it comes to the stock market, time is money. One quick and easy way to get your hands on that filing is to access the EDGAR database using the World Wide Web, a software tool that enables you to work with a hypertext-based interface to a wide variety of Internet information resources. There are two ways to work with the Web: You can wander around until you find the information you seek or you can connect directly to the site you desire.

To access EDGAR's Web site directly, connect to your Internet access provider and use the open location or open URL option of your Web browser to enter http://edgar.stern.nyu.edu/EDGAR.html. You'll see the screen shown in Figure 17.1.

Selecting Get Corporate SEC Profiles takes you to the next page, where you can choose Company Search to look for information on Sun Microsystems. Dave entered Sun Microsystems to search EDGAR's Archives. A minute or two later, he was presented with a list of documents related to the company that were in the database. With a bit more research, he discovered that the quarterly financial results were called 10-Q filings, and he could extract quickly from the search results the data he needed, as shown in Figure 17.2.

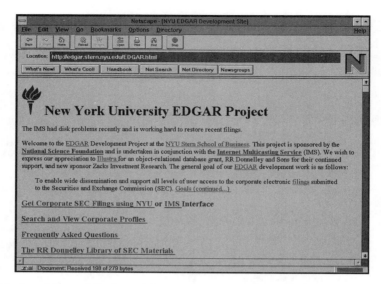

Figure 17.1. Securities and Exchange Commission data from the Internet via EDGAR.

Figure 17.2. Valuable information and insight about Sun Microsystems from SEC EDGAR Data.

Being a harried executive, you're actually too busy to wait for the results of a search. You've already done an e-mail query and found out the exact name of the file you seek. Through the FTP program, you can connect directly with the EDGAR database and extract the specific document. At your Internet account shell prompt, you connect by typing `ftp ftp.town.hall.org` and log in as anonymous using your electronic mail address as your password. (For example, Rosalind would use `resnick@harrison.win.net` as her password)

Once you've entered the database, you double-check the filename specified in the e-mail message from EDGAR and see that the file in question is called `/edgar/data1/709519/0000891618-94-000031.txt`. This means that you'll want to change to the `data1/709519` directory and then retrieve the specified file. We recommend cut and paste rather than trying to type it correctly!

In terms of the simple ftp interface, here's what you'll want to type and how it'll look on the screen:

```
ftp> cd edgar
250-
250- Welcome to the Internet EDGAR Dissemination project. Get the
250- file named general.txt for an introduction to this data archive.
250-
250-This project is funded by a grant from the National Science Foundation
250-to the New York University School of Business in conjunction with the
250-Internet Multicasting Service. Additional support for this project
250-has been provided by Sun Microsystems and UUNET Technologies.
250-
250-
250 CWD command successful.
ftp> cd data1/709519
250 CWD command successful.
ftp> get 0000891618-94-000031.txt
200 PORT command successful.
150 Opening ASCII mode data connection for 0000891618-94-000031.txt (58659 bytes ).
226 Transfer complete.
local: 0000891618-94-000031.txt remote: 0000891618-94-000031.txt
59816 bytes received in 10 seconds (5.7 Kbytes/s)
ftp> quit
221 Goodbye.
```

Suppose that you didn't know where the EDGAR Gopher site was located. All you knew was that you wanted to find financial data, and you had a hunch that it was on the Internet somewhere. That's where a system such as Lycos can prove invaluable. You can use Lycos to search by keyword through a huge database of Web, Gopher, and FTP archives. Here you could search for, say, `edgar` and sift through all the entries that match. You would have to do a little digging, but eventually, you would find what you're looking for. The other nice thing about Lycos and its brethren is that, once you select a choice from the menu, you're instantly whisked away to the Web, Gopher, or FTP server that holds the data you seek.

Figure 17.3 shows an example of what you might see on your screen if you used a different Web search system, Yahoo (`http://www.yahoo.com/`), to look for information on EDGAR and related SEC databases on the Web. In this case, we simply looked in, from the top, `Economy`, `Markets and Investments`, and `Stocks` for information.

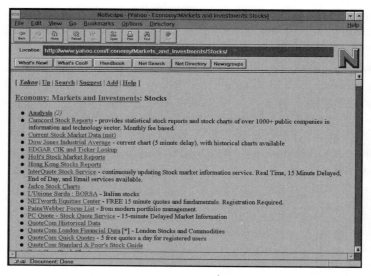

Figure 17.3. Stock related information on Yahoo.

Globe-Trotting with Telnet

Now that you've made a killing in the stock market (the Internet doesn't offer online brokerage services yet, though it will soon), let's look at how you can use the Internet to help your company crack overseas markets. The database we're talking about now is the U.S. Commerce Department's Economic Bulletin Board, an electronic warehouse containing thousands of files, more than 700 of them updated daily. The board offers information about current economic conditions, economic indicators, employment, monetary matters, and more in 20 general subject areas. One of the most valuable files is a list of trade leads from other countries—overseas purchasing requests for everything from footwear to computers.

Commercial users without Internet access dial the Economic Bulletin Board directly, at a cost of $45 a year plus per-minute connection charges. And that's not including the long-distance phone charges you'll pay if you live anywhere other than Washington, D.C.

That's where Internet users have an advantage. By accessing the bulletin board through the Internet, you can log on for free and download a wide variety of files without incurring a single charge. The Internet access tool that you use to do this is called *telnet*. To use telnet, connect to your local Internet account and then enter the electronic address of the computer you seek. The main U.S. Commerce Department's Economic Bulletin Board computer is called `ebb.stat-usa.gov`, so the command you would enter is `telnet ebb.stat-usa.gov`. Once you log in as `guest`, you can use the bulletin board to select menu items and download files as if you had dialed it directly.

Suppose that your company makes and distributes personal computers and peripherals. You've heard that demand for computers is exploding in Latin America, and you're looking for some sales leads. You log onto your Internet account, type telnet ebb.stat-usa.gov at the prompt and log into the Economic Bulletin Board as guest.

Here's what you'll see on your screen:

```
WELCOME TO THE ECONOMIC BULLETIN BOARD

                    THE ECONOMIC BULLETIN BOARD (R)
                               of the
                    UNITED STATES DEPARTMENT OF COMMERCE

                       RONALD H. BROWN, Secretary

          Operated by STAT-USA   | Data lines: 300/1200/2400 202-482-3870
                                  |              9600 bps       202-482-2584
    Director:          Ken Rogers |             14,400 bps      202-482-2167
    EBB Manager:   Forrest Williams| Telnet access:          ebb.stat-usa.gov
    System Operators:  Bruce Guthrie| Orders and info:         202-482-1986
                      Richard Brace | Fax number:              202-482-2164

  The Economic Bulletin Board is a registered Trademark of the Dept. of Commerce

            Subscribers:  use your account number as your User ID
            Nonsubscribers:     please use GUEST as your User ID

User ID? guest

TBBS Welcomes GUEST
Your last time on was 06/13/95 09:06
You are authorized 20 mins this call

                    IT'S OUR BIRTHDAY BUT
                    YOU GET THE GIFTS!

It's our 10th Anniversary and we want you to help us celebrate!  Everyone's
invited!

          *   The ECONOMIC BULLETIN BOARD'S BIRTHDAY BASH *

             WHEN:  June 16, 1995; Midnight to Midnight
             WHAT:  FREE ACCESS to everyone!
             HOW :  Sign on with our special User ID and Password!
                       User ID  = tenth
                       Password = birthday

That's right - FREE ACCESS for one day only, June 16, 1995 when you use our
special access code.  This is our way of saying THANK YOU for sticking with
us for ten years.  We hope to be able to serve you for *at least* ten more.

                        - The staff of STAT-USA
```

```
June 9, 1995
Detailed Bank Credit data, BCDETAIL.EXE, from the Federal Reserve Board will
not be available until Monday at 10:30am.

************ IT'S OUR BIRTHDAY BUT ** YOU GET THE GIFTS! **************
We're celebrating our 10th Anniversary!  STAT-USA's Economic Bulletin Board (EBB
) has provided the latest economic information available from the federal govern
ment every day for the last ten years.  Call now and say, "HAPPY BIRTHDAY EBB,"
and you'll get 15 months of access for the price of 12.  This means an extra thr
ee months of access to over 5,000 files every day!  Hurry, this offer is for new
 subscribers only and ends June 30, 1995.  Call us at (202)482-1986.

ECONOMIC BULLETIN BOARD      Local time in Washington DC: 09:07 on 06/13/95
======== ======== =====      Connect time for this call: 00:00:32
        MAIN MENU            Port: 47    Speed: 9600
        ==== ====
<B>ulletins         View or list system bulletins
<F>iles             Download or search for files on system
<T>rade Promotion   Export promotion files and resources
<P>residential      Presidential Announcements (including US Budget)
<N>ews              New files and updates expected this week, news flashes
<R>egister          Sign up for EBB
<U>tilities         Set default download protocol, change keyword, etc
<C>omments          Send comments to EBB staff or read mail
<L>ogon again       Logon again using another userID

==><G>oodbye    <?>Help!!

Command:
```

Press F (for Files) at the command prompt to get into the files directory. Then download the bulls.exe file (the one containing the most recent trade leads) using your communications software. Once you've opened that self-extracting file, you can search for computer-related trade leads using the search command in your word-processing software.

You can also use *telnet* to get free legal information for your company. Suppose that, for example, you run a home business, and you've just released a new antivirus program that's selling like crazy on the local computer bulletin boards where you've uploaded it. One day, when you're online poking around, you notice another antivirus program. After downloading it and checking the code, you see some unsettling similarities between that program and the one you just wrote. You reach for the phone to call your lawyer, but then you put it down when you remember how much he charged you the last time you called.

Instead, you connect to your local Internet access provider and telnet to the Cornell Law School Legal Information Institute. You bone up on a little copyright law, so you won't waste time asking dumb questions that rack up big legal bills. While you're there, you might also want to dip into West Publishing Company's online legal directory; maybe there's an attorney who's better (and cheaper) than the one you're using now.

> **Tip:** Connect to the Cornell Law School through telnet by requesting
> the host `fatty.law.cornell.edu`. For example, from a dialup account,
> you could enter `telnet fatty.law.cornell.edu` to connect. Log in with
> `guest`. Alternatively, try visiting the list of Law School libraries via
> the World Wide Web at `http://www.yahoo.com/Law/Libraries/`.

Finding Your Way with WAIS

Another helpful tool for finding information on the Internet, albeit one that many
people find confusing, is Wide-Area Information Servers (WAIS). As do Gopher
and the Web, WAIS simplifies hunting for data sources on the Internet. However,
WAIS actually does the searching for you. Currently, more than 500 databases
are available through WAIS servers, including a fair amount of information on
business-related topics. Searches completed through WAIS are easy to work with,
because the program orders all matched documents based on the number of search
words that occur, putting the most relevant document on the top of the pile.

Here's what popped up when we did a keyword search for business on the WAIS
server at Thinking Machines Corporation. (Telnet to the system with `telnet`
`quake.think.com`, logging in as `wais`.):

```
SWAIS                                Search Results                         It
  #     Score      Source                     Title                       Lines
001:   [1000] (directory-of-se)  Health-Security-Act                        296
002:   [ 778] (directory-of-se)  ersa                                        55
003:   [ 667] (directory-of-se)  ANU-Australian-Economics                    99
004:   [ 667] (directory-of-se)  ANU-CAUT-Academics                          80
005:   [ 667] (directory-of-se)  ANU-CAUT-Projects                           84
006:   [ 667] (directory-of-se)  ANU-SSDA-Australian-Census                 106
007:   [ 667] (directory-of-se)  ANU-SSDA-Australian-Opinion                114
008:   [ 667] (directory-of-se)  ANU-SSDA-Australian-Studies                126
009:   [ 667] (directory-of-se)  ASK-SISY-Software-Information               34
010:   [ 667] (directory-of-se)  IAT-Documents                               33
011:   [ 667] (directory-of-se)  National-Performance-Review                 62
012:   [ 667] (directory-of-se)  academic_email_conf                         61
013:   [ 667] (directory-of-se)  agricultural-market-news                    23
014:   [ 667] (directory-of-se)  cerro-1                                     23
015:   [ 667] (directory-of-se)  journalism.periodicals                      58
016:   [ 667] (directory-of-se)  usda-csrs-pwd                               47
017:   [ 667] (directory-of-se)  world-factbook                              21
018:   [ 667] (directory-of-se)  wu-wien-phonebk                             20

<space> selects, arrows move, w for keywords, s for sources, ? for help
```

The way to think about WAIS is to imagine it as a database of databases. To use a metaphor, it's comparable to the library card catalog, which contains books specifying where other books can be found. Once you have searched it, you need to search a second time within the databases matched—the reference books—to actually find the information you seek.

Who's on First?

One of the biggest problems on the Internet is finding names and addresses. Even though a number of firms are compiling Internet "yellow" and "white pages," it's still easier to call somebody on the phone than search the network for an e-mail address. But what if you can't make that phone call? Perhaps the person you're trying to reach lives in another country, many time zones away, a place where a long-distance phone call would be time-consuming and expensive.

Fortunately, there's a Gopher site at the Texas Tech University Computer Science Department that might have just what you're looking for. Type `gopher gopher.cs.ttu.edu`, and you'll see a menu that looks like this.

```
-->    1.  Search Netfind for E-mail addresses <?>
       2.  Search Netfind for Internet Domain addresses <?>
       3.  Search for a Country's Top Level Internet Domain Code <?>
       4.  Verify Someone's Internet E-Mail Address <?>
       5.  Inter-Network E-mail From-To Information/
       6.  Country Specific E-Mail Information/
       7.  Netfind - (Internet-wide E-Mail address searches)/
       8.  Phone Books at Other Institutions/
       9.  USENET E-Mail Addresses/
      10.  WHOIS Gateway/
      11.  X.500 Gateway/
      12.  U.S. Zip Code Directory <?>
      13.  U.S. Postal Codes Directory <?>
      14.  U.S. Telephone Area Code Directory <?>
      15.  U.S. Geographical Information by City or Zip <?>
      16.  Local Times Throughout the World/
      17.  CIA World Factbook, 1993 edition <?>
      18.  World Telephone Area Code Directory/
      19.  Search US State Department Travel Advisories <?>
```

From there, you can access a wide variety of Internet tools and databases that can help you find the person you're looking for. The Texas Tech Gopher also contains some other nifty features. For example, it searches U.S. Postal Zip Codes plus telephone area codes in both the United States and overseas, separating foreign area codes by country instead of zone.

Alternatively, if you prefer the Web as your interface, you can connect to `http://www.yahoo.com/Reference/White_Pages/` and search through a variety of different online phone books.

Is Company X on the Internet?

One question that might pique your interest now and again is whether a particular firm is connected to the Internet. The best way to answer this is through a simple little program called *whois*, a program that can search for users, computers, or even tell you information about any hostname on the network.

Is Prentice-Hall on the Internet? The command you type to find out is `whois prentice-hall`, and here's what you would see on the screen:

```
Prentice-Hall Legal & Financial Services (NET-PHLFS)
   15 Columbus Circle
   New York, NY 10023

   Netname: PHLFS
   Netnumber: 165.160.0.0

   Coordinator:
      Sangiorgi, Adelaide  (AS18)  [No mailbox]
      212-373-7565

   Record last updated on 24-Jun-93.
```

That's not right, so we try again without the hyphen and have a completely different result.

```
Prentice Hall (PRENHALL-DOM)
   Route 9W
   Englewood Cliffs, NJ 07632

   Domain Name: PRENHALL.COM

   Administrative Contact:
      Reichlin, Seth  (SR146)  BOOKS@PRENHALL.COM
      (201) 592-2358
   Technical Contact, Zone Contact:
      Jenkins, Colin  (CJ2)  JENKINS@PRENHALL.COM
      (201) 461-7091

   Record last updated on 01-Sep-93.

   Domain servers in listed order:

   HYDRA.PRENTICE.COM          192.251.132.3
   NS.UU.NET                   137.39.1.3
```

As with many Internet services, it's always worth trying a slightly different tactic if your first attempt fails to yield the results you seek.

Another strategy for finding companies, particularly those that might be on the Web, is to try opening a URL that seems logical given the name of the firm. Most companies have servers that conform to the naming convention of `http://www.company-name.com/`, so to find Microsoft, for example, you could try `http://www.microsoft.com/`, or Specialized Bicycles with `http://www.specialized.com/`. Both of these companies are, in fact, on the Web at the addresses indicated.

> **Tip:** You can use *whois* to find out about one of the authors too: try `whois DT135`.

So Many Databases, So Little Time

Now that you've got a sense of how to search for free information on the Internet, it's time to find out what's out there for you and your company. As you might expect from a computer network that was spawned by the federal government, there's lots of government information available. Besides the SEC and the Commerce Department, government data available on the Internet includes information from the Census Bureau, the Patent Office, the Federal Deposit Insurance Corporation, the Federal Communications Commission, and the Bureau of Labor Statistics, just to name a few. State governments from New York to Michigan to California make their data available, too. More and more foreign governments and intergovernmental agencies are also making their information available to Internet users.

Gumprecht in his introduction to *Internet Sources of Government Information* writes

> Internet users can now access hundreds of sources of current government information from around the world—Census data, Supreme Court decisions, world health statistics, company financial reports, weather forecasts, United Nations information, daily White House press briefings and much more. You can now e-mail the President, and enactment by Congress last year of the Government Printing Office Electronic Information Access Improvement Act assures the U.S. government's role in distributing information electronically will increase. A variety of other proposals suggest that in the future, more and more information produced by state, local and international governmental organizations will also be available online, sometimes exclusively.

An excellent example of free enterprise at work, entrepreneurs and universities have rushed in to offer government information on the network when the agencies have been slow to join the information highway directly. Indeed, if you scan back over some of the references cited earlier in this chapter, you'll notice how many of them "live" on nongovernment computer systems. It's also worth noting that private parties can offer government information in this way because the majority of government documents cannot be copyrighted by law.

What kind of information is available on the network? Here's a fascinating background document we recently retrieved from the Census Department's Gopher site at `gopher.census.gov`, the kind of information that can help any business decide what new markets to target for future products, offices, and campaigns.

pop, "Mother's Day Statistics" (5/14/95)

                    EMBARGOED UNTIL: MAY 14, 1995 (SUNDAY)

Public Information Office   CB95-89
301-457-2794
301-457-4067 (TDD)

Martin O'Connell (Demographics)
301-457-2416

Arlene Saluter
301-457-2465

Paul Zeisset (Economics)
301-457-4116

                    CENSUS BUREAU STATISTICS
                       ABOUT MOTHERS

    EMBARGOED UNTIL: MAY 14, 1995 (SUNDAY) - The Census Bureau
culled the following statistical facts from its many demographic
and economic reports on the occasion of Mother's Day 1995:

The numbers on mothers

    -    Of the estimated total of 103.4 million women 15 years of age and over
         in the United States in 1993, 73.9 million of them were mothers.

    -    As of 1993, these mothers had given birth to an average of 2.7 childre
         n in their lifetimes.

    -    The average age of the nation's mothers in 1993 was 48.1 years old.

    -    In 1993, mothers then living had given birth to 196 million persons o
         ut of a total population of 258 million.

Mothers are forever

    -    Mothering takes a little longer nowadays: 5.1 million sons and daught
         ers age 25 to 34 lived at home with their parents in 1993 compared wit
         h 2.0 million in 1970.

    -    Sons tended to prefer the comforts of home more than daughters. Of th
         e 25- to 34-year-olds living at home with their parents, 3.3 million w
         ere male; 1.8 million, female.

How we celebrate our mothers

    -    The value of manufacturers' shipments of Mother's Day greeting cards j
         umped from $80 million in 1987 to $148 million in 1992, an increase of
         84 percent across the 5-year period.

```
Where the mothers are

     -    Regionally, more mothers were living in the South (25.3 million) in 19
          93 than in any other region, while the fewest were in the Northeast (1
          4.7 million).

     -    The state with the highest number of mothers by far was California, wi
          th 8.6 million; New York was second with 5.2 million and Texas third,
          with 4.8 million.

Surrogate mothers

     -    Stay-at-home dads who care for children of their employed wives have d
          eclined as the economy picks up and the fathers return to full-time wo
          rk.  From a high of 20 percent in 1991, the percentage of children unde
          r five cared for by their homebound fathers fell to 16 percent in 1993.

     -    The number of preschool-age children of working women in organized day
          -care or nursery schools came to 30 percent in 1993—the highest perce
          ntage since the Census Bureau began tracking child-care arrangements i
          n the 1970s.

     -    Grandparents are assuming a larger role in the care of their children'
          s children.  In 1993, about 17 percent of these children under five we
          re being cared for by grandparents, either in the children's homes or
          at the grandparents' homes.

Sources:

     -    Unpublished data from the Fertility Statistics Branch, Population Divi
          sion, U.S. Census Bureau

     -    "Marital Status and Living Arrangements:  1993"

     -    "1992 Census of Manufactures Preliminary Industry Series:  Greeting Ca
          rds; Book-Binding; Printing Trade Services"

                              -X-
```

If you'd like to access the Census department data via the Web, use the Web address `http://www.census.gov/` to get there.

Universities throughout the world provide access to everything from library card catalogs to course catalogs and free software. The Library of Congress and The New York Public Library are among the hundreds of private libraries available through the network; you can't read or check out books through the network—yet—but being able to search the world's libraries for reference works can be an invaluable strategic resource.

And there's more! These days, hundreds of private companies, Internet access providers, and commercial online services are making business-oriented databases available to Internet users. The World, for example, provides a gateway to 15 commercial online services providers including CompuServe, Datastar, Delphi, Dialog, and Dow Jones News/Retrieval. Though you still have to pay to use them, you can access them for the cost of a local phone call without logging off to dial each one of them separately.

Here's what you would see if you choose `Commercial Services via the Internet` after using Gopher to connect to the World in Boston, Massachusetts (use `gopher world.world.com`):

```
Commercial Services via the Internet

  -->  1.   Information about the Commerical Services menu.
       2.   BRS (Bibliographic Retrieval Service) [McLean, VA] <TEL>
       3.   BioTechNet - +1 508 655 8282 <TEL>
       4.   Compuserve // via hermes <TEL>
       5.   Datapac information +1-800-267-6574 // via hermes <TEL>
       6.   Datastar <TEL>
       7.   Delphi <TEL>
       8.   Dialog [Palo Alto, CA] <TEL>
       9.   Dow Jones News/Retrieval [Princeton, NJ] <TEL>
      10.   EBSCONET <TEL>
      11.   LEXIS/NEXIS (Mead Data General) [Dayton, OH] <TEL>
      12.   Legi-Slate Info Service <TEL>
      13.   Newsnet // via hermes <TEL>
      14.   OCLC <TEL>
      15.   Research Library Information Network (RLIN) [Stanford, CA] <TEL>
      16.   WLN - Western Libraries Network (free til 1 Oct 1992) <TEL>
```

The Financial Economics Network (FEN), an Internet discussion group where subscribers swap information via e-mail about banking, accounting, stocks, bonds, options, small business, corporate finance, and emerging markets, delivers a daily report to its members that provides a market summary of 29 indices and averages. The free report includes the Dow Jones industrial average and the Standard & Poor's 500-stock index and a list of the most actively traded stocks and changes in foreign currency prices.

Tip: Join FEN yourself by sending mail to either editor Wayne Marr (`marrm@clemson.clemson.edu`) or John Trimble (`trimble@vancouver.wsu.edu`).

Microsoft Corporation last year debuted a public database containing financial information about the company, enabling Internet users to download free of charge Microsoft's 10-K annual and 10-Q quarterly reports and recent press releases. Bell Atlantic has done the same. You can connect to these services through the Web or Gopher at `microsoft.com` and `bell-atl.com`. Curious about whether your favorite firm has information publicly available? Use whois to see whether they're on the network and then try connecting to their site with a couple of different tools: For ftp access, try `ftp.`*`their domain name`*, for Gopher, try `gopher.`*`their domain name`* or just connect to their server directly, and for the World Wide Web, try URL `http://www.`*`domain name`*`.com/`, as shown previously.

For example, here's how you could search for public information that's available from Cisco Systems: Step one would be to log in to your Internet access account and type `whois cisco`. Whois reveals that the company has a registered domain name of `cisco.com`. Armed with that information, you could explore what information is available by entering `ftp cisco.com` and `ftp ftp.cisco.com` to see whether either lets anonymous users in—log in with `anonymous`. Use Gopher with `gopher cisco.com` or `gopher gopher.cisco.com`; or even try connecting to a Web server by using the generic URL `http://www.cisco.com`. There's no guarantee it will work, of course, but you might find out that the company has a variety of information available to the public through ftp and the Web.

Business Databases on the Internet

To help you get started, we've compiled a list of business-oriented databases available for free on Internet-connected computers. Many of them are listed in Gumprecht's guide; others come from recent postings on Net-happenings, the Internet mailing list and Usenet group devoted to spreading the word about new Internet resources; and still others are those we stumbled across in various searches, discussions, and articles in the media. As a rule of thumb, we encourage you to skim any Internet-related article you might come across. You never know what you'll find!

Reference

FedWorld: National Technical Information Service system provides access to more than 100 U.S. government computer bulletin boards, many of them previously accessible only by modem. Also includes full text of select U.S. government publications, statistical files, federal job lists, satellite images, and more. The system often is difficult to access because the number of available connections is limited. Connect with `telnet fedworld.gov`. The full text of select documents is also available from FedWorld's FTP archive. Try `ftp ftp.fedworld.gov` with user `anonymous` and your e-mail address as the password. Finally, this is also a great World Wide Web site at `http://www.fedworld.gov/`.

Library of Congress Information System: Provides access to the Library of Congress online catalog, U.S. government copyright files, databases containing current information about federal legislation and foreign law, a catalog of sources available in Braille or audio format, a national directory of organizations, and more. Connect with `telnet locis.loc.gov` or visit `http://www.loc.gov/`.

Library of Congress Marvel: One-stop source for a multitude of government material taken from a variety of sources: census data, Congressional information, White House documents, crime statistics, State Department reports, and more. You can use `gopher marvel.loc.gov`, `gopher://marvel.loc.gov/`, or `telnet marvel.loc.gov` (login as `marvel` if you telnet).

National Trade Data Bank: Comprehensive business and economic site on the Internet. More than 300,000 documents and more than 130 information programs from 20 federal sources, including the Department of Commerce Foreign Trader's Index, the Export Yellow Pages, the Trade Opportunities Program, and Market Research Reports. Other agencies will also release data, including the White House and the Departments of State, Treasury, Defense, Agriculture, Labor, Transportation, and Energy. Other major sources of information include the Central Intelligence Agency, the U.S. International Trade Commission, the Export-Import Bank of the U.S., the Federal Reserve Board, the Overseas Private Investment Corporation, the Office of the U.S. Trade Representative, the U.S. Trade and Development Agency, the U.S. Agency for International Development, the U.S. Small Business Administration, and the Social Security Administration. Connect through three means: `ftp ftp.stat-usa.gov`, `gopher.stat-usa.gov`, or `http://www.stat-usa.gov/` from a Web browser.

SunSITE Archives: University of North Carolina system is the best first source for the full text of important new government reports. Also provides access to White House documents, NATO information, North Carolina Supreme Court decisions, full text of the North American Free Trade Agreement, and much more. Use `http://sunsite.unc.edu/`, `gopher sunsite.unc.edu`, or `telnet sunsite.unc.edu` with the login of `gopher`. Whichever way you use, choose `worlds of sunsite` to get started.

U.S. Government Gophers: Provides one-stop access to nearly 100 U.S. government Gopher systems. Connect with your favorite gopher client program to `gopher peg.cwis.uci.edu` and then navigate through `individuals`, `information sources`, `cjboyer`, `gophers`, and finally to `United States government gophers`.

U.S. Government Publications Index: Provides keyword access to citations for U.S. government publications issued through the Government Printing Office since 1976. Connect using the main system of the Colorado Alliance of Research Libraries (CARL) with telnet by typing `telnet database.carl.org` and then choosing `carl systems library catalogs`, `carl systems libraries - western u.s.`, `carl`, `library catalogs`, `government publications`.

Zip Codes: Database of U.S. zip codes, searchable by keyword. The data is made available through the University of Oregon for Gopher and telnet access. Connect through `gopher gopher.uoregon.edu` and then choose `Desktop Reference, Geographic and Travel Information`. To access the data through telnet, type `telnet gopher.uoregon.edu` and log in as `gopher`. Alternatively, go directly to the U.S. Postal Service with your Web browser at `http://www.usps.gov/ZIP4Form.html`.

Demographics and Market Research

Census Information: Provides one-stop access to a broad range of Bureau of the Census-compiled data through Rice University in Texas. Connect with `gopher riceinfo.rice.edu` and then choose `Information By Subject Area, Census`.

Census of Population and Housing: 1990 Census data available in text and Lotus 1-2-3 spreadsheet formats for U.S. cities, counties, metropolitan areas, states, and the nation, with comparisons from 1980. This information is housed at the University of Missouri. Access it by typing `gopher bigcat.missouri.edu` and then looking in `Reference and Information Center`. (For an archive of historical Pennsylvania Census data, see the listing for the "Economic Development Information Network" in the "Economics and Business section.") You also can get to the 1990 Census information at `http://www.census.gov/cdrom/lookup`.

Public Opinion Item Index: Though not government information, public opinion polls provide valuable insight into the American public view on a variety of topics, including views on the government, its officials, and policies. This University of North Carolina system enables users to search an archive of data from polls conducted by *USA Today*, Louis Harris, *The Atlanta Constitution,* and others. Get to it with `telnet uncvm1.oit.unc.edu` and then log in as `irss1` with the password `irss`. Once there, look in `IRSS` for the section labeled `Public Opinion Item Index`.

U.S. Department of Agriculture Economics and Statistics Gopher: USDA-Cornell University system provides access to statistics on a wide variety of agricultural topics—consumer food spending, milk and dairy sales, ozone levels, meat consumption, fertilizer use, and more. Most data can be downloaded in Lotus 1-2-3 format or as text. Connect with the command `gopher usda.mannlib.cornell.edu` or try `telnet usda.mannlib.cornell.edu` with the password `usda`. There's also a tremendous amount of USDA information on the Web at `http://www.yahoo.com/Government/Agencies/Department_of_Agriculture__USDA_/`.

Technology

High Performance Computing and Communications: An effort toward a National Information Infrastructure. This site offers the full text of the federal government's report on the proposed National Information Infrastructure, the formal name of what we know today as the `information highway`. Use gopher to connect at `gopher gopher.hpcc.gov` and then choose `HPCC-Toward a National Information Infrastructure`.

Another interesting paper is *Realizing the Information Future, The Internet and Beyond* which is available on the Web at `http://xerxes.nas.edu/1/nap/online/rtif`.

Information Infrastructure Task Force Gopher: Provides access to task force directories, press releases, calendars, committee reports, as well as the full text of speeches, documents, and select legislation relevant to the National Information Infrastructure. Connect with `gopher iitf.doc.gov`.

National Information Infrastructure Agenda: Full text of a Clinton administration report describing the role of government in promoting the development of the telecommunications and information infrastructure by the private sector. Again, use Gopher to find `gopher ace.esusda.gov` and then step through `Americans Communicating Electronically`, and `National Policy Issues` to find the information. Using the Web, you can also see this document—with graphics—at `http://sunsite.unc.edu/nii/NII-Table-of-Contents.html`.

Merit Network Information Center: The Michigan-based MERIT consortium provides information about the Internet, NSFNet, and MichNet, including General Accounting Office reports, Office of Management and Budget reports, National Research and Education Network activity, conference proceedings, newsletters, statistical reports, policy statements, user's guides, and more. Use `gopher nic.merit.edu` or `http://nic.merit.edu/`.

Economics and Business

Basic Guide to Exporting: Full text of a U.S. International Trade Administration introduction to exporting; use `gopher umslvma.umsl.edu` and then choose `the library, government information`.

Commerce Business Daily: Full text of the 10 most recent issues of the *Commerce Business Daily*, a U.S. government publication that invites private bids on projects proposed by federal agencies. You also can search the information here by keyword to find whether there are any bids invited for a specific product or service. Check it on the Web at `http://cos.gdb.org/repos/cbd/cbd-intro.html` or connect with `gopher cns.cscns.com` and select `Special-Commerce Business Daily`.

Country Reports on Economic Policy and Trade Practices: Full text of detailed U.S. Department of State reports describing the economic policy and trade practices of individual countries around the world. Connect to the University of Missouri at St. Louis `gopher umslvma.umsl.edu`, `The Library`, `Government Information`.

EconData: University of Maryland archive of economic time series statistics prepared by U.S. government agencies. Data from this site must be downloaded and reformatted on your own computer. They provide downloading instructions and tools. The path is `gopher info.umd.edu` and then `educational resources`, `economic data`. Through telnet: `telnet info.umd.edu`.

Economic Bulletin Board: The Department of Commerce offers easy access to thousands of data files, more than 700 of them updated daily. Includes information about current economic conditions, economic indicators, employment, foreign trade, monetary matters, and more in 20 general subject areas. Connect with `telnet ebb.stat-usa.gov` and log in as `guest` or use the University of Michigan Gopher server to connect at `gopher gopher.lib.umich.edu` and then `social sciences resources`, `economics`. Alternatively, you can use `gopher://una.hh.lib.umich.edu/11/ebb` from within your Web browser.

EDGAR: New York University continues with the Security and Exchange Commission to make a wide variety of stock and corporate information available to Internet users. Current data only encompasses information on companies that file reports electronically. Try `http://edgar.stern.nyu.edu/EDGAR.html` or `gopher vaxvmsx.babson.edu` and then look in `business resources`. Alternatively, use ftp—as shown earlier in this chapter—with `ftp town.hall.org` and a login of `anonymous` and your own e-mail address as the password.

Empowerment Zones and Enterprise Communities: This site provides information about a new government program to designate up to nine empowerment zones and 95 enterprise communities for the purpose of helping to create jobs and improve conditions in the nation's poorest urban neighborhoods and rural areas. Learn more at `gopher ace.esusda.gov` and then choose `americans communicating electronically`.

The Financial Economics Network (FEN): FEN is an Internet discussion group where subscribers swap information via e-mail on banking, accounting, stocks, bonds, options, small business, corporate finance, and emerging markets. FEN delivers Holt's Stock Market Reports, also by e-mail, to subscribers. The daily report provides a market summary of 29 indices and averages, including the Dow Jones industrial average and the Standard & Poor's 500-stock index. It also lists the most actively traded stocks and changes in foreign currency prices. To sign up, contact editor Wayne Marr (`marrm@clemson.clemson.edu`) or John Trimble (`trimble@vancouver.wsu.edu`).

General Agreement on Tariffs and Trade (GATT): Full text of the final version of the GATT agreement, incorporating all changes made at the Uruguay round of negotiations. An executive summary written by the U.S. trade representative is also available. Connect to gopher ace.esusda.gov and look in americans communicating electronically, national policy issues. There are two Web alternatives. Various GATT information and papers can be found in Norway, of all places, at http://ananse.irv.uit.no/trade_law/gatt/nav/toc.html, and you can find the documentation of the final Uruguay round of the talks (dated 24 May, 1994) at http://heiwww.unige.ch/gatt/final_act/.

Gross State Product Tables: U.S. Bureau of Economic Analysis tables estimating the value of goods and services for 61 industries in 50 states. Use gopher gopher.lib.umich.edu and then social sciences resources, economics (2/94) or connect with telnet una.hh.lib.umich.edu and log in as gopher.

Industry Profiles: Full text of a series of Small Business Administration reports that describe the trends and opportunities for small businesses in select industries. This one is at the University of Missouri, St. Louis. gopher umslvma.umsl.edu and then look in the library, government information, small business administration industry profiles. You can also visit the Small Business Administration itself directly on the World Wide Web, at http://www.sbaonline.sba.gov/.

International Business Practices: Full text of a Department of Commerce reference work that provides overviews of import regulations, free trade zones, foreign investment policy, intellectual property rights, tax laws, and more, for 117 countries. Try: gopher umslvma.umsl.edu the library, government information.

Labor News: Department of Labor bulletin board that provides access to labor statistics, daily news releases, OSHA information, abstracts of articles in the Monthly Labor Review, and more. Via telnet telnet fedworld.gov and then choose gateway system and connect to gov't systems.

LabStat: Bureau of Labor Statistics system that provides access to current and historical employment and unemployment data, occupational injury and illness rates, consumer and producer price index figures, as well as other labor and economic data. Only available through ftp directly from the Bureau at ftp stats.bls.gov, log in with user anonymous and your e-mail address as the password. Start with directory pub. This can also be accessed from a Web browser as ftp://stats.bls.gov/.

National Export Strategy: Full text of a report to Congress by the Trade Promotion Coordinating Committee outlining 60 actions designed to strengthen U.S. export promotion efforts. Available through ftp at ftp sunny.stat-usa.gov, log in as anonymous with your e-mail address as the password. Start in pub/export. Better yet, use your Web browser to visit http://sunny.stat-usa.gov/.

North American Free Trade Agreement: Full text of NAFTA and related documents, available through the World Wide Web at `http://www.nafta.net/naftagre.htm` or from two different Gopher sites: `gopher ace.esusda.gov` and then `americans communicating electronically, national policy issues (2/94)`, or if that doesn't seem to work, `gopher umslvma.umsl.edu, the library, government information`.

Occupational Outlook Handbook: Full text of a U.S. Department of Labor annual that provides detailed information about more than 300 occupations, including the nature of the work, working conditions, training and education requirements, job outlook, average salaries, and more. Connect with `gopher umslvma.umsl.edu` and then look in `the library, government information` or go directly by `gopher://marvel.loc.gov/11/federal/fedinfo/byagency/executive/labor/`.

Overseas Business Reports: Full text of U.S. International Trade Administration reports describing the economic and commercial climate in individual countries around the world. At the University of Missouri, St. Louis: `gopher umslvma.umsl.edu` and then `the library, government information`.

President Clinton's Economic Plan: Full text of A Vision of Change for America, a summary of the President's economic plan. Connect with Gopher at `gopher wiretap.spies.com` and then search in `government docs` for `clinton's economic plan`, or you can see it via Web at `gopher://wiretap.spies.com/11/Gov/Economic`.

Quote.com: Various sites offer stock information, but few are better and more interesting than this one. You can visit it at `http://www.quote.com/` but be warned that only a portion of the information it offers is available without charge.

Regional Economic Information System (REIS): This Department of Commerce system offers statistics on employment by industry, income and earnings by industry, and transfer payments for states and counties. Try `http://sunny.stat-usa.gov/` or `gopher sunny.stat-usa.gov` and then choose `economic conversion information, regional statistics`.

State Small Business Profiles: Full text of a series of Small Business Administration reports that provide statistical overviews of the economy in each of the 50 states, focusing on the small business sector. Connect via Web at `http://www.sbaonline.sba.gov/` or with `gopher umslvma.umsl.edu, the library, government information, small business administration state profiles`.

Uniform Commercial Code: Full text of the Uniform Commercial Code, including a keyword search system, available at Cornell University. Connect through telnet by typing `telnet www.law.cornell.edu` with the login `www`. It's also available directly, though the connection is a bit hit-or-miss: `http://www.law.cornell.edu/ucc/ucc.table.html`.

U.S. Industrial Outlook: The Department of Commerce annually examines recent trends and provides five-year projections for the top 350 industries in the United States. Connect with `gopher gopher.lib.umich.edu` and then look in `social sciences resources, economics, industrial outlook`. Alternatively, try `telnet una.hh.lib.umich.edu` with the login of `gopher` or visit the Department of Commerce at `http://www.doc.gov/`.

Government Regulation

Ambient Monitoring Technology Information Center: This Environmental Protection Agency system provides information and the full text of regulations concerning ambient air quality monitoring. Use `telnet ttnbbs.rtpnc.epa.gov` with the login of `amtic` or visit the EPA's beautiful Web site at `http://www.epa.gov/`.

Americans With Disabilities Act: The full text of the 1990 Americans with Disabilities Act is available through Gopher from the University of California at Santa Cruz. Connect with `gopher scilibx.ucsc.edu` and then look in `the library,` for `electronic books`. You can also find this at `gopher://wiretap.spies.com/00/Gov/disable.act`.

Clean Air Act Amendments Bulletin Board System: EPA system provides access to information relevant to 1990 Clean Air Act Amendments, including full text of the act. Connect `telnet ttnbbs.rtpnc.epa.gov` with the account `caaa`.

Clean Water Act: Full text of the Clean Water Act, as taken from the U.S. Regulatory Code. Use `gopher sunny.stat-usa.gov` and then search in `economic conversion information exchange, adjustment programs and laws`. Use Web `http://www.epa.gov/docs/great_lakes`.

Clearinghouse for Inventories/Emission Factors (CHIEF): This EPA system provides information about air emission inventories and emission factors and provides access to tools for estimating emissions of air pollutants and performing air emission inventories. Use `telnet ttnbbs.rtpnc.epa.gov` and then log in as `chief`.

Environmental Protection Agency: The EPA system provides access to a directory of environmental information resources, a database containing information about environmental regulations governing the closure of military bases, proposed new rules for the pulp and paper industry, pesticide regulatory information, and more. Use `gopher gopher.rtpnc.epa.gov` or Web to `http://www.epa.gov/`.

National Air Toxics Information Clearinghouse: EPA system provides access to a directory of government air toxics control officials, descriptions of regulatory programs, emissions guidelines and inventory data, and more. Connect with `telnet ttnbbs.rtpnc.epa.gov` and then log in as `natich`.

Food and Drug Administration Bulletin Board System: Full text of FDA news releases, enforcement reports, import alerts, drug and product approval lists, Federal Register summaries, agency publications, articles from FDA Consumer and more. Use `telnet fdabbs.fda.gov` with login `bbs` or use your Web browser to visit `http://www.fda.gov/`.

Food Labeling Information: This FDA database that provides information about new food labeling regulations and activities related to the Nutrition Labeling and Education Act. Use `gopher zeus.esusda.gov` and then look in `usda and other federal agency information` for `food labeling information`. An overview can be found at `http://www.fda.gov/hpage,food.html`.

Health Care Reform Information: Full text of the Clinton administration's health care reform proposal, a detailed section-by-section explanation of the Clinton plan, along with related reports and press releases. Connect with `http://sunsite.unc.edu/nhs/NHS-T-o-C.html` or look at `gopher ace.esusda.gov` and then look in `americans communicating electronically`, `national policy issues` for `health care reform agenda`.

Occupational Safety and Health Administration Regulations: Full text of current OSHA standards and regulations, as taken from the Federal Register and Code of Federal Regulations. Use your Web browser to connect to `http://www.osha.gov/` or gopher to: `gopher stellate.health.ufl.edu` then choose `OSHA`.

TOXNET: This system at the National Institutes of Health will allow you access to a database with information about the toxicology of hazardous chemicals. It's being built as we write this, and in the future is also expected to offer a variety of other databases, including the Toxic Chemical Release Inventory (TRI), the Registry of Toxic Effects of Chemical Substances (RTECS) and the Chemical Carcinogenesis Research Information System (CCRIS). Try connecting: `gopher tox.nlm.nih.gov`.

International Trade

Background Notes: Full text to a series of U.S. Department of State reports that provide brief overviews of the people, history, government, economy, and foreign relations of individual countries around the world. Use `gopher umslvma.umsl.edu` and then choose `the library` and `government information`.

Country Studies and Area Handbooks: Full text of select Army Area Handbooks, such as *Japan: A Country Study*, which present in-depth discussion of the political, economic, and social conditions of countries around the world. This is accessible through `gopher umslvma.umsl.edu`: choose `the library`, `government information`, and then `army area handbooks`.

Also available at `http://lcweb.loc.gov/homepage/country.html`.

International Organizations: Provides access to general information about more than two dozen major international organizations, from the Food and Agriculture Organization to the World Bank. Connect to the University of Vermont at `gopher mirna.together.uvm.edu` and then choose `united nations, UN organizations`. Even better, connect to an extensive database of United Nations-related information on the Web at `http://www.undcp.or.at/unlinks.html`.

State Department Travel Advisories: Full text to a series of U.S. Department of State reports that provide travel information and travel advisories for countries around the world. Arranged by country, files include current conditions, country descriptions, entry requirements, embassy and consulate locations, information about registration, medical facilities, drug penalties, crime, and more. Use `http://www.stolaf.edu/network/travel-advisories.html` or `gopher gopher.stolaf.edu` and then choose `internet resources, us-state-department-travel-advisories`.

World Bank Public Information Service: Full text of World Bank policy papers, environmental reports, project information documents, country economic reports, publications catalogs, and more. Try `http://www.worldbank.org/` or `gopher gopher.worldbank.org`.

Law

Code of Federal Regulations: Commercial systems enable users to browse the Code of Federal Regulations or search it by keyword. Access to the complete CFR is not yet available. The system places limits on the amount of information non-subscribers can retrieve, however. Use `gopher gopher.internet.com` and then choose `counterpoint publishing (2/94)` or `telnet gopher.internet.com` with the log in `gopher`. Finally, you can also try `gopher://gopher.counterpoint.com:2001/` from a Web browser.

Computer Law: Australian FTP archive includes a variety of files containing information on computers and the law, including the text of many U.S. state laws. Use `ftp sulaw.law.su.oz.au` and then log in as `anonymous` with your e-mail address as your password.

Copyright Information: The Library of Congress enables users to search a database of information about works registered since 1978 in the U.S. Copyright Office. Also includes files that provide general information about copyright. Connect at `telnet locis.loc.gov` or `http://www.loc.gov/`.

Cornell Law School Legal Information Institute: Uses the World Wide Web to search and retrieve information from numerous legal texts, including the U.S. Copyright Act, Supreme Court decisions, and the Uniform Commercial Code. Use Mosaic or another Web browser to connect with URL `http://www.law.cornell.edu/` or `telnet` `fatty.law.cornell.edu.`

Internet Patent News Service: List of all U.S. patents issued during the previous week, available by free subscription via electronic mail. To sign up or to find out more about the mailing list, send e-mail to `patents@world.std.com.`

Patent and Trademark Office Bulletin Board System: Provides access to Official Gazette notices, information about new patents, patent and trademark fee schedules, agency directories, full text of PTO news bulletins, press releases, brochures, and more. Use `telnet fedworld.gov` and then `gateway system, connect to gov't systems` or visit `http://www.uspto.gov/` or the sometimes easier to use `http://www.eds.com/patent.html.`

Patent Office Reform Panel Final Report: Full text of a U.S. Patent and Trademark Office report recommending that U.S. patent procedures be changed to follow policy held by most industrialized nations. Try `gopher wiretap.spies.com` and then look in `government docs.`

Supreme Court Decisions: High court decisions updated nightly and available through the World Wide Web. Use the URL `http://archive.orst.edu:9000/supreme-court` or check out `http://www.law.cornell.edu/supct/.`

Venable, Baetjer, Howard & Civiletti: Washington law firm specializing in information law. One of the first law firms in the country to offer a World Wide Web server. See what they have to offer the Internet with URL `http://venable.com/vbh.htm.`

Contrast that listing with the Web pages from Ice, Miller, Donadio & Ryan of Indianapolis (the legal representatives for one of the authors) at their Web site `http://www.imdr.com/imdr/.`

## CHAPTER 18

PROVIDING CUSTOMER SUPPORT

If you are selling a product or service, there are two basic ways to approach your customers—either as faceless folk who simply give you money or as unique individuals with problems, ideas, and a need for what you are selling. If you fall into the first camp, customer support probably is not a priority. If you genuinely care about the people who help you stay in business, however, the Internet can offer an unparalleled opportunity to build and strengthen your customer relationships. Through the Internet, you can offer customers easy access to your sales and development team, free updates and information sheets, even extra copies of documentation or technical notes—all with minimal fuss and cost.

By posting product and technical information on a newsgroup, a Gopher server, or a Web or FTP site, even the smallest company can stay in touch with customers and provide up-to-the-minute technical assistance without costly international telephone calls or overseas offices. Through the Internet, customers can ask questions, receive upgrades and bug fixes for their software programs, demonstrate performance problems to an online engineer, and offer ideas for future enhancements and future products—without ever leaving their offices or picking up the telephone.

It is no surprise that today hundreds of businesses offer customer support online. For many hardware and software vendors, high-tech hand-holding on the Internet is a logical addition to the dialup bulletin boards or forums they maintain on commercial online services such as CompuServe, America Online, and Prodigy. For example, Digital Equipment Corp., Sun Microsystems, Hewlett-Packard, Wingra Technology, and Silicon Graphics use the network to interact with customers. High-tech companies might seem a logical fit for the network, but even noncomputer-related businesses are starting to exploit the Internet for customer support. These companies include bookstores, newspapers, and even an underwear manufacturer.

At its simplest, the Internet offers companies the advantage of worldwide access to customers, but there's more. Through the Internet, companies can use search-and-navigation tools such as e-mail-based servers, WAIS, Veronica, and Gopher to provide customers access to information about products and other business information, or even a database of frequently asked questions and answers.

This chapter is designed to show you how a wide variety of companies—large and small—are using Internet tools to provide customers with cost-effective service and support. We also take a look at the costs involved in setting up a customer support site on the Internet and how you can integrate Internet support with the support that you already offer through telephones, faxes, and computer bulletin boards.

Evaluating Customer Support Options

Most companies today offer customer support in one of four ways—telephone, fax, postal mail, or a computer bulletin board—either through direct dial to the corporate office or through a commercial online service. Many companies rely on some combination of all four methods.

Each delivery method has its advantages and disadvantages. Telephone support, often via a toll-free number, gives the customer direct access to a live technician with whom he can discuss a problem until it is resolved. The disadvantage is that at a busy company, telephone support often results in busy signals, lengthy waits on hold, and a high degree of customer frustration.

Fax support, in which a customer writes up a short summary of the problem and faxes it to the customer service center, can take even longer than phone support to resolve a problem. It is less effective because the suggestion that the customer receives by fax might not solve his problem completely. Of course, postal mail is slower than either telephone or fax, although it is often a less costly way to provide documents or computer files that are not time-sensitive. Most software firms distribute application upgrades through postal delivery, for example—a strategy we consider later in this chapter.

By contrast, computer bulletin boards or forums on commercial online services can be an ideal customer service solution—especially for technology companies whose customers are knowledgeable about computing. By logging on to a computer bulletin board, a customer can tack up a note any time of day or night and receive a response within hours. Large companies such as Microsoft and IBM assign paid technical support staffers to answer questions on their forums on CompuServe and other commercial online services. Customers can go online to download software upgrades and bug fixes and to search technical documentation.

There are a number of disadvantages to opening a forum on a commercial service or launching a dialup BBS, however. Most significant is that the burden of dealing with the complexities of the technology is placed on the customer. (Just configuring a modem can be a significant obstacle for many customers.) Another problem with commercial services is that customers who are not subscribers to that service find themselves in limbo: Customers who don't subscribe to that particular service are left in the cold. Finally, dialup services—whether they rely on computers at the home office or through a commercial service—can be expensive to maintain. Many customers find it frustrating to pay to obtain a product and then have to pay extra to get things working properly.

The Internet, meanwhile, offers all the advantages of a computer bulletin board plus the convenience of offering a support strategy that integrates smoothly and seamlessly with the way your customers already do business. The Internet also offers the advantage of being accessible worldwide through a local phone call. Too, the Internet makes it easy for customers to communicate with you directly, offering advice and suggestions that can help improve your products and your bottom line. It's like having a 24-hour-a-day focus group consisting of your best, brightest, and most committed customers.

Providing technical support through the Internet can also be far less expensive than any of the other support options, particularly if a large volume of information is involved. In August 1993, Sun Microsystems, of Mountain View, California, started a program called SunSolve to answer its customers' technical questions through Internet e-mail and to distribute software fixes through the network. Previously, the company had relied on a toll-free telephone number for questions and a staff of technicians who would package, address, and mail CD-ROM updates to each customer.

Since SunSolve was introduced, use of the company's toll-free telephone support line has dropped by over 90%. At the same time, the company has cut its support costs by $1,000,000 a year and managed to offer more information to more customers and increase customer satisfaction—a critical gauge of any support strategy. Even better from a company perspective is that fewer staffers are now required to offer this higher level of support and service.

On the other hand, it's important to note that use of Sun's toll-free telephone number did not drop to zero. There are always cases in which getting support online is not a practical solution—for example, when your computer or modem is down. Remember that offering customer support on the Internet doesn't automatically enable you to pull the plug on your toll-free hotline or to scrap other customer support options. If nothing else, many customers—even computer owners—are not yet on the Internet, so it is vital to maintain telephone, fax, and postal mail support services as well. With the growing popularity of the Web, however, it may soon be possible to phase out your computer bulletin board in favor of a Web site.

Remember that the goal of any customer support system should be to make it easier for customers to get help, not simply to reduce time and trouble for your company. If your company benefits—and it should through proper use of the Internet—all the better. But don't make cutting costs the primary impetus for implementing changes to your customer support strategy.

Net Results: Why Internet Support Is Good Business

A growing number of companies are discovering another advantage to offering customer support through the Internet—it is excellent public relations. One example is small-time software developer InterCon Systems of Herndon, Virginia. InterCon Systems develops Internet software for PCs and Macs. Through its aggressive use of the Internet, the company has developed a worldwide reputation for providing top-notch customer support. Typically, InterCon developers spend several hours a week reading Usenet newsgroups covering computer-related topics. They respond to any posted query they can answer, regardless of whether it has anything to do with InterCon products.

Developer Amanda Walker, known around the office as the Net Goddess, has even begun to get fan mail from Internet users who rave about the calm, smart, and nontechnical way in which she pens her postings. One man liked Walker's style so much that he said that he wanted to read her description of how to boil an egg. The end result: new customers for InterCon's products.

Getting Feedback with E-Mail

Providing customer support through the Internet can be as simple as letting your customers contact you through e-mail. These days, many newspapers and magazines solicit letters to the editor via Internet e-mail. *The Boston Globe, The Sacramento Bee, The San Jose Mercury News, Business Week, The New Republic, Playboy,* and *Wired* are all on the Internet. Others use commercial online services, which Internet users can reach through gateways. Not only does this enable the publications to receive and publish reader letters more quickly, but it also eliminates the need to have them typed into the computer for layout. Moreover, by creating an Internet mail-server, the newspaper can automatically send each reader an acknowledgment of receipt at far less cost than stuffing an envelope and paying for postage.

To see how this works, consider the automatic message that *The Boston Globe* sends out in response to the e-mail it gets:

```
This is to confirm that your electronic mail message to The Boston Globe has bee
n received. Thanks for taking the time to write to us. Although we cannot respon
d individually to all the messages we receive, we encourage you to watch the app
ropriate spot in the paper if you have submitted a letter or question to a Globe
editorial department. For your reference, here are the other e-mail addresses at
The Globe:
   news@globe.com
        story ideas, suggestions
   circulation@globe.com
        circulation requests/problems, vacation stops, subscription info
   classified@globe.com
        information about placing a classified ad
   letter@globe.com
        letters to the editor (please include full name and address)
   voxbox@globe.com
        submissions to the Living section's "Voxbox" column
   ombud@globe.com
        comments on our coverage (to Globe Ombudsman)
   ask@globe.com
        submissions to "Ask The Globe"
   list@globe.com
        event listings for Thursday's Calendar section
   howwhy@globe.com
        Health and Science section
   chat@globe.com
        submissions to "Confidential Chat"
   ciweek@globe.com
        City Weekly section
   religion@globe.com
        religion editor
   arts@globe.com
        arts editor
When sending e-mail to the Globe, please include your full name, address and pho
ne number.  Thank you.
```

Some companies answer their Internet e-mail manually. You might think that a clothing manufacturer is an unlikely candidate for electronic customer support, but Joe Boxer Corporation, a California designer and manufacturer of underwear, has ditched its toll-free telephone line for an Internet e-mail box in an attempt to reach the twenty-something market that cut its teeth on the Internet. Joe Boxer's billboards and advertisements all now read, "Contact us in underwear cyberspace. Internet `joeboxer@jboxer.com`." The company gets 15 to 20 messages a day, and each one receives a personal response.

Spreading the News with Usenet Newsgroups

As InterCon's experience shows, companies can successfully offer customer service through the Internet simply by responding intelligently to messages posted on Internet discussion groups. Many businesses, however, prefer to stay within Usenet newsgroups focused on their own products—the Internet equivalent of the bulletin boards and forums offered on the commercial online services.

One company that closely monitors Usenet newsgroups focused on its product line is Silicon Graphics. It participates in eight different Usenet newsgroups under the `comp.sys.sgi` newsgroup umbrella—including `comp.sys.sgi.apps`, `comp.sys.sgi.hardware`, and `comp.sys.sgi.bugs`, which are focused on applications, hardware, and technical discussions.

What kinds of discussion are found on a newsgroup? Here is a list of recent messages posted in `comp.sys.sgi.hardware`, a newsgroup focused on hardware problems and solutions:

```
ATM boards for SGI?
Advice on Contem Cyber, Periph Sol?
Archiving Devices
Are there any DSP boards for the Indy's?
BIT3 VME-VME Adaptor
Bezels for drive sleds?
Block to inode-number
Brand New Fuji 8mm Exabyte $7 each
Causes of Exabyte servo failure?
Composite or separate H/V syncs on an RGB monitors??
DAT vs. QIC..
Disabling Indy power button
E&S dialboxes
EISA FDDI card?
EXABYTE HOWTO FOR SGIs
Exabyte 8505 on Indigo2 with IRIX 5.2
Experience with VME-based reflective memory on Challenge?
Fast Ethernet : WHEN & WHAT ??
Filming a monitor
Galileo board installation
HP 2.1 GB disk in 4D/25
```

```
HP 35450A 4mm DAT tape drive on Indigo 2
HP DAT drive problem on indy
How To Control Audio
How do I hook up a PC monitor to an indy?
I want 2 use CDdrive under Linux to read SGI-IRIX-efs-CD
INFO on Internal HD for SGI IRIS INDIGO
IRIX 6.0 64 bit support for R4400?
Important .. at least for me
Indy 4600 upgradeable like other indies?
Indy R4600 SIMMs
Indy forsale
Jumpers —> New Sys Disk ? HOW ??
MP cache miss cycle times
NEC CDROM <-> Indigo
Need Dataglove for Indigo2
Need HP 650c driver
Novice questions - what do we need to develop programs?
Opinions wanted: >= 3 GB drives? (Especially Seagate or Micropolis)
PC EISA FDDI board on Indigo 2?
Panic Error: ECC
Pinnacle Rewritable Optical disk problems with IRIX 4.0.5H
Problem exorcising bad block
Q: swap of ID-Chip from PI to R3K-Indigo possible ?
R4400 upgrade problem - help!
R6000 (Was: R8000 in an Indy?)
R8000 in an Indy?
RAID-5 on SGI
Recomendations for 4D-25 4M sims?
Recommendations wanted for UPS systems
Recovery from Graphics Error ?
SGI 'n DAT
SGI Audio over SCSI?
SGI pointer Frequently Asked Questions (FAQ)
SGI serial cable problems
Searching Third-party disk for Challenge
Stereo glasses
Stipled pattern on SGI display
Students price for a 4600 indy?
Subject: EXABYTE HOWTO FOR SGIs
Swap of ID-Chips from PI to Indigo1 ?
Technical manual or whitepaper for RE^2
Thermal Problems - Onyx RE2
Upgrade PrimCache to SecCache
Upgrading RAM on an INDY
Using SGI Drives on PCs
Video capture on INDY?
WANTED: Used Indy or Indigo
XS24 upgrade: HELP NEEDED !!!!!
[Q] Serial communication library
adding sharp MO drive
checking things out
comp.sys.sgi.misc
disk sled price markup - is this a record
lots of audio channels
need help adding sharp MO drive
parallel port and INDY
seeking fault tolerant system solution
```

```
serial port bug in 5.2 ?
setting up gateway from Magnum 3000 via SLIP
sgi peripherals on sparcstation?
swap of sys_id chip from PI to Indigo1 ?
```

Notes posted to the company's newsgroups come from customers all over the world. This note posted by a Silicon Graphics customer in Japan is fairly typical:

```
From: suzuki@cim.pe.u-tokyo.ac.jp (SUZUKI Hiromasa)
Subject: Question: Serial Port Connection
Date: 23 Apr 95 05:44

I want to connect a 3D digitizer to Indy via Serial Port (RS232C).
Unfortunately the digitizer is designed for IBM PC and we got no
information about how to connect it to Indy.
The only information that I could find in Indy's manual is a document
about the pin arrangement of the serial port connector.
Can anybody tell me where I can find more information, how to write
programs to read/write data via Serial Port and so on?
Your help will be much appreciated.
--
Hiromasa SUZUKI
-------------------------------------------------
suzuki@cim.pe.u-tokyo.ac.jp
Department of Precision Machinery Engineering
The University of Tokyo, JAPAN
```

By responding to newsgroup postings, Silicon Graphics assists not only the customer who posted the note but also other customers who encounter the same problem. Here is a response posted by Silicon Graphics' Dave Olson to a question posted by a customer from Denmark:

```
From: olson@sgi.com (Dave Olson)
Subject: Re: HP35480 on Indy - Having problems
Date: 24 Apr 1995 19:27

Ottmar Roehrig (or@silicon.hanse.de) writes:

>       wd93 SCSI Bus=0 ID=4 LUN=0: SCSI cmd=0x8 disconnected \
>       on non-word boundary (addr=c0044402, 0x7bfe left), can't DMA.\
>       Resetting SCSI bus

This means the 'no disconnect during data phase' DIP switch isn't set.  I have h
eard that the DIP switches for this might be different with different model or f
irmware revs, with no further info.  I think your best bet is to call your distr
ibutor for the drive, and try to get an answer as to which DIP switch.  If you a
re successful, pleaselet us know.  You might also ask (including the firmware re
v) oncomp.periphs.scsi, as some of the HP Bristol folks responsible for DAT ofte
n answer questions there.
```

```
(The firmware rev should be displayed as part of the inquiry by 'mt stat'). Also
, since bru seems to work, you could try dropping the i/o size from64K (last mem
ber of struct) to 32K or 20K (bru uses 20K), and see if that Also, since bru see
ms to work, you could try dropping the i/o size from 64K (last member of struct)
to 32K or 20K (bru uses 20K), and see if that works around the problem, or expli
citly give something like 'tar cb 64' when making tapes.
--
The most beautiful things in the world are          |   Dave Olson
those from which all excess weight has been         |   Silicon Graphics
removed.  -Henry Ford                               |   olson@sgi.com
```

Newsgroups are only one facet of the customer support services that Silicon Graphics provides on the Internet. Research and development manager Jennifer Cantele, head of the Silicon Surf team, which developed Silicon Graphics' World Wide Web server, says that the company also enables customers to send questions to technical support staffers via e-mail. Through the company's "customer profile" service, also available via the Internet, customers can continually update information about their location, e-mail address, and computer system. They can receive the appropriate software from the company automatically.

The future, as Cantele sees it, is the company's Web server, which enables customers to browse through information about the company and its products and to use hyperlinks to explore its ftp archives and other data. The server, in operation since March, 1994, is one of the busiest spots on the entire World Wide Web (see Figure 18.1). You can check it out at `http://www.sgi.com/`. Cantele says, "As the Internet has opened up to what we feel is more commercialization, we see this as the perfect opportunity to use it to provide support to our customers. We've really just scratched the surface."

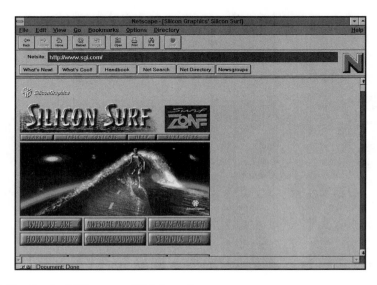

Figure 18.1. Don't miss SGI on your Web travels.

Anticipating Questions with FAQs

In addition to answering individual customers' questions, many companies also post FAQs, or Frequently Asked Questions lists, on the Internet. Companies post FAQs on their own newsgroups and on newsgroups that discuss related topics. The idea is to anticipate general questions that customers might have, which frees up the customer support staff to focus on solving less common problems.

Long-time computer manufacturer Digital Equipment Corp. produces two FAQ documents for its customers throughout the world, accessible through electronic mail, ftp, or the `comp.unix.ultrix`, `comp.sys.dec`, `comp.unix.osf.osf1`, `news.answers`, and `comp.answers` Usenet newsgroups. Here is an excerpt from that document:

```
S1. How can I get lots of free software for ULTRIX and OSF/1? The main FTP serve
r for DEC is gatekeeper.dec.com, which maintains a large selection of sources fr
om the net in general, as well as publiccode for ULTRIX, such as "monitor", "top
" and other system-specifictools. /pub/DEC has sources for several packages writ
ten by employeesat Digital (though they are not supported Digital products), as
well as some programs that required special changes to port to ULTRIX. None of t
hese sources or utilities are "supported" by anyone other than their authors. Th
e directory /pub/DEC/Alpha/apps has several programs to have been ported to Alph
a OSF/1. In addition, Digital's "European UNIX Competency Circle" produced a CDR
OM of free software for UNIX. To get a copy, speak to a local person from Digita
l. For questions or suggestions about it, except about availability, write to fr
eeware@univriv.vbo.dec.com Because the disk is in ISO 9660 format, it can be moun
ted and used in almost any UNIX system and many proprietary systems, including U
LTRIX, OSF/1, Solaris, DOS, and VMS.
Answer A1 in the OSF/1 FAQ says how to order the Alpha OSF/1 Freeware CD.

S4. How do I play music CDs on DEC CD-ROM drives? Music CDs can be played throug
h a speaker jack on RRD42 CD-ROM drives, which is the one contained in the DECst
ation 5000/{120,125} box. The are three different programs available. A command
line version and a Motif-based version can be found in: gatekeeper.dec.com or de
cuac.dec.com in /pub/DEC:
        cdp.c[.Z]           /* command line version */
        xcd_source.tar.Z    /* Motif version. */
            [Timothy Williams, williams@nvl.army.mil]

M6.**NEW** How do I contact Digital Customer Relations? If you are having a prob
lem dealing with Digital that you cannot satisfactorily resolve through your loc
al Digital office, please contact US Customer Relations at:
    Internet: response@mkots3.enet.dec.com
    Phone:    800-DEC-INFO or 603-884-0915
    FAX:      603-884-4692
    Mail:     US Customer Relations
              Digital Equipment Corporation
              Digital Drive, MKO2-2/D15
```

```
P.O. Box 9501
Merrimack, NH 03054-9501
```

If you opt to provide a FAQ for your products and services—a strategy that we recommend—remember these guidelines:

- Keep the questions and answers succinct.
- Include a summary of all the questions at the top of the document.
- Be sure to include valuable information.

Over 2,200 FAQ documents are available on a wide variety of topics, and the Internet community is familiar and comfortable with them. It is also a good idea to have an e-mail address that automatically responds to any e-mail with the FAQ document. We suggest `faq@yourcompany`. Finally, don't let the information in your FAQ document become stale. Try to include up-to-date information about release schedules, the latest versions of software, and contact information for current corporate executives and product specialists.

> **Tip:** Check out some of the bewildering variety of FAQ documents available by visiting either the Web archive at `http://www.lib.ox.ac.uk/internet/news/faq/by_category.index.html` or the Gopher server at `sol.csd.unb.ca`.

Do-It-Yourself Support with ftp Sites

One of the most common problems for software companies today is distributing fixes, patches, and updates to existing programs to customers. Most firms rely on registration cards and charge anywhere from $20 to $150 for an upgrade—which usually includes only a stack of floppy disks. With the Internet, the cost associated with these updates can be eliminated. The customer database can become an e-mail list—which is also useful for company newsletters and press releases of new products. The cost of disk duplication vanishes. Manuals can be offered online for free, with a supplemental charge for printed, bound documentation.

By setting up your computer as an ftp site, your customers can access a library of software programs and documentation effortlessly. Because Web browsers can access ftp archives, even companies that have not yet made the leap to the Web can still be easily accessed by customers who prefer a graphical, point-and-click interface. Customers connect to the site's Internet location, search the directory for the appropriate text or file, and download it to their own computers.

Digital Equipment Corp., which operates one of the largest FTP sites on the Internet, makes over 9,000 company documents and software programs and more than 300,000 public domain software programs available to Internet users. Russ Jones, the company's Internet program manager, estimates that Internet users access more than 20,000 documents a month from DEC's archives.

Here is a partial list of the kinds of files, documents, and programs available in the `contrib` directory of the ftp archive at `gatekeeper.dec.com`:

```
Alpha/        VMS/            database/       micro/          sf/
BSD/          X11/            doc/            misc/           standards/
DEC/          X11-contrib/    editors/        multimedia/     sysadm/
Digital/      athena/         forums/         net/            text/
GNU/          case/           games/          news/           usenet/
Mach/         comm/           graphics/       plan/           usenix/
NIST/         conferences/    mail/           published/
UCB/          data/           maps/           recipes/
```

Although DEC has been hooked into the Internet for over ten years, Jones says that the company started aggressively using the network as a way to reach customers only two years ago. "So many of our customers were on the Internet that it just became obvious that the time was ripe to do it."

Prior to the Internet customer support system, DEC required customers to use their modems to dial in to one of the many DEC bulletin boards around the world to download software updates and technical documentation. Now they can obtain the same support through the company's ftp site on the Internet without needing any special hardware or software other than the existing Internet connection.

Like Silicon Graphics, DEC participates in company-related Usenet newsgroups. Current estimates suggest that over 80,000 people read the discussion occurring in the Usenet group `comp.sys.dec`, the main Digital newsgroup. Digitals' World-Web Wide server, launched in October 1993, attracted over 9,000 visitors in its first four months in operation. You can see it for yourself at `http://www.digital.com/home.html`.

DEC also operates what it calls the Electronic Connection, an online ordering service that customers can access through telnet. Try it yourself by typing in the command `telnet order.sales.digital.com`. Since DEC opened the service in February 1994, online orders have increased at a rate of $1 million per month.

Here is an example of what you see when you enter DEC's online store:

```
List            Net  Days Lead
    Model No    Description                      Price  Disc      Price
Time
1.    QT001-3M FORTRAN-20,SOURCES MT9 1600       1404 10.00      1263.60
2.+   QT001-3Z FORTRAN-20, SVC RTC UPD            468 10.00       421.20
```

```
3.     QT001-8M FORTRAN-20,SOURCES MT9 1600       2244 10.00      2019.60
4.     QT001-9M FORTRAN-20,SOURCES MT9 1600       4572 15.00      3886.20
5.     QT001-DZ FORTRAN-20,SRC LICENSE ONLY       2100 10.00      1890.00   30
6.     QT001-IM FORTRAN-20,SOURCES MT9 1600        760  0.00       760.00
7.     QT001-NM FORTRAN-20,UDP MT9 1600           2678 10.00      2410.20   30
8.     QT001-NZ FORTRAN-20, RT TO COPY             599  0.00       599.00   30
9.     QT001-XM FORTRAN-20,SOURCES MT9 1600      12075 10.00     10867.50   30

+ fast ship product                    Total of   9 model numbers found
- - - - - - - - - - - - - - - - - - - - - - - - - - - - - - - - - - - - - - - - - -
- - -
  Type a selection number or command letter, then press <RETURN>:

Commands:   Order   Help   Back   Main   Quit
```

DEC enables customers to test-drive its OSF/1 AXP server directly by logging on to it through the Internet. The system, in place since December 1993, receives roughly 360 logins a day, or one every four minutes. The AXP test drive program has been so successful that the company has expanded it to include an OpenVMS AXP server and an Alpha AXP Workstation Farm.

"What we're trying to do is use every mechanism on the Internet to reach customers," Jones says. "We don't care if a customer has access to a newsreader, telnet, or a Web browser. We want him to be able to reach our information no matter which tool he's using."

We heartily agree and endorse DEC's wise strategy of using a variety of Internet-based means to disseminate, distribute, and circulate information about the company and its products. So don't be fooled into thinking that the Web is the end-all of the Internet. Customers use a variety of different tools based not only on what they can access but also on their technological comfort level.

Publishing Information with Gopher and WAIS

Thanks to the Internet, companies can publish large databases of technical information in searchable format by using Internet tools such as Gopher and WAIS. Many companies set up Web servers to enable customers to browse through support information more easily.

Sun Microsystems is a pioneer in using the Internet to provide customer service. Sun operates SunSITE, an Internet server at the University of North Carolina that serves as a repository for information about Sun products and public domain software, White House papers, and other data. Use of the system has reached 100,000 transfers a day. Additional SunSITE "mirror" servers have been set up in Tokyo and London. By locating document archives around the world, Sun hopes to help its overseas customers reduce the long waits to access data from the North Carolina server.

Here are some of the many SunSITE offerings available:

```
-->   1.  SunSITE Sustainable Agriculture Information/
      2.  Sunsite Political Science Archives/
      3.  Worlds of SunSITE — by Subject/
      4.  What's New on SunSITE/
      5.  Music - The American Music Resource - Via Sunsite Gopher Server/
      6.  Sunsite Gopher Server/
      7.  Poetry - Poetry and Creative Writing - Via Sunsite Gopher Server/
      8.  National Information Infrastructure Information (from sunsite)/
      9.  National Health Security Plan (from sunsite)/
     10.  Pictures - White House Pictures - Via Sunsite Gopher Server/
     11.  Sustainable Agriculture Information - Via Sunsite Gopher Server/
     12.  Welsh Language and Culture Archive - Via Sunsite Gopher Server/
     13.  GNU Software (Sunsite)/
     14.  University of North Carolina at Chapel Hill  (Ogphre..site archives)/
     15.  SunSITE gopher/
     16.  Sunsite Gopher Server/
     17.  Russian coup information on sunsite.
     18.  Usage stats from sunsite.unc.edu.
     19.  sci.econ.research Archives (from sunsite.unc.edu)/
     20.  Virtual Reality - Via Sunsite Gopher Server/
     21.  Multimedia - University of North Carolina SUNsite/
     22.  Pictures - Univ. of N. Carolina SUNsite White House Pictures/
     23.  New files on sunsite.unc.edu.
     24.  Re: Patches removed from sunsite.
     25.  New uploads to sunsite.unc.edu.
     26.  Talk Radio on sunsite.unc.edu.
     27.  Linux WAIS databases on sunsite.
     28.  New files on sunsite.unc.edu.
     29.  newspak-2.0 uploaded to sunsite.
     30.  Slackware now mirrored on sunsite.
     31.  New files on sunsite.
     32.  printing.how-to uploaded to SunSite:Incoming.
     33.  New files on sunsite.
     34.  Sunsite Update (more then new files!).
     35.  New files on sunsite.unc.edu.
     36.  fvwm-0.985 X-11 Window Manager is available on sunsite.
     37.  Sunsite ftpmail return.
     38.  SunSITE.unc.edu now gopher-ed!.
     39.  New files list on sunsite.unc.edu.
     40.  sunsite/
     41.  sunsite.ls-lR.gz.
     42.  New files on sunsite.unc.edu.
     43.  Re: Patches removed from sunsite.
     44.  New uploads to sunsite.unc.edu.
     45.  Talk Radio on sunsite.unc.edu.
     46.  Linux WAIS databases on sunsite.
     47.  New files on sunsite.unc.edu.
     48.  newspak-2.0 uploaded to sunsite.
     49.  Slackware now mirrored on sunsite.
     50.  New files on sunsite.
     51.  printing.how-to uploaded to SunSite:Incoming.
     52.  New files on sunsite.
     53.  Sunsite Update (more then new files!).
     54.  New files on sunsite.unc.edu.
     55.  fvwm-0.985 X-11 Window Manager is available on sunsite.
```

```
56. Sunsite ftpmail return.
57. SunSITE.unc.edu now gopher-ed!.
58. New files list on sunsite.unc.edu.
59. sunsite/
60. National Health Security Act on SunSITE.
61.     Usage stats for sunsite.unc.edu.
62. Z39.50 Archives at sunsite.unc.edu/
63. SunSITE (Sun Software, Information, and Technology Exchange).
64. 93-11-01-18: Usage stats from sunsite.unc.edu.
65. 93-09-14-19: Populus on sunsite.unc.edu.
66. 93-09-15-19: Re: Populus on sunsite.unc.edu.
67. 93-09-16-10: Re: Populus on sunsite.unc.edu.
68. SunSITE.unc.edu 152.2.22.81  unknown/
69. US Budget Source on sunsite.
70. SunSITE.unc.edu now gopher-ed!.
71. Usage stats from sunsite.unc.edu.
72. Russian coup information on sunsite.
73. sunsite.unc.edu/
74. sunsite.unc.edu/
75. SunSITE gopher.
76. Pictures from the Smithsonian (copied from sunsite.unc.edu)/
77. SunSITE ip number change (fwd).
78. UNC Sun Archive (sunsite.unc.edu)/
79. sunsite.unc.edu/
80. White House Papers on sunsite.unc.edu.
81.     J. SunSITE.
82. SunSITE software archive.
83. Re: Patches removed from sunsite.
84. Re: Patches removed from sunsite.
85. 35) FTP: sunsite.unc.edu@pub..c/political-science/whitehouse-papers//
86. UNC Sun Archive (sunsite.unc.edu)/
87. SunSite software archives (sunsite.unc.edu)/
88. SunSite software archives (sunsite.unc.edu)/
89. SunFlash archives (sunsite)/

90. SUNsite ftp server.
```

Here is what you see when you log on to the main menu of the SunSITE Gopher server at the University of North Carolina. To access it, type gopher sunsite.unc.edu at the system prompt.

```
              Root gopher server: sunsite.unc.edu
 -->  1.  About Ogphre/
      2.  Sun and UNC's Legal Disclaimer.
      3.  Surf the Net! - Archie, Libraries, Gophers, FTP Sites./
      4.  Internet Dog-Eared Pages (Frequently used resources)/
      5.  Worlds of SunSITE — by Subject/
      6.  SUN Microsystems News Groups and Archives/
      7.  NEWS! (News, Entertainment, Weather, and Sports)/
      8.  UNC Information Exchange (People and Places)/
      9.  The UNC-CH Internet Library/
     10.  UNC-Gopherspace/
     11.  What's New on SunSITE/
```

To access customer information about Sun, select menu item 6. Here is what appears on your screen:

```
-->  1.  About Sun Microsystems Archives.
     2.  Browse Sun Related Information And Archives/
     3.  SUN Flash product announcements (1989 - present)/
     4.  SUN related news groups/
     5.  Search  Postscript copies of Sun Technical White-papers <?>
     6.  Search  SUN Spots Archives <?>
```

Sun's WAIS server is more confusing to use, but it enables customers to use a high-power search tool to zero in on the documents they need. The following list of documents was retrieved by a keyword search using the word OpenLook, which is the name of one of Sun's leading software products:

```
Sun Fixes WAIS Archives: openlook
-->  1.  100451-09.README    /packages/wais/wais-data/sun-fixes/.
2.   100826-01.README    /packages/wais/wais-data/sun-fixes/.
3.   100451-30.README    /packages/wais/wais-data/sun-fixes/.
4.   100451-61.README    /packages/wais/wais-data/sun-fixes/.
5.   100928-01.README    /packages/wais/wais-data/sun-fixes/.
6.   100451-47.README    /packages/wais/wais-data/sun-fixes/.
7.   100451-55.README    /packages/wais/wais-data/sun-fixes/.
8.   100451-48.README    /packages/wais/wais-data/sun-fixes/.
9.   100451-56.README    /packages/wais/wais-data/sun-fixes/.
10.  100393-01.README    /packages/wais/wais-data/sun-fixes/.
11.  100394-01.README    /packages/wais/wais-data/sun-fixes/.
12.  100451-58.README    /packages/wais/wais-data/sun-fixes/.
13.  100451-59.README    /packages/wais/wais-data/sun-fixes/.
14.  100451-60.README    /packages/wais/wais-data/sun-fixes/.
15.  100451-43.README    /packages/wais/wais-data/sun-fixes/.
16.  100451-52.README    /packages/wais/wais-data/sun-fixes/.
17.  100451-62.README    /packages/wais/wais-data/sun-fixes/.
```

To round out its Internet offerings, Sun launched its own Web server in April 1995. To see what the firm has done, use a Web browser and connect to URL http://www.sun.com. By using the technology that underlies the World Wide Web, customers can click SunSITE and access the server.

Surfing a Web of Support

Like Silicon Graphics, Digital Equipment Corp., and Sun Microsystems, many companies are looking to the Web these days to give their customers an easier way to browse through technical information. Hewlett-Packard, for example, has added a Web server to its HP SupportLine electronic support services. By surfing the HP Web site, customers can resolve software problems quickly by searching up-to-date support and problem-solving information, browsing news and current announcements, and subscribing to mailing lists that automatically deliver the latest Hewlett-Packard support information to their electronic mailboxes.

According to Doug Levitt of Hewlett-Packard's Response Center Lab in Mountain View, California, HP SupportLine began providing customer support over the Internet in 1991—before the Web existed. The first thing the group did, he says, was to set up an ftp site from which customers could download software patches. Customers previously had to call the Response Center by telephone and order a diskette through the mail. That was not the optimal solution: "When you're a large company and you want to deliver software to thousands of customers, the costs can become prohibitively expensive," he says.

After getting its ftp site up and running, Hewlett-Packard set up an Internet mail link to enable customers to obtain software patches by requesting them via e-mail. The company launched a group of eight mailing lists to disseminate information to existing and potential HP customers. Although it is hard to estimate how many people read the mailing lists—many people subscribe and then pass them on—Levitt says, it is a cost-effective way of distributing information to Hewlett-Packard's customers.

In the future, Levitt says, Hewlett-Packard is looking at offering Internet support involving multimedia—enabling customers to communicate through voice instead of by clicking buttons on a screen or by typing commands on a keyboard.

For now, however, HP SupportLine's Web site is state-of-the-art. Figure 18.2 shows the HP home page (URL `http://support.mayfield.hp.com`). Customers can click buttons to read news and announcements, search problem-solving databases, browse software patches, and subscribe to electronic digests.

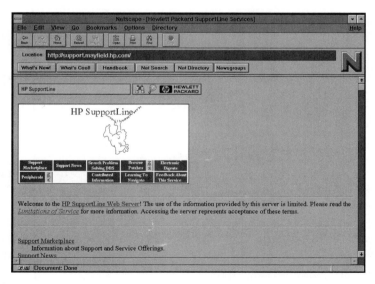

Figure 18.2. Hewlett-Packard offers customer support through the Web.

Clicking the Support News button displays a hyperlinked menu that connects customers to documents containing information about new products, HP discounts and promotions, technical tips, and other information (see Figure 18.3).

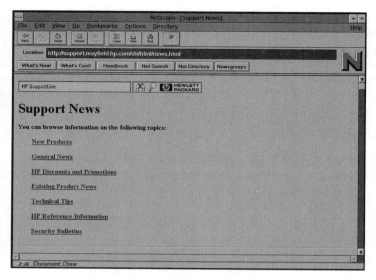

Figure 18.3. HP's Support News area offers new-product information, discounts, and promotions.

In HP's problem-solving database, customers can find answers to their technical questions (see Figure 18.4).

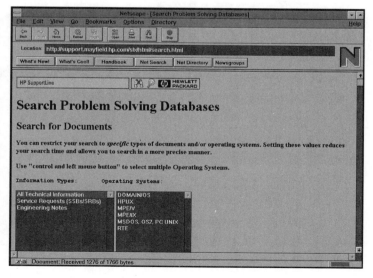

Figure 18.4. HP's database offers solutions to technical problems.

HP's Web setup makes it easy for customers to subscribe to a variety of HP mailing lists, which keep them informed of new products, technical tips, security, and general news (see Figure 18.5).

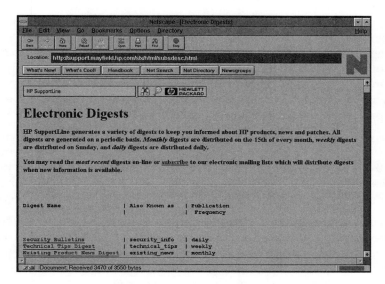

Figure 18.5. HP lets customers subscribe to mailing lists through its Web site.

Customers can also browse information contributed by others, such as the documents supplied by Ohio State University, as shown in Figure 18.6.

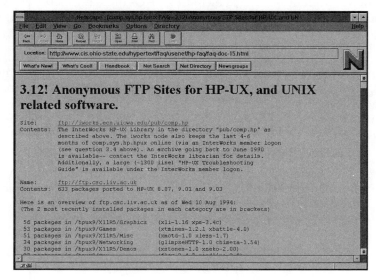

Figure 18.6. HP's Web site also provides links to related resources.

The Bottom Line: The Cost of Providing Customer Support on the Internet

How much does it cost to provide customer support over the Internet? Some customer support options, such as responding to customer queries via e-mail or setting up newsgroups and mailing lists, cost practically nothing apart from the cost of obtaining Internet access, which your company might already have. You also must factor in the time that your technical support personnel spend interacting with customers electronically. This can be a real time-saver if your company had previously been providing support by telephone, fax, or postal mail.

The cost of setting up a Web site, Gopher database, or ftp archives on the Internet varies depending on how much information you have in electronic format already. If you have a computer bulletin board up and running, offering that information on the Internet can be as simple as establishing a telnet link to your company's computer system or uploading the data to an Internet-connected server.

Indeed, many ftp and Gopher servers are so simple to set up that you can drop all the files you want to offer in a single directory, point the server to that directory, and start advertising the new capability. More sophisticated organization is not much more difficult either. Divide the information into categories, as you saw with the Gopher examples, and assign each category a subdirectory in the main server directory. Just make sure that you include mnemonic names.

It's also important to give something back to the Internet community. If your firm sells modems, for example, offer space for public information on modems and telecommunications—perhaps including FAQs on dialup services. A few dozen megabytes of disk space can mean the difference between customers perceiving you as just another vendor offering tech sheets on the wire and customers steering others to your site and spreading goodwill.

The most expensive means of offering customer support via the Internet is by setting up your own Web server—though you can rent Web space for much less. Sun Microsystems, for example, dedicated a $50,000 SparcCenter 1000 UNIX server and several full-time employees to its Web site, says Eric Schmidt, the company's chief technology officer. The projected cost is $150,000 to $250,000 a year.

You can even use dialup accounts to distribute information through the Internet to your customers. Netcom Communications Services, for example, grants all dialup users 5MB of space in its anonymous ftp archive site. That is plenty of space for a few spec sheets, press releases, and an FAQ document.

Another alternative is to configure an inexpensive PC with a dedicated 19.2 kbaud connection, perhaps through SLIP. The cost of this connection is approximately $160 per month. Add in the expense of the appropriate modem and the telephone line. A quick glance in any computer publication will show that you can easily find a 486-based PC with a gigabyte of disk space for under $2,500. The server and communications software required is free and is probably available directly from your Internet access provider. The total setup cost is $3,000, and the typical monthly running cost is $200. Compare that to the cost of just a single direct mailing and you can see why customer support on the Net is catching on in a big way.

Keys to Good Customer Support

When setting up a customer support site on the Internet, we suggest you keep in mind two important ideas:

> Use a variety of Internet tools—from e-mail autoresponders to Web sites and newsgroups—to enable all your customers to access your information.

> Offer valuable free information to encourage Internet users who aren't already customers to visit your site and find out more about your products and services.

In this chapter, you have seen examples of companies that have applied these techniques to gain customers and reap public relations benefits on the Internet. By following their examples, you can do it, too!

NETWORK SECURITY

Any business that links its computer system to the Internet exposes itself to crackers and electronic joy-riders able to vandalize data, pilfer passwords, and steal systems for fun or profit.

What makes the Internet so vulnerable to electronic mischief? Unlike centralized networks operated by commercial online services, such as CompuServe and Prodigy, the Internet is a decentralized system spread across hundreds of thousands of computers world-wide. Each of these machines has its own passwords and security procedures—or lack thereof. In some cases, subnets of the Internet are only as strong as their weakest link. Intruders who break into one part of a local network on the Internet can rapidly gain access to much of the rest of the local network and sometimes to other networks too. There have been some steps in the right direction, however. Internet security issues are now being addressed by the government-funded Computer Emergency Response Team, or CERT—an Internet security investigation squad—and by the Internet Engineering Task Force—a volunteer group that is working on developing standards for message encryption and authentication. Don't be fooled, though. The Internet remains far from secure.

Given its problems, is the Internet a safe place to do business? The answer is both yes and no—although the security risks have not stopped more than 50,000 companies worldwide from hooking up their internal networks to the Internet. Do the potential rewards of doing business on the information highway outweigh the risks? They do indeed, particularly for companies that take proper precautions. The goal of this chapter is to show you the risks and realities of doing business on the Internet. You'll get hard facts about crackers, viruses, and other Internet security risks, and you'll find out how unauthorized users can gain access to your company's financial information and your customers' credit-card numbers. You'll also learn how to ward off network intruders and obtain information from leading security experts, information that can help you build the best Internet security plan for your business.

The History of Internet Security

Despite its origins at the Defense Department, the Internet was never designed to be a completely secure system, certainly not as secure as most of the commercial online services. Because it was created to help academic researchers and government officials interact with one another, the Internet was designed for maximum openness and interoperability—that is, the ability for people and computers on different networks to communicate easily and seamlessly. And that's one of the big reasons why the Internet has attracted such a large following. The Internet never would have been as successful if it had been balkanized, or broken up into smaller subnetworks.

Keep in mind that when the Internet was launched in 1969, network security was not a big issue, and far fewer people were on the Net than there are today. Back then, the Internet resembled a small town where people did not have to lock their doors when they went out for the evening. In fact, some computers on the network purposely left their "doors" open to enable anonymous visitors to pick up or leave files. This still happens to some extent—that is what anonymous ftp is all about—but now it is impossible to know who else is on the network interacting with your corporate computer system.

Today, with more than 30,000,000 users throughout the world, the Internet is hardly a small town anymore, and the small-town ethos that members of the network once enjoyed has given way to big-city problems in need of big-city solutions. As a result, Internet security breaches have become more and more common in recent years. In November 1988, Cornell University graduate student Robert T. Morris Jr., launched the first major Internet virus, an insidious program that ended up crashing over 6,000 machines on the network and shutting down the network for days on end while it was being eradicated. Morris, who became the first person ever charged with violating the federal Computer Fraud and Abuse Act, stated at the time that he did not realize his rogue program would be destructive. He was fined $10,000 and ordered to perform 400 hours of community service.

More recent break-ins have had a more sinister overtone. In November 1991, the United States General Accounting Office revealed that between April 1990 and May 1991 computer crackers in the Netherlands broke into various computer systems via the Internet and accessed sensitive U.S. military data. Some of the data included information on Gulf War personnel, the type and number of military equipment being moved, troop deployments, and the development of new weapons systems.

Even though there is little evidence that the crackers destroyed any data, evidence does suggest that in several instances they modified and copied it. Jack L. Brock Jr., director of government information and financial management in GAO's Information Management and Technology division, told the Senate Governmental Affairs Subcommittee on Government Information and Regulation that the crackers were able to break into the Internet-connected systems because of three problems: vendor-supplied accounts with well-known default passwords, easily guessed individual account passwords, and vulnerable operating systems.

Commercial Internet networks have been vandalized, too. In October 1993, Public Access Network Corp. (panix.com) was infiltrated by an unauthorized system cracker who obtained high-level access to the system, forcing it to shut down for three days. As an Internet access provider, Panix sells access to the Internet. The intruder stole account names and passwords of those Panix users who were connecting through telnet and other services to other machines on the Internet. Officials said afterwards that the full magnitude and consequences of the breach were still unknown, because the cracker's programs were hidden within the Panix operating system and had collected the secret information for many weeks.

In early 1994, CERT spotted what might be the largest computer security breach on the Internet so far and urged tens of thousands of Internet users to change their passwords. CERT, set up in the aftermath of Morris virus in 1988, said that it was not certain whether the crackers who broke into the network had vandalized computer systems or unleashed damaging viruses.

Meanwhile, security experts have speculated that recent break-ins might have been connected to a group of students, known as the Posse, who had been taunting Internet systems operators and taking down systems just for the thrill of it. Whoever the crackers really were, they apparently broke into the network on January 1 and installed a sniffer program—a program that watches the network wires and logs passwords on computers at the University of California at Berkeley. The program collected more than 3,000 account and password combinations between 7 a.m. and 9 p.m. Once noticed, the security violation forced system administrators to send notices to all logged users, telling them to change their passwords immediately. "We haven't identified who did it," James Settle, special agent for the Federal Bureau of Investigation, told *The Wall Street Journal* at the time. "There are so many people out there who can do this."

And just this February, notorious hacker Kevin Mitnick was arrested and accused of stealing an estimated 20,000 credit-card numbers and thousands of data files from the Internet.

Internet Risks and Realities

With no universal security standard yet in place, the Internet continues to be a somewhat perilous place to do business, and the Internet is likely to become more dangerous as it gets bigger and as the volume of commercial traffic rises. Dain Gary, manager of CERT, indicates that his group logs three or four security breaches on the Internet each day. In 1995, Gary expects a 50% increase over the previous year's 1,000 reported intrusions. The real numbers are probably even higher. Fearing embarrassment and loss of public confidence, businesses rarely report break-ins, and experts estimate that only 15% of breaches are reported to law-enforcement authorities. That suggests that there will be 40 to 50 security violations or break-ins on the Internet every day by the time you read this chapter.

Internet vandals are also becoming more sophisticated. The typical Internet intruder these days is less likely to be a teenager out for an electronic joyride. Many intruders are now industrial spies motivated by financial gain. Using special software, these crackers probe for weaknesses in a network's operating system, the underlying program that manages all other software programs. Once they detect a loophole, the criminals spread the news through underground publications, at cracker conventions, and on computer bulletin boards. Cracker-designed programs that exploit these defects and search for crucial information are distributed in much the same way. In the Panix break-in in November, 1993, for example, system administrators eventually found the sniffer program that the cracker had installed to watch and take notes as Panix users logged onto other computer networks. By monitoring those activities, the cracker stole the passwords to those other networks as well.

Businesses that connect their computer systems to the Internet put themselves at risk in three principal ways:

> The e-mail that they send and receive through the Internet can be intercepted and read.

> The business and financial records that they store on their computer systems can be viewed, tampered with, or destroyed.

> The credit-card numbers of their online customers can be stolen and used illegally to ring up unauthorized charges.

Real-Life Experience

We deal with security issues on a daily basis. Rosalind often receives orders for her electronic newsletter through e-mail, which include credit-card data and other information. Dave offers information on a wide variety of commercial Internet ventures to Internet users through ftp, e-mail, and other sources. These services are possible security threats that can have disastrous consequences.

It is tempting to think that there is just too much traffic for any individual transaction to be found, and Dave notes that he has transacted dozens of online purchases by sending his credit-card information, all without a glitch. With so much data on the wire, there is no problem. Or is there?

One danger that retail businesses on the Internet face is that, as their sites attract more shoppers, it becomes increasingly likely that their e-mail messages might contain a credit-card number. Credit card numbers contain a set number of digits and most cardholders are likely to enter them in a pattern identical to that on their credit cards, both of which can add up to potential trouble.

But the potential for credit-card theft is not the only security risk on the Internet. Perhaps the most obvious is to ensure that your machine and account are secure. If you have a dialup account with an Internet access provider, make sure to choose a good password for your account and keep it secret. Later, we offer some helpful tips for choosing secure passwords. If you have a SLIP, PPP, or other direct Internet connection, make sure that every account on the system has a secure password—even diagnostic accounts and others set by the factory.

Talk with your system vendor to find out about any security problems, bugs, or patches. You'll probably need to make only minor changes, but a simple upgrade today could spare you considerable anguish tomorrow.

Creating a Secure Environment

One of the best ways to safeguard the security of your computer system is to build a firewall, employ an encryption software program, and ensure that all user accounts on your system have complex passwords. For example, a firewall—a computer that acts as a buffer between your company's computer system and the Internet—can be used to keep outsiders from accessing your data. Data encryption can ensure the privacy of your transmissions and the security of documents stored on the system in the event that someone gains access.

Not all companies are equally conscientious about network security, however. A 1992 study conducted by USA Research in Portland, Oregon, tells an alarming tale. Among the respondents who had experienced at least one attack, 34% indicated that they had no idea how the cracker had gained access to the system, and almost 20% said that they has taken no measures to prevent the attacks. Although close to 70% said that they used password procedures to prevent the attacks, only 9% reported using encryption to safeguard sensitive data on their systems.

No matter which security methods you choose, remember that network security begins at home. Start by ensuring that security on your own internal computer system is up to snuff. Experts say that your policy should dictate at least a minimum level of security for all computers attached to your networks and include procedures for checking and maintaining the security of each attached computer. Just as important as any policy, however, is that you regularly verify that your account, password, system, and network are all secure.

The good news is that there are many security software programs on the market that can help you make your system secure. Sun Microsystems' ASET program involves the use of uncrackable passwords, and you can use the public-domain COPS software to search a variety of UNIX systems for security problems. The Tripwire auditing package from Purdue University and the Tiger module in the TAMU toolkit from Texas A&M University can help you manage individual systems. Commercial packages, such as Securemax from Demax Software, are designed both to automate the process and to collect data from distributed nodes, centralizing these security checks. A small investment of this nature can save considerable headaches and problems later.

However, be careful that in your efforts to make your system secure, you don't build a fortress so impregnable that nobody can get in or out. The value of the Internet, after all, is its open linkages to a worldwide computer network. Although the security precautions that you take must be strong enough to protect your company's network, they should not be so strong that they bar legitimate access by employees, vendors, or customers. Information managers who want to open their networks to their company workers also need to design a security system that is easy to use.

"The key concept in all security, including Internet network security, is to make the cost of attack higher than the value of the asset," says Pat Farrell of American Management Systems in Fairfax, Virginia. "Firewalls, one-time passwords, encryption, and so on, simply raise the cost of attack. Nothing will safeguard with certainty."

Staying Off the Net

Without a doubt, the safest way to avoid Internet security problems is to stay off the Internet completely—to send e-mail and other vital data either through a wide area network routed through a major telecommunications carrier or to rely on a commercial online service such as CompuServe, America Online, or MCI Mail. Although commercial online services enable you to send and receive Internet mail, these networks are considered fairly safe because they offer only gateways to the Internet—essentially, doors that periodically open and close only for e-mail.

Another important difference between a centralized online service and an Internet access provider is that on a centralized system like CompuServe, if you send an electronic mail message to another user, it never leaves the computer system, avoiding any potential network security problems. On the Internet, it is unlikely that another user is on the same system. As a result, messages and data travel through a variety of machines. Therefore, you can trust just a single machine; but you are forced to place your trust in all the systems en route.

Because the Internet is not a single network, but a network of networks, some portions of the Net are actually safer than others. Jeffrey Shapard of the University of California at Berkeley explains that the academic networks are notoriously full of security holes—open access subnetworks, poorly administered systems, and, as he phrases it, "lots of eyes and ears that can tap into your bitstream without a great deal of cleverness." He continues, "On the other hand, commercial Internet providers such as Performance Systems International (PSI) have tight central network management, careful routing, extensive training available for customers on security mechanisms, and even enhanced services with encryption built-in."

As we explained earlier, security considerations and the level of administrative sophistication are important selection criteria to use when you choose an Internet access provider. Most of the larger access providers are quite secure with continual monitoring, frequent spot checks, and explicit usage guidelines. All services should be able to help you ensure maximum security for your business.

An alternative approach is to keep your systems away from the prying fingers of the Internet community by paying for an inexpensive dialup account. This is the least expensive way to connect to the Internet. This way, your company transmits and accesses Internet data through a UNIX line-oriented interface—a shell—rather than connecting to the Internet directly through a SLIP/PPP connection or a leased line. Yet another approach is to limit your use of the Internet to e-mail. With its store-and-forward nature, e-mail is not interactive. Therefore, it cannot easily be used to transmit viruses or worms.

The drawback to these strategies is that you greatly reduce your access to the Internet and its many tools and features. Dialup accounts also have their limitations, as discussed earlier in this book.

Passwords

The face of modern banking transactions has changed dramatically since the introduction of the automated teller machine. What really made the system work was the personal identification number. Your PIN, as you know, is a secret multiple-digit number that you use in combination with an ATM card to verify that you are authorized to use the card. If someone steals your card, it is useless to him if he does not know your PIN. Simple but effective.

Computer systems offer a similar security strategy through account passwords—a system by which users can uniquely and positively identify themselves as the owner of the specified account with minimal fuss. Unlike an ATM system, however, users are free to opt not to have passwords or to choose passwords that are ineffective. To understand this, how secure would you feel if the PIN for your account were as simple as 1234 or, even worse, were not even needed to use your bank card? Choosing a poor password or not having any password at all is an incredibly bad idea, and we strongly urge against this practice. The reason is simple. The single most effective way to stymie Internet intruders is to have your account and system require a password for access.

For various reasons that inevitably seem inane after a break-in, users and systems managers frequently either ignore or circumvent this important facet of system security. Others, not realizing the danger, use vendor-supplied passwords that come with the system, establish a password, and never change it, or else they write down their password and leave it on a desk or taped to the computer itself. All these are akin to leaving the keys in your car and the door unlocked when you are in a dangerous neighborhood.

Following are some simple guidelines that can help you and the rest of your company choose individual, meaningful passwords that are both mnemonic and secure. Keep these questions in mind when choosing a password:

Is it at least six characters long?
Does it have both digits and letters?
Is it mixed upper and lower-case letters?
Is it a non-dictionary word?
Has it been changed within the last 60 days?
Is it a name or word that is not associated with you or the account?

Examples of poor, easily guessed passwords include your Social Security number, driver's license, dog's name, and any word that might appear in a dictionary. Excellent passwords, by contrast, are those that combine characters and digits in a mnemonic fashion. For example, hi2all and 2logIN! are impossible for a program to guess.

In setting up a password security system, it is important to make sure that an intruder who penetrates a single computer cannot gain access to the entire local area network. Computers at a site often provide easy access to others at the same site. One possible protective measure, which carries the drawback of inhibiting local networking, is to set up each computer in a system with its own password and security procedures. Certainly, any computer storing sensitive corporate information should have more extensive security and constantly changing passwords.

Firewalls

Unlike its namesake in firefighting, a network firewall is a combination of hardware and software that examines network traffic and permits only approved packets of information to pass through. It creates a controllable gateway between your internal network and the potentially hostile intruders that might be lurking on the Internet.

The simplest form of a firewall is to use packet filters in your network-connection router. By programming the router, you can tell it to discard any packets requesting information or services that you deem a potential security threat or to funnel requests for a certain service, such as e-mail, to a particular computer. You can also use routers to break your networks into segments called subnets and to restrict packets passing between those subnets. This assists in managing internal corporate security and network traffic.

Another approach to firewalls is to use actual computers as routers and gateways, making them the funnel through which all external data arrives on your internal gateway. Commercial solutions, including Digital Equipment Corporation's SEAL product and Eagle Technology's Raptor, use workstations to monitor network connections. By using a workstation as the router, not only is there no direct connection between your internal network and the Internet, but all traffic can be carefully monitored, which ensures that potential security problems are detected automatically. The gateway computer can be configured to permit only a subset of all Internet services onto or off the Internet. Systems like this create extensive audit trails that are helpful in checking for intruders. Sun Microsystems offers a slightly different approach with its Itelnet, a software-only firewall gateway. Public domain solutions are also available, including the Drawbridge portion of the TAMU package.

> **Tip:** A good place to check for firewall information and current products on the Web is Yahoo. Use URL `http://www.yahoo.com/Business/Products_and_Services/Computers/Networking/Firewalls/`.

Security experts remind us that there are typically trade-offs to firewalls in terms of money, access, and convenience. Jonathan Heiliger of the San Francisco Bay Area Regional Research Network (BARRnet) observes, "Firewalls are highly effective only when constructed properly. It's a major capital investment to set up a proper firewall, and there are always tradeoffs and considerations for the users. Usually, the more extreme the firewall, the more difficult or cumbersome it is for users of the system to access the outside world."

Data Encryption

Another important security measure is data encryption. This extends far beyond just working with the Internet. If you have any sensitive data on your computer, we recommend that you encrypt it even without a network connection. Encrypted data is useless without the key to decrypt it, even if someone breaks into your office. The Internet is worse, however, because it is a nonswitched public network—you have little control over where your data goes once you send it on its journey. It is not so different from dropping a letter in a mail box—you have no say over the post offices through which your letter will be routed.

Regarding security and encryption, there are two main areas to consider—messages in transit and data stored on the disk. Like other forms of mail, e-mail has some subtle security problems that are not apparent at first glance, the most important of which for businesses is whether the message is really from the person you think it is from. To solve this problem, computer scientists have invented something called digital signatures, the computer equivalent of the legally binding signature required at the bottom of a purchase order or contract. The technology is intriguing. In its simplest form, a digital signature is a numeric summary of the entire contents of the message or file. Change a single character and the summary changes. Therefore, if the sender adds a digital signature to a message, the recipient should be able to compute a digital signature for the message and compare the two. If they are different, the signature has been modified en route. Unfortunately, there are still no widely distributed mechanisms for irrefutable digital signatures on the Internet.

Data encryption is vital because it is the only way to ensure that your communications are kept private—especially as wireless pathways become more widely available. Encryption works by translating your message into what appears to be gibberish if viewed and then sending the data on to the recipient. Once received, the recipient enters either the same key—private key encryption—or a different key—public key encryption—and the gibberish is automatically translated back into readable text or other data. Encryption of this form can also be used for files and data that you are not planning to send to anyone but would like to keep private anyway.

Most encryption is based on either the Data Encryption Standard (DES) or the Rivest, Shamir, and Adleman (RSA) specification and consists of a mathematically complex sequence of substituting a new character for each character in the original text. The complexity of the substitution strategy is what makes these standards so secure. Without the secret password that unlocks the file, crackers could spend weeks trying to read the text, without success.

Public versus Private Key Encryption

Imagine that any electronic mail or file that Rosalind and Dave send to each other is automatically encrypted with their electronic mail software. It sounds like a great idea, particularly because they have agreed on a secure password to use for the transaction. What happens, though, if Dave wants to send a secure e-mail message to his friend, James, but the two have not agreed on password? Clearly, you cannot send a password through e-mail, since that would defeat the whole purpose of encrypting the message in the first place. Likewise, if you must telephone the recipient of your message to tell him or her the password, you are wasting time—and losing many of the benefits of going electronic in the first place.

A number of bright cryptographers thought about this problem and, in 1976, introduced a fascinating scheme known as *public key encryption*. With public key encryption, the key that you use to encrypt text is different from the one needed to decrypt it. In the real world, it would be like Rosalind having a two-key secure mailbox. One key, the public key, is needed to drop mail off; the second key, her secret key, is required to open the box and read the messages inside.

The computer equivalent is identical. People can send e-mail to Rosalind if they know her public key, which they use as the key for encrypting the message. If seen in transit, the message would make no sense to anyone and even applying her public key would not unlock the text. Once Rosalind receives the message and types in her private key, the message is instantly decrypted and readable. If you are looking for a solution for secure electronic mail and data transfer, public key encryption is unquestionably the answer.

Tip: A great place to learn more about encryption on the Internet is the Encryption FAQ document. It is available through anonymous FTP at `rpub.cl.msu.edu` in `/pub/crypt/sci.crypt/`. Specific sections of the document are available via anonymous ftp at `rtfm.mit.edu` in `/pub/usenet/news.answers/cryptography-faq`. The FAQ is posted to the Usenet newsgroups `sci.crypt`, `talk.politics.crypto`, `sci.answers`, and `news.answers` every 21 days. You can also find the information on the Web at URL `http://www.lib.ox.ac.uk/internet/news/faq/by_category.cryptography-faq.html`.

Encryption at Work

Consider this typical scenario, which Dave has encountered more than once with his clients. The client company has an inexpensive dialup Internet account with a local access provider and wants to send a company newsletter to its customers by e-mail. To accomplish this, the company maintains its database of e-mail addresses on a local system disconnected from the Internet and transmits a copy of the list of addresses to its Internet account. There it is used to address a copy of the newsletter and is encrypted, making it unreadable and secure until the next time when the company needs the information. Most encryption today is based on software algorithms, which are notoriously slow—certainly too slow for any sort of on-the-fly encryption of network traffic—but hardware encryption has proven to have many political and technological problems of its own too. How much will it cost? How pervasive will it be?

Several commercial e-mail programs, such as Lotus' cc:Mail, already incorporate encryption. Other programs in the UNIX environment, notably Elm, offer a simple message-scrambling capability. Microsoft's Remote Access System (RAS) and Apple's System 7 both offer built-in encryption. Most versions of UNIX include the powerful crypt encryption program with the system. Racal-Guardata of Herndon, Virginia; Morning Star Technologies of Columbus, Ohio, and UUNET Technologies of Falls Church, Virginia, all sell hardware for encrypting data before it leaves your site.

Another solution is Kerberos, developed by Project Athena at the Massachusetts Institute of Technology. Using separate keys and messages, known as secrets, Kerberos operates in such a way that users on the MIT campus-wide network or any other network with Kerberos facilities do not have to send passwords or any other sensitive information in unencrypted text—known as *cleartext*—which makes it impossible for electronic eavesdroppers to get hold of the key to the network's security system.

An up-and-coming encryption system is Privacy-Enhanced Mail, or PEM, which uses digital signatures for security and authentication purposes. Perhaps the most promising system is PGP—short for Pretty Good Privacy. It is a more secure version of public key encryption, because it enables secure message transmission. Here is how you can use it in your business: You first publish a public key. When customers want to send a message containing sensitive information to your firm, they enter the public key and their own private key. PGP uses a combination of both to encrypt the data suitable for transmission through e-mail. When the message is received, your representative could decode the message with a combination of the public key from the other company and your firm's private key. With this system, you do not need to know the key that your customer used. Likewise, no customers ever learn the PGP key that you use.

Encryption Lingo

The more you learn about data encryption, the more acronyms and lingo you are likely to encounter. To help you out, here are explanations of four of the most common terms. The information comes in part from a frequently asked questions (FAQ) document maintained by Marc VanHeyningen. You should pay close attention to the comments about which encryption systems are acceptable for export from the United States and which are restricted by the Department of Defense.

RIPEM—short for Mark Riordan's Internet Privacy Enhanced Mail—is a developing privacy-enhanced mail software application based on pending international PEM standards.

RIPEM offers four security features: disclosure protection, originator authenticity, message integrity, and nonrepudiation of origin. Nonrepudiation of origin ensures that the message cannot be read en route, which guarantees that no portions of the message are lost during transmittal. Most of the code is in the public domain, except for certain encryption routines that come from a library licensed from RSA Data Security.

To obtain a copy of RIPEM, you can use the ftp program to connect to the computer `ripem.msu.edu`, which is open to ftp for users in the United States and Canada. To find out how to obtain the application itself, you must ftp to the system, change to the `pub/crypt` directory with the `cd` command, and read the file GETTING_ACCESS. Or use URL `ftp://ripem.msu.edu/pub/crypt/GETTING_ACCESS`.

RSA—short for Rivest, Shamir, and Adleman, its inventors—is a public key cryptographic system. This means that there are two different, related keys. One key encrypts, and the other one decrypts. Because each key cannot be derived from the other one, users can publish their encryption (public) key widely and keep their decryption (private) key to themselves. Anyone can use your public key to encrypt a message, but only you hold the private key needed to decrypt it.

To find out more about RSA and modern cryptography in general, use the ftp program to obtain any of the various related documents available on `rsa.com`. Look in `pub/faq/`. Or, use the URL `ftp://rsa.com/pub/faq/`.

DES—short for Data Encryption Standard—is unlike RSA and other public key encryption systems. DES requires that the same encryption key be used at both ends of the process. If you want people to send you data encrypted with DES, you must tell them your private encryption key. If anyone else learns the key, he can decrypt your files with impunity. The big advantage to DES, particularly with UNIX and dialup Internet accounts, is that the UNIX `crypt` program is widely available. Like all other DES implementations, it is considerably faster than RSA.

DES is sometimes considered to make data less secure because it is older and uses an internal key length considered too short by current standards. However, it should be reasonably safe against an opponent smaller than a large corporation or government agency.

PGP—short for Pretty Good Privacy—is a cryptographic mail program based on public key encryption. PGP has been around longer than RIPEM and is sufficiently different so that the two are incompatible and mutually exclusive. If your colleagues use RIPEM, you need to use it as well or you won't be able to read their messages.

You may have noticed that RIPEM and PGP seem to be implementations of the same encryption system, and you are absolutely right. The main difference between the two is that RIPEM has been designed to conform with a new privacy-enhanced mail standards specification document, whereas PGP is noncompliant. What this means is that today you need to make the same program available to both sender and recipient. Down the road, though, you should expect RIPEM to be more likely to work than PGP. Which is actually better? We recommend you try both and talk with your customers and clients to see what they use. Ultimately, the more popular program is the better choice for your company.

Although PGP and RIPEM may not be legally sent outside the United States and Canada without an export license, the PGP program has already been distributed through the networks—potentially illegally—and is widely available throughout the world.

Emergency Measures: What to Do If a Break-In Occurs

Despite all the Internet security measures now available, break-ins do occur. If you have a computer system or local area network on the Internet and believe that security has been breached, contact CERT immediately at its 24-hour hotline: (412) 268-7090. Be prepared to supply the following information:

The names of the computers compromised at your site.

The kind of computers that were compromised, including details on operating systems and related software.

Whether security upgrades, modifications, or vendor-supplied patches have been applied to the compromised systems. If yes, were patches applied before or after the intrusion?

The accounts that were compromised.

Other hosts or sites that might be involved in the intrusion and whether you have already contacted the sites about the security violation.

The contact information used for contacting sites, if you contacted them.

The contact information for other sites that might have been affected so that CERT can contact them directly.

Whether law enforcement agencies have been contacted.

Excerpts from any potentially relevant system logs, including available timestamps.

What assistance you would like from the CERT Coordination Center.

Additional Resources

This chapter has discussed the importance of good security and a variety of approaches to achieving it. There are many additional sources of information on encryption, public key systems, Internet security, and timely bulletins on potential security problems and break-ins. Here are some of the best:

Computer Bulletin Boards and Discussion Groups

VIRUS-L mailing list. VIRUS-L is a moderated Internet mailing list with a focus on computer virus issues. Instead of sending dozens of messages every day, this mailing list distributes information in digest form. It is essentially an electronic newsletter that compiles all recent messages. For more information, including a copy of the posting guidelines, use the ftp program to connect to `cert.org`. Look for the `virus-l.README` file in the `/pub/virus-l` directory. To be added to the mailing list, send an e-mail message to `listserv@lehigh.edu` with the message body stating SUBSCRIBE VIRUS-L *yourname*.

VALERT-L mailing list. VALERT-L is a quick way to share urgent virus warnings with other Internet computer users. Any message sent to VALERT-L also appears in the next VIRUS-L digest. To be added to the mailing list, send e-mail to `listserv@lehigh.edu`. In the body of the message, type SUBSCRIBE VALERT-L *yourname*.

`comp.security.announce.` This Usenet newsgroup is used solely for the distribution of CERT advisories. It is necessary reading for anyone interested in security on the Internet.

`comp.security.misc.` This Usenet newsgroup offers a forum for the discussion of computer security, especially as it relates to the UNIX operating system.

`alt.security.` This Usenet newsgroup discusses computer security. Security issues unrelated to the Internet, such as car alarms, locks, and personal security systems, are often discussed as well.

`comp.virus.` This Usenet newsgroup focuses on computer virus issues. Much of the information that arrives here is a copy of the messages sent to the VIRUS-L mailing list. To obtain a copy of the newsgroup guidelines, use the ftp program to connect to `cert.org`. Look for the `virus-l.README` file in the `pub/virus-l` directory.

comp.risks. This Usenet newsgroup discusses the risks to the public from computers and related systems. One of the oldest newsgroups, comp.risks, is a terrific place to learn about the latest break-ins and security problems in the world around us. You'll soon start to realize that things are much less secure than you would think!

Web sites. The Web has a number of interesting sites to visit if you want to learn more about security. Starting with the comp.security.misc Usenet group FAQ file is a good bet:

//www.lib.ox.ac.uk/internet/news/faq/comp.security.misc.html

You can glean an amazing amount of information from a visit to Yahoo. Start at

//www.yahoo.com/Science/Mathematics/Security_and_Encryption/

The Computer Emergency Response Team (CERT)

Because it is so vital to Internet security, it is worth discussing CERT in more detail. CERT was formed by the Defense Advanced Research Projects Agency (DARPA) in November 1988, immediately following the Internet worm attack, when it became painfully clear that there was no effective way quickly to disseminate security information to the Internet community and no agency charged with tracking and maintaining a history of security incidents. The CERT charter is to work with the Internet community to facilitate its response to computer security events involving Internet hosts, to help raise the community's awareness of computer security issues, and to conduct research targeted at improving the security of existing systems.

CERT products and services include 24-hour technical assistance for responding to computer security incidents, product vulnerability assistance, technical documents, and seminars. In addition, the team maintains a number of mailing lists—including one for CERT advisories—and it provides an anonymous ftp server—cert.org—where security-related documents, past CERT advisories, and tools are archived and available for viewing.

In cooperation with a number of leading computer and operating systems vendors, CERT advisories provide information on how to obtain a patch or the details of a workaround for known security problems. For obvious reasons, CERT does not publish vulnerability information until a workaround or patch is available. These advisories are published on the Usenet newsgroup comp.security.announce and are distributed via the cert-advisory mailing list. To join the list, send a note to cert-advisory-request@cert.org. If you can receive the Usenet group, we recommend that you use it instead to ease the load on the CERT computers.

Throughout the year, members of the CERT Coordination Center give presentations at various technical conferences, seminars, and meetings of regional network organizations. Periodically, special arrangements can be made to tailor the presentation to fit the requirements of the specific site. For information regarding presentations, contact the CERT Coordination Center.

Address:

CERT Coordination Center
Software Engineering Institute
Carnegie Mellon University
Pittsburgh, PA 15213-3890
U.S.A.

Internet e-mail address: `cert@cert.org`
Telephone number: (412) 268-7090 (24-hour hotline)
Fax number: (412) 268-6989
Information online: `ftp://ftp.cert.org/pub/cert_faq`

Books

There are a wide variety of different books on UNIX and Internet security. We recommend the following:

Bryant, R. Bringle. *UNIX Security for the Organization*. Sams, 1994.

Curry, David A. *UNIX System Security: A Guide for Users and System Administrators*. Addison-Wesley, 1992.

Denning, Peter J., ed. *Computers Under Attack: Intruders, Worms, and Viruses*. Addison-Wesley, 1990.

Garfinkel, Simson, and Gene Spafford. *Practical UNIX Security*. O'Reilly & Associates, 1991.

Hafner, Katie, and John Markoff. *Cyberpunk: Outlaws and Hackers on the Computer Frontier*. Simon and Schuster, 1991.

Neumann, Peter G. *Computer Related Risks*. ACM Press, 1994.

Siyan, Karanjit, and Chris Hare. *Internet Firewalls and Network Security*. NRP, 1995.

Summary

What needs to be done to make the Internet safe for business users? Perhaps the biggest change is ensure that all users of the Internet—business, educational, governmental, or recreational—focus on effective security measures that they can implement on their own accounts and computer systems. A surprising number of break-ins occur because of problems that could have been easily fixed with a bit of precaution and security savvy.

Experts in security focus on specific data security. Even with public key encryption standards and RSA encryption, two fundamental problems remain: making sure that the encryption software is widely distributed and extending it to include an unbreakable digital signature—an area particularly important in electronic commerce.

The good news is that many security experts are addressing this problem. The IP Security working group of the Internet Engineering Task Force is actively working on how to make the Internet truly secure. The result of this work is already beginning to show up. Soon sending information over the Internet will be much more secure soon than talking on the telephone or handing your American Express card to a clerk at the local shop. (See Chapter 16, "Getting Paid (Safely)," for more information about credit-card encryption, digital cash, and other secure ways of transacting business online.)

Evidence of the improvements in Internet security is the growing number of turnkey-secure server systems available from companies such as Netscape Communications, Terisa, Sun Microsystems, Silicon Graphics, and Digital Equipment Corp. If you do not have access to security experts and want to ensure that what you want private stays safe, they can be a terrific alternative.

THE COMMERCIAL NETS

Business Opportunities on the Commercial Nets

When you hear the term *information superhighway*, you likely think of the Internet. Although we believe that the Internet is the best choice for doing business online, other networks might be better suited to your company's needs.

Although smaller than the Internet, the three big online services— America Online, CompuServe, and Prodigy—had 6.3 million subscribers at the end of March 1995, nearly double their headcount of a year ago, according to Electronic Information Report. The breakdown: America Online—2.2 million subscribers, up from 700,000; CompuServe—2.8 million members, up from 1.8 million; and Prodigy—1.3 million members, up from 1.13 million. SIMBA Information, Inc., a market research firm, predicts that by 1998 close to 15 million people throughout the United States will subscribe to commercial online services.

For businesses, the commercial networks offer several advantages over the Internet—at least for now. One big plus is ease of use. Although there are now plenty of graphical interfaces for the Internet, many Internet users—especially people who log in through universities and community free-nets—must make do with terminal screens and UNIX prompts. The three big online services offer free or inexpensive graphical front-ends so that users can bypass the confusing text-based interfaces that bog down so much of today's Internet usage. They also feature directories of databases, bulletin boards, and members, which makes them far easier than the Internet to search and navigate.

Another advantage for businesses is the capability to set up secure online shopping malls on the networks and to transact business there—although, as you saw in Chapter 16, "Getting Paid (Safely)," it is far safer to send credit card data through the Internet now than it was a year ago. Moreover, you can advertise on welcome screens that point shoppers directly to your store—unlike the Internet, on which you must post notes about your online shop in dozens of different directories and discussion groups, with no guarantee that anybody will find you.

The third advantage to using commercial online services is cultural. Although the commercial online services try to restrict blatant advertising to the "classified" sections of their services, they are typically less strict than Internet newsgroups and mailing lists about what constitutes an ad. Likewise, the people who use commercial online services tend to be more tolerant of thinly disguised sales pitches than some of the purists on the Internet. As a result, flame wars are far less common.

So what's the catch? The biggest drawback to doing business on the commercial online networks is financial: Commercial online services are far more expensive than the Internet. In the commercial world, online time is metered, although prices have dropped considerably. Some services charge fees for sending and receiving e-mail. Many databases are steeply surcharged. After all, the commercial networks are private-sector companies that are out to make a profit, not just to have fun.

As we wrap up this book, we think that you will find it useful to learn how the three big online services stack up against the Internet. You will also find out about new services, such as Apple's eWorld, AT&T Interchange, and the Microsoft Network. This chapter takes a look at what each service offers for businesses and analyzes its strengths and weaknesses. The next chapter profiles the virtual communities found on the services. You will find out how much the networks charge for e-mail, advertising, storefronts, and other services. You will also learn how to craft a successful online marketing and communications strategy that combines the best of what the Internet and the commercial online services have to offer. That, after all, is the bottom line—finding the best online solution for your business, no matter what kind of product or service you sell.

Commercial Online Services versus the Internet

Like the Internet, commercial online services provide e-mail, file transfer, discussion groups, and sales and marketing capabilities. Both types of networks can be accessed through modems and local-area networks. Both reach an international user base.

That is where the similarities end. Here are some of the key business differences between the Internet and its commercial cousins:

Demographics. The commercial online services, with the exception of CompuServe, attract primarily home computer users, not business owners, government officials, or academics. Unlike the Internet, the commercial networks tend to reach a predominantly domestic subscriber base. CompuServe, the online service with the biggest international presence, has only one million subscribers outside the United States.

Culture. Subscribers to commercial online services tend to be less averse to advertising and solicitation than Internet users are. As a result, advertisers on commercial services can put up display ads and storefronts. In some cases, they can send targeted mailings to subscribers who express interest in their products.

Infrastructure. Commercial networks provide a ready-made infrastructure complete with mainframe computers, a nationwide (or worldwide) network of local-access telephone numbers, a well-advertised market presence, hundreds of bulletin boards, and the capability to set up a gateway to databases. Therefore, there is no need to set up your own shop as you would on the Web. The downside is that commercial networks typically take a hefty cut of the online revenues generated by their business partners, or they charge steep setup fees.

Pricing. Unlike Internet access, which typically offers users unlimited access to e-mail and other services for a flat monthly fee, subscribers to commercial networks pay based on actual usage. Though prices have come down dramatically over the last year—the Big Three have slashed their rates to under $3 an hour—you could end up spending much more for online access than you would if you opened an account with an Internet access provider.

E-mail. Unlike the Internet, on which users pay a flat fee to send an unlimited number of e-mail messages, the two largest commercial networks, CompuServe and Prodigy, levy per-message surcharges after the subscriber has exceeded his monthly allotment of free e-mail. Although that allotment might be more than sufficient for individual users, businesses that rely on e-mail as their primary communications tool can be in for an unpleasant surprise when they receive their bill at the end of the month. Moreover, CompuServe charges a minimum of ten cents per message to receive Internet e-mail, which means that you could end up spending a pretty penny if you subscribe to a busy mailing list.

Discussion groups. Commercial networks offer computer bulletin boards, similar to Internet newsgroups, on thousands of topics from pet care and scuba diving to small business and computing. In fact, many leading hardware and software companies provide technical support bulletin boards on the commercial services. Commercial services, however, lack the equivalent of the Internet's mailing lists through which companies can automatically distribute postings, press releases, brochures, and product announcements to colleagues and customers.

Databases. Although the Internet offers a wealth of free government, university, and technical information, the commercial services offer gateways to the world of pay-as-you-go information sources, such as Dow Jones News/Retrieval, S&P Online, Disclosure, Predicasts, and Ziff-Davis' Computer Database Plus. (Many of these fee-based databases, however, are now available through the Internet. See Chapter 17, "Mining for Business Information.")

Walls. Unlike the Internet, on which you can telnet from one computer to another to order a book or download a file, you cannot travel freely from one commercial service to another. If you are a CompuServe subscriber, for instance, you cannot access an America Online bulletin board. Likewise, if you are a Prodigy member, you cannot search a CompuServe database or read the latest electronic issue of *Time* magazine on America Online. The walls that still exist between the commercial services for competitive reasons mean that it is impossible for a company to make a single media "buy" that reaches all subscribers, as you can on the Internet.

Making Money on the Commercial Networks

There are a variety of ways for businesses to use the commercial online networks to promote, advertise, and sell their products. In fact, there are many more options than currently on the Internet. Here are seven of them:

Networking. Just as you can post notes on Internet newsgroups or mailing lists, you can tack notes on commercial network bulletin boards, which can be an excellent way to market your products and boost company awareness. If you sell software to mail-order vendors, for example, you might want to put a note on CompuServe's Entrepreneur's Forum. If you sell baby gifts, you might want to post a note on Prodigy's Homelife Bulletin Board. It is important to keep your postings more informational than promotional, however. Posting a list of "10 Ways to Save Money on Your Taxes" goes over better than a blatant ad for your accounting firm.

> **Tip:** Cultures vary in cyberspace, but as a general rule, users respond more favorably to advertisements that contain useful and interesting information rather than empty hype.

Targeted e-mail. Some commercial services permit—and even encourage—targeted mailings to subscribers based on interests or demographic criteria. This means that you can send an ad for your new pet food to anybody who belongs to the service's Pet Lovers Bulletin Board. It also means that you can send reminder notices a week before Mother's Day to all the people who placed an order at your online flower shop within the last year. True, you could do the same with an Internet flower shop, but it is impossible to know who subscribes to a particular Usenet newsgroup.

Advertising. The three big commercial networks offer classified advertising, the same as you would find in the Classifieds section of a daily newspaper. All three also offer full-color display advertising similar to glossy ads in magazines. Commercial networks permit advertisers to post notices on the welcome screen that appears when the subscriber logs on. Choosing the number next to it automatically transports the user to the vendor's online area.

Online storefronts. Prodigy and CompuServe feature large online shopping malls with hundreds of merchants hawking everything from computers to CDs to flowers. Subscribers can browse through merchandise, find out pricing and product information, and place orders online by typing their credit card numbers. The price of setting up shop can be steep, however.

Sponsorship. Commercial networks offer companies the opportunity to sponsor an online area, a less obtrusive form of advertising that enhances their online presence without peddling a specific product. Microsoft, for example, sponsors the Microsoft Small Business Center on America Online. Advertising sponsorships have become popular on the Internet over the last year, as you saw in Chapter 14, "Is Anybody Making Money on the Net?"

Joint ventures. These days, dozens of newspapers, magazines, and other media companies are hooking up with commercial networks to publish online editions. *The New York Times, Time, Road & Track, The San Jose Mercury-News, The Chicago Tribune, The Atlanta Journal and Constitution, U.S. News & World Report*, and *The Detroit Free Press* have joined forces with commercial networks within the last few years. Typically, the print publication gets a 10% to 15% share of the revenues generated by the online area through users' connect-time charges, although profit splits and revenue guarantees are coming into vogue as the online services compete to sign up print publishers and lure their large subscriber base.

Once they are online, the newspapers and magazines can sell advertising space and subscriptions to their print publications, books, software, and other products.

Database gateways and publishing. The commercial networks offer gateways to specialized databases that contain financial, research, travel, directory, and other information. The database provider typically receives a share of the revenues generated by the online service's subscribers.

How the Commercial Online Services Stack Up

Now that you know how commercial services differ from the Internet, it is time to look at the business opportunities that each service offers. Remember that advertising and setup fees that seem expensive by Internet standards should be judged by their effectiveness in ringing up sales. If Prodigy can bring your business $4 million each year in sales as it does for PC Flowers, it might be worth the price that you would pay to set up an online storefront.

CompuServe

Advertisers in CompuServe's Electronic Mall pay approximately $50,000 to set up a store online plus a 2% commission on each sale. This includes 200 products with descriptions, 500 products without descriptions, 100 graphics with quarterly updating, 52 Mall Marquees, 500 $5 usage credits, and a $15,000 CompuServe Magazine advertising credit toward a minimum commitment. This fall, CompuServe plans to open its Mall to Internet users as well. Figure 20.1 shows a special Mother's Day area that enables CompuServe subscribers to shop for clothes, flowers, food, gifts, and other items.

CompuServe also maintains a Classified Ads area. As with placing a classified ad in a newspaper, the cost of putting a classified ad on CompuServe varies depending on the size of the message and the length of time it is displayed. A 7-day listing costs $1.00 per line; a 14-day listing costs $1.50 per line; a 56-day listing costs $5.20 per line; and a 182-day listing costs $14.30 per line. Each line can consist of up to 65 characters.

CompuServe works with online publishers on a revenue-sharing basis, paying them a small portion of the connect-time revenues that their online areas bring in.

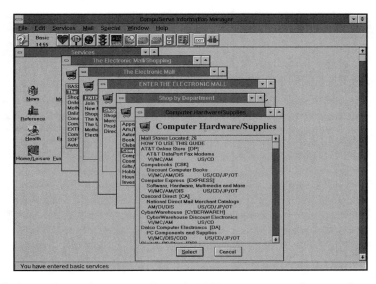

Figure 20.1. CompuServe charges merchants $50,000 to set up an online storefront in its mall.

Prodigy

Prodigy charges premium prices for display advertising on its service. A five-screen Standard Advertising Unit—that is, a full-screen ad with multiple access points—costs $27,500 per month. A 15-screen buy costs $37,500 per month, and a 30-screen buy costs $54,200 per month.

Now that Prodigy has rolled out Web access, the service has established a rate card for its home page (http://www.astranet.com). It charges $4,000 per week for a premium listing on its home page—an example of which is shown in Figure 20.2—and $2,000 per week for a standard listing. The weekly fee for an ad on Prodigy's Best of the Net pages is $1,000 for a premium listing and $500 for a standard listing. Budget-minded businesses can pay from $150 to $250 each week to list their Web site on Prodigy's Shopping pages.

Prodigy allows advertisers to send targeted e-mailings to subscribers, based on a variety of demographic and interest-group criteria. Creative and production fees cost extra. For targeted mailings, the service charges a cost-per-thousand of $300 to $500, depending on the number of mailings sent. Prodigy charges additional fees for printable coupons, dealer locators, informational databases, advertiser-sponsored bulletin boards, and other promotional services.

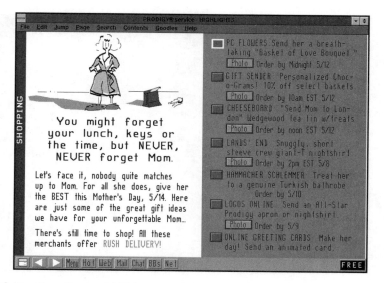

Figure 20.2. Prodigy charges $4,000 per week for a premium listing on its home page.

Prodigy's business classified advertising rates range from $75 a screen for a two-week display to $200 a screen for a three-month display. Additional screens cost $5 each.

Prodigy hosts online newspapers and magazines on its service both on a revenue-sharing basis and on a profit-splitting basis. A profit-splitting basis is one in which both the publisher and Prodigy bear their own costs and split any profits.

America Online

Thanks to its new multimedia Rainman software, America Online offers display advertising on its service. Unlike Prodigy, however, America Online does not run display ads across the bottom of its screen, although some of its online newspapers and magazines have started selling advertising in their forums. Two examples are *Bicycling* magazine and *Time Online,* shown in Figure 20.3. In some cases, publishers keep all the ad revenues that they generate, and sometimes they split them with the service. America Online pays publishers royalties of 10% to 20% based on connect-time revenues generated by their online areas plus sign-up bonuses of around $15 for each new member whom they recruit to the service.

America Online's shopping area is smaller than those of its two larger rivals. As for the cost of establishing a commercial presence on the service, America Online says that it does not publicly disclose the details of its arrangements with its information partners. Unlike the other commercial services, however, it does not charge a fee for placing classified ads online.

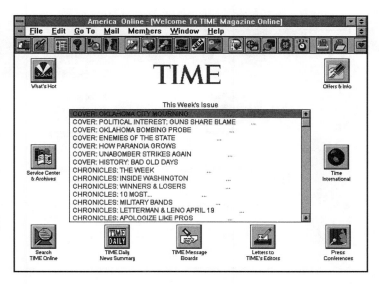

Figure 20.3. America Online allows online newspapers and magazines, such as *Time Online*, to sell advertising in their forums.

eWorld

For now, there are no ads on eWorld, Apple's new online service, although publications can sell subscriptions and other products. Later this year, eWorld will unveil a plan to reward publishers based on factors such as metered rates, download fees, transaction charges, and display ads.

Even though the service has not signed up any newspapers yet, it recently snared two national magazines: *Inc.*, shown in Figure 20.4, and *Writer's Digest*. eWorld publishers get a royalty based on usage, typically around 15%. Although eWorld's revenue splits are no more generous than many of its online rivals, publishers will be able to reap higher revenues by offering surcharged services such as software downloads and other interactive components for which subscribers might want to pay extra. eWorld will also permit publishers to set up individual gateways, thereby enabling them to own their own subscribers. eWorld offers sign-up bonuses and, in some cases, revenue guarantees.

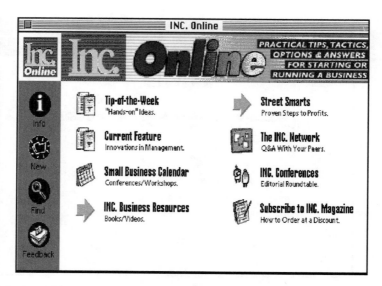

Figure 20.4. eWorld hosts several online publications, including *Inc.* magazine.

AT&T Interchange

If Interchange were in the business of flipping burgers, its motto would probably be "Have it your way." Billing itself as a next-generation publishing platform, Interchange, launched by Ziff-Davis and recently purchased by AT&T, was designed to enable newspapers and magazines to build their own online services on its network.

So far, the service has signed up *The Washington Post* (Digital Ink), *The Minneapolis Star-Tribune* (Star Tribune Online), Ziff-Davis Publishing Co., and Cowles Business Media. Rather than link up with the service as information providers, publishers are invited to join Interchange as publishing partners, keeping 75% to 80% of the revenue that they bring in, minus fees associated with acquisitions, support, and telecommunications. It's up to the publishers to build circulation. These alliances enable publishers to control every aspect of their online destiny, from a publication's appearance to pricing and advertising. Publishers also bear significant financial risks, such as the cost of acquiring and maintaining their own subscribers.

Interchange, shown in Figure 20.5, offers publishers more flexibility in terms of pricing. The first five hours of connect time are a flat rate set by the publisher. Any additional connect-time charges are allocated between the publisher and the network based on the amount of time that the user spends in the publisher's online area. For example, if a *Washington Post* reader spent all his time in the *Washington Post* area, the *Post* would keep all the money generated. Interchange is expected to go live this summer.

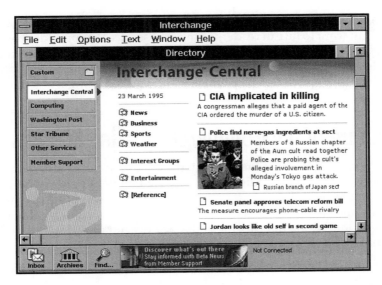

Figure 20.5. If Interchange were in the business of flipping burgers, its motto would probably be "Have it your way."

Microsoft Network

Looming like a dark cloud over the Big Three is the Microsoft Network, expected to debut in August with the launch of Windows 95. At the April Internet World show in San Jose, attendees crowded around as a Microsoft demonstrator seamlessly dragged and dropped files and images from the Internet to his hard drive and back again over a 28.8 kbps connection that seemed much faster. "All you need to know is how to double-click it," he told his mesmerized audience. "You don't need to know anything else." Because MSN looks and feels just like any other Windows 95 application, it became difficult to tell during the demo whether the data was being retrieved from MSN, the Internet, or the computer's hard drive—which presumably is what Microsoft is counting on.

What may be bad news for CompuServe, Prodigy, and America Online presents exciting opportunities for businesses, especially for publishers and other information providers. Rather than splitting connect-time revenues with Microsoft as newspapers and magazines do on the other services, publishers will get a cut of the sales they ring up. Each time a publisher sells information through the network, it will pay Microsoft a commission of 5% to 45% to provide the transaction services.

Suppose that your company publishes stock quotes. On the Microsoft Network, you might want to lure in readers with a free service that provides basic financial news. Once a reader who owns, for example, 100 shares of Exxon, reads that his stock has dropped, he might want to pay $2 to read a more in-depth story to find out why. Rack up enough $2 payments and you're talking real money!

The Future of the Commercial Online Services

With the rapid growth of the Internet, the demise of commercial online services such as CompuServe, Prodigy, and America Online is being widely predicted. The reasoning goes like this: If online users can get everything they want—from live chat and special-interest bulletin boards to cool graphics and mountains of information—on the Internet for under $20 per month, why should they waste their time with for-profit services that charge them by the hour?

Personally, we think that reports of the impending death of commercial services are greatly exaggerated. We are willing to bet that the three big for-profit networks will be alive and kicking a year from now—and enjoying record growth and healthy profits.

These are four reasons why we think that the commercial online services are here to stay:

1. Nobody wants to sift through 14,000 newsgroups and 27,000 Web servers.

   You could sit home and watch CNN and C-Span all day and save a couple hundred bucks a year by not buying a newspaper, but do you? Of course not. You have a life—not to mention a job to go to. The same is true with the Internet. If you really wanted, you could surf the Net for hours on end and scoop up information on just about anything you ever wanted to know. Most people, though, don't have the time or patience to do that.

   That's where the commercial services come in. They take the chaos of the Internet and give it structure and order. America Online, for example, offers an area called Internet Connection that organizes the Internet's unruly mass of information so that members can quickly zero in on only those things that interest them. Looking for a place to talk about online marketing? Just type in the word `marketing`. Within seconds, you get a list of all the Internet's marketing-related discussion groups.

2. People like a place to hang their hat.

   Even in cyberspace, where nobody knows whether you are a dog and where you can try on new personalities and disguises, people prefer to hang out where they feel they belong. All the major commercial services—not to mention thousands of smaller, for-profit bulletin board systems—feature forums, or special interest groups, that are really online communities.

For the quilters who hang out on CompuServe's Crafts Forum, for instance, CompuServe isn't just a place to bone up on the latest needle-craft techniques. It is a long-distance support group where friends who have never met can share news of births, deaths, and marriages. These people are not going to switch to the Internet's `alt.crafts.quilting` newsgroup—or one just like it that's certain to spring up—just because it costs a few bucks less.

3. The Internet is still too hard to get around.

Imagine New York City without street signs, the Kalahari Desert without a map, and hieroglyphics without the Rosetta stone and you're starting to get an idea of what it's like to navigate the Internet if you don't know where you are going. Despite new point-and-click interfaces like Internet in a Box that make surfing the Net a whole lot easier, finding your way around the Net is still a challenge.

But getting around is only half the battle. The other problem is installing the software that you need to get onto the Internet in the first place—if you want to surf the Web, that is. Even experienced online users often have trouble installing the TCP/IP software that enables your personal computer to access the network directly and to talk to other Internet computers in a language that they can understand. Then you have to find, retrieve, and install a copy of Mosaic, Netscape, or some other browser software to view the Web in graphical format. That's a tall order, considering that many computer users have trouble downloading a file.

Again, this is where commercial services have the edge. On Prodigy, the first commercial service to make Web access available to its members, you click one button and Prodigy automatically ships you a copy of its Web browser while you wait. You don't have to install TCP/IP software or get a direct Internet connection. Prodigy's computer goes onto the Web and sends you a copy of any Web page that you want—without your computer ever having to talk to the Internet directly.

4. Commercial services are a better, safer place to shop.

The Internet is still not ready for prime time when it comes to online retailing. Because nobody organizes the Internet's many shops and shopping malls, it is hard to find the stores that have what you are looking for. Moreover, mall security is lax on the Internet, making it relatively easy for hackers to filch your credit card number when you place an online order. Compare that to the commercial online services, where mall security is tight. Nobody gets in unless he or she is a registered user.

Should You Put Your Money on the Commercial Services?

Where is all this headed? In the coming months, watch for Internet merchants to pay big money to the commercial services to steer online users their way through hyperlinked mentions on the Internet hotlists and home pages that they are setting up for their services. Internet merchants probably will be willing to pay the online services to give them valuable demographic data about the shoppers who visit their sites.

It's instructive to note that CompuServe started out in the 1970s selling time-share services on its mainframes. When the market changed, CompuServe entered the online service business, hosting interactive forums and providing access to databases and other information. Recently, CompuServe bought Spry, the developer of Internet in A Box, and now is poised to become one of the world's largest Internet access providers.

Don't count the Big Three out.

HOW THE OTHER HALF LIVES

In the late 1980s, fewer than 1,000,000 Americans subscribed to commercial online services. Today, the total number of people online with the various commercial services is close to 7,000,000. The number is likely to double within the next four years—and that doesn't count the tens of thousands of people who dial up independently owned bulletin board systems (BBSs) nationwide.

Other demographic trends are also encouraging. According to Link Resources' Annual Home Media Survey, 36.4% of U.S. households now own personal computers, 53% of personal computer owners have modems, and 24% of modem users log onto online services. These numbers clearly illustrate that the online marketplace is no longer a futuristic fantasy.

This chapter is designed to acquaint you with the diversity of communities that exist on the major commercial online services and to help you market to these communities sensitively and effectively. The more you know about what makes people tick on CompuServe, Prodigy, America Online, and eWorld, the better positioned your company will be to sell to them—on the online service to which they subscribe and on the Internet.

Tapping into Virtual Communities

Just as there are thousands of distinct "virtual communities" on the Internet, there are just as many on the commercial online services. A young mother who seeks advice on Prodigy's Homelife Bulletin Board is unlikely to warm to the same sales pitch directed to a middle-aged executive on CompuServe who likes to download shareware that will make his PC run better and faster.

Here is a quick tour of the major online services and the people you'll find there.

CompuServe

CompuServe Information Service, a unit of H&R Block, is the most business-oriented of the commercial online services.

An information treasure chest that doubles as one of the world's busiest online communications hubs, CompuServe offers access to more than 2,000 databases, including newspaper and magazine libraries, stock market and financial data, an online stock brokerage, an online shopping mall, and an online travel agency, along with communications links to the Internet, MCI Mail, AT&T Mail, the NetWare MHS Local-Area Network, and fax and Telex machines around the world.

By entering key words or phrases, CompuServe's Executive News Service subscribers can clip news stories from, among other sources, the Associated Press, United Press International, *The Washington Post*, Reuters Financial, and OTC NewsAlert (an information service on over-the-counter stocks).

CompuServe enjoys an especially strong following among the small business and entrepreneurial crowd. It is also the most cosmopolitan of the commercial services, with close to 2,000,000 subscribers in the United States and Canada, 700,000 subscribers in the Pacific Rim, 300,000 in Europe, and 80,000 in the rest of the world.

In addition to the standard online staples of news, weather, sports, and computer games, CompuServe offers hundreds of special-interest bulletin boards, called forums (pictured in Figure 21.1), where its 3,000,000 members gather to discuss everything from quilt making to fantasy baseball, and to download free and low-cost software. CompuServe's forums provide free technical support for most major hardware and software vendors, and its CB Simulator chat area provides a forum for real-time conversations.

Until recently, CompuServe had two main drawbacks—difficulty of use and high cost. For novice users, the service's complex command structure and text-based interface were difficult to navigate. Its connect-time charges—$12.80 per hour for 2,400bps access and $22.80 per hour for 9,600bps and 14.4Kbps access—were far higher than its competitors.

These drawbacks have been mitigated, however. CompuServe Information Manager (CIM), a graphical front-end program for DOS, Windows, and Macintosh platforms, makes the service much easier to navigate. Subscribers can click icons, pull-down boxes, and other on-screen options with a mouse instead of typing commands at the system prompt. On CIM, subscribers can compose mail and set up file transfers before logging on, thereby saving time and money.

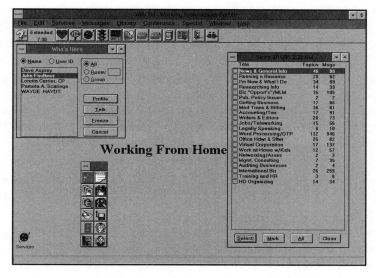

Figure 21.1. CompuServe enjoys a strong following among the business crowd.

CompuServe has also taken steps to bring its pricing more in line with the rest of the pack by introducing a $9.95-per-month flat fee plan that includes unlimited access to 120 of its basic services. Although CompuServe still charges $4.80 per hour for access to its bulletin boards, members now get three hours of Internet access, which includes access to the World Wide Web. Additional Internet usage is billed at $2.95 per hour. Access to CompuServe's extended services, such as special-interest bulletin boards (forums), is billed at $4.80 per hour for all modem speeds up to and including 14.4 kbps. CompuServe's Internet Club enables members pay an additional $15 per month—that is, $24.95 per month total—for 30 hours of Internet access. Additional Internet usage costs $1.95 per hour.

Demographics

Here is how CompuServe's demographics break down:

Membership: 3,000,000
Gender: 83% male, 17% female
Median age: 40.8 years

Education: 71% have a college degree or higher
Marital status: 70% are married
Average annual household income: $90,340

Prodigy

Designed with the novice user in mind, Prodigy revolutionized the online world when it burst on the scene in 1989. The brainchild of IBM and Sears, Prodigy is part user-friendly videotext service and part Home Shopping Network, reflecting both sides of its unusual lineage.

A family-oriented online service that works hard to maintain its G rating, Prodigy serves up wholesome fare guaranteed to delight, amuse, and entertain even the youngest computer user. Of the big three online services, Prodigy offers by far the largest and most varied array of information and services for children. Prodigy also boasts the largest percentage of women users—38% at last count—of any of the major commercial networks.

Subscribers can use the Prodigy Mall to browse through hundreds of online stores hawking everything from CDs to flowers and to view real-time drawings and photographs of the products available.

Over the last few years, Prodigy has taken steps to broaden its appeal to more technologically sophisticated computer users—and to prevent its existing members from moving on. In January 1995, Prodigy became the first major commercial online service to offer its members access to the Web (see Figure 21.2). It now has over 500,000 Web users. In April, Prodigy signed an agreement with three Baby Bell companies to provide high-speed ISDN (Integrated Services Digital Network) access to its online service and to the Internet. Prodigy members in Boston, Nashville, San Jose, and Woodland Hills, California, will be the first to get ISDN access. IBM, Prodigy's co-owner, will begin offering a consumer-grade ISDN modem called the Wave Runner to Prodigy members for $495.

Meanwhile, Prodigy's new Windows interface, called P2, is expected to be available by the time this book is published. The new interface will be written completely in HTML and will improve navigation between Prodigy and the Internet. Prodigy's current interface has been widely criticized as cartoonish and clunky.

Prodigy has taken steps to solidify its popularity among the mainstream consumers that form its core membership base. Lower prices, real-time chat rooms, faster modem speeds, and joint ventures with companies such as ESPN, *The Los Angeles Times,* and Cox Newspapers have enhanced its content and have attracted new subscribers.

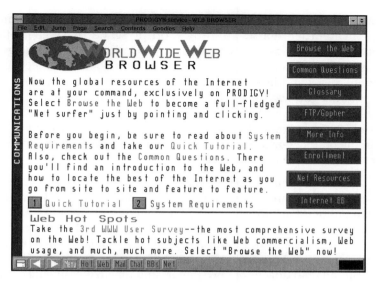

Figure 21.2. Prodigy's Web browser has helped attract new subscribers to the service.

Demographics

Here is how Prodigy's demographics break down:

Membership: More than 2,000,000. Some analysts say the number is actually closer to 1,300,000 if only primary account holders are counted and not other family members who sign on.

Gender: 62% male, 38% female

Median age: 41 years

Education: 77% have attended or graduated from college

Marital status: 66% are married

Median annual household income: $72,600

America Online

Logging onto America Online is like hanging out at the coolest watering hole in town without ever leaving your living room.

Over the last year, America's fastest-growing online service has zoomed past the 2,000,000-member mark, rivaling CompuServe in size—not counting CompuServe's overseas subscribers. America Online owes its rapid growth to an ample mix of live chat rooms, topical message boards, software stockpiles, online magazines, news and finance databases, a kids-only area, a senior citizens' center, an Internet gateway, and other features—all wrapped up in one easy-to-use package. The price is right, too. At $9.95 per month for five hours of basic services and $2.95 per hour after that, America Online has long been one of the best deals in the online world—although it will have to lower its prices if it wants to compete with flat-fee Internet access providers.

Part of America Online's appeal is that it offers something for everyone. Simply click a colorful icon and jump into a discussion on anything from genealogy to Christian politics. Each forum contains a related bulletin board, and subscribers who want to talk live can do so in hundreds of lively chat rooms with names like Over Forty, Romance Connection, and Teen Chat—or create their own. If you are looking for news you can use, America Online offers a fully stocked newsstand, where you can read dozens of newspapers and magazines, including *The Chicago Tribune, Time* magazine, and *Woman's Day*. America Online's reference desk offers encyclopedias, dictionaries, and even information about the White House. Its software center is free to all subscribers and contains hundreds of files that can be searched by category or keyword.

Over the last year, America Online has improved the service by rolling out a jazzy new multimedia interface that features on-screen photos and a new "departments" structure that makes it easier for users to locate areas of interest. The service's new Flash Sessions feature enables you to log on, send and retrieve your mail, and log off.

Like its rivals CompuServe and Prodigy, America Online has improved its Internet gateway and recently rolled out a preview version of its Web browser. However, it is primitive and needs work. If you have never surfed the Internet before, America Online is an excellent place to get your feet wet. The point-and-click interface and colorful icons offer a fun, easy way to access Internet e-mail, newsgroups, Gopher and WAIS databases, file-transfer protocol (FTP), and the Web (see Figure 21.3). Its Internet Connection offers a variety of resources—from a message board to an online version of *Wired* magazine—to help Internet novices tap into Net culture.

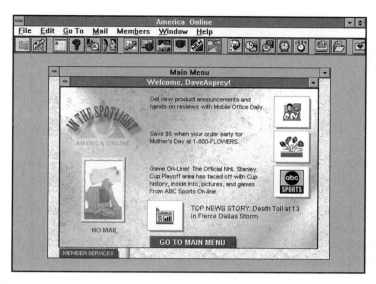

Figure 21.3. Logging onto America Online is like hanging out at the coolest watering hole in town without ever leaving your living room.

Demographics

Here is how America Online's demographics break down:

> **Membership:** 2,000,000
> **Gender:** 84% male, 16% female
> **Average age:** 40 years
> **Education:** 60% are college graduates
> **Marital status:** Not available
> **Average annual household income:** Greater than $50,000

eWorld

If you are marketing to Macintosh users, you have come to the right place. eWorld, Apple's new online service, has 75,000 of them signed up so far, and until the service rolls out a Windows version, there won't be a PC user in sight.

eWorld, pictured in Figure 21.4, has a laid-back California feel to it—hardly surprising considering the service's West Coast roots. Like its larger competitors, eWorld offers subscribers a wide variety of information and communications resources.

Members can read news bulletins from Reuters and UPI, research grants and funding assistance, search Grolier's Encyclopedia, get investment data, and browse online editions of *Inc.* and *Advertising Age.* For those in the mood for lighter fare, an online recipe catalog and video clips from newly released movies are available.

Figure 21.4. eWorld invites visitors to a quaint, leafy world that houses chat rooms, bulletin boards, and online publications.

Shoppers can choose from caviar, books, and other goodies in eWorld's marketplace. Members can also tack up for-sale notices in the eWorld classifieds and play a variety of online games—although they cannot yet play one another online. Hundreds of software programs and pictures can be downloaded.

Demographics

eWorld's demographic data was not available at presstime.

The Future of Commercial Online Services

Despite the soaring popularity of the Internet, the future of commercial services appears to be bright as well. Emboldened by the success of CompuServe, Prodigy, and America Online, Microsoft, AT&T, Apple, Hearst, Ziff, Bell Atlantic, and other technology and communications powerhouses are investing heavily in developing online networks. At the same time, *The Washington Post, The New York Times,* ESPN, Hachette Fillipache, Scholastic, CMP Publications, Home Shopping Network, QVC, and Viacom are jumping into the online fray to leverage their offerings in other media.

Boosting the fortunes of the commercial networks is the prohibitive cost of wiring the nation's households for interactive television. Even with total cooperation and under the best of prevailing market conditions, it would take at least five years to expand bandwidth and communications for television and to build the links that are missing from cable, telephone, and data communications networks, according to Gene DeRose, vice president of Jupiter Communications Co., a New York-based media research and consulting firm.

In the meantime, both subscribers and businesses are beginning to believe that commerce through the commercial services is the next-best thing for now. The commercial services, meanwhile, are rapidly making the transition to multimedia, continuing extensive testing of ISDN and cable-modem delivery in order to speed service and allow for the video, graphics, and sound that greater bandwidth permits.

Online shopping and transaction-based services are also beginning to take off on the commercial networks. Sales of products and services through the commercial services totaled $50,000,000 to $200,000,000 in 1994, according to SIMBA Information of Wilton, Connecticut. SIMBA predicts that online sales will soar as high as $2,500,000,000 to $5,000,000,000 by 1998.

DeRose, too, predicts that retail and transaction services will grow rapidly over the next few years, especially as online access is combined with television shopping networks, CD-ROM software publishing, television infomercials, telephone-based product ordering, and credit card processing.

Integrating Commercial Networks and the Internet

For most businesses, choosing to do business on the Internet or on the commercial networks is not an either/or decision. Once a business has converted its promotional or informational data into electronic format, there is no reason not to explore all online avenues, and the additional cost is minimal.

Here are several ways to integrate the Internet and the commercial networks in your company's marketing plans:

- **E-mail and networking.** Set up accounts on the Internet and on several large commercial networks so that potential customers on these services can reach you quickly and conveniently. When you have an account on each network, you can participate in online discussion groups and post press releases and product announcements.
- **Sales and marketing.** Set up a storefront on the Web. Rent space in the CompuServe or Prodigy Malls, if your company can afford it.
- **Customer service.** Set up an FTP site and a mailing list on the Internet to post FAQ lists and field customer questions. Set up a technical support forum on a commercial network, such as CompuServe or GEnie.

- **Publishing.** Publish an online edition of your newspaper or magazine on a commercial online service. Post free excerpts of your publication on the Internet as a way of promoting it.

- **Databases.** Hook up with a commercial network to provide a gateway to your database. Allow Internet users to access it via telnet or the Web.

Pricing and Contact Information

America Online
8619 Westwood Center Drive
Vienna, VA 22182
(800) 827-6364

America Online costs $9.95 a month, which includes five hours of connect time. After that, connect time is billed at $2.95 an hour.

CompuServe Information Service
5000 Arlington Centre Boulevard
Post Office Box 20212
Columbus, OH 43220
(800) 848-8199

CompuServe members pay $9.95 a month for unlimited access to more than 120 basic services, such as news and weather. They also get three hours of Internet access, which includes access to the World Wide Web. Additional Internet usage is billed at $2.95 an hour. Access to CompuServe's extended services, such as special-interest bulletin boards, is billed at $4.80 an hour for all modem speeds up to and including 14.4 kbps. With CompuServe's Internet Club, members pay an additional $15 a month for 30 hours of Internet access. Additional Internet usage is billed at $1.95 an hour.

Prodigy Services Co.
445 Hamilton Avenue
White Plains, NY 10601
(800) 284-5933

Basic Prodigy service costs $9.95 a month, which includes five hours of usage. Prodigy's Value Plan costs $14.95 a month and includes unlimited access to hundreds of core features and five hours of "plus" features, such as bulletin boards. The 30/30 Plan charges members $29.95 a month for 30 hours' usage. Additional usage costs $2.95 an hour.

eWorld
1 Infinite Loop
Cupertino CA 95014
(800)775-4556

eWorld charges an $8.95 monthly membership fee, which includes four hours of online time. Additional usage costs $2.95 an hour.

PART VIII

THE FUTURE OF INTERNET BUSINESS

HURDLES TO BE OVERCOME

At this point in the book, you might think that there is nothing but blue sky for business on the Internet. The Internet is unquestionably an exciting new place to look for customers and to sell products, but it has its share of problems.

This chapter looks at what we consider the most significant obstacles to pervasive, widespread acceptance of the Internet as a cornerstone of future commercial ventures. Underlying much of our analysis is our belief that the Internet will continue to grow and ultimately become a cornerstone of the so-called information superhighway or as it is commonly known in the United States, the National Information Infrastructure.

The transition from academic computer network to massive, secure international network is by no means guaranteed, even though plenty of individuals and companies are working toward that end. Multi-billion-dollar investments by the major cable and telephone companies in competing technologies raise the distinct possibility that the company that supplies your cable television signal will merge or form a partnership with the company that provides you with telephone service. One day soon, you'll be able to surf the Net through your television and use your PC to make and receive phone calls.

The main advantage of using television and cable as a basis for an information superhighway, rather than new and alien technologies such as PPP/SLIP modem connections or ISDN, is that they are already familiar and pervasive. The number of people who have access to the Internet is dwarfed by the millions who have cable television and want more—and better—programming. And although we would prefer to contemplate a future in which people seek interactive entertainment, many people are content to sit back and passively absorb signals from their television sets.

Here are the five greatest challenges that we see shaping up for the Internet in the coming decade.

Common Access

The greatest obstacle for the growth of the Internet is offering access to everyone who wants to participate. If the information highway is going to become a force for democracy worldwide, it must be accessible even to people who cannot afford to buy a computer to hook up to their telephone line.

One approach that is gaining popularity is offering public access Internet terminals at public libraries and other institutions. Seattle has enjoyed some success with this, and other public libraries around the nation are seeking to copy its model, as funds permit. And there lies part of the public policy dilemma: Should funds for the development of the information superhighway being funneled to projects seeking universal or common access, or should they aid businesses in joining the network?

Today, most of the public funds for Internet-related projects are aimed either at creating a friendlier business environment—with chambers of commerce and government offices online—or helping schools and other educational institutions gain access to the network. Universal access is low on the list of priorities.

But universal access is not strictly a public policy consideration.

The fact is that businesses won't start making serious money on the Internet until the network encompasses a larger, broader, and more diverse audience that includes not only affluent white males but also minorities, women, and lower-income groups. That can happen only as Internet access becomes more universal, as technological barriers fall away, and as online merchants and service providers serve up sufficiently compelling content to convince today's couch potatoes to go online. Frankly, it's hard for us to envision a day when people would log onto the Internet purely to read the ads and surf corporate Web sites. Only if interactivity can be fostered through free information services, chat rooms, and message boards will the Internet and the information superhighway capture the imagination and the pocketbooks of the buying public.

Bandwidth and Technology

Common access is an important barrier, but just as important are faster connection speeds. Currently, most Internet users have 14.4kbps or slower modems and lack direct SLIP, PPP, or T1 access to the network. This means that viewing graphics, audio, and video on the Web remains a slow and tedious process.

The way we see it, it's a game of leapfrog. As modem speeds get faster and faster, more graphics-intensive Internet sites will demand more and more bandwidth; in other words, by the time you finally get a 56kbps line to your home PC, accessing the Net's coolest sites will require no less than a T1. By the time you get a T1, you'll need a T3. And so on. As a result, many people will simply never catch up. This is why we encourage all companies that want to build an effective online presence to make their information available not only through the graphics-intensive Web but also through simple e-mail autoresponders.

Recently, some companies have introduced services offering real-time audio and video that don't require users to download the entire data file before hearing or viewing the material. However, these services generally require higher bandwidth and faster Internet connections than the vast majority of existing Internet users possess. As more people connect, this gap in technological capabilities could deeply divide the online world. Together with age, gender, income, and geographic region, it's important to consider your customers' technological capabilities when positioning your products and services online.

Finding What You Seek on the Net

A well-designed Web site containing valuable information and interactive features is of little value if potential customers cannot find it. Another problem is the seemingly simple problem of locating information on the network. Despite what you read in newspapers and magazines, there's more to surfing the Net than jumping on your board and catching a wave. For the Internet truly to succeed for businesses and consumers alike, there must be a quick and easy way to find things without wandering about and wasting time. Few people would patronize a bookstore with clerks who waved vaguely towards the far wall and answered all queries with, "I think what you want is somewhere around here."

Recognize that search tools like Yahoo, Lycos, and InfoSeek, discussed in Chapter 9, "The Electronic Schmooze," are only part of the answer. Sure, Yahoo may contain some 40,000 entries, but that's not a tremendous number compared to the more than *4,000,000* documents available on the Internet. A single entry for each Usenet group, mailing list, and FAQ document would account for almost 25,000 entries alone. Yahoo works, however, because it offers a catalog of catalogs, just as the Internet Mall is really a mall of malls, listing stores that exist elsewhere on the network.

Unfortunately, this approach to information retrieval—catalogs of catalogs—doesn't scale very well. For a few thousand entries, it's fine. But when any search can result in thousands of matches across a database with millions of entries, as you saw with Lycos in Chapter 9, it becomes difficult for most people to find what they're looking for.

As a result, we predict that more companies will sell information look-up services and simple, but timely, catalogs of information available elsewhere on the Internet. InfoSeek is the first of many to adopt this strategy.

As we've stressed throughout this book, the key to publicizing your Internet site is listing your site in the right databases—just as success in traditional marketing depends on advertisements in magazines and commercials on television programs that reach your target market. The good news is that there are plenty of Web sites and newsgroups that let you announce your site and many of them focus on a specific topic or interest.

Target Marketing—Or Not?

Another challenge to doing business on the Internet is the difficulty in targeting specific markets. On the Internet, there's no easy way to advertise or send direct mail to specific demographic slices. If you sell a product of interest to teenage boys but no one else, there's no easy way to target that specific demographic group on the network. Other media, by contrast, offer more precise ways of target marketing, such as special-interest magazines and sponsorships of television shows and sponsoring sporting events.

On the Internet, companies have dealt with this problem in various ways, offering give-aways, games, and discounts on products in an effort to lure a listening audience. What matters, of course, is not how many people stop by your site. What matters is getting the *right people* to visit your site and learn about your business.

For too many people hyping the potential of the Internet for business, a large number of visitors is a clear indication of success—a measure that we see as far too simplistic. If you want lots of people to come to your Web site, just sign a deal with Sports Illustrated to offer an online edition of the magazine's popular swimsuit issue. Your visitors probably won't pay much attention to your product, but they will definitely come to your site.

Fact is, lots of traffic does not necessarily translate into lots of sales.

One way to avoid stumbling over this hurdle is to orient your message and the theme of your site around your company's product line. If you sell cruise berths for your cruise line, for example, offer maps and information on the destinations visited by your ships and perhaps a brief history of the cruise line.

Display pictures of the ship and the ports. If you can attract the audience interested in cruises, you will have gained a qualified market segment—that is what target marketing is all about.

On the Internet, target marketing is about building an audience, creating a subculture, and transforming customers into fans. As Dave says to his clients, it's not the first or second visit to your site that matters; it's the third. When people begin to come back to your site over and over again, you'll know that you have built a successful Internet business presence.

Solving the Security Puzzle

The final hurdle for the long-term success and growth of the Internet is the lack of individual and commercial security. For the last few decades, the Internet has remained fairly secure thanks primarily to a lack of criminals seeking to break in and wreak havoc. Small-scale attempts have been made with varied success, but the Net remains secure mostly through luck. Once big business gets online and business-to-business financial transactions begin, we believe that better-organized and more sophisticated criminal ventures will try to get their piece of the action in cyberspace.

That said, security on the Internet will undoubtedly improve over the next few years, especially as businesses seek the chance to do commercial transactions on the Net directly. Dozens of different solutions will become available this year, with banks and other financial institutions experimenting with everything from micro-purchases with digital cash to letting Internet users view their bank balances online. Remember, though, that the final responsibility for Internet security, however, rests with you.

Too Many Hurdles to Jump?

We believe that the hurdles outlined in this chapter are serious but not insurmountable. Some of them, such as the issue of universal access, involve important national policy issues for the public to decide. If the past few years are any indication, however, we believe that the interest and excitement surrounding the Internet will prove sufficient to solve any hurdle.

We also doubt that the Internet will ever replace traditional commerce—the local mall will continue to be a spot where people will congregate for social activities and shopping—but, over the next few years, the online world will mature into an important venue. Many small businesses will make a fortune on the Net, whereas many larger companies will spend inordinate amounts of money building massive edifices that few will visit.

Trends and Predictions

By now, you have learned the *pros* and *cons,* the pit-falls, and the potential of doing business on the Internet. You have also discovered that although the Internet might not yet be the much-vaunted information-tion highway, it is closer to reality than just mere hype—and it becomes more real by the minute. Though a relatively small percentage of the world's households and businesses are currently on the Net, millions of home computer users and thousands of companies, some as tiny as the corner delicatessen, are giving the Internet a try.

What the future holds for companies doing business on the Internet is anybody's guess. Although no one knows whether shoppers will flock to the Internet cybermalls or whether executives and professionals around the world will start doing business on an electronic handshake, plenty of money is betting that the answer will ultimately be a resounding yes.

The following sections describe ten Internet business trends worth watching.

Continued Population Growth on the Internet

With all the changes swirling around the worldwide network of networks these days, the only certainty about the Internet appears to be growth.

The Internet now has over 30,000,000 users and is estimated to be growing at a rate of more than 1,000,000 new users a month. If the population of the Internet continues to expand at its current pace, practically everyone in the world will be on the Net by the year 2000, according to projections by the Internet Society. Although the Internet's growth will eventually bump up against barriers such as literacy, network access, and computer ownership, observers agree that the Internet still has plenty of room to grow.

Much of this growth is coming from the commercial, as opposed to the university or government, sector. At current rates, two new Internet accounts are added to the network every four minutes—one of which is from a commercial site—according to Dataquest, a market research firm in San Jose, California. Subscribers to commercial online services such as Prodigy, CompuServe, and America Online will continue to pour into the Internet, accelerating the commercialization trend and drowning out the objections of long-time Internet denizens.

Fueling much of this growth is the Internet's World Wide Web hypermedia system. Jupiter Communications, a New York market research firm, predicts that 40,000,000 home computer users will be on the Web by 1999.

The Internet's continued growth is good news for just about everybody trying to make money on the Internet—from the access providers who rent the "pipes" to the marketers to the publishers who provide the content that Internet users want to read. On the other hand, the recent entry of MCI, AT&T, and Microsoft into the Internet access market may signal the start of an industry-wide consolidation that could ultimately doom hundreds of local Internet access providers.

Lower Network Access Costs and Wider Availability of Internet Tools

With computers, modems, and Internet access plummeting in price, Internet connections—even the high-powered PPP connections needed to run Netscape or Mosaic—are becoming more widely available.

For about $200, you can get a high-speed 28.8kbps modem. For $60 to $150, you can buy a top-line communications software package. You can obtain a PPP connection from a local Internet access provider for as little as $20 per month; a regular dialup, or shell, account starts at less than $10 per month. The price of a T1 line—the Internet connection of choice for many large companies—has come down to less than $500 a month in some parts of the country. Integrated Digital Services Network (ISDN) is now another viable alternative in some regions for high-speed connections. Commercial online services such as CompuServe, America Online and Delphi offer Internet connectivity as well. Refer to Appendix A for a list of Internet access providers.

A host of new and soon-to-be-released software interfaces will open up the Internet to even more users. For example, commercial versions of the Internet's popular Mosaic and Gopher programs that are fast and easier to use and that contain more features are now available. Microsoft will incorporate TCP/IP software into Windows 95, due out in August, 1995, and the Mac already includes built-in TCP/IP support.

Easier On-Ramps

With so many new users descending on the Internet, the race is on to come out with graphical interfaces that enable Internet novices to send mail and to access data with the click of a mouse.

Popular packages today include Internet in A Box, a software package billed by its developers as "the first shrink-wrapped package to provide a total solution for PC users to get on to the Internet." Developed by O'Reilly & Associates and Spry, Internet in A Box provides a multimedia Windows interface, a suite of Internet applications such as e-mail, newsgroups, telnet, Gopher, and Mosaic. It also includes O'Reilly's Global Network Navigator, an interactive guide to the Internet. Internet in A Box requires a SLIP or PPP connection and works with both PCs and local area networks.

A remarkable number of alternative interfaces are also available, including Pipeline (shown in Figure 23.1), Netscape, NetCruiser, TCP/Connect II, Internet Chameleon, and InterRamp. The three major commercial online services offer graphical Net interfaces, too. Almost all these programs include some free connect time, and many are free for subscribers of specific Internet services such as NetCom and Hooked.

Commercial versions of Mosaic, the popular graphical browser, are available, even as the National Center for Supercomputing Applications (NCSA) at the University of Illinois at Urbana-Champaign continues to upgrade the public domain version of the program available to Internet users at no charge. Spyglass, Inc., of Savoy, Illinois, has an agreement with NCSA to enhance and re-license Mosaic to Internet users. Versions for Windows, the Macintosh, and X Window systems (UNIX) are available from Spyglass. Figure 23.2 shows the Spyglass Mosaic.

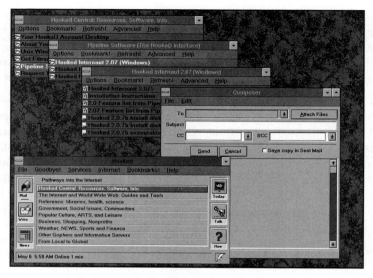

Figure 23.1. Pipeline offers an easier way to navigate the Net.

Figure 23.2. Spyglass Mosaic is another Web browser.

Essentially, Spyglass has redesigned Mosaic so that it is a more robust and full-featured browsing tool. Enhancements include improved installation, better memory management, increased performance, new forms capabilities, on-line hypertext-based help, support for a proxy gateway, and user interface improvements such as support for multiple windows. Future versions will include enhanced security and authentication that will enable credit-card and other types of business transactions to take place on the Internet, filters that will enable documents from popular document readers to be read seamlessly by Mosaic, and integration with emerging editing and document management tools.

Then there's Netscape Navigator, the coolest browser on the block—hardly surprising considering that it was created by the same talented team that pioneered the original program at the NSCA. Their long experience shines through in every feature of Netscape, from its new, easy-to-use navigational buttons to the way it loads pages onto the screen while you watch. Other Web browsers make you wait until a page is completed before you can start viewing it, but with Netscape, you can view pages while the download is still in progress. Unlike other Web browsers, Netscape doesn't limit you to the Web alone. It also enables you to access e-mail, newsgroups, Gopher, FTP, and other Internet tools. Netscape is free to download, or $39 for registration and technical support from the company; the company recently announced a retail version that will sell in computer stores.

Buckets Of E-Mail

Although fax machines still outnumber e-mail boxes in offices around the world, e-mail is gathering steam thanks to the Internet. According to Book Marketing Update in Fairfield, Iowa, as much as 75% of business-to-business correspondence will take place by fax or e-mail by the year 2000. Probably half of all consumer-to-consumer and business-to-consumer correspondence will be through fax or e-mail, predominantly the latter. One example of the more powerful e-mail programs we're starting to see is Eudora, available on both Mac and PC, as shown in Figure 23.3

Even the U.S. Postal Service is hedging its bets. Postmaster General and CEO Marvin Runyon, in his annual report to the Senate Governmental Affairs Committee in May 1995, suggested, "Post office lobbies could serve as on-ramps providing access to anyone who wants to be on the electronic highway. We can help certify electronic messages and safeguard their privacy, securing one company's market-sensitive information from the intruding eyes of its competitors."

Internet addresses are fast becoming a fixture on business cards. Sporting an Internet address carries a high-tech caché. Having an Internet address with your company's domain name on it—for example, yourcompany.com—is considered even classier.

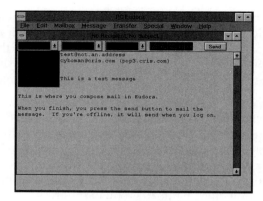

Figure 23.3. Eudora is a popular graphical interface for e-mail.

Bells, Whistles, and Multimedia

The Internet today is still a mostly silent, text-based expanse of cyberspace with only the quiet clacking of computer keys to break the silence. Audio, video, and other multimedia applications remain rarities on the Internet for a host of technological reasons, despite innovations such as Internet Phone (with which you can use the Internet for voice calls) and RealAudio (which plays real-time sound clips).

In the past year, however, that has finally begun to change. Soon, Internet video conferencing will be widely available at a fraction of the cost of using regular telephone networks. The reason is that there is no need to pay a phone carrier $100 per minute to transmit images. Once your company is connected to the Internet, there is no extra fee for transmitting video. Besides facilitating virtual business meetings, Internet video offers the potential to enhance the feasibility of telecommuting, telemedicine (remote diagnostics), remote collaboration between workgroups, and distance learning on the network.

Facilitating Internet video transmissions is the Multicast Backbone (MBone), a virtual multimedia network developed by researchers from the University of Southern California Information Services Institute. The service, available through the Internet, provides users with efficient use of bandwidth because a single data packet takes up the same amount of bandwidth whether it is received by one workstation or many. MBone applications such as net video, visual audio tool, and whiteboard can be downloaded from a variety of anonymous FTP locations at no charge. MBone applications must be run over T1 lines for maximum video performance, however.

For now, Internet video conferencing still has a long way to go before it is ready for prime time. Right now, it is much slower than the video conferencing offered by the phone networks—about 15 frames per minute—and the images that appear on conferees' computer screens are rather small—about a quarter of a screen. Some Internet observers also fear network-wide traffic jams if too many companies attempt to use the Internet for video conferencing at the same time.

Nevertheless, some interesting new software programs promise to revolutionize Internet video conferencing and to make it more widely accessible than it is today. CU-SeeMe, shown in Figure 23.4, was developed at Cornell University. It enables multiple video windows to operate on a single PC or Macintosh screen simultaneously with each window able to transmit and receive text and audio. The black-and-white video is far from perfect—as the number of windows open increases, more bandwidth is used and the video becomes slower—and audio is available only for Mac users. Even so, the prospect of "live video conferencing from around the globe is more than just a little bit intriguing," writes Brian Gallagher in the June, 1994, issue of *Boardwatch* magazine. Although it is possible to run the program through a modem, a T1 or T3 connection is preferable, say its developers. CU-SeeMe is available for free via anonymous FTP from `gated.cornell.edu` in the `pub/video` directory. The program requires TCP/IP software and a SLIP connection or higher. By the end of 1995, there will also be a commercial version of CU-SeeMe from White Pine Software.

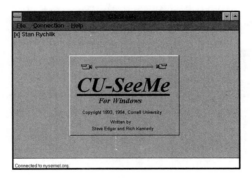

Figure 23.4. CU-SeeMe live video over the Internet.

Tighter Security

One of the biggest stumbling blocks to Internet commerce is the lack of a secure way of handling credit card, banking, and other financial transactions. Because of growing demand on the part of businesses, however, software programs featuring encryption and digital signatures are becoming available. According to *The*

Internet Letter, a monthly newsletter for business users, Bank of America is banking on the Internet to facilitate electronic transactions. The bank is a participant in CommerceNet—the World Wide Web-based marketplace that plans to release a secure Mosaic later this year—and hopes to use the Internet as a vehicle for payments, wire transfers, and investments. Wells Fargo, the second largest bank in California, recently became one of the first banks in the United States to offer customers Internet access to their checking and savings accounts, credit lines, and credit card information.

New encryption technologies are also coming on the scene, making secure credit card transactions a reality. In April, Netscape Communications Corporation, America Online, CompuServe, Prodigy, and IBM announced their investment in Terisa Systems, a Menlo Park, California, company that licenses and markets technologies that enable secure transactions on the Internet. Terisa will develop a unified approach designed to integrate both Enterprise Integration Technologies' Secure HTTP protocol and Netscape's Secure Sockets Layer. This means that Internet shoppers will soon be able to safeguard their credit card numbers when making purchases, no matter which Web browser they use.

Besides facilitating commercial transactions, encryption is also making possible new forms of Internet business, such as book publishing. A company called Bibliobytes, for example, offers hundreds of books through the network. Within 30 seconds of ordering, Internet users can have an entire book delivered to their computers. You can visit for yourself at `http://www.bb.com/`. Figure 23.5 shows Bibliobytes' home page.

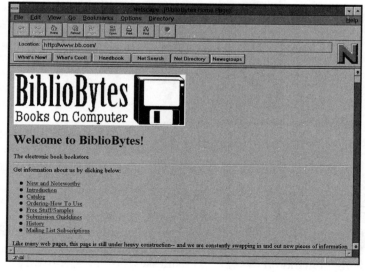

Figure 23.5. Bibliobytes' home page.

The Rise of Politically Correct Advertising

Probably the biggest controversy on the Internet right now is the issue of commercialization. How can companies market, advertise, and sell their products and services on the Internet without offending the very customers they hope to attract? And how can businesses zero in on their target markets without sending out direct mailings and getting flamed?

"Advertisers will quickly figure out that they must abandon the old flood-the-world-with-direct-mail approaches that were considered successful if they realized a three percent response rate," Bill Washburn, former director of the Commercial Internet Exchange, told *Internet World* magazine in an interview. "Valuable commercial information delivered in narrow, highly customized rifle shots to exactly the right small group of individuals at precisely the right time might be the key."

One advertising model that is catching on is passive advertising, or sponsorship— that is, posting marketing and advertising information on a World Wide Web server and inviting potential customers to come in and browse for free. One company that has latched onto this concept in a major way is HotWired, an online version of the popular *Wired* magazine.

Unlike the unwelcome postings splattered throughout the Internet by attorneys Canter & Siegel, HotWired offers a "politically correct" advertising forum for companies that want to share information about their products and services. HotWired charges sponsors $30,000 for a two-month advertising spot in its magazine. Readers can access HotWired for free, though they must first register and select a user i.d. and password, a system that helps the magazine and its advertisers track site traffic and demographics. To visit HotWired, shown in Figure 23.6, go to URL http://www.hotwired.com/.

Another commercial initiative on the Internet is the Internet Shopping Network, which has been selling computer software on the Internet for over a year. Like Home Shopping Network, which enables consumers to order products displayed on television, members can use Internet Shopping Network to browse more than 20,000 software and hardware products and other items from a personal computer or workstation with the click of a mouse. Like the PC Catalog available on Prodigy and CompuServe, ISN enables shoppers to search products organized by platform (Macintosh, DOS, Windows, or UNIX) or by category (for example, children or programmers). Orders are processed within 15 minutes of receipt and are shipped the next business day from one of 12 distribution centers throughout the United States. To avoid the security problems associated with making purchases over the Internet, shoppers must first fax the company a registration card with their credit card number and expiration date. Purchases are charged to that card.

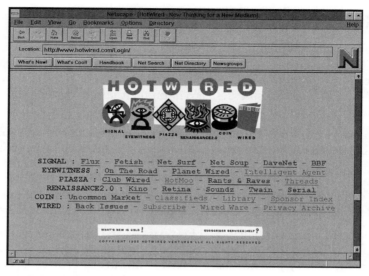

Figure 23.6. HotWired on the Web.

By eliminating the overhead associated with conventional retailing, ISN claims to offer some of the best prices around for the high-tech products it sells. Moreover, members of the ISN network get free online access to the entire previous year's contents of *InfoWorld* magazine to help them make better buying decisions. Future services will include more publications, more stores, and electronic downloading of software titles. To visit ISN, shown in Figure 23.7, go to `http://shop.internet.net/`.

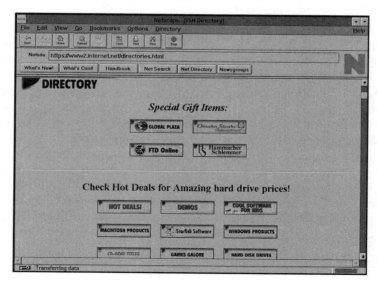

Figure 23.7. Internet Shopping Network on the Web.

More In-Your-Face Advertising

At the same time that the Internet's major players are rallying around politically correct advertising platforms like HotWired, renegade entrepreneurs are trying more blatant sales pitches with varying degrees of success. Canter & Siegel, the Arizona immigration law firm that gained Internet-wide notoriety by plastering Usenet newsgroups with green card notices last year, claims it earned $100,000 on a minimal investment. The law firm has set up a company called Cybersell to help other companies market their products on the Internet by using the same techniques—and has even written a no-excuses book about its own experience with Internet marketing.

In May of last year, another marketer tried the same thing in Florida. According to *The Miami Herald*, an advertisement for a Miami-based company called U.S. Health, Inc., offering a $29.95 thigh-thinning cream went out over Internet to over 850 electronic mailing lists. The practice, which has become known as spamming, resulted in nearly half a million complaints to the sender and to Shadow Information Services, the Miami company that provided it access to Internet. U.S. Health's attorney told the *Herald* that he knew nothing about the ad and little about the company.

Does this mean that advertisers can break the unwritten rules of netiquette and get away with it? Maybe not. Although companies like this may profit in the short run, blatant advertisers run the risk of turning into Internet pariahs—companies with which no one will do business.

When NETCOM Communications Services canceled Canter & Siegel's account, NETCOM's president, John Whalen, posted a public note on the Internet explaining the company's decision.

"NETCOM believes that we can and will refuse service to people who have demonstrated that they do not respect the guidelines preventing posting advertisements to inappropriate Usenet newsgroups," Whalen wrote. "As a commercial Internet service provider, NETCOM encourages commercial activity on the Internet and believes it to be an important part of a complete service. However, NETCOM also believes that commercial activities need to be undertaken in an orderly and thoughtful manner, with attention to appropriate usage and sensitivity to the cooperative culture of the Internet community."

Whalen goes on to say, "Our position is that NETCOM can be compared to a public restaurant, where a customer may be refused service if he is not wearing shoes. For the health of the other customers and the good of the restaurant, that customer may be turned away. NETCOM believes that being a responsible provider entails refusing service to customers who would endanger the health of the community. Customers, commercial or not, who will contribute to the health of the community and respect the laws of the land and the rights of others will be welcome."

Other companies, meanwhile, are taking a different approach to direct advertising on the Internet. Instead of attempting to wipe it out completely, The Internet Company, the Cambridge, Massachusetts, consulting firm that operates the Electronic Newsstand, tried to set up a new Usenet hierarchy of market newsgroups to accommodate commercial postings in what the company deems a culturally acceptable way. Its logic was that if Internet users don't want to read commercial postings, they don't have to. The community was uninterested, and the project has since faded away.

Geographic Specialization

Although the Internet is a worldwide marketplace separated less by geographical boundaries than by interest groups, local Internet access providers are beginning to offer advertising services to hometown businesses seeking to break into the global marketplace.

Two years ago, CyberGate, an Internet access provider in Deerfield Beach, Florida, launched a Gopher site called CyberStore on the Shore, designed to be a marketplace for Florida companies. To see CyberStore on the Shore, which is shown in Figure 23.8, type gopher gopher.gate.net at the system prompt or visit its URL at http://inca.gate.net/marketplace/. CyberGate also offers Web services to commercial customers.

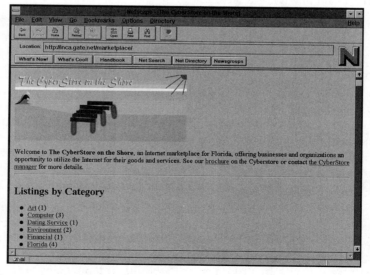

Figure 23.8. CyberStore on the Shore.

Internet Is Here to Stay

Despite all the hype about interactive television and its 500 channels, the prohibitive cost of the set-top boxes and fiber optic cable necessary to make that vision a reality means that the Internet is not likely to be replaced for at least the next few years. In fact, many observers believe that the Internet will never become obsolete. Regardless of the networking technology that emerges in the future, the Internet as a virtual community of individuals, universities, governments, and businesses will continue to prosper.

"Worldwide, old and new information service organizations are plugging into the Internet and drawing sustenance from its vast and uncharted seas of information and delivering their services to its rising millions of users," Vinton Cerf, president of the Internet Society, wrote last year in *Internet Society News*. "Access to the 23,000 networks that make up the Internet is increasingly viewed as a national priority around the world in the research and education sectors, and many governments see the Internet as a microcosm of national and global information infrastructure that is emerging from the rich interplay of ideas, experiments, and collaborations among computer and telecommunications enterprises."

The Future of the Internet for Your Company

So what does all this mean for your company?

Although businesses that drive onto today's prototype of the information highway have no guarantee that they will strike it rich, companies that turn their backs on it will likely be left behind. Although it may be a long time before dispatching an e-mail message over the Internet becomes as commonplace as dialing a telephone, the trend is increasingly clear. The competitive edge will belong to those entrepreneurs prepared to log on, tap in, and reach out to the vast, chaotic, and virtually untapped electronic marketplace called the Internet.

It is our hope that this book will help you navigate the wilderness of Internet commerce, although as we warned you many pages ago, doing business on the Internet remains far from an exact science. If you want to contact either of us personally, send an e-mail message to Rosalind Resnick at rosalind@netcreations.com or to Dave Taylor at taylor@netcom.com. You can visit the *Internet Business Guide* on the Web at http://www.netcreations.com/ibg/. We would be delighted to hear from you.

INTERNET ON-RAMPS

This appendix lists companies and organizations that provide dialup Internet accounts for individuals and organizations. It includes providers in the United States, Canada, and other countries.

If you already are connected to the Internet but are searching for alternatives, check online at ftp:// nis.nsf.net/internet/providers/ or http:// www.internic.net/internic/provider.html. The National Science Foundataion (NSF) and InterNIC maintain lists of providers that are updated frequently. Web addresses, however, are subject to change, so it is possible that these addresses might have changed by the time you read this. If you are not already connected, other good sources are your local newspaper and Yellow Pages.

Geographical and Area-Code Summary of Providers in the United States and Canada

This section lists the names of North American Internet providers grouped by state or province, by area code, and alphabetically by provider name. Details and contact information for each provider follow in the next section. The first portion of this list presents providers that supply standard access. At the end of the list are the providers that supply packet/network or toll-free access.

Standard Access

Alabama—205

InterQuest, Inc.
Nuance Network Service
Planet Access Networks

Alaska—907

Internet Alaska

Alberta—403

Alberta SuperNet Inc.
CCI Networks

Arizona—602

ACES Research
CRL Network Services
Evergreen Internet
Internet Direct, Inc.
Internet Express
Network 99, Inc.
New Mexico Technet, Inc.
Primenet

Arkansas—501

Sibylline, Inc.

British Columbia—604

Cyberstore Systems, Inc.
DataFlux Systems Limited
Wimsey Information Services

California—209

Sacramento Network Access
West Coast Online

California—213

CRL Network Services
CSUnet (California State University)
DHM Information Management, Inc.
DigiLink Network Services
Earthlink Network, Inc.
KAIWAN Corporation
Primenet

California—310

CERFnet
CRL Network Services
CSUnet (California State University)
DHM Information Management, Inc.
DigiLink Network Services
Earthlink Network, Inc.

KAIWAN Corporation
Lightside, Inc.
Netcom On-Line Communication
   Services

California—408

Aimnet Information Services
Best Internet Communications, Inc.
   (BEST)
CSUnet (California State University)
ElectriCiti Incorporated
Internet Connection
InterNex Information Services, Inc.
Netcom On-Line Communication
   Services
Portal Communications Company
Scruz-Net
South Valley Internet
West Coast Online
zNET

California—415

Aimnet Information Services
APlatform
Best Internet Communications, Inc.
   (BEST)
CERFnet
CRL Network Services
CSUnet (California State University)
ElectriCiti Incorporated
Institute for Global Communica-
   tions (IGC)
InterNex Information Services, Inc.
LineX Communcations
Netcom On-Line Communication
   Services
QuakeNet
Scruz-Net

The Well
West Coast Online

California—510

Access InfoSystems
Aimnet Information Services
Best Internet Communications, Inc.
   (BEST)
CCnet Communications
CERFnet
Community ConneXion
CRL Network Services
CSUnet (California State University)
ElectriCiti Incorporated
HoloNet
InterNex Information Services, Inc.
Netcom On-Line Communication
   Services
Sacramento Network Access, Inc.
West Coast Online

California—619

CERFnet
CSUnet (California State University)
CTS Network Services (CTSNet)
ElectriCiti Incorporated
ESNET Communications
Netcom On-Line Communication
   Services
Network Link, Inc.

California—707

Access InfoSystems
CRL Network Services
CSUnet (California State University)
Northcoast Internet
Pacific Internet
West Coast Online

California—714

CERFnet
CSUnet (California State University)
DHM Information Management, Inc.
DigiLink Network Services
Digital Express Group (Digex)
KAIWAN Corporation
Lightside, Inc.
Netcom On-Line Communication
   Services
Network Intensive

California—805

Dataware Network Services
KAIWAN Corporation

California—818

CERFnet
CSUnet (California State University)
DHM Information Management, Inc.
DigiLink Network Services
Earthlink Network, Inc.
KAIWAN Corporation
Lightside, Inc.
Netcom On-Line Communication
   Services
Primenet

California—909

CSUnet (California State University)
Digital Express Group (Digex)
KAIWAN Corporation
Lightside, Inc.

California—916

CSUnet (California State University)
Netcom On-Line Communication
   Services

Sacramento Network Access, Inc.
Sierra-Net
West Coast Online

Colorado—303

CNS
Colorado Internet Cooperative Asso-
   ciation
Colorado SuperNet
DASH - Denver Area Super Highway
Internet Express
Netcom On-Line Communication
   Services
New Mexico Technet, Inc.
Nyx
Rocky Mountain Internet, Inc.

Colorado—719

CNS
Colorado SuperNet
Internet Express
Old Colorado City Communications
Rocky Mountain Internet, Inc.

Connecticut—203

Connix: The Connecticut Internet
   Exchange
I-2000
New York Net
PCNet
The Dorsai Embassy

Delaware—302

SSNet, Inc.

District of Columbia—202

CAPCON LibrARY Network
Capitol Area Internet Service (CAIS)

Clark Internet Services, Inc.
  (ClarkNet)
NovaNet, Inc.
US Net, Inc.

Florida—305

Acquired Knowledge Systems, Inc.
CyberGate
Florida Online
Gateway to the World, Inc.
IDS World Network
SatelNET Communications

Florida—407

Florida Online
IDS World Network

Florida—813

CENTURION Technology, Inc.
Florida Online
PacketWorks, Inc.

Florida—904

Florida Online
SymNet

Georgia—404

CRL Network Services
Internet Atlanta
MindSpring Enterprises, Inc.
Netcom On-Line Communication
  Services
Ping

Georgia—706

Mind Spring Enterprises, Inc.

Hawaii—808

Hawaii OnLine

Idaho—208

WLN

Illinois—217

FGInet, Inc.

Illinois—312

American Information Systems, Inc.
  (AIS)
InterAccess Co.
MCSNet
Netcom On-Line Communication
  Services
Ripco Communcations, Inc.
Tezcatlipoca, Inc.
WorldWide Access

Illinois—708

American Information Systems, Inc.
  (AIS)
CICNet
InterAccess Co.
MCSNet
Ripco Communcations, Inc.
Tezcatlipoca, Inc.
WorldWide Access
XNet Information Systems

Illinois—815

American Information Systems, Inc.
  (AIS)
InterAccess Co.
MCSNet
WorldWide Access

Indiana—317

IQuest Network Services
Network Link, Inc.

Indiana—812

IgLou Internet Services

Iowa—319

INS Info Services
Planet Access Networks

Iowa—515

Cyberlink Communications
INS Info Services

Iowa—712

INS Info Services

Kansas—316

Southwind Internet Access, Inc.
Tyrell Corp.

Kansas—913

Tyrell Corp.
SkyNET Corp.

Kentucky—502

IgLou Internet Services

Kentucky—606

IgLou Internet Services

Louisiana—504

Neosoft, Inc.
Tyrell Corp.

Maine—207

maine.net, Inc.

Manitoba—204

MBnet
Traveller Information Services

Maryland—301

CAPCON LibrARY Network
Capitol Area Internet Service (CAIS)
ClarkNet (Clark Internet Services, Inc.)
Digital Express Group (Digex)
FredNet
NovaNet, Inc.
US Net, Inc.

Maryland—410

CAPCON LibrARY Network
Capitol Area Internet Service (CAIS)
Clark Internet Services, Inc. (ClarkNet)
Digital Express Group (Digex)

Massachusetts—508

Inter Access Company
intuitive information, inc.
Schunix
The World
UltraNet Communications, Inc.

Massachusetts—617

BIX (Delphi Internet Services)
Inter Access Company
Internet Access Company
Netcom On-Line Communication
  Services
North Shore Access
Pioneer Global

The World
Wilder Systems, Inc.
Xensei Corporation

Michigan—313

CICNet
ICNet/Innovative Concepts
Innovative Data (ID-Net)
MichNet
Msen

Michigan—517

ICNet/Innovative Concepts
MichNet
Msen, Inc.

Michigan—616

ICNet/Innovative Concepts
MichNet
Msen, Inc.

Michigan—810

ICNet/Innovative Concepts
Innovative Data (ID-Net)
MichNet
Msen, Inc.
Rabbit Network, Inc.

Michigan—906

ICNet/Innovative Concepts
MichNet
Msen, Inc.

Minnesota—218

Minnesota Regional Network
    (MRNET)
Red River Net

Minnesota—507

Millenium Communications
Minnesota Regional Network
    (MRNet)

Minnesota—612

Cloudnet
Millenium Communications
Minnesota MicroNet
Minnesota Regional Network
    (MRNet)
StarNet Communications, Inc.
    (Winternet)

Missouri—314

Neosoft, Inc.

Missouri—816

SkyNET Corp.
Tyrell Corp.

Montana—406

WLN

Nebraska—402

INS Info Services
Internet Nebraska Corp.

Nevada—702

Evergreen Internet
Great Basin Internet Services
Network 99, Inc.
Sacramento Network Access, Inc.
Sierra-Net

New Hampshire—603

MV Communications, Inc.

New Jersey—201

Internet Online Services
Neighborhood Internet Connection
New York Net
Planet Access Networks
The Dorsai Embassy
Zone One Network Exchange
(ZONE)

New Jersey—609

Digital Express Group (Digex)
New Jersey Computer Connection
New York Net

New Jersey—908

Digital Express Group (Digex)
I-2000
New York Net
Planet Access Networks
Zone One Network Exchange
(ZONE)

New Mexico—505

Internet Express
New Mexico Technet, Inc.

New York—212

Blythe Systems
Creative Data Consultants
CRL Network Services
Echo
Escape (Kazan Corp)
Ingress Communications, Inc.
Internet Online Services
Interport Communications Corp
Maestro Technologies, Inc.
Netcom On-Line Communication
    Services

Network 23, Inc.
New York Net
NYSERNet
Panix
Phantom Access Technologies, Inc.
Pipeline Network
The Dorsai Embassy
Zone One Network Exchange
(ZONE)

New York—315

NYSERNet

New York—516

Creative Data Consultants
I-2000
LI Net, Inc.
Long Island Information, Inc.
Maestro Technologies, Inc.
Network Internet Services
New York Net
NYSERNet
Panix
Phantom Access Technologies, Inc.
The Dorsai Embassy
Zone One Network Exchange
(ZONE)

New York—518

Internet Online Services
NYSERNet
Wizvax Communications

New York—607

NYSERNet

New York—716

NYSERNet

New York—718

Blythe Systems
Creative Data Consultants
Echo
Escape (Kazan Corp)
I-2000
Ingress Communications, Inc.
Interport Communications Corp.
Maestro Technologies, Inc.
New York Net
NYSERNet
Phantom Access Technologies, Inc.
The Dorsai Embassy
Zone One Network Exchange
    (ZONE)

New York—914

Cloud 9 Internet
I-2000
New York Net
NYSERNet
Phantom Access Technologies, Inc.
The Dorsai Embassy
TZ-Link
WestNet
Zone One Network Exchange
    (ZONE)

New York—917

Network 23, Inc.
New York Net
Zone One Network Exchange
    (ZONE)

North Carolina—704

FXnet
Interpath
Northcoast Internet
VNet Internet Access, Inc.

North Carolina—910

Interpath

North Carolina—919

Interpath

North Dakota—701

Red River Net

Ohio—216

APK Public Access UNI*
Exchange Network Services, Inc.

Ohio—513

EriNet Online Communications
Freelance Systems Programming
IgLou Internet Services

Ohio—614

OARNet

Oklahoma—405

GSS Internet

Oklahoma—918

GSS Internet
South Coast Computing Services, Inc.

Ontario—416

UUNorth Incorporated

Ontario—519

Hookup Communication Corporation

Oregon—503

Agora
Hevanet Communications
Internetworks
Netcom On-Line Communication
  Services
Teleport
Teleport, Inc.
WLN

Pennsylvania—215

Prometheus Information Corp.
  (FishNet)
VoiceNet/DCS
You Tools Corporation (FAST.NET)

Pennsylvania—412

Telerama

Pennsylvania—610

Prometheus Information Corp.
  (FishNet)
SSNet, Inc.
You Tools Corporation (FAST.NET)

Pennsylvania—717

You Tools Corporation (FAST.NET)

Rhode Island—401

IDS World Network

Quebec—514

Communications Accessibles
  Montreal, Inc.

South Carolina—803

A World of Difference, Inc.
FXnet
Global Vision, Inc.
SIMS, Inc.
South Carolina SuperNet, Inc.

Tennessee—615

Edge

Texas—210

Freeside Communications

Texas—214

DFW Internet Services, Inc.
Metronet, Inc.
Neosoft, Inc.
Netcom On-Line Communication
  Services
Texas Metronet

Texas—409

Info-Highway International, Inc.
Internet Connect Services, Inc.
Neosoft, Inc.

Texas—512

Eden Matrix
Freeside Communications
Illuminati Online
Internet Connect Services, Inc.
Netcom On-Line Communication
  Services
Onramp Access, Inc.
Real/Time Communications
Zilker Internet Park

Texas—713

Black Box
Info-Highway International, Inc.
Internet Connect Services, Inc.
Neosoft, Inc.
South Coast Computing Services,
    Inc.

Texas—817

ACM Network Services
DFW Internet Services, Inc.
Metronet, Inc.
Texas Metronet

Texas—915

New Mexico Technet, Inc.

Utah—801

Evergreen Internet
Internet Direct of Utah
XMission

Virginia—703

CAPCON LibrARY Network
Capitol Area Internet Service (CAIS)
Clark Internet Services, Inc.
    (ClarkNet)
Digital Express Group (Digex)
Netcom On-Line Communication
    Services
NovaNet, Inc.
PSI
US Net, Inc.

Virginia—804

Global Connect, Inc.
Widowmaker Communications

Washington—206

Cyberlink Communications
Eskimo North
Netcom On-Line Communication
    Services
NorthWest CommLink
Northwest Nexus, Inc.
Pacific Rim Network, Inc.
Pacifier Computers
Skagit On-Line Services
Teleport
Teleport, Inc.
Townsend Communcations, Inc.
WLN

Washington—509

Internet On-Ramp, Inc.
WLN

Wisconsin—414

BINCnet
Exec-PC BBS
FullFeed Communications
Internet Connect, Inc.
MIX Communications
WorldWide Access

Wisconsin—608

BINCnet
FullFeed Communications

Wisconsin—715

BINCnet
FullFeed Communications

Packet Network/Toll-Free Access

CompuServe Packet Network

IDS World Network

PSINet

HoloNet

SprintNet

Neosoft, Inc.
Portal Communications Company

Tollfree/800 Access

AlterNet (UUNET Technologies)
American Information Systems, Inc.
    (AIS)
BIX (Delphi Internet Services)
CENTURION Technology, Inc.
CERFnet
CICNet
CNS
CRL
Denver Area Super Highway (DASH)
Digital Express Group (Digex)
Exec-PC BBS
Freeside Communications
FXnet
Hookup Communication Corporation
IgLou Internet Services
Info-Highway International, Inc.
INS Info Services
InterAccess Co.
Internet Express

Internet Online Services
Interpath
IQuest Network Services
Msen, Inc.
Neosoft, Inc.
Netcom On-Line Communications
    Services
Network Intensive
New Mexico Technet, Inc.
OARNet
Pacific Rim Network, Inc.
PCNet
Ping
Primenet
Rabbit Network, Inc.
Rocky Mountain Internet, Inc.
Sacremento Network Access, Inc.
Scruz-Net
South Coast Computing Services,
    Inc.
Traveller Information Services
Tyrell Corp.
UltraNet Communications, Inc.
VNet Internet Access, Inc.
VoiceNet/DCS
West Coast Online
WLN
Zone One Network Exchange
    (ZONE)

Tymnet

Holonet

Alphabetical List of Providers

This section presents an alphabetical list of providers grouped by country and provider name. Countries included are the United States, Canada, Australia, Germany, the Netherlands, New Zealand, Switzerland, and the United Kingdom.

United States and Canada

The following is a list of North American Internet providers arranged in alphabetical order by provider name.

A World of Difference, Inc.

Area code(s):	803
Voice phone:	(803) 769-4488
E-mail address:	info@awod.com
Services provided:	Shell and PPP

Access InfoSystems

Area code(s):	707 and 510
Voice phone:	(707) 422-1034
E-mail address:	info@community.net
Services provided:	Shell, SLIP, and PPP

ACES Research

Area code(s):	602
Voice phone:	(602) 322-6500
E-mail address:	sales@aces.com
Services provided:	SLIP and 56-T1

ACM Network Services

Area code(s):	National and international
Voice phone:	(817) 776-6876
E-mail address:	account-info@acm.org
Services provided:	Shell, SLIP, PPP, and T1

Acquired Knowledge Systems, Inc.

Area code(s):	305
Voice phone:	(305) 525-2574
E-mail address:	samek@aksi.net
Services provided:	Shell, SLIP, and PPP

Agora

Area code(s):	503
E-mail address:	info@agora.rain.com
Dialup number:	(503) 293-1772
Services provided:	Shell, Usenet, FTP, telnet, Gopher, Lynx, IRC, and mail; SLIP/PPP is coming

Aimnet Information Services

Area code(s):	408, 415, and 510
Voice phone:	(408) 257-0900
E-mail address:	info@aimnet.com
Services provided:	Shell, SLIP, PPP, and DNS

Alberta SuperNet, Inc.

Area code(s):	403
Voice phone:	(403) 441-3663
E-mail address:	info@supernet.ab.ca
Services provided:	Shell, e-mail, Usenet, FTP, telnet, Gopher, and SLIP/PPP

AlterNet (UUNET Technologies)

Area code(s):	National and international
Voice phone:	(800) 4UU-NET4
E-mail address:	info@uunet.uu.net
Services provided:	Telnet only, SLIP, PPP, 56, 128, T1, and 10Mps

American Information Systems, Inc. (AIS)

Area code(s):	312, 708, 800, and 815
Voice phone:	(708) 413-8400
E-mail address:	schneid@ais.net
Services provided:	Shell, SLIP, PPP, and leased lines

APK Public Access UNI*

Area code(s):	216
Voice phone:	(216) 481-9428
E-mail address:	support@wariat.org
Services provided:	Shell, SLIP, and PPP

APlatform

Area code(s):	415
Voice phone:	(415) 941-2641
E-mail address:	support@aplatform.com
Services provided:	Shell, SLIP, and PPP

Best Internet Communications, Inc. (BEST)

Area code(s):	408, 415, and 510
Voice phone:	(415) 964-2378

E-mail address:	info@best.com
Services provided:	Shell, SLIP, PPP, and leased lines

BINCnet

Area code(s):	608, 414, and 715
Voice phone:	(608) 233-5222
E-mail address:	ward@binc.net
Services provided:	SLIP, PPP, and 56–T1

BIX (Delphi Internet Services)

Area code(s):	National and international
Voice phone:	(800) 695-4775 or (617) 354-4137
E-mail address:	info@bix.com
Services provided:	Shell

Black Box

Area code(s):	713
Voice phone:	(713) 480-2684
E-mail address:	info@blkbox.com
Services provided:	Shell, SLIP, PPP, and ISDN

Blythe Systems

Area code(s):	212 and 718
Voice phone:	(212) 348-2875
E-mail address:	accounts@blythe.org
Services provided:	Shell

CAPCON LibrARY Network

Area code(s):	202, 301, 410, and 703
Voice phone:	(202) 331-5771
E-mail address:	info@capcon.net
Services provided:	Shell, SLIP, and PPP

Capitol Area Internet Service (CAIS)

Area code(s):	202, 301, 410, and 703
Voice phone:	(703) 448-4470
E-mail address:	dalston@cais.com
Services provided:	Shell, SLIP, PPP, ISDN, and 56–T1

CCI Networks

Area code(s):	403
Voice phone:	(403) 450-6787
E-mail address:	info@ccinet.ab.ca
Services provided:	Shell, e-mail, Usenet, FTP, telnet, Gopher, WAIS, WWW, IRC, Hytelnet, and SLIP/PPP

CCnet Communications

Area code(s):	510
Voice phone:	(510) 988-0680
E-mail address:	info@ccnet.com
Dialup number:	(510) 988-7140
	Login as guest.
Services provided:	Shell, SLIP/ PPP, telnet, e-mail, FTP, Usenet, IRC, and WWW

CENTURION Technology, Inc.

Area code(s):	813
Voice phone:	(813) 572-5556
E-mail address:	jablow@cent.com
Services provided:	Shell, PPP, 56, 128, and T1

CERFnet

Area code(s):	619, 510, 415, 818, 714, 310, and 800
Voice phone:	(800) 876-2373
E-mail address:	sales@cerf.net
Services provided:	Full range of Internet services

CICNet

Area code(s):	313, 708, and 800
Voice phone:	(800) 947-4754 or (313) 998-6703
E-mail address:	info@cic.net
Services provided:	SLIP, FTP, telnet, Gopher, e-mail, and Usenet

Clark Internet Services, Inc. (ClarkNet)

Area code(s):	410, 301, 202, 703
Voice phone:	(800) 735-2258 or (410) 730-9764
E-mail address:	info@clark.net
Dialup number:	(301) 596-1626
	Login as guest. No password.

Services provided: Shell/optional menu, FTP, Gopher, telnet, IRC, news, Mosaic, Lynx, MUD, and SLIP/PPP/[C]SLIP

Cloud 9 Internet

Area code(s):   914
Voice phone: (914) 682-0626
E-mail address: scottd@cloud9.net
Services provided: Shell, SLIP, PPP, ISDN, and 56 and up

Cloudnet

Area code(s):   612
Voice phone: (612) 240-8243
E-mail address: info@cloudnet.com
Services provided: Shell

CNS

Area code(s):   303, 719, and 800
Voice phone: (800) 748-1200
E-mail address: service@cscns.com
Dialup number: (719) 520-1700 or (303) 758-2656
Services provided: Shell/menu, e-mail, FTP, telnet, all newsgroups, IRC, 4m, Gopher, WAIS, and SLIP

Colorado Internet Cooperative Association

Area code(s):   303
Voice phone: (303) 443-3786
E-mail address: contact@coop.net
Services provided: SLIP, PPP, 56, T1, ISDN

Colorado SuperNet

Area code(s):   303, 719
Voice phone: (303) 273-3471
E-mail address: info@csn.org or help@csn.org
Services provided: Shell, e-mail, Usenet news, telnet, FTP, SLIP/PPP, and other Internet tools

Communications Accessibles Montreal, Inc.

Area code(s):   514
Voice phone: (514) 931-0749
E-mail address: info@cam.org

Dialup number: (514) 596-2255
Services provided: Shell, FTP, telnet, Gopher, WAIS, WWW, IRC, Hytelnet, SLIP/[C]SLIP/PPP, and news

Community ConneXion

Area code(s):   510
Voice phone: (510) 841-2014
E-mail address: info@c2.org
Services provided: Shell and SLIP/PPP

Connix: The Connecticut Internet Exchange

Area code(s):   203
Voice phone: (203) 349-7059
E-mail address: office@connix.com
Services provided: Shell, SLIP, PPP, and leased lines

Creative Data Consultants

Area code(s):   718, 212, and 516
Voice phone: (718) 229-0489, ext. 23
E-mail address: info@silly.com
Services provided: Shell

CRL

Area code(s):   213, 310, 404, 415, 510, 602, 707, and 800
Voice phone: (415) 837-5300
E-mail address: support@crl.com
Dialup number: (415) 705-6060
    Login as newuser. No password.
Services provided: Shell, e-mail, Usenet, UUCP, FTP, telnet, and SLIP/PPP

CSUnet (California State Unversity)

Area code(s):   All California area codes
Voice phone: (310) 985-9445
E-mail address: maryjane@csu.net
Services provided: 56, 128, 384, and T1

CTS Network Services (CTSNet)

Area code(s):   619
Voice phone: (619) 637-3737
E-mail address: support@cts.com

Dialup number: (619) 637-3660
Services provided: Shell, e-mail, Usenet, FTP, telnet, Gopher, IRC, MUD,
and SLIP/PPP

CyberGate

Area code(s):   305
Voice phone: (305) 428-4283
E-mail address: `sales@gate.net`
Services provided: Shell, e-mail, Usenet, FTP, telnet, Gopher, Lynx, IRC, and
SLIP/PPP

Cyberlink Communications

Area code(s):   206
Voice phone: (206) 281-5397 or 515-945-7000
E-mail address: `sales@cyberspace.com`
Services provided: Shell, SLIP, and PPP

Cyberstore Systems, Inc.

Area code(s):   604
Voice phone: (604) 526-3373
E-mail address: `info@cyberstore.ca`
Dialup number: (604) 526-3676
                     Login as `guest`.
Services provided: E-mail, Usenet, FTP, telnet, Gopher, WAIS, WWW, IRC,
and SLIP/PPP

Denver Area Super Highway (DASH)

Area code(s):   303
Voice phone: (800) 624-8597 or (303) 674-9784
E-mail address: `info@dash.com, custserv@dash.com`
Services provided: Shell, SLIP, PPP, and leased lines

DataFlux Systems Limited

Area code(s):   604
Voice phone: (604) 744-4553
E-mail address: `info@dataflux.bc.ca`
Services provided: Shell, e-mail, Usenet, FTP, telnet, Gopher, WAIS, WWW,
IRC, and SLIP/PPP

Datawave Network Services

Area code(s):	805
Voice phone:	(805) 730-7775
E-mail address:	sales@datawave.net
Services provided:	56

DFW Internet Services, Inc.

Area code(s):	214 and 817
Voice phone:	(817) 332-5116
E-mail address:	sales@dfw.net
Services provided:	Shell, SLIP, PPP, and 56–T1

DHM Information Management, Inc.

Area code(s):	213, 310, 714, and 818
Voice phone:	(310) 214-3349
E-mail address:	dharms@dhm.com
Services provided:	LAN, PPP, SLIP, 56–T1, and Shell

DigiLink Network Services

Area code(s):	213, 310, 714, and 818
Voice phone:	(310) 542-7421
E-mail address:	info@digilink.net or bob@digilink.net
Services provided:	ISDN and PPP

Digital Express Group (Digex)

Area code(s):	301, 410, 609, 703, 714, 908, and 909
Voice phone:	(800) 969-9090
E-mail address:	info@digex.net
Dialup numbers:	(301) 220-0258
	(410) 605-2700
	(609) 348-6203
	(703) 281-7997
	(714) 261-5201
	(908) 937-9481
	(909) 222-2204
	Login as new.
Services provided:	Shell, SLIP/PPP, e-mail, newsgroups, telnet, FTP, IRC, Gopher, and WAIS

Earthlink Network, Inc.

Area code(s):	213, 310, and 818
Voice phone:	(213) 644-9500
E-mail address:	info@earthlink.net
Services provided:	Shell, SLIP, PPP, ISDN, 56, T1, and DNS

Echo

Area code(s):	212, 718
Voice phone:	(212) 255-3839
E-mail address:	info@echonyc.com
Dialup number:	(212) 989-3382
Services provided:	Conferencing, e-mail, shell, telnet, FTP, and SLIP/PPP

Eden Matrix

Area code(s):	512
Voice phone:	(512) 478-9900
E-mail address:	jch@eden.com
Services provided:	Shell, SLIP, PPP, and T1

Edge

Area code(s):	615
Voice phone:	(615) 455-9915 or (615) 726-8700
E-mail address:	info@edge.net
Services provided:	Shell, SLIP, PPP, ISDN, and 56

ElectriCiti Incorporated

Area code(s):	619, 408, 415, and 510
Voice phone:	(619) 338-9000
E-mail address:	info@electriciti.com
Services provided:	SLIP, [C]SLIP, and PPP

EriNet Online Communications

Area code(s):	513
Voice phone:	(513) 436-1700
E-mail address:	info@erinet.com
Services provided:	Shell, SLIP, and PPP

Escape (Kazan Corp)

Area code(s):	212 and 718
Voice phone:	(212) 888-8780

E-mail address: info@escape.com
Services provided: Shell, SLIP, PPP, and 56

Eskimo North

Area code(s): 206
Voice phone: (206) 367-7457
E-mail address: nanook@eskimo.com
Services provided: Shell

ESNET Communications

Area code(s): 619
Voice phone: (619) 287-5943
E-mail address: steve@cg57.esnet.com
Services provided: Shell

Evergreen Internet

Area code(s): 602, 702, and 801
Voice phone: (602) 230-9339
E-mail address: evergreen@libre.com
Services provided: Shell, FTP, telnet, SLIP, and PPP

Exchange Network Services, Inc.

Area code(s): 216
Voice phone: (216) 261-4593
E-mail address: info@en.com
Services provided: Shell

Exec-PC BBS

Area code(s): 414
Voice phone: (800) EXECPC-1 or (414) 789-4200
E-mail address: info@earth.execpc.com
Services provided: Shell

FGInet, Inc.

Area code(s): 217
Voice phone: (217) 544-2775
E-mail address: newuser@mail.fgi.net
Services provided: Shell, SLIP, and PPP

FishNet (Prometheus Information Corp)

Area code(s):   215 and 610
Voice phone: (610) 337-9994
E-mail address: `info@pond.com`
Services provided: Shell, SLIP, PPP

Florida Online

Area code(s):   407, 305, 904, and 813
Voice phone: 407-635-8888
E-mail address: `jerry@digital.net`
Services provided: Shell, SLIP, PPP, ISDN, and 56–T1

FredNet

Area code(s):   301
Voice phone: (301) 698-0238
E-mail address: `info@fred.net`
Services provided: Shell and SLIP

Freelance Systems Programming

Area code(s):   513
Voice phone: (513) 254-7246
E-mail address: `fsp@dayton.fsp.com`
Services provided: Shell and SLIP

Freeside Communications

Area code(s):   210 and 512
Voice phone: (800) 968-8750
E-mail address: `sales@fc.net`
Services provided: Shell, SLIP, PPP, ISDN, and 56–T1

FullFeed Communications

Area code(s):   608, 414, and 715
Voice phone: (608) 246-4239
E-mail address: `info@fullfeed.com`
Services provided: Shell, PPP, 28.8, 56, 384, and T1

FXnet

Area code(s):   800, 704, and 803
Voice phone: (704) 338-4670
E-mail address: `info@fx.net`
Services provided: Shell, SLIP, PPP, ISDN, 56, and T1

Gateway to the World, Inc.

Area code(s):   National and international
Voice phone: (305) 670-2930
E-mail address: mjansen@gate.com
Services provided: Shell

Global Connect, Inc.

Area code(s):   National and international
Voice phone: (804) 229-4484
E-mail address: info@gc.net
Services provided: SLIP, [C]SLIP, PPP, and DNS

Global Vision, Inc.

Area code(s):   803
Voice phone: (803) 241-0901
E-mail address: derdziak@globalvision.net
Services provided: Shell, SLIP, PPP, ISDN, and 56–T1

Great Basin Internet Services

Area code(s):   702
Voice phone: (702) 829-2244
E-mail address: info@greatbasin.com
Services provided: UUCP, SLIP, and PPP

GSS Internet

Area code(s):   405 and 918
Voice phone: (918) 835-3655
E-mail address: info@galstar.com
Services provided: Shell, SLIP, and PPP

Hawaii OnLine

Area code(s):   808
Voice phone: (808) 246-1880 or (808) 533-6981
E-mail address: info@aloha.net
Services provided: Shell, SLIP, PPP, 56–T1, DNS, and ISDN

Hevanet Communications

Area code(s):   503
Voice phone: (503) 228-3520

E-mail address:	info@hevanet.com
Services provided:	Shell, SLIP, PPP, and telnet

HoloNet

Area code(s):	510, PSINet, and Tymnet
Voice phone:	(510) 704-0160
E-mail address:	support@holonet.net
Dialup number:	(510) 704-1058
Services provided:	Complete Internet access

Hookup Communication Corporation

Area code(s):	All Canadian area codes
Voice phone:	(800) 363-0400
E-mail address:	info@hookup.net
Services provided:	Shell, e-mail, Usenet, FTP, telnet, Gopher, WAIS, WWW, IRC, Hytelnet, Archie, and SLIP/PPP

I-2000

Area code(s):	203, 516, 718, 908, and 914
Voice phone:	(516) 867-6379
E-mail address:	mikef@i-2000.com
Services provided:	SLIP and PPP

ICNet/Innovative Concepts

Area code(s):	313, 810, 616, 517, and 906
Voice phone:	(313) 998-0090
E-mail address:	info@ic.net
Services provided:	Shell, SLIP, PPP, DNS, ISDN, 56K, and T1

IDS World Network

Area code(s):	401, 305, 407, and CompuServe Network
Voice phone:	(401) 885-6855
E-mail address:	info@ids.net
Dialup number:	(401) 884-9002
Services provided:	Shell, FTP, Gopher, telnet, Talk, Usenet news, and SLIP

IgLou Internet Services

Area code(s):	502, 812, 606, and 513
Voice phone:	(800) 436-IGLOU
E-mail address:	info@iglou.com
Services provided:	Shell, SLIP, PPP, and ISDN

Illuminati Online

Area code(s):	512
Voice phone:	(512) 462-0999 or (512) 447-7866
E-mail address:	admin@io.com
Services provided:	Shell, SLIP, PPP, and ISDN

Info-Highway International, Inc.

Area code(s):	409 and 713
Voice phone:	(713) 447-7025 or (800) 256-1370
E-mail address:	smcneely@infohwy.com
Services provided:	Shell, SLIP, and PPP

Ingress Communications, Inc.

Area code(s):	212 and 718
Voice phone:	(212) 679-8592
E-mail address:	info@ingress.com
Services provided:	Shell, SLIP, PPP, and 56–T1

Innovative Data (ID-Net)

Area code(s):	313 and 810
Voice phone:	(810) 478-3554
E-mail address:	info@id.net
Services provided:	Shell, [C]SLIP, PPP, and 56–T1

INS Info Services

Area code(s):	800, 319, 402, 515, and 712
Voice phone:	(800) 546-6587
E-mail address:	service@ins.infonet.net
Services provided:	Shell, SLIP, and 56–T1

Institute for Global Communications (IGC)

Area code(s):	415
Voice phone:	(415) and 442-0220
E-mail address:	support@igc.apc.org
Dialup number:	(415) 322-0284
Services provided:	E-mail, telnet, FTP, Gopher, Archie, Veronica, WAIS, and SLIP/PPP

InterAccess Co.

Area code(s):	312, 708, and 815
Voice phone:	(800) 967-1580
E-mail address:	info@interaccess.com
Dialup number:	(708) 671-0237
Services provided:	Shell, FTP, telnet, SLIP, and PPP

Internet Access Company

Area code(s):	617 and 508
Voice phone:	(617) 276-7200
E-mail address:	info@tiac.net
Services provided:	Shell, SLIP, PPP, ISDN, and 56

Internet Alaska

Area code(s):	907
Voice phone:	(907) 562-4638
E-mail address:	info@alaska.net
Services provided:	Shell and 56-T1

Internet Atlanta

Area code(s):	National and international
Voice phone:	(404) 410-9000
E-mail address:	info@atlanta.com
Services provided:	UUCP, SLIP, PPP, ISDN, 56, and T1

Internet Connect Services, Inc.

Area code(s):	409, 512, and 713
Voice phone:	(512) 572-9987 or (713) 439-0949
E-mail address:	staff@icsi.net
Services provided:	Shell, SLIP, PPP, ISDN, and 56–T1

Internet Connect, Inc.

Area code(s):	414
Voice phone:	(414) 476-4266
E-mail address:	info@inc.net
Services provided:	Shell, SLIP, PPP, ISDN, and 56–T1

Internet Connection

Area code(s):	408
Voice phone:	(408) 461-INET
E-mail address:	sales@ico.net
Services provided:	SLIP, PPP, ISDN, and 56–T1

Internet Direct of Utah

Area code(s):	801
Voice phone:	(801) 578-0300
E-mail address:	johnh@indirect.com
Services provided:	Shell, SLIP, PPP, and 56–T1

Internet Direct, Inc.

Area code(s):	602
Voice phone:	(602) 274-0100 or (602) 324-0100
E-mail address:	sales@indirect.com
Services provided:	Shell, SLIP, and PPP

Internet Express

Area code(s):	719, 303, 505, 602, and 800
Voice phone:	(800) 592-1240
E-mail address:	service@usa.net
Services provided:	Shell, SLIP, PPP, and dedicated lines

Internet Nebraska Corp.

Area code(s):	402
Voice phone:	(402) 434-8680
E-mail address:	info@inetnebr.com
Services provided:	Shell, SLIP, and PPP

Internet On-Ramp, Inc.

Area code(s):	509
Voice phone:	(509) 927-7267
E-mail address:	info@on-ramp.ior.com
Services provided:	Shell, SLIP, [C]SLIP, PPP, and leased lines

Internet Online Services

Area code(s):	201, 212, 518, and 800
Voice phone:	(800) 221-3756

E-mail address: accounts@ios.com
Services provided: Shell, SLIP, PPP, DNS, and leased lines

Internetworks

Area code(s):   National and international
Voice phone: (503) 233-4774
E-mail address: info@i.net
Services provided: SLIP, PPP, ISDN, and leased lines

InterNex Information Services, Inc.

Area code(s):   415, 408, and 510
Voice phone: (415) 473-3060
E-mail address: sales@internex.net
Services provided: ISDN

Interpath

Area code(s):   919, 910, and 704
Voice phone: (800) 849-6305
E-mail address: info@infopath.net
Services provided: Full shell for UNIX, and SLIP and PPP

Interport Communications Corp.

Area code(s):   212 and 718
Voice phone: (212) 989-1128
E-mail address: sales@interport.net or info@interport.net
Services provided: Shell, SLIP, PPP, and dedicated lines

interQuest, inc.

Area code(s):   205
Voice phone: (205) 464-8280
E-mail address: paul@iquest.com
Services provided: Shell, SLIP, and PPP

intuitive information, inc.

Area code(s):   508
Voice phone: (508) 342-1100
E-mail address: info@iii.net
Services provided: Shell, [C]SLIP, PPP, and 56

IQuest Network Services

Area code(s):	317
Voice phone:	(317) 259-5050 or (800) 844-UNIX
E-mail address:	info@iquest.net
Services provided:	Shell, SLIP, PPP, ISDN, 56, and T1

KAIWAN Corporation

Area code(s):	714, 213, 310, 818, 909, and 805
Voice phone:	(714) 638-2139
E-mail address:	sales@kaiwan.com
Services provided:	Shell, SLIP, PPP, and 56–T1

LI Net, Inc.

Area code(s):	516
Voice phone:	(516) 476-1168
E-mail address:	questions@li.net
Services provided:	Shell, SLIP, 56, and T1

Lightside, Inc.

Area code(s):	818, 310, 714, and 909
Voice phone:	(818) 858-9261
E-mail address:	lightside@lightside.com
Services provided:	Shell, SLIP, PPP, and 56–T1

LineX Communcations

Area code(s):	415
Voice phone:	(415) 455-1650
E-mail address:	info@linex.com
Services provided:	Shell

Long Island Information, Inc.

Area code(s):	516
Voice phone:	(516) 248-5381
E-mail address:	info@liii.com
Services provided:	Shell and SLIP

Maestro Technologies, Inc.

Area code(s):	212, 718, and 516
Voice phone:	(212) 240-9600

E-mail address:	staff@maestro.com or rlekhi@maestro.com
Services provided:	Shell, SLIP, and PPP

maine.net, Inc.

Area code(s):	207
Voice phone:	(207) 780-6381
E-mail address:	atr@maine.net
Services provided:	SLIP, PPP, 56, and T1

MBnet

Area code(s):	204
Voice phone:	(204) 474-9590
E-mail address:	info@mbnet.mb.ca
Dialup number:	(204) 275-6132.
	Login as mbnet. Use guest for password.
Services provided:	Shell, e-mail, Usenet, FTP, telnet, Gopher, WAIS, WWW, IRC, Archie, Hytelnet, and SLIP/PPP

MCSNet

Area code(s):	312, 708, and 815
Voice phone:	(312) 248-8649
E-mail address:	info@mcs.net
Services provided:	Shell, SLIP, PPP, ISDN, and dedicated lines

Metronet, Inc.

Area code(s):	214 and 817
Voice phone:	(214) 705-2900 or (817) 543-8756
E-mail address:	info@metronet.com
Services provided:	Shell, SLIP, and PPP

MichNet

Area code(s):	313, 616, 517, 810, and 906
Voice phone:	(313) 764-9430
E-mail address:	recruiting@merit.edu
Services provided:	SLIP, PPP, host services, 56, and T1

Millennium Communications

Area code(s):	507 and 612
Voice phone:	(507) 282-8943 or (612) 338-5509
E-mail address:	info@millcom.com
Services provided:	Shell, SLIP, and PPP

MindSpring Enterprises, Inc.

Area code(s):	404 and 706
Voice phone:	(404) 888-0725
E-mail address:	sales@mindspring.com
Services provided:	Shell, SLIP, and PPP

Minnesota MicroNet

Area code(s):	612
Voice phone:	(612) 681-8018
E-mail address:	info@mm.com
Services provided:	SLIP, SLIP, and PPP

Minnesota Regional Network (MRNet)

Area code(s):	612, 507, and 218
Voice phone:	(612) 342-2570
E-mail address:	sales@mr.net
Services provided:	SLIP, 56, and T1

MIX Communications

Area code(s):	414
Voice phone:	(414) 228-0739
E-mail address:	sales@mixcom.com
Services provided:	BBS, SLIP, and PPP

Msen, Inc.

Area code(s):	800, 313, 517, 616, and 906
Voice phone:	313-998-4562
E-mail address:	info@msen.com
Services provided:	Shell, SLIP, PPP, ISDN, 56, and T1

MV Communications

Area code(s):	603
Voice phone:	(603) 429-2223
E-mail address:	info@mv.mv.com
Services provided:	Shell, SLIP, PPP, and 56

Neighborhood Internet Connection

Area code(s):	201
Voice phone:	(201) 934-1445

E-mail address: info@nic.com and combes@nic.com
Services provided: Shell

NeoSoft, Inc.

Area code(s):   800, 713, 409, 214, 504, and 314
Voice phone: (713) 684-5969
E-mail address: jmw3@neosoft.com
Services provided: Shell, SLIP, PPP, ISDN, 56, and T1

Netcom On-Line Communications Services

Area code(s):   206, 212, 214, 303, 310, 312, 404, 408, 415, 503, 510, 512,
617, 619, 703, 714, 818, and 916
Voice phone: (800) 501-8649
E-mail address: info@netcom.com
Dialup numbers: (206)547-5992
(212) 354-3870
(214) 753-0045
(303) 758-0101
(310) 842-8835
(312) 380-0340
(404) 303-9765
(408) 261-4700
(408) 459-9851
(415) 328-9940
(415) 985-5650
(503) 626-6833
(510) 274-2900
(510) 426-6610
(510) 865-9004
(512) 206-4950
(617) 237-8600
(619) 234-0524
(703) 255-5951
(714) 708-3800
(818) 585-3400
(916) 965-1371
Login as guest.
Services provided: Shell, e-mail, Usenet, FTP, telnet, Gopher, IRC, WAIS,
and SLIP/PPP

Network 23, Inc.

Area code(s):   212 and 917
Voice phone: (212) 786-4810
E-mail address: info@net23.com
Services provided: Shell

Network 99, Inc.

Area code(s):   National and international
Voice phone: (800) NET-99IP
E-mail address: net99@cluster.mcs.net
Services provided: 56K-T3

Network Intensive

Area code(s):   714
Voice phone: (800) 273-5600
E-mail address: info@ni.net
Services provided: Shell, SLIP, PPP, 56, ISDN, and T1

Network Internet Services

Area code(s):   516
Voice phone: (516) 543-0234
E-mail address: info@netusa.net
Services provided: Shell, SLIP, and PPP

Network Link, Inc.

Area code(s):   619 and 317
Voice phone: (619) 278-5943
E-mail address: stevef@tnl1.tnwl.com
Services provided: Shell, NNTP, IDSN, 56, and T1

New Jersey Computer Connection

Area code(s):   609
Voice phone: (609) 896-2799
E-mail address: info@pluto.njcc.com
Services provided: Shell, SLIP, and PPP

New Mexico Technet, Inc.

Area code(s):   505, 602, 303, 915, and 800
Voice phone: (505) 345-6555

| E-mail address: | granoff@technet.nm.org |
| Services provided: | Shell, SLIP, PPP, and leased lines |

New York Net

Area code(s):	201, 203, 212, 516, 609, 718, 908, 914, and 917
Voice phone:	(718) 776-6811
E-mail address:	sales@new-york.net
Services provided:	SLIP, PPP, 56, 64, and 128–T1

North Shore Access

Area code(s):	617
Voice phone:	(617) 593-3110
E-mail address:	info@shore.net
Dialup number:	(617) 593-4557
	Login as new.
Services provided:	Shell, FTP, telnet, Gopher, Archie, and SLIP/PPP

Northcoast Internet

Area code(s):	707
Voice phone:	(707) 444-1913
Services provided:	Shell, FTP, telnet, Gopher, and SLIP/PPP

NorthWest CommLink

Area code(s):	206
Voice phone:	(206) 336-0103
E-mail address:	gtyacke@nwcl.net
Services provided:	Shell, SLIP, PPP, and 56–T1

Northwest Nexus, Inc.

Area code(s):	206
Voice phone:	206-455-3505
E-mail address:	info@nwnexus.wa.com
Services provided:	Shell, SLIP, PPP, 56, and T1

NovaNet, Inc.

Area code(s):	703, 202, 301
Voice phone:	703-524-4800
E-mail address:	sales@novanet.com
Services provided:	Shell, SLIP, PPP, 56–T1

Nuance Network Services

Area code(s):   205
Voice phone: (205) 533-4296
E-mail address: `info@nuance.com`
Services provided: Shell, Usenet, FTP, telnet, Gopher, and SLIP/PPP

NYSERNet

Area code(s):   212, 315, 516, 518, 607, 716, 718, and 914
Voice phone: (315) 453-2912
E-mail address: `info@nysernet.org`
Services provided: Shell and 56–T3

Nyx

Area code(s):   303
Voice phone: (303) 871-3308
E-mail address: `info@nyx.cs.du.edu`
Services provided: Shell and semi-anonymous accounts

OARNet

Area code(s):   614
Voice phone: (800) 627-8101
E-mail address: `info@oar.net`
Services provided: Shell and SLIP/PPP

Old Colorado City Communications

Area code(s):   719
Voice phone: (719) 528-5849
E-mail address: `thefox@oldcolo.com`
Services provided: Shell and 56

Onramp Access, Inc.

Area code(s):   512
Voice phone: (512) 322-9200
E-mail address: `info@onr.com`
Services provided: SLIP and PPP

Pacific Internet

Area code(s):   707
Voice phone: (707) 468-1005

E-mail address: `info@pacific.net`
Services provided: Shell, SLIP, PPP, and 56K–T1

Pacific Rim Network, Inc.

Area code(s):   206
Voice phone: (206) 650-0442
E-mail address: `sales@pacificrim.com`
Services provided: Shell, SLIP, PPP, ISDN, and 56K–T1

Pacifier Computers

Area code(s):   206
Voice phone: (206) 693-2116
E-mail address: `sales@pacifier.com`
Services provided: Shell, SLIP, and PPP

PacketWorks, Inc.

Area code(s):   813
Voice phone: (813) 446-8826
E-mail address: `info@packet.net`
Services provided: PPP and ISDN

Panix Public Access UNIX and Internet

Area code(s):   212 and 516
Voice phone: (212) 787-6160
E-mail address: `info@panix.com`
Dialup number: (212) 787-3100 or (516) 626-7863
     Login as `newuser`.
Services provided: Shell, Usenet, FTP, telnet, Gopher, Archie, WWW, WAIS, and SLIP/PPP

PCNet

Area code(s):   203
Voice phone: (800) 66-4INET
E-mail address: `sales@pcnet.com`
Services provided: Shell, SLIP, PPP, ISDN, 56, and T1

Phantom Access Technologies, Inc.

Area code(s):   212, 718, 516, and 914
Voice phone: (212) 989-2418
E-mail address: `info@phantom.com`
Services provided: Shell, SLIP, PPP, and 56–T1

Ping

Area code(s):   404 and 800 (including Alaska and Hawaii)
Voice phone: (800) 746-4835 or (404) 399-1670
E-mail address: bdk@ping.com
Services provided: Shell, SLIP, PPP, and 56

Pioneer Global

Area code(s):   617
Voice phone: (617) 375-0200
E-mail address: sales@pn.com
Services provided: Shell, 28.8, 56, and T1

Pipeline Network

Area code(s):   National and international
Voice phone: (212) 267-3636
E-mail address: staff@pipeline.com
Services provided: Shell

Planet Access Networks

Area code(s):   201, 908, 319, and 205
Voice phone: 201-691-4704
E-mail address: fred@planet.net
Services provided: Shell, SLIP, PPP, dedicated lines

Portal Communications Company

Area code(s):   408 and SprintNet
Voice phone: (408) 973-9111
E-mail address: info@portal.com
Services provided: Shell, e-mail, Usenet, FTP, telnet, Gopher, IRC, and
                    SLIP/PPP

Primenet

Area code(s):   602, 213, and 818
Voice phone: (800) 4 NET FUN
E-mail address: info@primenet.com
Services provided: Shell, SLIP, PPP, 56, 128, and T1

PSI

Area code(s):   North America, Europe, and Pacific Basin
                    Send e-mail to numbers-info@psi.com for list

Voice phone: (703) 709-0300
E-mail address: `all-info@psi.com`
Services provided: Complete Internet services

QuakeNet

Area code(s):   415
Voice phone: (415) 655-6607
E-mail address: `info@quake.net` (autoreply) or `admin@quake.net` (human)
Services provided: SLIP, PPP, DNS, and 56–T1

Rabbit Network, Inc.

Area code(s):   810 and 800 (including the entire U.S. and Canada)
Voice phone: (800) 456-0094
E-mail address: `info@rabbit.net`
Services provided: Shell, SLIP, PPP, and leased lines

Real/Time Communications

Area code(s):   512
Voice phone: (512) 451-0046
E-mail address: `info@realtime.net`
Services provided: Shell, SLIP, PPP, IDSN, and custom services

Red River Net

Area code(s):   701 and 218
Voice phone: (701) 232-2227
E-mail address: `lien@rrnet.com`
Services provided: Shell, SLIP, 56, and T1

Ripco Communcations, Inc.

Area code(s):   312 and 708
Voice phone: (312) 665-0065
E-mail address: `info@ripco.com`
Services provided: Shell

Rocky Mountain Internet, Inc.

Area code(s):   303 and 719
Voice phone: (800) 900-RMII
E-mail address: `mountr@rmii.com, jimw@rmii.com`
Services provided: Shell, SLIP, PPP, 56, and T1

Sacramento Network Access, Inc.

Area code(s):   916, 209, 510, and 702
Voice phone: (916) 565-4500
E-mail address: sales@sna.com
Services provided: Shell, SLIP, and PPP

SatelNET Communications

Area code(s):   305
Voice phone: (305) 434-8738
E-mail address: martinson@satelnet.org
Services provided: Shell, SLIP, and PPP

Schunix

Area code(s):   508
Voice phone: (508) 853-0258
E-mail address: info@schunix.com
Services provided: Shell, SLIP, PPP, ISDN, 56, 128, and T1

Scruz-Net

Area code(s):   408 and 415
Voice phone: (800) 319-5555
E-mail address: info@scruz.net
Services provided: SLIP, PPP, ISDN, 56, and T1

Sibylline, Inc.

Area code(s):   501
Voice phone: (501) 521-4660
E-mail address: info@sibylline.com
Services provided: Shell, SLIP, PPP, 56, 128, T1, DNS, and advertising

Sierra-Net

Area code(s):   702 and 916
Voice phone: (702) 832-6911
E-mail address: info@sierra.net
Services provided: Shell, SLIP, PPP, and 56–T1

SIMS, Inc.

Area code(s):   803
Voice phone: (803) 762-4956

E-mail address: `info@sims.net`
Services provided: Shell, SLIP, PPP, ISDN, 56, 128, and 256

Skagit On-Line Services

Area code(s):   206
Voice phone: (206) 755-0190
E-mail address: `info@sos.net`
Services provided: Shell, SLIP, and PPP

SkyNET Corp.

Area code(s):   816 and 913
Voice phone: (816) 483-0002
E-mail address: `info@sky.net`
Services provided: Shell, SLIP, PPP, and 56–T1

South Carolina SuperNet, Inc.

Area code(s):   803
Voice phone: (803) 748-1207
E-mail address: `info@scsn.net`
Services provided: SLIP, PPP, 56, and T1

South Coast Computing Services, Inc.

Area code(s):   713 and 918
Voice phone: (800) 221-6478
E-mail address: `sales@sccsi.com`
Services provided: Shell, SLIP, PPP, 56, and T1

South Valley Internet

Area code(s):   408
Voice phone: (408) 683-4533
E-mail address: `info@garlic.com`
Services provided: Shell, SLIP, PPP, dedicated lines, and leased lines

SouthWind Internet Access, Inc.

Area code(s):   316
Voice phone: (316) 263-7963
E-mail address: `staff@southwind.net`
Services provided: Shell and TIA-SLIP

SSNet, Inc.

Area code(s):	302
Voice phone:	(302) 378-1386
E-mail address:	info@ssnet.com or sharris@ssnet.com
Services provided:	Shell, SLIP, PPP, and UUCP

StarNet Communications, Inc.(Winternet)

Area code(s):	612
Voice phone:	(612) 941-9177
E-mail address:	info@winternet.com
Services provided:	Shell, SLIP, and PPP

SymNet

Area code(s):	904
Voice phone:	(904) 385-1061
E-mail address:	info@symnet.net
Services provided:	Shell, SLIP, and PPP

Teleport

Area code(s):	503 and 206
Voice phone:	(503) 223-4245
E-mail address:	info@teleport.com
Dialup number:	(503) 220-1016
Services provided:	Shell, e-mail, Usenet, FTP, telnet, Gopher, and SLIP/PPP

Teleport, Inc.

Area code(s):	503 and 206
Voice phone:	(503) 223-0076
E-mail address:	sales@teleport.com
Services provided:	Shell, SLIP, PPP, and ISDN

Telerama

Area code(s):	412
Voice phone:	(412) 481-3505
E-mail address:	sysop@telerama.lm.com
Dialup number:	(412) 481-4644
Services provided:	Shell, e-mail, telnet, Usenet, FTP, telnet, Gopher, IRC, and SLIP/PPP

Texas Metronet

Area code(s):   214 and 817
Voice phone: (214) 705-2900
E-mail address: info@metronet.com
Dialup number: (214) 705-2901 or (817) 261-1127
                       Login as info. Use info for password.
Services provided: Shell, e-mail, Usenet, FTP, telnet, Gopher, IRC, and
                       SLIP/PPP

Tezcatlipoca, Inc.

Area code(s):   312 and 708
Voice phone: (312) 850-0181
E-mail address: ilixi@tezcat.com
Services provided: Shell and TIA

The Dorsai Embassy

Area code(s):   718, 212, 201, 203, 914, and 516
Voice phone: (718) 392-3667
E-mail address: system@dorsai.dorsai.org
Services provided: Shell, SLIP, and PPP

The Well

Area code(s):   415
Voice phone: (415) 332-4335
E-mail address: info@well.com
Services provided: Shell

The World

Area code(s):   617 and 508
Voice phone: (617) 739-0202
E-mail address: staff@world.std.com
Services provided: Shell and DNS

Townsend Communcations, Inc.

Area code(s):   206
Voice phone: (206) 385-0464
E-mail address: inquiries@olympus.net
Services provided: PPP and 56

Traveller Information Services

Area code(s):   204
Voice phone: (800) 840-TNET or (204) 883-2686
E-mail address: info@traveller.com
Services provided: Shell, [C]SLIP, PPP, and ISDN

Tyrell Corp.

Area code(s):   816, 913, 504, and 316
Voice phone: (800) TYRELL-1
E-mail address: support@tyrell.net
Services provided: Shell, [C]SLIP, and PPP

TZ-Link

Area code(s):   914
Voice phone: (914) 353-5443
E-mail address: drew@j51.com
Services provided: Shell

UltraNet Communications, Inc.

Area code(s):   508
Voice phone: (508) 229-8400 or (800) 763-8111
E-mail address: info@ultranet.com
Services provided: SLIP, PPP, ISDN, 56, 128, and 384

US Net, Inc.

Area code(s):   301, 202, and 703
Voice phone: (301) 572-5926
E-mail address: info@us.net
Services provided: Shell, SLIP, PPP, DNS, and 56–T1

UUNorth Incorporated

Area code(s):   416
Voice phone: (416) 225-8649
E-mail address: uunorth@north.net
Dialup number: (416) 221-0200
                     Login as new.
Services provided: E-mail, Usenet, FTP, telnet, Gopher, WAIS, WWW, IRC,
                     Archie, and SLIP/PPP

VNet Internet Access, Inc.

Area code(s):	704
Voice phone:	(800) 377-3282
E-mail address:	info@vnet.net
Dialup number:	(704) 347-8839
	Login as new.
Services provided:	Shell, e-mail, Usenet, FTP, telnet, Gopher, IRC, SLIP/PPP, and UUCP

VoiceNet/DCS

Area code(s):	215
Voice phone:	(215) 674-9290
E-mail address:	info@voicenet.com
Services provided:	Shell, SLIP, PPP, and ISDN

West Coast Online

Area code(s):	415, 510, 707, 408, 916, and 209
Voice phone:	(800) WCO INTERNET
E-mail address:	info@calon.com
Services provided:	Shell, SLIP, PPP, ISDN, and 56–T1

WestNet

Area code(s):	914
Voice phone:	(914) 967-7816
E-mail address:	staff@westnet.com
Services provided:	Shell

Widowmaker Communications

Area code(s):	804
Voice phone:	(804) 253-7621
E-mail address:	bloyall@widomaker.com
Services provided:	Shell, SLIP, and PPP

Wilder Systems, Inc.

Area code(s):	617
Voice phone:	(617) 933-8810
E-mail address:	info@id.wing.net
Services provided:	Shell, pipeline, PPP, SLIP, ISDN, and 56–T1

Wimsey Information Services

Area code(s):   604
Voice phone: (604) 936-8649
E-mail address: admin@wimsey.com
Services provided: Shell, e-mail, Usenet, FTP, telnet, Gopher, WAIS, WWW,
                        IRC, Archie, and SLIP/PPP

Wizvax Communications

Area code(s):   518
Voice phone: (518) 271-6005
E-mail address: root@wizvax.com
Services provided: Shell, SLIP, [C]SLIP, PPP

WLN

Area code(s):   800, 206, 509, 503, 208, 406, and 360
Voice phone: 800-DIAL-WLN, 800-342-5956, 206-923-4000
E-mail address: info@wln.com
Services provided: Shell, SLIP, PPP, and 56–T1

WorldWide Access

Area code(s):   312, 708, 815, and 414
Voice phone: (708) 367-1870
E-mail address: support@wwa.com
Services provided: Shell, SLIP, PPP, ISDN, and leased lines

Xensei Corporation

Area code(s):   617
Voice phone: (617) 773-4785
E-mail address: sales@xensei.com, terri@xensei.com
Services provided: SLIP, PPP, ISDN, and 56K

XMission

Area code(s):   801
Voice phone: (801) 539-0852
E-mail address: support@xmission.com
Services provided: Shell, SLIP, PPP, and leased lines

XNet Information Systems

Area code(s):	708
Voice phone:	(708) 983-6064
E-mail address:	info@xnet.com
Dialup number:	(708) 983-6435 or (708) 882-1101
Services provided:	Shell, e-mail, Usenet, FTP, telnet, Gopher, Archie, IRC, SLIP/PPP, and UUCP

You Tools Corporation (FAST.NET)

Area code(s):	610, 215, and 717
Voice phone:	(610) 954-5910
E-mail address:	internet@youtools.com
Services provided:	SLIP, PPP, ISDN, and 56–T1

Zilker Internet Park

Area code(s):	512
Voice phone:	(512) 206-3850
E-mail address:	info@zilker.net
Services provided:	Shell, SLIP, PPP, and ISDN

zNET

Area code(s):	408
Voice phone:	(408) 477-9638
E-mail address:	info@znet.com
Services provided:	SLIP, PPP, ISDN, and DNS

Zone One Network Exchange (ZONE)

Area code(s):	800, 718, 212, 914, 516, 917, 201, and 908
Voice phone:	(718) 549-8078
E-mail address:	info@zone.net
Services provided:	UUCP, SLIP, PPP, and 56–T1

Australia

Aarnet

Voice phone:	+61 6-249-3385
E-mail address:	aarnet@aarnet.edu.au

Connect.com.au P/L

Areas serviced: Major Australian capital cities (2, 3, 6, 7, 8, and 9)
Voice phone: +61 3-28-239
E-mail address: `connect@connect.com.au`
Services provided: Shell, SLIP/PPP, and UUCP

Germany

Contributed Software

Voice phone: +49 30-694-69-07
E-mail address: `info@contrib.de`
Dialup number: +49 30-694-60-55
Login as `guest` or `gast`.

Individual Network e.V.

Area serviced: All of Germany
Voice phone: +49 0441-808556
E-mail address: `in-info@individual.net`
Dialup number: +49 02238 15071
Login as `info`.
Services provided: UUCP throughout Germany. FTP, SLIP, telnet and other services in some major cities.

Inter Networking System (INS)

Voice phone: +49 2305 356505
E-mail address: `info@ins.net`

Netherlands

Knoware

E-mail address: `info@knoware.nl`
Dialup number: +31 030 896775

NetLand

Voice phone: +31 020 6943664
E-mail address: `Info@netland.nl`

Dialup number: +31 020 6940350
Login as `new` or `info`.

Simplex

E-mail address: `simplex@simplex.nl`
Dialup number: +31 020 6653388
Login as `new` or `info`.

New Zealand

Actrix

Voice phone: +64 04-389-6316
E-mail address: `john@actrix.gen.nz`

Switzerland

Swiss Academic and Research Network (SWITCH)

Voice phone: +41 1 268 1515
E-mail address: `postmaster@switch.ch`

United Kingdom

Almac

Voice phone: +44 324 665371
E-mail address: `alastair.mcintyre@almac.co.uk`

Cix

Voice phone: +44 49 2641961
E-mail address: `cixadmin@cix.compulink.co.uk`

Demon Internet Limited

Voice phone: +44 81 3490063 (London)
    +44 31 5520344 (Edinburgh)
E-mail address: `internet@demon.net`
Services provided: SLIP/PPP accounts

The Direct Connection (UK)

Voice phone: +44 81 3170100
E-mail address: helpdesk@dircon.cu.uk
Dialup number: +44 81 3172222

Note to Providers

If you would like to be included in future versions of this list, for use in subsequent editions of this book and other Sams.net Internet books, send an e-mail message to Mark Taber at mtaber@netcom.com.

TOOLS AND RESOURCES

This appendix contains information on tools for the World Wide Web, Gopher, e-mail, and news. It also includes information on platform-specific tools.

World Wide Web Tools

If you decide to include support for the thousands of World Wide Web users on the Internet with your Internet marketing plans, you must grapple with the issue of transforming your brochures, product descriptions, price lists, pictures, and other information into the hypertext language that Web browsers such as Mosaic can read. If you opt for a commercial service as your Web server, you might find that the operators will perform this format translation for a fee or as part of the setup charge.

You can also produce your own Web-readable hypertext documents in-house by using hypertext markup language (HTML). An outside designer or a technician at your firm can create them directly, write them with the aid of an HTML editor, or convert by hand documents in other formats to HTML. An HTML document can be created with any text editor. If you are accustomed to marking up text in any way—even red-penciling it—HTML should be fairly intuitive.

Fortunately, a number of Web tools are available on the Internet, including *A Beginner's Guide to HTML* at URL `http://www.ncsa.uiuc.edu/General/Internet/WWW/HTMLPrimer.html`. An alternate HTML primer is available from Nathan Torkington of New Zealand through the network at the URL `http://www.vuw.ac.nz/who/Nathan.Torkington/ideas/www-html.html`.

Many people, however, prefer an HTML editor because it is graphical and easier to use than writing HTML documents directly in a standard editing environment. Some of the available editors are graphically oriented, offering a "what you see is what you get" metaphor. Others simply assist you in writing HTML by plugging in the desired markup tags from a menu.

The third option is converting documents created in other formats to HTML. Various filters that can accomplish this task automatically are available for free on the Internet. The best way to learn about the possibilities is to obtain a copy of the filter list at CERN. It is maintained by Rich Brandwein and Mike Sendall, and its URL is `http://www.w3.org/hypertext/WWW/Tools/Filters.html`.

Web tools include everything from Web browsers for surfing the Web to HTML editors for designing and creating your own Web pages. The sections that follow describe some of the best ones.

Mac

Netscape

Netscape is the world's most popular and powerful WWW browser. Download it from `ftp://ftp.netscape.com/netscape1.1/`.

NCSA Mosaic

This Web browser started it all. Download it from `ftp://ftp.ncsa.uiuc.edu/Mosaic/Mac/`.

Spyglass Enhanced NCSA Mosaic

A better version of NSCA Mosaic is available from a variety of resellers. For more information, visit `http://www.spyglass.com/`.

Mac Web

This Web browser for Macs is also available for Power Macs. Download it from `ftp://ftp.wustl.edu/systems/mac/info-mac/comm/tcp/mac-web-100a3.hqx`.

SHE (Simple HTML Editor)

SHE is a simple editor for creating HTML documents. It requires a HyperCard or HyperCard Player. Download it from `ftp://ftp.lib.ncsu.edu/pub/software/mac/simple-html-editor.hqx`.

PC

Netscape

Netscape is the world's most popular and powerful WWW browser. Download it from `ftp://ftp.netscape.com/netscape1.1/`.

NCSA Mosaic

This Web browser started it all. Download it from `ftp://ftp.ncsa.uiuc.edu/Mosaic/Windows`.

Spyglass Enhanced NCSA Mosaic

A better version of NSCA Mosaic is available from a variety of resellers. For more information, visit `http://www.spyglass.com/`.

HTML Assistant

This HTML editor works with Microsoft Windows. Download it from `ftp://ftp.cs.dal.ca/htmlasst/inst14.exe`.

WinWeb

WinWeb is a simple, easy-to-use—but stripped down—WWW browser. Download it from `http://galaxy.einet.net/EINet/WinWeb/WinWebHome.html`.

UNIX

Netscape

Netscape is world's most popular and powerful WWW browser. Download it from `ftp://ftp.netscape.com/netscape1.1/`.

NCSA Mosaic

This Web browser started it all, and it is still popular. Download it from `ftp://ftp.ncsa.uiuc.edu/Mosaic/unix`.

Spyglass Enhanced NCSA Mosaic

A better version of NSCA Mosaic is available from a variety of resellers. For more information, check out `http://www.spyglass.com/`.

ASHE

ASHE is an HTML editor for X Window with WYSIWYG. Download it from `ftp://ftp.cs.rpi.edu/pub/puninj/ASHE/`.

tkWWW (X Window)

This is an interface for the WWW that enables you to edit HTML. Download it from `ftp.w3.org.ch/pub/www/src`.

Gopher Tools

The World Wide Web isn't the only way to use the Internet to distribute information to potential customers and clients. This section takes a closer look at Gopher, a text-based distribution tool that enables users to navigate the Web through searchable menus.

Mac

Turbo Gopher

Turbo Gopher is one of the best Gopher clients for the Mac. Download it from `ftp://ftp.wustl.edu/systems/mac/info-mac/comm/tcp/turbo-gopher-20b8.hqx`.

GopherApp++

This is another Gopher client for the Mac. Download it from `ftp://ftp.wustl.edu/systems/mac/info-mac/comm/tcp/gopher-app-22b43.hqx`.

PNL Info Browser

This is a full-featured Macintosh Gopher client. Download it from `ftp://ftp.wustl.edu/systems/mac/info-mac/comm/tcp/pnl-info-browser.hqx`.

PC

Gopher Book

This gopher client for Windows uses a book analogy to represent the gopher's structure. Download it from `ftp://sunsite.unc.edu/pub/micro/pc-stuff/ms-windows/winsock/apps/`.

Hgopher

Hgopher is a popular Windows-based gopher client. Download it from `ftp://lister.cc.ic.ac.uk/pub/wingopher/`.

UNIX

Xgopher

Xgopher is a good X Window gopher client. Download it from `ftp://boombox.micro.umn.edu/pub/gopher`.

E-Mail Tools

For businesses, being able to connect with many people is a boon. For many companies, though, the greatest advantage to Internet e-mail is its low cost. Not only do you save on postage and printing compared to postal mailings, but by paying a monthly fee to an Internet access provider, you can send and receive all the e-mail you want without paying extra for messages or the time you spend online composing them.

The following are some popular tools that make sending and receiving Internet e-mail a snap.

Mac

Eudora

Eudora is the most famous and perhaps the best freely available e-mail program. Download it from `ftp://ftp.wustl.edu/systems/mac/info-mac/comm/tcp/mail/eudora-151.hqx`.

PC

Eudora

Eudora is one of the best PC e-mail programs around. Download it from `ftp://ftp.iquest.com/pub/windows/papa/mail/eudor144.exe`.

Elm

This is Dave Taylor's popular UNIX e-mail program ported to Microsoft Windows. Download it from `ftp://ftp.iquest.com/pub/windows/papa/mail/winelm.zip`.

Pegasus Mail

Pegasus Mail Works over both the Internet and Novell networks. Download it from `ftp://ftp.iquest.com/pub/windows/papa/mail/winpm2b2.zip`.

UNIX

Elm

This text-based e-mail reader comes with most shell accounts. Download it from `ftp://wuarchive.wustl.edu/packages/mail/elm/`.

Pine

Pine is a slightly more capable e-mail reader than Elm. It comes with most shell accounts. Download it from `ftp://wuarchive.wustl.edu/packages/mail/pine/`.

News Tools

If mailing lists are like a post office that can automatically make copies of your message and distribute it worldwide, Usenet is the public library, where each book covers a discussion on a specific topic. Newsreader interfaces range from text-based UNIX programs that require you to type complex commands at the system prompt to easy-to-use point-and-click interfaces that make sending a message as easy as clicking a menu item or an icon.

Mac

NewsWatcher

NewsWatcher is one of the best newsreaders around. Download it from `ftp://ftp.wustl.edu/systems/mac/info-mac/comm/tcp/news-watcher-20b24.hqx`.

TheNews

TheNews is another newsreader for the Mac. Download it from `ftp://ftp.wustl.edu/systems/mac/info-mac/comm/tcp/the-news-236.hqx`.

InterNews

InterNews is a newsreader from Dartmouth University. Download it from `ftp://ftp.wustl.edu/systems/mac/info-mac/comm/tcp/inter-news-105.hqx`.

NetNews Grazer

This set of AppleScript applications makes handling news much easier. Download it from `ftp://ftp.wustl.edu/systems/mac/info-mac/comm/tcp/netnews-filter-agent.hqx`.

PC

WinVN

WinVN is an nntp newsreader for Windows 3.1. Download it from `ftp://titan.ksc.nasa.gov/pub.win3.winvn/`.

Free Agent

This popular newsreader for Windows works online or offline. Download it from `ftp://ftp.forteinc.com/pub/forte/`.

News Express

News Express is another newsreader available for Windows. Download it from `ftp://ftp.iquest.com/pub/windows/papa/news/nx10b3.zip`.

UNIX

nn

nn is a popular text-based newsreader that runs on most shell accounts. Download it from `ftp://wuarchive.wustl.edu/packages/news/readers/nn/`.

rn

This older text-based newsreader comes with most shell accounts. It is generally considered inferior to nn. Download it from `ftp://wuarchive.wustl.edu/packages/news/readers/rn/`.

tin

tin is a screen-based newsreader based on the same metaphor as Elm. Download it from `ftp://wuarchive.wustl.edu/packages/news/readers/tin/`.

xrn

xrn is an X-based version of the rn newsreader. Download it from `ftp://wuarchive.wustl.edu/packages/news/readers/xrn/`.

Platform-Specific Tools

Some Internet tools run on only specific platforms such as UNIX, Windows, or the Macintosh. Here is a grab bag of tools for any occasion.

Mac

NCSA Telnet

You can use this simple text-based program to access other computers on the Internet. Download it from `ftp://ftp.ncsa.uiuc.edu/Mac/Telnet/Telnet2.7/`.

Fetch

Fetch is a user-friendly file transfer program for the Macintosh. Download it from `ftp://ftp.wustl.edu/systems/mac/info-mac/comm/tcp/fetch-212.hqx`.

Ircle

This easy-to-use IRC client is used for chatting. Download it from `ftp://ftp.wustl.edu/systems/mac/info-mac/comm/tcp/ircle-151.hqx`.

Homer

Homer is an unusual and humorous IRC client that can synthesize sound. Download it from `ftp://ftp.wustl.edu/systems/mac/info-mac/comm/tcp/homer-0934.hqx`.

PC

Winqvt/net

This Windows-based program combines telnet, ftp, and e-mail. Download it from `ftp://biochemistry.cwru.edu/pub/qvtnet)`.

WinWAIS

This WAIS client program can use network packet drivers or Winsock programs. Download it from `ftp://ridgisd.er.usgs.gov/software/wais`.

Serv-U

Serv-U is a Windows-based ftp server program. Download it from `ftp://ftp.iquest.com/pub/windows/papa/daemons/ftpsrv11.zip`.

Windows NCSA Httpd

Use this server to display Web pages from a PC running Windows. Download it from `ftp://ftp.iquest.com/pub/windows/papa/daemons/whtpd14p.zip`.

WinSMTP Daemon

This Windows-based SMTP server can handle mailing lists. Download it from `ftp://ftp.iquest.com/pub/windows/papa/daemons/snew106d.zip`.

UNIX

EMBOT

EMBOT is a powerful, self-configuring mail autoresponder program that works on any UNIX system. For more information, send e-mail to `embot@northcoast.com`. Use `list` for the subject line.

XWAIS

XWAIS is an X Window WAIS client. Download it from `ftp://sunsite.unc.edu/pub/wais`.

GN Release 2.0

This is a free server for Gopher and WWW pages. Download it from `ftp://ftp.acns.nwu.edu/pub/gn/`.

INDEX

Symbols

56K connections, 27

A

academic networks
  (security), 327
acceptable use policies
  (AUPs), 20, 158
access
  Archie, 93
  costs, 374
  e-mail, 61
  Gopher, 83
  graphical access to the
    Web, 88
  hits, 204
  Internet, 368
  mailing lists, 67
  WWW (World Wide
    Web), 87
access providers
  (Internet)
  cost, 15
  local phone access,
    20-21
  online accounts, 23
  performance, 19
  reliability, 18-19
  restrictions, 20
  security, 19-20

  user services and
    support, 21
addressing
  domains, 120
  e-mail, 62-64, 114,
    120-121
  hosts, 120
ADMDs
  (ADministration
    Management
    Domains), 115
adult entertainment
  (profitability), 221
Advanced Research
  Projects Agency
  (ARPAnet), 5
  cost, 15
advertising, 8-9, 203,
  381-384
  commercial online
    services, 345
  cost, 203-205
  display advertising,
    169-172
  exposure, 203
  free advertising,
    198-203
  home pages, 9

Q-R

X-Y-Z

Add to Your Sams Library Today with the Best Books for Programming, Operating Systems, and New Technologies

The easiest way to order is to pick up the phone and call

1-800-428-5331

between 9:00 a.m. and 5:00 p.m. EST.

For faster service please have your credit card available.

ISBN	Quantity	Description of Item	Unit Cost	Total Cost
0-672-30617-4		The World Wide Web Unleashed	$35.00	
0-672-30667-0		Teach Yourself Web Publishing with HTML in a Week	$25.00	
0-672-30466-x		Internet Unleashed (Book/Disk)	$39.95	
0-672-30718-9		Navigating the Internet, Third Edition	$25.00	
0-672-30761-8		Navigating the Internet with CompuServe	$19.99	
0-672-30764-2		Teach Yourself Web Publishing with Microsoft Word in a Week	$29.99	
0-672-30599-2		Tricks of the Internet Gurus	$35.00	
0-672-30595-X		Education on the Internet	$25.00	
0-672-30627-1		Plug-N-Play Mosaic	$29.99	
0-672-30594-1		Programming WinSock	$35.00	
0-672-30669-7		Plug-N-Play Internet	$35.00	
0-672-30638-7		Super CD-ROM Madness! (Book/CD-ROM)	$39.99	
❏ 3 ½" Disk		Shipping and Handling: See information below.		
❏ 5 ¼" Disk		TOTAL		

Shipping and Handling: $4.00 for the first book, and $1.75 for each additional book. Floppy disk: add $1.75 for shipping and handling. If you need to have it NOW, we can ship product to you in 24 hours for an additional charge of approximately $18.00, and you will receive your item overnight or in two days. Overseas shipping and handling adds $2.00 per book and $8.00 for up to three disks. Prices subject to change. Call for availability and pricing information on latest editions.

201 W. 103rd Street, Indianapolis, Indiana 46290

1-800-428-5331 — Orders   1-800-835-3202 — FAX   1-800-858-7674 — Customer Service

Book ISBN 1-57521-004-5

PLUG YOURSELF INTO...

THE MACMILLAN INFORMATION SUPERLIBRARY™

Free information and vast computer resources from the world's leading computer book publisher—online!

FIND THE BOOKS THAT ARE RIGHT FOR YOU!

A complete online catalog, plus sample chapters and tables of contents give you an in-depth look at *all* of our books, including hard-to-find titles. It's the best way to find the books you need!

- **STAY INFORMED** with the latest computer industry news through our online newsletter, press releases, and customized Information SuperLibrary Reports.

- **GET FAST ANSWERS** to your questions about MCP books and software.

- **VISIT** our online bookstore for the latest information and editions!

- **COMMUNICATE** with our expert authors through e-mail and conferences.

- **DOWNLOAD SOFTWARE** from the immense MCP library:
    - Source code and files from MCP books
    - The best shareware, freeware, and demos

- **DISCOVER HOT SPOTS** on other parts of the Internet.

- **WIN BOOKS** in ongoing contests and giveaways!

TO PLUG INTO MCP: ➤ WORLD WIDE WEB: **http://www.mcp.com**

GOPHER: gopher.mcp.com
FTP: ftp.mcp.com

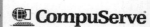